Wired for Sound

Wired for Sound

ENGINEERING AND TECHNOLOGIES IN SONIC CULTURES

EDITED BY PAUL D. GREENE AND THOMAS PORCELLO

WESLEYAN UNIVERSITY PRESS
Middletown, Connecticut

Published by Wesleyan University Press, Middletown, CT 06459

Printed in the United States of America

5 4 3 2 1

Library of Congress Cataloging-in-Publication Data

Wired for sound : engineering and technologies in sonic cultures / edited by Paul D. Greene and Thomas Porcello.—1st ed.
p. cm. — (Music/culture)
Includes bibliographical references and index.
ISBN 0-8195-6516-4 (cloth : alk. paper) — ISBN 0-8195-6517-2 (pbk. : alk paper)
1. World music—History and criticism. 2. Sound—Recording and reproducing. 3. Ethnomusicology. I. Greene, Paul D. II. Porcello, Thomas. III. Series.
ML3545.W57 2004
780'.9'05—dc22 2004016021

Contents

Acknowledgments

We wish to express our gratitude to several individuals and institutions who have inspired, facilitated, and supported the development, production, and publication of this book. During the 1999 annual meeting of the Society for Ethnomusicology, we convened a panel titled "Sound Engineering as Cultural Production," involving Cornelia Fales, Boden Sandstrom, Jeremy Wallach, and the two editors of this volume. Our discussions on and surrounding this panel were very stimulating and helpful, as we drew together and compared ethnographic and cultural perspectives on sound engineering. We are grateful to the Society for Ethnomusicology, which has not only provided the venues for this and other important panels and forums but also served more generally as a scholarly network and intellectual home for the development of this volume. It is impossible to mention by name all of the individuals whose insights have contributed to this project. With their intellectual support it has grown from a five-person panel to a thirteen-chapter book. We thank the authors who contributed their findings and insights to this volume. We are grateful not only for their original manuscripts but also for their ongoing efforts and patience throughout the process of preparing this book for publication.

We also thank our home institutions of Pennsylvania State University and Vassar College, which have provided support on many important levels. They have supported us as scholars and researchers, and numerous colleagues have offered valuable intellectual guidance. Through our home institutions we have also benefited from access to library and computer resources that have enabled us to conduct the necessary research and editing work for this volume.

We would like to thank Carfax Publishing Company for making it possible for us to publish Timothy D. Taylor's "Music and the Rise of Radio in Twenties America: Technological Imperialism, Socialization, and the Transformation of Intimacy," which first appeared in *The Historical Journal of Film, Radio and Television,* volume 22, number 3, in October 2002. We thank the American Anthropological Association for allowing us to publish Thomas Porcello's "Music Mediated As Live in Austin: Sound, Technology, and Recording Practice," which originally appeared in *City & Society,* volume 14, number 1, in 2002. And we thank Cambridge University Press for allowing us to publish Paul D. Greene's "Mixed Messages: Unsettled Cosmopolitanisms in Nepali Pop," which originally appeared in the journal *Popular Music,* volume 20, number 2, in 2001.

Finally, we thank the editorial board, series editors, and editorial staff of Wesleyan University Press, and especially Suzanna Tamminen and Leonora Gibson, for all of their efforts, guidance, and insights in seeing this volume through to final publication. They have been supportive throughout the process, from a handful of manuscripts to the printed volume.

Wired for Sound

CHAPTER ONE

Introduction
Wired Sound and Sonic Cultures

Paul D. Greene

A new and understudied means of music making has emerged within and among the world's musical cultures. It is driven not so much by the vibrations of membranes, chords, hard surfaces, or molecules of air but rather primarily by the manipulation of electrical impulses.[1] In the contemporary paradigm the sound waves' measurements, rather than the sound waves themselves, travel across metal filaments as differentials in electrical charge, and sound information—also encoded as electrical charge—is manipulated by means of computer interfaces. Our jam sessions today increasingly play out in information bits encoded as differences in electrical charge, and distinctions between musician and engineer have become blurred. Musical agents creating and manipulating sounds in this wired form harness unprecedented expressive powers as they simulate entire orchestras from information stored in tone banks; as they record, alter, and mix together any number of tracks of live performance; and as they sample any timbre or sound quality they encounter instantly for use in their own music making. Wired sound is at the basis of digital sound editing, effects processing, multitrack recording, and MIDI sequencing, practices that have powerfully impacted musical cultures and soundscapes around the world.

In addition, sound converted into electrical charges enters the wires and cables of the Internet (e.g., MP3 file exchange) and is given forms of electromagnetic radiation in radio waves and (as light) along fiberoptic cables. Because of the sheer velocity of wired sound, global musical synergies have accelerated and become more complex. Musics now travel faster and farther than was possible before, and the feedback loops of sound communication and musical influence back and forth from music's production centers to local settings of reception have accelerated dramatically. Recording studios have become, among other things, spongelike centers where the world's sounds are quickly and continually absorbed, reworked, and reincorporated into new musics. Music can now no longer be adequately modeled as something that happens in a local context and employs only the expressive means specific to a locality. Instead, music making increasingly employs technologies produced elsewhere and is informed by a heightened awareness of sounds that are traveling rapidly around the world. *Wired sound* therefore refers not only to music created by harnessing the new powers of wired technologies but also to the contemporaneous fact that many of the world's musical practices are increasingly wired together. Music (including even music that resists globalization) happens along a global circuit of rapid communication and varying influence: an accelerating and disjunctive global cultural flow, in Arjun Appadurai's sense (1990).

Although technologies of wired sound are not altogether new, they have become prevalent around the world only in recent years (and more so in some places than in others), due to the rapid expansion of middle classes in many societies, the accelerating mobilization of people, capital, and objects in the global cultural economy (ibid.), and reductions in the cost of sound technologies. In fact, following state deregulations (Manuel 1993), emergence of less expensive multitrack digital formats (Théberge 1997; Greene, this volume), and the falling prices of direct-to-disk recording software, sound production and reproduction technologies that were once prohibitively expensive are now within the financial grasp of many of moderate means. Analytic research on sound technology and the engineering of sonic culture has so far been conducted primarily in western cultural contexts, with a focus on western subject positions, yet the phenomenon has had a greater impact, in many ways, on the non-western world. Remarkably, the musical voice that has been most frequently recorded in all of the world's music history is not that of an American pop or European opera singer but rather of the Hindi filmsong playback singer Lata Mangeshkar.[2] It is quite likely that today there are more people working in studios to engineer sounds in Asia, Africa, and Latin America than in the West, and there are certainly more people listening to engineered musics in the non-western world. Although primarily of western origin and innovation, technologies of music production and distribution have come into their own in the non-western world, where high-tech sounds saturate many musical cultures today.

This book is about technological music making in global perspectives, about the extensions of control and assertions of creativity that ensue as technologies invented and produced in western societies are incorporated into and used by world cultures, and about both the nuancing and the revolutionizing of cultural forms and practices that have been brought about through wired sound. In some ways the new technologies seem to extend western influence and bring about a homogenization of the world's musics and musical practices. For example, these technologies make it possible for a small collection of musical genres to resonate powerfully over large portions of the world, where they are frequently imitated (the wide reach and influence of Indian filmsong and western rock genres come to mind).

But technologies of wired sound also have the potential (whether fully realized or not) of opening up new directions for musical expression and evolution, inspiring new logics of music creation and empowering local cultural and expressive values. Ethnographic evidence presented in this volume shows that people around the world today are merging technological engineering with traditional "musicking" (Small 1998) in unpredicted ways, and they are producing a wide array of musics that is only beginning to be studied. And while some studio products are fastidiously quantized at the expense of creativity ("The first technician [in the sense of technique] of music was the first to stop being a good musician" [Adorno 1958: 197]), many engineerings ("high-tech" musickings) around the world are quite creative, varied, and expressively powerful. For example, in Indonesian sound studios, a new style called "brutal ethnic" fuses traditional Javanese melodic and rhythmic elements, Indian filmsong rhythms, and death metal: sound qualities from diverse cultural worlds are thus for the first time musically drawn together, transgressively crossing boundaries of distance and cultural division. In American ambient and techno music, sound qualities are deliberately engineered to play tricks on listener perceptions, to seem at one moment to be completely artificial and at the next thoroughly natural—as if produced by actual performers—thus playfully but powerfully invoking and calling into question the relationship between body and machine. Around the globe, different engineers and studios develop reputations for particular "sounds," and many engineers keep their most innovative techniques secret.

A new modality of human music making has emerged, and its full range of meanings and cultural functions has yet to be assessed. As wired sound travels back and forth through what has become a global circuit, are we witnessing a worldwide assimilation of music making practices and a dissolution of meaningful distinctions among musics, aesthetics, and practices? Or is this in some ways the flashpoint of an explosion of new, technologically facilitated world musics? Might assimilation and differentiation both be underway at once? To address such questions there is a great need for ethnographic studies that discover and document the world's new musics, musical practices, and sonic cultures.

Ethnomusicologists and ethnographers who study world musical cultures have until recently tended to ignore electricity-based technologies in their studies of music making, community building, and performativity. We have tended, for example, analytically to favor technologies (such as instruments) made of organic components over those that originate with a western electronic hardware manufacturer, even when such technologies are used with immense creativity. And studies of recording technology and its relationship to music and culture (e.g., Zak 2001; Théberge 1997; Frith 1996: 226ff; Jones 1992; Cutler 1984) have examined primarily western subject positions and cultural contexts. Given the recent advent of wired sound to much of the world, researchers are just now reaching a point where it is possible to document, analyze, and theorize about the world's new technology-intensive musics. Tim Taylor (2004, 1997) is among the first scholars to extend analysis beyond western societies to study and theorize, in sustained ways, the implications of technology and globalization. This trajectory is extended further in Lysloff and Gay's *Music and Technoculture* (2003), a volume that examines music technologies from non-western as well as western perspectives and includes three ethnographic chapters on technologies in non-western cultures. *Wired for Sound* extends ethnographic study to all six inhabited continents and draws together global perspectives on sound engineering and its relationship to sonic culture.

The methods employed by the authors are primarily ethnographic but also include historical and psychological examinations. We investigate the mutually influencing and often interpenetrating practices of production, reproduction, reception, and perception of studio-produced and technology-facilitated sound qualities and musical patterns. We examine "sound engineering," not merely in the narrow sense of manipulating levels in a recording studio but also in the important broader sense of agency: "sound engineering" defined as the practice—by individuals, groups, institutions, corporations, or governments—of using sound technologies to engineer meanings, functions, and social strategies in musical cultures and in the world at large for strategic cultural, aesthetic, political, and economic ends (Greene 1999: 460–461). The volume draws emic viewpoints more centrally into scholarly discourse on music and technology in order to give voice to those with whom we work as ethnographers and to present local understandings of social and cultural institutions and practices. Together with the writings of scholars who voice perspectives from many parts of the world (for example, from Japan, Hosokawa 1990, 1984; from China, Chow

1993), ethnographic data on sound engineering (in the broader sense) offer new, global perspectives on music and technology.

Hard Wires

Although sound engineering clearly has great potential for "rational" and deliberate control over every detail of sound (Théberge 1997; Born 1995), engineering practice quite frequently does not progress rationally at all. Sometimes it progresses arduously, as engineers encounter stonewall after stonewall before perhaps experiencing a time of successful creativity. Engineers must tangle with their machines, often in a dumbfounded state: this is the "Can you hear me now?" phase of so many recording sessions. It is not just that technology may be complex or nonfunctional; instead, mismatches inevitably emerge between the engineering logics of actual cultural agents and the logics imposed on them, those hardwired into the machine from afar. As sound engineers plug themselves into the music technology and seek to be creative, they must grapple with fixed operating systems and unalterable programs that run on computers, synthesizers, tone modules, and effects processors designed in the United States, Japan, Europe, and also, in some cases, China.[3]

Every technology brings with it a particular logic, a structure that, among other things, is a means of bringing order to the world (Winner 1999: 32). This logic reflects its particular social history; as Lysloff and Gay point out (2003: 15–16), the logic of a particular technology depends upon the logics of the related technologies and preceding technologies that prefigure it (e.g., the electronic keyboard is prefigured by the piano, which in turn is prefigured by the harpsichord) and also on the shifting social and economic contexts (Mackenzie and Wajcman 1999) in which the technology is sold, used, and consumed (Théberge 1997). The sound engineering technologies analyzed in this volume have evolved and taken their current shape in the context of western musical and social history, and they are coded with a logic that reflects this history. Musicians creating music that flows from a different history or involves significantly different ways of patterning sound frequently encounter mismatches of musical-engineering logics as they use the technologies.

For example, in most studio technology pitch is mapped out onto western equal-tempered scales, and it is often difficult to reconfigure the technology so that it offers easy access to pitches in non-western tunings, such as those of the Javanese *pelog* and *slendro* scales. And because the technology is based on the model of distinct pitch levels triggered by discrete keys (as on an electronic keyboard, which is based on the western piano), it is generally more difficult and complicated to perform or encode Indian *gamaks* — slides, trills, and other performative features — using western-designed technology.[4] By design, some sound qualities and techniques are easier to produce and others more difficult. As a result, in many places the advent of western sound-engineering technologies has reinforced trends toward western equal-tempered scales with discrete pitches. Thus as western sound technologies are drawn into music making around the world, their hardwirings begin to structure local musical practices in certain ways, imposing their own musical logics onto the societies that adopt them. Hardwirings constitute a (sometimes subsonic) vehicle of control in the world's musical praxis, and technological musicking — perhaps more so than traditional musicking — becomes a struggle that engages with the translocal.

But in many cases, musical engineers develop innovative techniques to overcome the technology's inherent configurations and move beyond their originally intended uses (see Penley and Ross 1991: x). For example, in order to produce certain pitches used in Arabic music, Arab American musicians supplement the electronic keyboard with a device that makes it possible to play pitches that are not included on it (Rasmussen 1996). Culturally situated agents sometimes aggressively refunction their hard technologies by, for example, overdriving preamps in heavy metal. Some technological innovations could be called *kluges:* inelegant but effective ways of bypassing technology's inflexible features for creative ends.

Occasionally, new models of hardware are designed that reflect or enhance the new musical-cultural-technological practices that have been innovated. For example, factory-produced sound distortion modules can now readily be purchased to approximate the sonic effects of overdriving a preamp. As sound technologies are increasingly consumed in the nonwestern world, it remains to be seen to what extent future hardware models will better reflect the expressive needs of musicians operating outside the creative limitations of current western-designed technologies.

Global Circuits

Music technology has tended to bring about a blurring (in the sense of a loss of distinction) of the spheres of music production and consumption. Almost as soon as new musical technologies become available and affordable, they are put to service in local musical cultures. And as quickly as new sounds are engineered in local cultures, they are copied and loaded into the next generation of synthesizers or tone banks to be produced and distributed by music technology factories. In the process, musicians have become not only producers of music but also significant consumers of technology (Théberge 1997). As musical products become so thoroughly and rapidly recycled, the distinction between production and consumption begins to blur. The musical sounds of the world (Théberge 2003; Taylor 1997) have been drawn more deeply than before into the synergies of consumer society.

Many examples can be found of blurrings of production, distribution, and reception. Rudy Vallee's "intimate" crooning style, a 1920s American music production practice, is so dependent on a distribution network, namely radio, to create intimacy by bringing his live voice into private homes that the "distribution" technology effectively merges with the "production" practice (Taylor, this volume). The experience of listening to different and often contrasting musics heard in Kathmandu soundscapes (radio and audiocassette sounds) has led to a new aesthetic in which engineers, influenced by their listening ("reception") practices, employ multitrack recording technologies deliberately to record music with abrupt juxtapositions of musical style and texture ("production"; Greene, this volume). The innovative hip-hop practices of turntabling and sampling collapse "reception" (purchasing, playing back, and listening to) and "production" (Rose 1994). In fact, with technologies of digital sampling, the previously stable categories of authorship and performance are now threatened (Bradby 1993: 162). In this volume we examine the shifting politics of identity construction, in which technologies that were innovated primarily in western societies become incorporated and "entangled" (in the sense of Thomas 1991) into numerous indigenous traditions, practices, and systems of value and meaning. Accordingly, this book engages musical production, distribution, and reception, as well as some of the ways in which the three practices interpenetrate each other today.

In *Strange Sounds: Music, Technology, and Culture* (2001), Tim Taylor historicizes and politicizes music transcription (notation) and points toward its importance for production, storage and distribution, and consumption. He pinpoints, in the late nineteenth century, the moment at which sound itself, rather than its representation, could be sold and moved. (Of course, with digitized sound, we now sell and move measurements of sound rather than sound itself; we have in a sense returned to transcription.) Taylor terms the electronic exchanges of today the first nonphysical mode of music distribution. I would argue that, with the emergence of nonphysical music distribution, the feedback channel between musical production and its reception has accelerated to such an extent that feedback is now approaching instantaneous, wired speeds.

The technological and social processes examined by Théberge and Taylor extend outward to encompass much of the globe, constituting a global circuit of production, reception, and distribution; of influence, subversion, and resistance; of pushes and pulls between local and translocal. The new technologies make it possible for local and translocal sounds to travel and interact at unprecedented speeds, to cross barriers of geographical distance and cultural difference, to facilitate powerful transformations of communities' musics (Jones 2000). As musicians and listeners around the world increasingly live lives plugged into this global circuit, they face new challenges and engage in new processes of identity construction. On the one hand, the accelerating synergies between local and global are facilitating an acceleration of western musical influence into world cultures and lifeways. But at the same time, as satellite television, radio, and the Internet increasingly reach musicians and listeners in previously isolated settings, many musicians, such as the Native Americans studied by Diamond, respond by making their own recordings, thus registering themselves and their music in the global circuit. Evidence also suggests that some "schismogenetic" processes (Feld 1994a) are taking place. Sound engineers and musicians often articulate new techniques they have invented to achieve local aims, and the emergence of distinct studio "sounds" (in the sense of Théberge 1997: 191) may reflect artistic *différence* (the drive toward difference and distinction) in technological music production.

One can also hear women differentiating themselves from men in their approaches to and styles of music making. In Diamond's interviews with and studies of Native American recording artists (in this volume) she finds that women, in comparison to men, voice greater concerns for collaboration and trust among performers and engineers and generally involve themselves less closely in the technological specifics of production. Native American women, like women in other settings around the world, often encounter barriers when they enter the sphere of sound recording; there is a persistent notion—possibly beginning in western societies and radiating outward with the spread of its technology—that technology is "masculine," in opposition to nature, which is "feminine" (see Bradby 1993: 156; Théberge 1997: 123). But Diamond finds that a collaborative vision of the musical product—a CD as "a documentation of our process [of working together]," as Sadie Buck puts it—can build considerable respect and prestige for female artists. Further, she points out that the trust that Native American women cultivate in the process particularly enables them, more so than men, to innovate their musical traditions: an expressive aim to which technology then becomes subservient. There are benefits, then, in thinking broadly about technology as part of a collaborative creative process (cf. Sandstrom 2000). New feminist perspectives seek ways of overcoming the binaries of nature/technology and feminine/masculine by exploring new "cyborg" mergings of humanity, nature, and technology in both fiction and cultural life (Haraway 1991; Marsh and West 2003).

And at the same time, new global music–based subcultures such as global heavy metal are emerging. These are new "counter-nodes of identity" formations (Appadurai 1990: 18–19) that are, in many ways, both transnational *and* marginalized. Global musical hybrids comprise another vehicle of identity formation within wired sound. Hybrid forms use sound-studio technology to combine musical elements from different traditions. Such forms often make use of studio sound's ability to invoke place: sounds that index certain geographic locales or particular world instruments or cultural groups are recorded, sampled, and combined in multitrack sound studios. Combinations of cultural places in hybrid multitracks facilitate cultural exploration (Greene, this volume), local microcultural constructions vis-à-vis a larger superculture (Slobin 1993), and transgressive social boundary crossing (Lipsitz 1994; Wallach, this volume). Deborah Wong's examination of Asian American expressivity in rap (1994) suggests that even in practices of intense cultural borrowing (enactment by Asian American performers of hip-hop gesturing and rapping into a microphone), identity assertion is possible. The microphone can become a powerful vehicle of the "eye/I": a process of self defining, identity asserting, and cultural positioning.

Charged Wires: Anxieties and Desires

The use of technology in musical practice is rarely neutral or transparent in the experience of musicians and listeners. Instead, technology's presence bears important meanings, and often leads to significant transformations in musical and aesthetic ideals. For Simon Frith, with the advent of electrical recording and amplification, perfection in western recordings "ceased to refer to a specific performance (a *faithful* sound) and came to refer . . . to a constructed performance (an *ideal* sound). The 'original,' in short, ceased to be an event and became an idea" (1996: 234; emphasis in the original; cf. Chanan 1995). One could also say that the aesthetic ideal now inheres in the sonic materiality of the recording itself (Wallach 2003). As engineered music has also become a ubiquitous presence in many non-western soundscapes, its technological nature has likewise inflected musical meanings and aesthetic expectations and in some cases sparked debates.

Concerns, criticisms, and celebrations of technology in music are particularly inflected by the anxieties and desires that emerge in immediate contexts in response to sound technology, and to technology in general. Some music genres showcase recognizably "high-tech" sounds, and technology's traces come to function as prestigious markers of modernity. In other musics, such traces are heard as warning signs of cultural co-optation, and engineers labor to mask or conceal the "studioness" of their products. Wired sound is thus culturally and politically charged: listeners and musicians around the world invest sound technologies and studio recordings with anxieties on the one hand, and desires on the other.

There are many anxieties and concerns inspired by—and indeed warranted by—wired sound. Recording technology has enabled the separation of musical sounds from musicians, which has resulted in the musicians' subsequent loss of control over their circulation, their meanings, and all too often their ownership. Understandably, Native American musicians are wary of the recording process: "We have to be sure of the recording process before we allow the sound," says Sadie Buck; "the atmosphere in which we're creating our work has to be a good environment or I won't sing," says Mishi Donovan (Diamond, this volume). Indeed, one might add to the list any of a number of anxieties that are articulated with regard to wired sound: it is too carefully controlled, it is too inhuman (but it also, ironically, reproduces the natural with perhaps too much precision), it is too preauthored (software packages are too invasive), it lacks "aura" (in the sense of Benjamin 1968), or it is too hegemonic (a western product that has entered the non-western world in a strategy to bring money to the West). There is also a wariness toward technologies that threaten to replace human labor. Many high-tech musics reflect a longing to erase (Eric Clapton unplugged) or exceed (metal guitar overdrive) music technologies. Also accompanying the spread of sound-studio technologies come anxieties of engineering fakery: that studio-altered or fabricated sound products can "dupe" listeners into thinking that they are hearing an "authentic" recording of a performance event. This raises concerns because for many listeners an originary presence of actual voices, bodies, instruments, or performances is very important; it functions, in some sense, as an anchor, a guarantor of the recording's meaning and value. (Some related concerns also come up in ethnomusicological field recordings: see Lysloff and Gay 2003: 2–6; Porcello's afterword to this volume.)

At the same time, technologically altered sound can also be an object of desire and pleasure (Frith 1996). In many instances, unintentional byproducts of certain music technologies, such as the compression, distortion, or audio echoes of magnetic tape (Porcello 1998/2003) or even the buzzes and pops of records, have become central to musical aesthetics: listeners, disc jockeys, and dancers take pleasure in the "warm" sounds of analog records and resist shifting to compact discs, in which such "limitations" are overcome (Wallach 2003: 44; Thornton 1996). Further, technology and its sonic traces can embody for listeners the hopes and dreams of modernity, of western technology and freedom from hardship and want. This desire for a technological utopia, a perhaps unrealizable vision of the "technological sublime" (Penley and Ross 1991: xii–xiii), is evident in certain dance clubs, among specific (often underground) groups, in particular age brackets, in certain geographic locales, and in particular venues where one longs for the self-consciously digitized music product.

A longing for technology is particularly evident in the ways in which people talk about it in Asia and elsewhere in the non-western world (Greene and Henderson 2000: 110–111). Sleeves of Tamil pop albums in Chennai marketplaces feature pictures and descriptions of the sound studios in which the music was produced, promoting a commercial recording by invoking its modernity (that is, its alignment with current technology, western marketing strategies, and so forth). The trappings of sound engineering—of the "high tech"—in Pakistan, Nepal, India, Malaysia, Indonesia, and elsewhere are aurally evident in the conspicuous use of digital effects (for example, reverb, delay, flange), quantized (computer-perfected) rhythms, perfectly balanced frequency response, and the frequent use of obviously synthesized or electronically manipulated sounds. Here, the desire for a "techno-sound" has often been less impeded than in the West by a sense of the immanence of real or imagined loss surrounding digitized musics. The positive associations of the new, the cutting edge, the cosmopolitan, the sophisticated, and so on are highly prized prestige markers. In the genres of Indonesian *dangdut* (Wallach, this volume) and Nepali pop (Greene, this volume), engineered sound qualities, and the explicit inclusion of the sounds *of* studio-based engineering, reassure listeners that their societies or states have entered a new, modern, global arena of culture and identity assertion. Sometimes positions vis-à-vis technology divide listeners along gender lines: in Nepal, I find that female Nepali pop listeners are generally less critical of the intrusion of audibly high-tech sounds into folksongs, perhaps because they generally have more to gain from the promises of technology and modernity and less to gain from traditional Nepali culture and gender expectations and restrictions.

The anxieties and desires that surround sound technology take different forms in different sonic cultures. Accordingly, many of the chapters in this volume engage with ways in which anxiety and desire shape notions such as "reality" (Meintjes), "sincerity" (Porcello), or "fidelity" (Shank 1994) of music in the cultural contexts in which it is produced and heard. What kinds of technological interventions and sound effects are permitted? What kinds are disallowed?

The evidence collected in this volume suggests that there are perhaps as many answers to these questions as there are studio production sounds.

This is because there are many locally constructed notions of "authenticity" that contradict each other in the immediate contexts of musicking (see Taylor 1997: 21–28). Moehn finds that in Rio de Janeiro musicians effectively navigate the desires and anxieties of sound recording by cultivating two different but interrelated samba music aesthetics — one for live performance and the other for studio recording. Groups of Native American musicians call for a strict clarity of drum sounds, for to obscure them through sound processing would "destroy the specificity of the timbral information about place and nation" (Diamond). In a Johannesburg recording session, a "real" Swaziland drum sound is accomplished through complex recording techniques involving seventeen microphones (Meintjes; see also Meintjes 2003). Thomas Porcello articulates the careful measures taken by sound engineers in recording the Austin sound and its sense of live, honest, genuine expression. The Austin strategy finds parallels in other American and Canadian musical production aesthetics: too much reverb, too much flange, too regular a rhythm, and so on strike a North American listener as inauthentic, in part because the sound is interpreted by listeners as overproduced. The ethnographies collected here suggest that matters of "authenticity" and "sincerity" are deeply caught up in *local* (as well as global) cultural discourses and ideologies of truth, value, anxiety, desire, and pleasure. While technologies that inspire these concerns, anxieties, and desires may be somewhat universal, the ensuing discourses, ideologies, and sound engineering practices are not. Indeed, as Porcello suggests (in the afterword), such discourses are becoming central to genre definition.

Some sound engineers seek to "enhance" the commercial viability of "authentic" musical sounds. One of the benefits of Neuenfeldt's rich accounts of producer Nigel Pegrum's studio practices (in this volume) is an illustration of how deeply intertwined concerns of authentic Australian Indigenous expressivity, commercial viability, and aesthetic appeal can become (see Erlmann 1996). Pegrum stresses, "I really was very careful about putting forward any opinions. But it soon become clear to me that David liked to be produced . . . I found myself almost talking David through some of the tracks." As Neuenfeldt holds an ethnographic lens to the specific, actual moments in which an ancient musical tradition is drawn into and transformed within a sound studio, he brings into sharp focus the specific processes through which the world's sounds are becoming technologically mediated. Tellingly, not only are aesthetic knowledge and skill subservient to commercial concerns but commercial concerns are thoroughly aestheticized in an emerging "industrial logic" of production. In Pegrum's engineering (especially in the creation of "didjeridu-friendly sections" — introductory additions performed on synthesizers and other instruments that frame the *didj* sound in its new technologically and commercially mediated form)—the sounds of the didj and of indigenous expressivity are wedded with outsiders' (perhaps New Age–inspired) conceptions and expectations of the didj, which has already become a well-known transnationally consumed sound bite. The important and contentious distinction between musical and cultural cooptation on the one hand and cooperative culture brokering on the other becomes blurred in the era of wired sound: as Neuenfeldt observes, "Everyone involved [in production] had something of value to add to the projects and it could also be viewed as a form of intercultural reconciliation through art and music."

Music-Wire-Body

As we examine our role as machine operators, we ask questions (that we have always asked) about the ontological status of the human body in a continuous material practice that extends from the eye, hand, and ear to the metal and plastic of machines. Cyborg metaphors have been invoked to model contemporary interfacings between human and machine, in both fiction and lived social reality (for example, Marsh and West 2003: 195–197; Haraway 1991). Cyborg models characterize the senses in which machines and bodies can ideally be made to work efficiently in tandem as well as the ways in which machines and bodies adapt to each other to facilitate cooperative work.

Like other technologies, global sound technologies influence or guide bodies in some senses and simulate bodies in other senses (see Manuel 1995), all in ways that warrant new examinations. Fales (this volume) discusses ways in which a sense of the corporeal presence of a human performer's voice can be simulated, altered, or "morphed" into other sounds through technological means. In contemporary musical cultures, engineers can produce what I call "Pygmalion moments" in which synthesized timbres suddenly begin to sound like and be perceived as those produced by a living human body; and, as well, such "human" sounds can be dismantled, before the listener's very ears, into sounds obviously produced through technological artifice.

One of the most globally widespread uses of digitized sound, particularly digitized drum tracks, occurs in dance clubs. Here, where drum sounds have often originated in the studio rather than by means of any actual drumming, the technologically produced rhythms set the pace for the movement of dancers' bodies (Fikentscher 2000; Thornton 1996; Rose 1994; Greene, this volume). At techno and drum & bass (or "jungle") raves it is the superhumanly fast and precise drumstrokes of rhythm machines that set a sometimes almost impossibly fast pace for the human dancers to follow.

In some cases, music technology facilitates new modes of experiencing one's own body and its relationship to the social world. Shuhei Hosokawa (1984), a Japanese scholar writing on the invention and uses of the Walkman, describes how the new technology creates a "personal theatre." The affective tensions and anticipations of Walkman music are so compelling that they in effect restructure one's real environment: listeners walk the real world to the beat of the Walkman. Writing from the perspective of the People's Republic of China, Rey Chow finds that the "miniaturizing" world of the Walkman offers an individual the ability to be "deaf to the loudspeakers of history" (1993: 49), which is both valuable and problematic.

Sound engineers in Nepal use digital delay echoes and noodling melodic shapes to simulate the effect of sounds heard high in the Himalayan mountains (Greene 2003). In Rio de Janeiro, sound amplifiers deployed along the avenues are differentially timed so that live sounds and their electrical amplification arrive at the same time, thus creating the sense that listeners and performers share a unified soundspace and participate in a shared musical event (Moehn, this volume). In the United States, Porcello (1996: 309–315) shows how engineers who recorded Van Halen's "Runnin' with the Devil" encoded new levels of meaning through the strategic use of stereo imaging and effects processing that invites listeners to hear sound shapes that unfold through three-dimensional space. Radio singers of the 1920s sang closely into a microphone in order to produce sound qualities that would normally be audible only in close spaces (Taylor, this volume). In these ways and many more, sound technologies are also used globally to enact corporeal simulations in the form of technologically constructed or technologically inflected spaces, bodies, and voices (see Lacasse 2000). These are also sound technology's animating moments, when perceptually persuasive sound products mimic or evoke physical environments. Through stereo imaging, effects processing, and the sampling of sounds that bring to mind certain kinds of places, engineers create virtual-cum-real cultural spaces audible in musical design.

The contributors to the present anthology all discuss wired sound in one sense or another, and all engage with a new global soundscape that is wired for sound. The authors represent the disciplines of ethnomusicology, cultural and linguistic anthropology, popular music studies, cultural studies, and communications, and they hail from the most distant expanses of the Western world: Sweden, Australia, and North America. Many of them also have considerable hands-on experience in sound-studio engineering. Our common focus has been to paint a world portrait (we collectively cover all six inhabited continents) from a position combining ethnographic detail and theoretical rigor. In this volume, many of the chapters foreground questions rooted in sound studios and the ways in which studio-produced sounds are used. Chapters 2 through 7 (by Meintjes, Moehn, Neuenfeldt, Porcello, Diamond, and Wallach) emphasize production practices, while chapters 8 through 12 (by Fales, Berger and Fales, Greene, Grandin, and Taylor) emphasize issues of reception; yet many of the chapters demonstrate in their very contents that a clear distinction cannot be drawn between the two.

In "Reaching 'Overseas': South African Sound Engineers, Technology, and Tradition," Louise Meintjes examines sound-studio practice, culture, and discourse in Johannesburg. "Overseas" (meaning the major European and American studios) represents for South African engineers a "trope of excellence," with associations of innovation, wealth, and stardom: "For sound engineers who are involved in shaping South African music styles, values about local traditions are co-constructed with ideas about sound production in high-end studios in the metropoles of the North." Meintjes, who also examines labor relations in view of the apartheid legacy, recounts an ongoing preference on behalf of one white engineer for a direct input of bass guitar, while black musicians preferred a slightly distorted miked sound "appropriate to a 'traditional' aesthetic." The solution: "Peter simultaneously miked the amp and patched the bass directly into the console, and he assured the musicians that he could get them the sound they wanted, 'only better,' with the clean DI signal." Disagreements over sound aesthetics (to distort or not to distort) are moments where the racial politics of studio production happen by way of studio decisions.

In "'The Disc Is Not the Avenue': Schismogenetic Mimesis in Samba Recording," Frederick Moehn explores a dichotomization of musical spheres that happens as Brazilian samba groups who perform elaborate and boisterous musical processions down the avenues (*sambódromos*) of Rio de Janeiro also produce marketable albums of their music in studios. With careful attention to what is captured and what is "cleaned up" in the studio tracks (*base*), he shows how the two spheres in some ways assimilate to each other and in other ways become sharply polarized. In studios, samba musicians and engineers seek ways to capture and encode some of the participatory energy of the avenue; however, they also pursue new ideals of a "professional sound." Remarkably, Moehn also finds that sound engineers alter the sound reinforcement technology deployed for samba processions specifically with the aim of making the long soundscape of the avenue function as a single sphere of shared musical experience. This is accomplished by a computer program that calculates the precise delay needed for each speaker such that the sound traveling through the air arrives at the same time as its electrical amplification.

In "Nigel Pegrum, 'Didjeridu-Friendly Sections,' and What Constitutes an 'Indigenous' CD: An Australian Case Study of Producing 'World Music' Recordings," Karl Neuenfeldt examines producer/engineer Nigel Pegrum's engineering of "indigenous authenticity." Neuenfeldt finds that the earthy, "real" sound of the didjeridu is juxtaposed by engineers with "unreal" (connoting artificial or inauthentic) synthesized sounds. The challenge for engineers is to blend the two kinds of sound in a way that does not result in a jarring juxtaposition. Neuenfeldt also finds that despite worldwide standardization there are "secret" aspects to recording processes, in that individual producers or engineers have particular ways of recording or mixing that arise from their particular aesthetic visions, or "sounds."

In "Music Mediated As Live in Austin: Sound, Technology, and Recording Practice," Thomas Porcello examines participatory discrepancies (defined as timbre, sound, and tone qualities), reverberant sound, and ideals of genuine and populist expression represented by live-sounding or live-seeming recording techniques. He identifies Austin's sound values in connection with the city's performance scene, and in the contrast between the music scenes of Austin and Nashville, perceived locally as a battle of ideologies. Porcello finds that the city of Austin "has actively traded upon this sound in promoting civic identity and using the live music scene to bolster the local economy," and that sincerity, place, musical style, and live performance constitute the Austin sound to such an extent that any recording process must realize these qualities. In particular, Porcello discusses how drum sounds are engineered to evoke "roominess" as an index of live performance, and how technological choices in the recording process are to a large extent driven by the fact that "liveness" is a political aesthetic for many Austin musicians.

In "Media As Social Action: Native American Musicians in the Recording Studio," Beverley Diamond studies Native American musicians, especially Native American women, as they enter the sound studio to craft their musical expressions. Women artists in particular consider the choice of engineers and musicians with whom they work to be highly important, and they speak of the "trust" that is a necessary prerequisite for recording. Diamond shows the problems that emerge when these artists find that the recording practice is organized around the common recording-studio assumption that music consists of separable parts that can be recorded in separate takes. In contrast, much Native American music requires "live" social interaction among musicians in order to unfold properly, and it relies upon cueing devices that are not easily incorporated into studio practice. Consequently, the musicians insist upon organizing themselves in circles as they perform. Native Americans express deep concerns about any studio effects or processes that would obscure the precise timbral and rhythmic features that make it possible to differentiate the music of one region or nation from another. Diamond's study elucidates ways in which the logic and assumptions behind sound technology and recording practices can become barriers to local expressive needs, and how musicians overcome such difficulties.

Jeremy Wallach's "Engineering Techno-Hybrid Grooves in Two Indonesian Sound Studios" examines how various ethnic and foreign sounds are layered in recording studios in Indonesia. While "influence" is a sine qua non of understanding nearly all aesthetic products, multitrack technology heralds an unprecedented fluency with hybridization: the creation of sounds under a rubric of the simultaneity (that is, the copresentation) of influence. Wallach also presents the Indonesian aesthetic anti-ideals of "left back" (Nepalis would say, and do say, "backward") in sound-studio aesthetics. Wallach argues that musical syncretism is representative of cultural syncretisms as experienced today by working-class youths in Jakarta.

Music perception researcher Cornelia Fales examines the acoustics of timbre and the perception of timbre in self-consciously high-tech sounds that "characterize the digital era." In "Short-Circuiting Perceptual Systems: Timbre in Ambient and Techno Music," Fales discovers that in terms of auditory processing, listeners encounter the timbres of electronic musics in ways different from those of acoustic music. Timbre, Fales explains, has a great deal to do with hearing a sound and then interpreting it, presumably by comparing it to known sounds or to whatever sound the listener expects to hear at a certain point in the listening process (see Feld's (1994b) study of "interpretive moves" in listening). Fales delineates a taxonomy of the sounds of ambient music based upon hearing, processing, interpreting, confronting expectations, and so on.

Cornelia Fales and Harris M. Berger collaborate in examining metal fans' perceptions of degrees of "heaviness" in metal songs. In "'Heaviness' in the Perception of Heavy Metal Guitar Timbres: The Match of Perceptual and Acoustic Features over Time," Berger and Fales work with findings published by Berger (1999) and Robert Walser (1993) that demonstrate that among metalheads, it is primarily the guitar timbres that define a "heavy" sound. Berger and Fales examine musics that metalheads characterize as less heavy and more heavy (i.e. earlier and later heavy metal music) and compare their acoustic measurements; in so doing, they both historicize heavy timbre and also describe its timbral qualities with greater nuancing. Working from the aesthetic values of heavy metal (power, intensity, heaviness, and so on) Berger and Fales discover that perception of heaviness corresponds to a flattened dynamic envelope, and that flatter and flatter envelopes sound heavier and heavier to metalhead listeners.

In "Mixed Messages: Unsettled Cosmopolitanisms in Nepali Pop," I examine the reception of Nepali mix music: studio-engineered sonic montages of abruptly juxtaposed musical styles heard in rapid succession. In the "mix" configuration, foreign and indigenous sounds often present themselves as inscrutable sound bites—suggestive, intriguing, but ultimately underdetermined cultural indices that are detached from their original histories and contexts. Kathmandu's "mix" musics, which have taken on a new shape since the early 1990s, suggest that one *ars combinatoria* is not the same as another. Unlike Chinese mix musics with their gritty rock timbre that indexes authenticity, or certain Indonesian mixes in which jazz's sophistication represents a cultural fit and thus a comfortable studio mix with gamelan's elite connotations of the court, Nepali mix music encodes with fanatic precision a montage of timbres, rhythms, and sound bites that cite and graph the West without integrating it. Urban listeners describe themselves as situated in contradictory worlds as they hear the mixture of East and West that characterizes the professional identities of Kathmandu's upper middle class.

Electromagnetic music encoding—wireless "wires" of radio broadcasting—form the basis of the soundscapes of Ingemar Grandin's "The Soundscape of the Radio: Engineering *Modern Songs* and Superculture in Nepal" and Tim Taylor's "Music and the Rise of Radio in Twenties America: Technological Imperialism, Socialization, and the Transformation of Intimacy." Grandin examines the sociocultural aspects, politics, and economics of radio sound production in Nepal in the 1970s. Articulating some well-founded skepticism toward theories that assume that music commodities will automatically lead to music industries, Grandin explains how economies of patronage and sponsorship guided the sound-studio production for Radio Nepal. Musical products such as audiocassettes were primary prestige markers for the featured musician rather than commodities that entered a market of consumers. The engineered sounds broadcast by Radio Nepal shaped both a national culture and a "superculture" (in the sense of Slobin 1993) that incorporated Nepal's multiple ethnicities, influences from outside Nepal, oppositional voices, and so on.

Timothy Taylor examines the culture of early radio, and the discourses of and surrounding radio, in the United States. The domestication of radio technology (its reach into private homes), Taylor argues, grew out of marketing strategies that urged consumers to purchase a necessary object of "civilized" peoples. In fact, "having technology" was rapidly becoming a means of labeling people on the radio and in other media, of separating Americans and American-ness from native peoples elsewhere and their technologically "deficient" lifeways.

Early radio took on uses that brought this technology into the deepest reaches of privacy and that are unheard of today: radio weddings, radio funerals, radio "prescriptions" as part of medical practice, and so on. Taylor argues compellingly that "even as radio was brought into these realms of social life . . . it was at the same time reconfiguring the nature of the private, of intimate space—it was being integrated into individual lives, into individual private fantasies." American radio then came to blur, or at least alter, the distinction between public and private in American life.

In his afterword, Thomas Porcello surveys several broad themes emerging in these chapters and suggests analytical trajectories for future research. He calls for a broad, multidisciplinary approach to the study of the world's contemporary high-tech sonic cultures and suggests that *Wired for Sound* represents a foray into examining what he calls local "techoustemologies" of sound. By this new term, which is also an analytic tool, he means to "foreground the implication of forms of technological mediation on individuals' knowledge of, sensations in, and consequent actions upon their acoustic environments as grounded in the specific times and places of the production and reception of sound."

In sum, I believe it is time for ethnomusicologists, anthropologists, communications and media theorists, sociologists, historians, and others to make a greater contribution to the study of sound engineering and the world's technological musics. Our scholarly inquiries should further engage with the ways that wired technologies influence and are entangled in today's many diverse sonic cultures, and with the creative, cultural, and musical ways locally situated agents use and refunction their technologies. As we increasingly make and listen to music through the interconnected machines of the globe, we open up new chapters in our notions of organology.

Notes

1. The Hornbostel-Sachs (1961) scheme of organology involving membranophones, chordophones, idiophones, and aerophones (exemplified by drums, zithers, gongs, and flutes, respectively) is sometimes extended to include electrophones—synthesizers or other instruments sounded electrically. But the system loses analytic utility in distinguishing among the many practices and technologies of electric music making. The scheme's criteria for organological distinction include the nature of the material that vibrates, and the immediate means by which the material is made to vibrate. These criteria are not useful in distinguishing among the many electric musical practices or technologies: in every case, woofers and tweeters at the final playback location are made to vibrate in response to electrical signals.

2. Alison Arnold (2000: 538) observes that Lata Mangeshkar is cited in the *Guinness Book of World Records* as the vocalist who has recorded the largest number of songs.

3. I have found that Chinese-made music technologies are increasingly used throughout South and Southeast Asia; most are interchangeable with established western technologies.

4. This echoes an earlier technology-related struggle, when the western keyboard–driven harmonium was introduced to India in the mid-nineteenth century. In much of the twentieth century the instrument was banned from Indian radio because it was incapable of producing *gamaks.*

References

Adorno, Theodor. 1958/1999. "Music and Technique." In *Sound Figures,* transl. Rodney Livingstone. Stanford: Stanford University Press, 197–216.

Appadurai, Arjun. 1990. "Disjuncture and Difference in the Global Cultural Economy." *Public Culture* 2(2): 1–24.

Arnold, Alison. 2000. "[Indian] Film Music: Northern Area." *Garland Encyclopedia of World Music,* vol. 5, pp. 531–541. New York: Garland.

Benjamin, Walter. 1968. "The Work of Art in the Age of Mechanical Reproduction." In *Illuminations,* trans. Hannah Arent. New York: Schocken Books, 217–251.

Berger, Harris M. 1999. *Metal, Rock, and Jazz: Perception and the Phenomenology of Musical Experience.* Hanover, N.H.: Wesleyan University Press/University Press of New England.

Born, Georgina. 1995. *Rationalizing Culture: IRCAM, Boulez, and the Institutionalization of the Musical Avant-Garde.* Berkeley: University of California Press.

Bradby, Barbara. 1993. "Sampling Sexuality: Gender, Technology, and the Body in Dance Music." *Popular Music* 12(2): 155–176.

Chanan, Michael. 1995. *Repeated Takes: A Short History of Recording and Its Effects on Music.* London: Verso.

Chow, Rey. 1993. "Listening Otherwise, Music Miniaturized: A Different Type of Question about Revolution." In *The Cultural Studies Reader,* ed. Simon During. New York: Routledge, 382–402.

Cutler, Chris. 1984. "Technology, Politics, and Contemporary Music: Necessity and Choice in Musical Forms." *Popular Music* 4: 279–300.

Erlmann, Veit. 1996. "The Aesthetics of the Global Imagination: Reflections on World Music in the 1990s." *Public Culture* 18(1): 467–488.

Feld, Steven. 1994a. "From Schizophonia to Schismogenesis: On the Discourses and Practices of World Music and World Beat." In *Music Grooves: Essays and Dialogues,* ed. Charles Keil and Steven Feld. Chicago: University of Chicago Press, 257–289.

———. 1994b. "Communication, Music, and Speech about Music." In *Music Grooves,* 77–95.

Fikentscher, Kai. 2000. *"You Better Work!" Underground Dance Music in New York City.* Hanover, N.H.: Wesleyan University Press/University Press of New England.

Frith, Simon. 1996. *Performing Rites: On the Value of Popular Music.* Cambridge, Mass.: Harvard University Press.

Greene, Paul. 1999. "Sound Engineering in a Tamil Village: Playing Cassettes as Devotional Performance." *Ethnomusicology* 43(3): 459–489.

———. 2001. "Authoring the Folk: The Crafting of a Rural Popular Music in South India." *Journal of Intercultural Studies* 22(2): 161–172.

———. 2003. "Nepal's *Lok Pop* Music: Representations of the Folk, Tropes of Memory, and Studio Technologies." *Asian Music* 34(1): 43–65.
Greene, Paul, and David Henderson. 2000. "At the Crossroads of Languages, Musics, and Emotions in Kathmandu." *Popular Music and Society* 24(3): 95–116.
Haraway, Donna J. 1991. *Simians, Cyborgs, and Women: The Reinvention of Nature.* New York: Routledge.
Hornbostel, Erich von, and Curt Sachs. 1961. "Classification of Musical Instruments." Trans. Anthony Baines and Klaus Wachsmann. Reprinted in *Galpin Society Journal* 14: 3–29.
Hosokawa, Shuhei. 1984. "The Walkman Effect." *Popular Music* 4: 165–180.
———. 1990. *Reko do no bigaku* [The Aesthetics of Recorded Sound], English summary. Tokyo: Keisó Shobó.
Jones, Steve. 1992. *Rock Formation: Music, Technology, and Mass Communication.* Newbury Park, Calif.: Sage Publications.
———. 2000. "Music and the Internet." *Popular Music* 19(2): 217–230.
Lacasse, Serge. 2000. "Voice and Sound Processing: Examples of Mise en Scène of Voice in Recorded Rock Music." *Popular Musicology Online.*
Lipsitz, George. 1994. *Dangerous Crossroads: Popular Music, Postmodernism, and the Poetics of Place.* New York: Verso.
Lysloff, René T. A., and Leslie C. Gay, eds. 2003. *Music and Technoculture.* Middletown, Conn.: Wesleyan University Press/University Press of New England.
Mackenzie, Donald, and Judy Wajcman, eds. 1999. *The Social Shaping of Technology,* 2nd ed. Buckingham: Open University Press.
Manuel, Peter. 1993. *Cassette Culture: Popular Music and Technology in North India.* Chicago: University of Chicago Press.
———. 1995. "Music as Symbol, Music as Simulacrum: Postmodern, Pre-modern, and Modern Aesthetics in Subcultural Popular Musics." *Popular Music* 14: 227–239.
Marsh, Charity, and Melissa West. 2003. "The Nature/Technology Binary Opposition Dismantled in the Music of Madonna and Björk." In *Music and Technoculture,* eds. René T. A. Lysloff and Leslie C. Gay. Middletown, Conn.: Wesleyan University Press/University Press of New England, 182–203.
Meintjes, Louise. 2003. *Sound of Africa! Making Music Zulu in a South African Studio.* Durham, N.C.: Duke University Press.
Penley, Constance, and Andrew Ross. 1991. *Technoculture.* Minneapolis: University of Minnesota Press.
Porcello, Thomas. 1996. *Sonic Artistry: Music, Discourse, and Technology in the Sound Recording Studio.* Ph.D. dissertation, University of Texas at Austin.
———. 1998/2003. "'Tails Out': Social Phenomenology and the Ethnographic Representation of Technology in Music-Making." *Ethnomusicology* 42(3): 485–510. Reprinted in *Music and Technoculture,* ed. René T. A. Lysloff and Leslie C. Gay. Middletown, Conn.: Wesleyan University Press/University Press of New England, 264–289.
Rasmussen, Anne. 1996. "Theory and Practice at the 'Arabic Org': Digital Technology in Contemporary Arab Music Performance." *Popular Music* 15: 345–365.
Rose, Tricia. 1994. *Black Noise: Rap Music and Black Culture in Contemporary America.* Hanover, N.H.: Wesleyan University Press/University Press of New England.
Sandstrom, Boden. 2000. "Women Mix Engineers and the Power of Sound." In *Music and Gender,* eds. Pirkko Moisala and Beverley Diamond. Urbana: University of Illinois Press, 289–305.
Shank, Barry. 1994. *Dissonant Identities: The Rock 'n' Roll Scene in Austin, Texas.* Hanover, N.H.: Wesleyan University Press/University Press of New England.

Slobin, Mark. 1993. *Subcultural Sounds: Micromusics of the West.* Hanover, N.H.: Wesleyan University Press/University Press of New England.
Small, Christopher. 1998. *Musicking: The Meanings of Performing and Listening.* Hanover, N.H.: Wesleyan University Press/University Press of New England.
Taylor, Timothy D. 1997. *Global Pop: World Music, World Markets.* New York: Routledge.
———. 2001. *Strange Sounds: Music, Technology, and Culture.* New York: Routledge.
Théberge, Paul. 1997. *Any Sound You Can Imagine: Making Music/Consuming Technology.* Hanover, N.H.: Wesleyan University Press/University Press of New England.
———. 2003. "'Ethnic Sounds': The Economy and Discourse of World Music Sampling." In *Music and Technoculture,* ed. René T. A. Lysloff and Leslie Gay. Middletown, Conn.: Wesleyan University Press/University Press of New England, 93–108.
Thomas, Nicholas. 1991. *Entangled Objects: Exchange, Material Culture, and Colonialism in the Pacific.* Cambridge, Mass.: Harvard University Press.
Thornton, Sarah. 1996. *Club Cultures: Music, Media, and Subcultural Capital.* Hanover, N.H.: Wesleyan University Press/University Press of New England.
Wallach, Jeremy. 2003. "The Poetics of Electrosonic Presence: Recorded Music and the Materiality of Sound." *Journal of Popular Music Studies* 15(1): 34–64.
Walser, Robert. 1993. *Running with the Devil: Power, Gender, and Madness in Heavy Metal Music.* Hanover, N.H.: Wesleyan University Press/University Press of New England.
Winner, Langdon. 1999. "Do Artifacts Have Politics?" In *The Social Shaping of Technology,* ed. D. MacKenzie and J. Wajcman. Buckingham: Open University Press.
Wong, Deborah. 1994. "'I Want the Microphone': Mass Mediation and Agency in Asian-American Popular Music." *The Drama Review* 38(3): 152–167.
———. 2003. "Plugged In at Home: Vietnamese American Technoculture in Orange County." In *Music and Technoculture,* ed. René T. A. Lysloff and Leslie Gay. Middletown, Conn.: Wesleyan University Press/University Press of New England, 125–152.
Zak, Albin J. III. 2001. *The Poetics of Rock: Cutting Tracks, Making Records.* Berkeley: University of California Press.

CHAPTER TWO

Reaching "Overseas"

South African Sound Engineers, Technology, and Tradition

Louise Meintjes

"Overseas," sound engineers do not have to cover for the producer, scramble around like a tape operator,[1] program any musician's keyboard, check any string tunings, rehearse any vocalists, or invent any lyrics. Seated in front of the console, they can concentrate on technically rendering the best sound possible for the job at hand.

In the U.K., "I was handed the lead—that's it, that's it, that's it!" British sound engineer Richard Austin exclaimed to me in Johannesburg, South Africa, in 1992. "I mark it up on the desk, and the tape op takes the leads and pops them in. And then you just concentrate on the sound. While the programmer's trying to work out 'Oh God, this has got to be changed'; the producer is saying 'I don't quite like that,' all I'm worried about is getting the right sound. Because you've only got that [one] area to worry about, obviously your product is going to sound better."[2]

"Overseas," a sound engineer is in a position to experience the process of technological production uncompromised and at its best: the toughest producers, absolute engineering at the console, super-creative technicians, the smartest design boffins behind the newest technological innovations, mythic star personalities backstage and in the throes of composition, and mediated public attention as glitzy as it gets. Once "overseas," an engineer can engage with these desirable features of the profession in their superlative, quality-producing forms.

"Overseas" is constructed as a value-laden discursive category through talk amongst engineers about their own work in foreign studios as well as through stories circulated about the studio experiences of others. South African Darryl Heilbrunn learned how to design and build studios while on a three-month course at the Recording Workshop in Trillacarthy, Ohio, in 1984. He then made his way to Los Angeles, where he helped build an eight-track studio. "Just as it was completed, [the owner's] husband had hooked up with some people in London and the Clash — Joe Strummer — wanted to do a demo in Los Angeles. So one of my first clients was a major British punk artist, Joe Strummer, which was a freak out! When we left the studio there would be hoards of fans outside, and limos and bodyguards and the whole Hollywood extravaganza — so I was hooked."[3]

To sustain a career and to cope with the daily pressures and strict hierarchies in an "overseas" studio, an engineer has to be "hooked" in some way, whether by the glitz, the sounds, or the technological puzzles involved in rendering sound to tape or disc. Conventional divisions of labor, organizational processes, and protocols of apprenticeship are rigorously upheld in those studios. As a seventeen-year-old initiate in British studios Richard Austin had to operate the tape recording machines. "For like three years he tape-op'ed — that's just sitting with the remote control for the tape machine," narrated Lance Longley, a new studio assistant who had many more tasks than that at Downtown Studios in Johannesburg. "Richard wasn't allowed to ask a question to the engineer about *anything*, about the desk, or what he was doing. All he had to do was just handle the tape machine. That was *it* for like three years!"[4] Such austere procedures need to be upheld if a studio is to deliver the goods, for "overseas" the intensity of the demand for sonic sophistication and the requisite standards of production are supreme. Over there, engineers are incrementally trained in the profession from the bottom up. In an ordered system, an engineer is socialized into its smooth operation. When Humphrey Mabote participated in an audio engineering course at Surrey University in the U.K. in 1984, the instructor "called a producer from Earth, Wind & Fire to come and give us a lecture about various producers that he had worked with. He will tell you how difficult the producers are, so you get yourself into it."[5] In other words, he warned novice engineers to brace themselves for working with renowned producers who might be divas or tyrants.

However tough and uncompromising "overseas" studio practice is, it presents opportunities for professional development and innovative work. An engineer may rub shoulders with music and industry elites, learning from them and perhaps absorbing some of their prestige. Part of Humphrey's thrill of learning in the U.K. came from "being taught by a person who made that particular machine. That guy will tell you straightforward

'I made *this* to correspond with *that*.' You actually see the guy who made an SSL actually teaching you how to work it out, and teaching you what major problems you can encounter on an SSL.[6] And the guys who made the Mitsubishi digital machines, they are all there [too]! The guys who use them—I'm talking of the big guys, you know—[they are all there]."[7] By working in studios "overseas" an engineer can participate in a global network of thoroughly cosmopolitan music makers who are constantly on the move, upward through the ranks of their profession, and outward around the world.

For all of these reasons—a rigorous work ethic, a keen systematic training and socialization procedure, a shared dedicated attention to sophisticated sound manipulation in the studio control room—"overseas" is artistically enabling.

After tape op'ing for three years without being permitted to interrupt the engineers with distracting questions, Richard Austen broke through, "and the guys would show him this and that. He's worked with a lot of very good bands: Phil Collins, Shakatak, Brian Eno from Roxy Music, a lot of very popular people. I mean to me," Lance professes, "that's what it is, hey. The music world is definitely overseas."[8]

By "overseas" Lance doesn't mean all of the places across the oceans. He doesn't mean Cape Verde, or Bombay, or Moscow, or Buenos Aires. He doesn't even mean Tokyo. "Overseas" refers to the Euro-American metropoles, the major centers of music production and distribution. It is constituted by the principal geographic nodes through which many forms of recorded music from across the globe filter in order to gain access to the wealthiest multinational markets, where music sales are the most profitable.[9] In addition to referencing a set of places unlike Johannesburg, "overseas" represents a trope of excellence. In the interviews I conducted and from which I quote above, the exaggerated talk of engineers working in South Africa elevates foreign studio processes into an ideal type. It is the character and significance of this ideal type that I will consider here.

"Overseas" is most likely a vigorous discursive category in many studios located away from the Euro-American metropoles. But how and when "overseas" is significant and what precisely its components are in each case arise from the peculiarities of the experience of studio practice at home. I posit that South Africa's history of racialized politics lends this ideal type its local distinction, even though the engineers do not present "overseas" in racialized terms. I unpack this below in order to argue that the specificities of a studio's political context as well as its technological history and position in the global market are implicated—and often audible—in the sounds the studio produces.

Based on my fieldwork in Johannesburg, which took place predominantly at Gallo Africa's Downtown Studios, I present my argument in three steps.[10] First I lay out the local conditions outside the studio at a particular South African historical moment falling between the unbanning of the liberation movement organizations in 1990 and the first democratic elections in 1994. This time produced intense challenges for local recording companies and studios, which were in the process of (re)entering a competitive global market. New risks and opportunities, coupled with the uncertainties of political upheaval and negotiation, prompted passionate comparative talk about foreign and domestic recording conditions amongst engineers.

Next I enter the studio control room, where I chronicle race, class, and gender configurations in order to profile the social and professional practices that shape a peculiarly South African work environment. This 1990s configuration emerges from apartheid's history, throughout which access to opportunities and capital was regulated on the basis of state-determined race categorizations.

Finally I detail some recording procedures for "traditional" music, as narrated by sound engineers. By traditional music, I mean music referred to as such by sound engineers as well as music marketed by the domestic industry under this rubric. Though Downtown Studio's sound engineers were all engaged in a variety of projects, the bulk of their work came from recording what they often referred to as "black stuff": low-budget, run-of-the-mill, township pop styles and traditional musics. As tokens of a characteristically South African sound, successful traditional music recordings probably best equipped South African studio practitioners with a commodity and a professional profile to help them reach overseas, each in their various capacities as performers, producer-managers, or engineers. It is also in the recording of traditional musics that struggles over rendering professional excellence rub most harshly against struggles over aesthetic preference. Moments of contestation over sound become available for the underlying racial politics to work themselves out, and hence my focus here. For sound engineers who are involved in shaping South African music styles, values about local traditions are co-constructed with ideas about sound production in high-end studios in the metropoles of the North.

Sound Shapers

With the exception of Edward Kealy (1979) it is only in the last decade that music scholars and trade press authors have recognized that the role of the studio sound engineer is an important musical one (Buskin 1991, Stone 1992, Porcello 1996, Théberge 1997, Porcello 1998, Cunningham 1998, Meintjes 2003). Yet engineers have increasingly assumed the creative authority once reserved for producers in the control room. Producers, once principally talent scouts, then artists and repertoire personnel, evolved into dominating—if not dictatorial—figures running production houses, ruling recording sessions, and becoming celebrities. Nowadays, in bids to maintain that level of creative control in the composition, arrangement, recording, and mixing processes, a number of producers have migrated to the seat of the sound engineer (for example, Daniel Lanois, who has produced and engineered albums by U2 and Robbie Robertson, among others). Others have begun to identify what they do as engineering rather than producing, as engineering gains in reputation as a compositional act and producing suffers from its association with big business (for example, Steve Albini, who engineered albums for bands such as Cordelia's Dad, Nirvana, and John Spencer Blues, among others). This blurring of engineering and production roles in the studio—sometimes with performing artists' roles as well—has come about with developments in audio technology that place artistic control increasingly in the hands of those who have the technological competence to manipulate electronic controls and to work through often complex user interface systems.

Trade press authors and scholars writing about studio-sound engineering have of course been captivated by the innovative and distinctive features of the subject under study, namely the technological gear and electronic advances that seem to make creative processes in the studio different from those on the stage or in the street. Thus writers have largely focused on professionals working in European or American metropoles, major centers for the consumption of high-tech equipment. State-of-the-art design and fully integrated use of electronics is assumed in the discussions. They have also tended to concentrate on high-sales, high-budget, high-tech productions in those metropoles, thus mostly in the pop, rock, r&b, and sometimes jazz styles.

Supported by a growing literature on the history of sound equipment (Daniel, et al. 1999), sociology and media studies have led the way in generating discussions about studio-based creativity. Historical accounts track changes in production procedures and sonic experimentation as they have been prompted by technological advances (Kealy 1979, Millard 1995, Cunningham 1998). In professional biographies of engineers and producers, writers trace career lineages by itemizing each person's progress in relation to specific studios, producers, stars, hits, and technology preferences (Martin 1979, Buskin 1991, Stone 1992). Sociological and media studies approaches situate music recording in the context of industrial organization, economic processes, and technological procedures (Gray 1988, Hennion 1989, Théberge 1997).

Summing up the current study of music technology, Théberge states that "recording technology must be understood as a complete 'system' of production involving the organization of musical, social, and technical means" (1997: 193). Ethnographers have begun to expand on what "the organization of . . . social means" in the studio entails, and ethnomusicologists have begun to detail how that organization is critical to the shaping of "musical means." For example, the absence of women behind the console and the difficulties of their entry into the trade have been discussed (Sandstrom 2000), as have issues of gender in relation to the deployment of studio technology, language use, and power (Porcello 1996). Thomas Porcello has also discussed issues of language and power in relation to the recording of differently valued music styles. Greene (2001) and Stolzhoff (2000) are among those who consider mixing in relation to issues of class and generation or ethnicity, though they do so in contexts of consumption/reception or of dance club performance, not in relation to social processes inside the studio.

What I can contribute here, in the spirit of Tim Taylor's reminder to consider agents and their specific practices in relation to the use of technologies (Taylor 2001: 25–38), is a further delineation of the "social" inside the studio. In a 1989 paper that importantly begins to tease out the industrial and creative processes enclosed in the control room, Antoine Hennion writes that in order to construct a sonic representation of the world, which he takes to be the "abstract task" of artistic production, one of the initial steps in the recording studio is that of "methodically rendering the world absent" (Hennion 1989: 411). Only by representing an ideal studio is it possible to erase from studio practice the power relations generated by forms of social difference operating in the social world outside the studio.

The ingenuity of technicians, advances in technology, individual talent of artists, and market pressures all need to be held in analytic view if we are to understand the innovative and creative decisions of music production. But without articulating in more detail what the "social means" in sound recording are, these engineers and production teams, and the aesthetic decisions they make in the studio, will continue to be represented as somehow free of social biographies and political positioning and unaffected by the contours of local histories.

An emphasis on "world music" production in a center located in the backwaters of the multinational industry (and in a politically unsettled state) prompts other kinds of considerations as well. It absolutely brings to the fore ways in which politics outside the studio are implicated in the creative processes that happen through the electronic manipulation of sound inside the studio. Such politics are affected both by the global location—hence, by their position in relation to transnational industrial power relations — and by the peculiarities of local conditions — hence by their position in relation to domestic market controls and state formations. National and transnational postcolonial and industrial drives converge in studio practice, and they are played out in negotiations among engineers, producers, and performing artists over the shaping of sound.

South Africa outside the Studio

Johannesburg is a high-rise industrial city, the center of South Africa's music industry, and the urban environment that produces the nation's highest crime statistics.

In the early 1990s South Africa was in the process of being welcomed back into the world community after decades of international declamation of the apartheid state as a pariah nation. In 1990, Nelson Mandela had just been released, and the African National Congress and other wings of the liberation movement had been unbanned. Multifarious political representatives were negotiating the terms for a transition to democratic governance, to be instantiated in 1994. Along with these acutely contested negotiations, multiple forms of violence fomented in the townships and rural areas (especially in the KwaZulu-Natal province), in informal settlements, single-men's hostels, and on the mines.[11] Eventually the violence spread right into the city centers. Covert state-supported action, labor disputes, political contestation, historical vendettas, police corruption, racial hatred, and criminal opportunism all played a part in producing an upsurge in the violent activity witnessed and experienced by citizens that was unprecedented at any point in the preceding four decades. This lengthy period of distraught and indelibly racialized social relations and widely discrepant class positions could not be erased overnight.

At the same time, political restructuring promised new beginnings for everyone alike: new markets, new professional opportunities, new associations, and new mobility. Though the cultural boycott of South Africa had never been complete — sound engineers, for one, had moved in and out of the country in their professional capacities — its demise through the late 1980s eased foreign barriers for South Africans working in cultural production who wanted to participate in global networks and foreign events.[12]

The breakdown of isolationist policies and ideologies expanded the possibilities of travel for South African cultural producers and their products. It also opened access to the South African market for foreign interests, and domestic industry soon faced the threat of powerful multinational imposition. For local musicians, producers, and engineers, the enticing potential of forging new relationships with high-profile artists and wealthy foreign individuals extending their creative projects and investments into the country was fraught with anxiety. "It's a melting pot at the moment; anything could happen. It's very exciting!" reckoned sound engineer John Lindemann in 1989. He explained, "The thing is, from the technical point of view, we're going to have to jack ourselves up. We've got a problem: our studios are good—they're very good—but we fall a little bit short of the international requirements. Okay, not that I'm in favor of a flood of engineers and producers coming here and just raping us. If we get raped, so will the musicians. We've got to be helluva careful of that. . . . What we need is overseas guys coming here—in limited amounts, okay—and working with the musicians, producers, engineers, and studios [so that we can] learn the little extras from them."

At the very time that the music industry was on the cusp of international reintegration, national economic stresses placed budgetary constraints on cultural producers' work. (For one, a national budget once mostly reserved for a white minority population now had to meet the needs of all of the country's citizens.) With industry and the nation as a whole not yet free of the constraints of the racialized past, not yet safely integrated into a new democracy, and not yet prosperously participating in an open global market, studio management and their engineers found themselves in an exciting though precarious position: how were they to make the shift from parochial to cosmopolitan status without losing control over the commodity (South African sounds) that they produced and that gave them their peculiar distinction? This was the dilemma upon which John Lindemann reflected. "Something's gonna happen," he continued. "I mean eighteen months ago we were in the total grip of sanctions—*total* grip—so we actually knew where we were going because we knew what the limitations were. I had fixed ideas as to how music should be." How were engineers to meet international production standards within the constraints of local codes of studio conduct that were shaped by the economic and political realities of an emerging nation?

To be competitive in a global market and to participate in a global network of production people, high standards in pitch accuracy and production quality, for a start, were of paramount importance. These qualities were the ticket of entry. When an opportunity arose to export the old African jazz band the Elite Swingsters, Gallo scrambled around to remix the new domestic release (Elite Swingsters 1992). Their artists and repertoire team required that the production team improve the sound, especially the weak and muddy bass, and cover up some pitch inaccuracies that were simply too "off" for the world to hear. In the local context, globally competitive production standards were harshly difficult to reach despite the skills of the engineers.

South Africa in the Studio Control Room

In South African recording studios throughout history—and still in the early 1990s—race, class, and gender hierarchies overlapped with the division of labor. On the whole, the engineers were white, middle-class men, while producers—especially of "traditional" styles—were usually black men. Those producers who produced market successes did well financially, becoming icons of an upwardly mobile black class fraction, and they were all thoroughly urban in their lifestyles. In contrast to the producers, traditional performing artists were generally working-class men and women. Some lived in the decrepit inner city or in satellite townships around Johannesburg, while others were rurally based, migrating regularly between town and countryside. Most of these musicians were only employed in temporary or part-time positions, or they were seeking work; few had opportunities for full-time employment in or out of the industry. Traditional recording musicians generally struggled to earn a living wage through musical activities alone.

These race and class positions in the studio derive their forms from apartheid's peculiar history. That men should be schooled to be adept and in control of technology is a widespread social practice;[13] that predominantly white men should be in control is not exclusive to South Africa, though the state's racist exclusion policies created an extreme case. That black producers became particularly powerful gatekeepers in South Africa derives from the idiosyncrasies of the white-controlled industry. Its executives and white employees lacked the necessary knowledge about local black music styles, languages, audiences, locations, practices, and so forth and thus had to rely on their black employees to scout for talent, negotiate with musicians, and promote their product, especially during those eras in which apartheid policies prohibited freedom of movement for whites as well. Black producers became crucial mediating figures, running huge production houses from the 1960s through the early 1980s (Allingham 1992 and 1999, Meintjes 2003). Though they no longer manage competitive houses of artists for recording companies, producers today have sustained some of the legacy of their predecessors and are still necessarily called on to play mediating roles.

In the ideal studio, the producer, as the studio's client, directs studio sessions and has final authority over the sound. The engineer serves the producer. But in South African studio practice, this was not always the case; the engineer—white, male, and at the controls of the console—wielded significantly more power than would probably be the case in studios elsewhere, especially "overseas." On the other hand, even though engineers often extended their contributions to a production beyond their stereotypical duties, their creative input went publicly and remuneratively unacknowledged. "That record reeks of me!" exclaimed Darryl Heilbrunn while complaining that he wasn't offered coproduction rights on an album.[14] As engineers who historically in the division of studio labor had been thought of as craftsmen and technicians (Kealy 1979), and as white, urban, middle-class people working on black artistic expression, they were positioned with a doubly negative status in the South Africa of the early 1990s. When it came to being recognized and valued for their musicality in the studio, they were caught in a nexus between debates about race and cultural ownership and debates about technical service versus definitive musical contribution. Lee Short explained the engineer's struggle for personal recognition in the studio and for professional recognition outside it: "Look, the bottom line with the engineer—and this is the truth—if it's a wonderful, successful great selling album, it's a wonderful producer. If the album dogs, and it's bad and nobody buys it, it's the engineer's fault."[15]

Language differences in the studio also overlapped with the division of labor, at times exacerbating the power differentials stemming from race and class divisions or from studio roles, and at other times strategically countering social and professional hierarchies. Control rooms were never monolingual, yet in traditional music sessions it was particularly rare that all participants would share competence in a common language. Humphrey, Downtown's black in-house engineer, was the only Downtown engineer who spoke local African languages in addition to English and Afrikaans.[16] On the other hand, producers were multilingual and well or adequately versed in English. Performers of traditional styles were also typically multilingual, though, with some exceptions, they spoke little English. Producers thus played a critical mediating role by translating discussions, concerns, and directives between engineer and performers. The fantastic variety of languages and varying levels of facility in the languages represented produced a unique situation, one rife with challenges for efficient collaboration and loaded with poetic means for discreetly contesting authorities. Virtuosic code-switching and choices of language were used in order to communicate but also at times to exclude, to joke, to mark an authorial position, or to undercut others' claims of authority.

The following vignette will serve as an example: the engineer, producer, and singers are getting ready for a take in the studio. It is the engineer's usual duty to announce the name of the band and song number onto the tape as an identifying measure before recording a song. "Well—you can say it this time," engineer Peter Pearlson tells West Nkosi, the producer; the band's name is Isigqi Sesimanje, and the correct pronunciation of "Isigqi" requires the sounding of a voiced alveolar-palatal "click." The ability to say this consonant "q" (here in the form "gq") is a distinct marker of Zuluness in the studio.

Producer West responds authoritatively: "You must say that, Peter."

Silence.

"I'm teaching you now. Isigqi, cut one," West says to Peter, who is meant to repeat the phrase after him. Silence. "Isigqi," says West. "Say it," he demands, playfully acting out his authority as producer over his engineer.

West repeats it till Peter reluctantly has to try. Peter sounds out "Isi—ke." No good.

West leans forward, looks him in the face, and prompts him syllable by syllable with perfect deliberation. Everyone in the studio laughs. West jostles with him. "Ah, come on, Peter, you must improve, man!"

At this point Peter draws out his professional card: "We've taken two hours to set up, and we're going to spend another two hours trying to start the first song." West relents.

While Peter checks if he's getting a reading, one of the singers in the recording booth quips in Zulu to her fellow waiting vocalists, "Can you hear them? White people talk like their tongues are burning!"

"Okay, standby!" calls Peter, his fingers poised on the record and play buttons.

West pronounces "Isigqi, cut one" onto the tape as it rolls and the recording begins.[17]

Thus a struggle that arose out of a recording procedure was waged playfully over discrepancies in linguistic skills. Nevertheless, it brought to the fore a deviation from standard ("overseas") practice as well as a (culturally specific) inadequacy of the engineer.

In addition to the particular multilingual dynamics in the studio, varying competences in technical vocabularies exacerbate differences among studio participants and generate other idiosyncratic recording practices as well. Few traditional performers have a facility in using scientific or acoustic terms to talk about sound recording and processing, the terms by which engineers render musical sounds into digital information to be stored on tape. Nor do producers of traditional recordings necessarily have competence in the operation of electronic studio technology and its concomitant technical vocabulary, though they are in charge of the studio sessions.[18]

"Know the desk, man!" exclaims Darryl in frustration. "[African American producers] could talk to you in technical terms; they were thoroughbred, qualified producers. Our guys just aren't educated in that manner. Yes, blame apartheid, blame the white man—whatever—but it's a fact, you know."[19] These "technical terms" encompass an understanding of the capabilities of technology and what it can offer in terms of sound repertoire, a command of the scientific terms that articulate ideas about sound quality and processing as precisely as possible, and a competence in English to communicate those ideas in the (unexamined) lingua franca of the studio. Darryl proposes that these skills are fundamentals of the trade and simply need to be learned. "There is no way that a producer can sit back and say 'I don't need to know anything about engineering because I'm a producer.' That is rubbish. That does not exist overseas!" It was thus sometimes the case in South African sessions that those with technical knowledge assumed authority over the producer. Engineers reported that they frequently mixed recordings, in whole or in part, in the absence of the producer (and with the producer's subsequent approval).

Communication in "traditional" recording sessions is thus socially and pragmatically complicated with respect to race and class positions and language use, with the former mapping onto the politics of the latter. Social position and (English) language competence bear on the creation of and access to particularized professional knowledge formations.

While sound engineers freely comment on the weaknesses in black performers' "technical" competence, they speak cautiously about their own authority over matters of local culture and tradition. "Culture" is constructed in studio talk as the domain of the performers; they might not have the gear, but they have the goods: songs, local voices, and tradition. In narrating to me the experience of recording the Tsongan artist Thomas Chauke,[20] Lee very carefully and persistently qualified his musical evaluations as technical considerations, even though they were clearly not only about production value. His care in speaking is marked not only in his emphatic repetitions but also in the way he hedges and qualifies his comments: "I was very unhappy with [the previous Thomas Chauke album]—technically—technically I was not happy at all. It was actually quite embarrassing. But the thing sold a hundred and fifty thousand units! Thomas was smiling, the record company was smiling, and the people out there apparently were smiling. So who am I to really judge it? . . . I must admit, I approached it differently this year [with the next album], with this whole sort of high-tech [approach] instead of from the live traditional kind of feel. I put a lot of new sort of feeling to it, and this year I was [a] helluva lot happier—technically. You know, the first album he didn't really know who I was, nor my approach and my feel, and I wasn't too sure about him. We had to get to know each other." Lee goes on to qualify his authority and the form it takes as professionally based and sufficiently within the bounds of his engineering status. But his reflection begins to less self-consciously recognize the extent of his socially accumulated power: "This time I was in a more fortunate position where I could actually call more of the shots, or not necessarily call more of the shots but maybe advise technically, just advise a little more, you know, and say 'Ah, be careful of that,' for this and this reason, and actually prove it to him. And he'd say 'No, you're dead right.' So this year's album far outstripped last year's album — technically. This one I could actually put on and the engineers can listen to it, and they can criticize or praise it as they wish. I was too embarrassed to put the last one on, because I just gave Thomas exactly what he wanted. As he wanted it, I gave it to him, which is not always the wisest thing. You've got to be careful — you've got to hit that right balance between the two. It's hard."[21]

Essentially Lee is talking about balancing between asserting an authority conferred on him by his race and class position and an authority appropriate to his studio role. The former would better enable him to deliver the production values that meet international standards and thereby protect his reputation in the world of engineering. The latter would express from the position of an engineer a respect for the authority of a star, a performing artist, and a client, and it would be sensitive to a history of white domination.

What Lee articulated as a technical and cultural divide was explained by Tom Mayberry, who engineered at a small studio elsewhere in the city, in terms based upon the conditions of race. He accounted for the discrepancies between his own and black studio performers' aesthetic preferences in terms of racially distinct psychologies that produce physiological differences in hearing. He interpreted the situation through a set of assumptions about African technological naiveté and lack of rational scientific perspective: "Whether you like him or he likes you or anything like that, that's all inconsequential [in the studio]. It's the end result that matters. So [African musicians] play at ear-shattering level, their ears become numb and damaged after a certain period of time. And then they start talking to you about a certain sound. Now if your ears are not numb and damaged, you can't hear that certain sound they're talking about. You're hearing a different sound. You're hearing what is actually the true sound. So the whole trick of recording is to actually listen, not to have it so loud that you don't have to listen, which is what these guys do. It's just like this presence around them, a wall of sound — that's what turns them on. But if you haven't been able to hear what you're recording, it'll just be a big mess. Again it's basically because they haven't got enough knowledge, you know, and perhaps we haven't got enough knowledge of them — let's be fair about it. I mean I try, I really do. I sit down and talk for hours with these guys. I really try to know what is going on inside their head."[22] Criticizing the hearing acuity and sensibilities of musicians who play in styles for which high volume is an aesthetic feature is not unusual; consider, for example, the slighting of heavy metal and punk artists by some Western art music elites. But here Mayberry speaks from within a South African ideological realm in which aesthetic otherness quickly gets explained in terms of a social otherness constructed in the course of a history of racism.

South Africa's sound engineers pinpoint access to equal education more than anything else as the root of the South African music industry's problem and the continuing weight dragging against its progress. Though none of the engineers working at Downtown Studios in the early 1990s condoned apartheid, they articulated social difference as it is expressed in music making, and especially in traditional performances, as a historical fact. While they understood racial categories as mere constructions attributable to years of irrational apartheid policy, they acknowledged and experienced them as deeply ingrained in the fabric of social relations, as thoroughly inhabited by South African citizens, and in some cases as having a permanent effect on the physiological conditioning of the body. The pivotal moment when Tom's conversation turns from his criticism of African musicians' rehearsal practices to his reflection about their difference is his suggestion that "it's basically because they haven't got the knowledge." For him, apartheid's constraints have consequences that register in the body and that limit the possibilities for communication across the color line.

Underlying social conflicts were often articulated in and as negotiations over competing ideas about sound quality and how best to achieve it. For example, Tom's talk about the African musicians' preference for a "wall of sound" over his own preference for a clarity and space in music achieved through painstaking sound separation is a criticism of "them" versus "us." In the studio itself on a couple of occasions I witnessed a disagreement over how to record the bass guitar. In both cases the moment was loaded with unspoken feelings about difference. The musicians wanted the bass amp miked. From their point of view, miking the amp reproduced the hard, slightly distorted, very heavy bass sound that was appropriate to a traditional aesthetic. The sound engineers wanted to use a direct input line, patching the bass guitar directly into the console, for this would minimize unwanted noise and give them the cleanest sound to manipulate at the desk. On one of these occasions, Peter simultaneously miked the amp and patched the bass directly into the console, and he assured the musicians that he could get them the sound they wanted, "only better," with the clean DI signal. The musicians were content with this proposition. On another occasion, Tom closed down the session. He refused to mike the bass amp because he did not want poorly recorded sound leaving his studio, for this would compromise his own standards and damage his reputation. The musicians left grumbling that he did not understand their tradition. (The social disruption was amended in a subsequent meeting.)

Using Technology and Representing Tradition

In addition to shaping studio practice, the intersecting dynamics around race, class, culture, and technological engagement had effects on the recorded sound. Engineers at Downtown Studios had at their disposal a wide range of analog and digital sound processing and recording gear in one of the best-equipped state-of-the-art facilities in South Africa. What they chose to use depended on the task at hand, the time and budget allocated to the project, and the aesthetic and social values they associated with the style.

When Darryl had the opportunity to record what he considered to be an authentically traditional instrument, he went to fantastic ends to capture and represent its sound accurately. This happened when he worked on an album in Johannesburg with Manfred Mann, who "got some guy from Swaziland[23] who had calabashes on sticks, and he pulled these strings, and I miked up this thing with seventeen microphones. That was a REAL traditional instrument! And it sounded great," he recounted.[24] As an engineering professional, he went to sophisticated technological ends to render his technological intervention as inaudible as possible, using a battery of electronic equipment to make the recorded performance sound as unmediated as he could. He wanted ultimately to give an impression of a live, face-to-face encounter between musician and listener. Using the techniques conventionalized in folk music recording, he wanted to represent a sound that he idealized as African in a way that he felt most accurately represented the truths of its origins (and hence, its performer). For him, this instrument was connected to the idea of a pristine African life where musicians were inherently divorced from the relations of industrial cultural production, and playing music was an acoustic and participatory social experience.

His creative decisions were influenced by other factors as well. Manfred Mann was visiting from overseas, and Darryl's ideas about appropriate engineering for a foreign star and audience kicked into action. As an international rock celebrity, a producer experienced in overseas production practices, a South African expatriate, and a professional with foreign currency, a foreign studio budget, foreign contacts, and foreign fans, Mann was an icon of success and musical excellence. He enabled elaborate miking and recording, and his prestige and positioning in the global industry commanded attention. While his presence gave reason and resources for sophisticated sonic processing, it also prompted inward glances at what South Africa's distinctiveness might be. Darryl segued from his exclamations about the authenticity of the calabash as an African instrument into a reflection on the fact that it takes foreign intervention to bring local attention—in the form of high production standards—to the (aesthetic and exchange) value of local expression: "Here it takes an ex–South African living in London to actually show us how to record our own music." In miking the calabash with seventeen microphones, homegrown values of local Others overlap with local ideas about "overseas," and the two positions are stylistically coherent in terms of their production values.

In sessions in which traditional musicians showed that they were creatively engaged with technology in their performances and in their ideas of music production, Darryl valued their sound very differently. He felt that Zulu traditional artists "use drum machines more than they should; they should actually be using live drums. You see, the whole irony of it is they come in and say 'We're a traditional Zulu band, record us.' But did their fathers have drums like we use in the studio? Did their forefathers have DX7s that go 'whirrp, whirrp'?[25] Did their forefathers have all these fancy machines that we use to create their music? No! So therefore they are not really traditional artists. A traditional Zulu band is animal drum skins, finger-piano,[26] guitars made out of tin cans, okay, natural percussion, and a group of people standing around and singing and chanting. THAT is traditional music. I have yet to record a traditional band that way. If they came in that way, I'd then have the respect for them. I'd say, 'Right, this is the real McCoy, I'm not using a modern Ludwig drum set here.'"

Darryl implies that black South African music that sounds mediated is contaminated culture that is neither good music nor authentic; traditional musicians who choose to use available contemporary technology as a creative resource lose their authenticity and mask their musicality. Earlier technologies like tin-can guitars do not necessarily disrupt Darryl's model. By incorporating signs of the recently outmoded (Taussig 1993), musicians who play in a Zulu-identified style are still not part of the contemporary postindustrial complex, for these musicians are drawing on styles that are out of fashion without seeming to know it. Nor does the presence of high technology disrupt Darryl's model. Indeed, in the Mann case he advocates playing into seventeen microphones. The issue concerns who has control over that technology. Who makes the decisions concerning its use? In what capacity and toward what ends is that technology employed? And who is its audience?

The use of a Ludwig drum set or a DX7 keyboard, by means of which musicians can introduce electronically produced effects ("whirrp whirrp") into their sound, is problematic in Darryl's articulation because it uses technology to produce sounds, not just to transmit them. In contrast to his seventeen-microphone scenario, the Ludwig drums and DX7 make the means of production audible in the sound. The musicians are heard to be part of a contemporary postindustrial world in which they use electronic technology creatively, and listeners might imagine them as having the skills and interests to be engaged in technological processes with a studio production team. The audible traces of the means of production are also traces of the relations of production.

In the idealized seventeen-microphone case, on the other hand, high-tech equipment and procedures lend more recording and processing control to the production team at the console — not to the performing artists — and the emphasis is placed on giving the transmission of sound from the source its purest chance. The sonic outcome of such control over transmission masks the very relations of production. It buries the history of contested race-based relations beneath the surface of the sound and renders the performance pristine.

In practice, in South African studios in the early 1990s it was rare that such delicate attention as in the Mann session was afforded to a "traditional" recording. In the two years during which I attended many studio sessions in Johannesburg, I did not witness such attention. The limited time and budget that studios could afford to spend on traditional recordings precluded it. Studios needed the revenues generated by booking multiple projects. Furthermore, many within the industry argued that it was not efficient to produce expensive high-tech projects when the targeted consumers (rural and working-class people) listened to music through lo-fi playback equipment such as cheap radios, small battery-operated cassette players, low-end integrated sound systems, or "ghetto blasters."[27] Some argued that traditional music simply didn't demand much studio time or dedicated professional skills at the console. In expressing frustration at the creative limitations of his job in South Africa in comparison to his experience in London, Richard Austen explained to me that "black traditional" music production is "not so-called trendy or modern production — it's a folk standard, production that has been around for about twenty five, thirty years! There's nothing special, it's just nice songs, played nicely by good musicians and that's it." You "come in, play the parts, mix it, mess with an echo here or there, and then it goes out."[28] Neil Kuny recognized the advantages that less-experienced engineers reaped from the way "traditional" music was positioned and treated in the studio setting: "The nice thing about that black music, which is quite raw, is that you don't have to be that good to engineer it, in a sense. When I was an engineer without much knowledge, they were confident enough to put me on a project on my own and say 'do it,' knowing that there's not much that could go wrong."[29] Within two years of beginning his career at Downtown Studios, Neil was engineering sessions on his own.

Other industry personnel and sound engineers not associated with Downtown Studios believed that the music itself wasn't worth the effort. Their disparaging criticisms of the quality of the music were sometimes underwritten by perjorative assumptions about the people who composed, performed, and enjoyed it: lo-tech production was adequate for low-quality music making for listeners and performers who wouldn't know the difference.

Reaching Overseas

Despite the struggle and frequent negativity about conditions of production at home, the potential for exciting studio experimentation and for uncovering and shaping new (international) stars in South Africa—or, more correctly, from South Africa—did not pass local South African music makers by. Even sound engineers imagined that they could make a "break" from where they were positioned, despite the odds against them. Peter Pearlson noted that "very few people realize that maybe the engineer and the producer sat twelve hours on one lead vocal, trying to get the guy to sing in tune or trying to get the guy to sing in time or trying to get the guy to deliver—to out-deliver himself—because it's got to be a memorable performance, you only do it once."[30] Like producers and "traditional" artists, engineers expressed a sense of being positioned in a particular kind of center—at a source of musical material. Sound engineers know that the uniqueness of local styles combined with their own wealth of experience at the console could make South Africa's studio production distinctive. They felt the pressure of the international industry's imminent influx. "Overseas" personnel could either bypass them and South Africa's domestic companies altogether, or else local studio practitioners (including engineers) could catch a ride with them to success. "One day I'm going back overseas, and people are going to ask me 'So what was it like working as an engineer for several years in a top South African recording studio? How's it going there? Tell us about all the guys who came in from the bush and came in with their animal skin drums,'" Darryl mused. However, the engineers rarely described themselves as structurally empowered to seize the moment, either on an individual basis or as a local professional group. "And I'm going to say 'What are you talking about? I haven't done that yet!'" Darryl continued. "I had one attempt at that, and that was with Manfred Mann." With the restrictions on their mobility through a grounded fear of violence and by work pressures that kept them bound to the studio for very long hours, as well as through the difficulties of professional communication in the studio, there was a sense of pending entrapment in a quagmire brought on by the way that local sociopolitics necessarily infiltrated the South African professional arena.

Some locals also were keenly aware of how the peculiarities of the South African work conditions, if they were exploited well and in conjunction with an overseas-directed effort, could enhance their careers, their expertise, and their reputations. Most of the engineers considered South African studios to usefully offer crash courses in music production. Engineer and artist and repertoire person Dave Segal noted how South Africa's backwardness could prepare him for a leap up the rungs overseas, just as overseas had brought him opportunity at home. Because of the discrepancies between home and foreign studio procedures, moves between them offered short cuts to enhancing his status and professional opportunities: "I went to study in the Institute of Sound Recording in San Diego for a year [1980], and I got my diploma there. I was planning on staying and working in the States, except I got a call from RPM Studios saying they need an engineer, urgently, and they'd heard about me studying there.[31] At that stage not many people had studied overseas—in fact, I don't think anybody had. I mean in the States you can't become a first engineer for like the first two and a half years. You have to be an assistant engineer for a very long time, and here was an opportunity for becoming a first engineer. Like, you know, I was a bit spoiled almost. But I thought, 'Huh, let me go for it!' I'd planned to come back here [to South Africa] and get experience as a first engineer and then go back to the States, but I've just never gone back."[32] Segal had moved from full-time engineering to an artist and repertoire position at Gallo Record Company.

Some engineers expressed a sense of shared isolation and shared deprivation with like professionals located in other places peripheral to the major production and distribution centers "overseas." But, as Peter reckoned, the South African industry developed particular dynamics that originated in its racially based social history and that fundamentally intensified the professional isolation while impeding the chances of breaking out of it. Flow out of a place like (white) Australia seemed easier from his perspective in South Africa.[33] "There are far fewer people in Australia, and the Australian music industry buzzes. They've produced some worldwide smashes—Midnight Oil, ACDC, Little River Band. There's a whole list of guys who've cracked it internationally. We've [also] got enormous talent here, on BOTH sides—on the black side, and the white side, and the crossover side. I see enormous potential. I don't think that there are many people who could deliver the sort of results that we deliver in the sort of time we've got, and the sort of budgets that we've got."[34] In Peter's South Africa internal pressures made it impossible to meet international production standards, and yet the ruthless international market and the legacy of foreign disapproval of (white) South Africa cut local production efforts no slack in this regard.[35]

When Darryl was recording Joe Strummer that time, Strummer "didn't like the sound of the studio that we had built—it didn't suit his voice. So we recorded him in the toilet. We put the microphone on the seat cover, and Joe sang all his demo songs in the toilet, and we ran the cable into the control room and recorded his album. Which was a lot of fun."[36] Darryl champions the lo-tech makeshift arrangement in L.A. with the same intensity of spirit that he did miking up a "calabash on strings" with seventeen microphones in South Africa.

Both choices demonstrate his virtuosity as a sound engineer. Both are worked from within settings endowed with technological resources. Both respond to style-specific production aesthetics. Strummer, a punk guitarist, was known for choosing lo-tech, "live-sounding" recording options that coincided with a political position that opposed the interventions and commercialization of music by the industry. The reverberant acoustic properties of bathrooms give sounds a particular personality that Strummer and the production team chose to exploit. These are all significant to Darryl's heralding of the toilet as L.A. recording booth. Along with the generosity, one might say, of allowing the vocal character of the individual named artist to determine the overall character of the acoustic event, Darryl surrenders some of his control at the console to capture the quirky liveness of the environment. Implicit too in this choice of acoustic recording space is the fact that Darryl has the professional and creative freedom to record Strummer's sound in the best way possible, even if it is in a bathroom. South Africa's history and contemporary struggles preclude that liberty. To record a traditional musician in a bathroom would run the risk of an aesthetic choice being first and foremost interpreted and experienced by the musicians as an ugly political act.

All of the music makers rationalize local problems in the studio and in the industry as the legacy of apartheid. It is in this context that "overseas" is idealized for its efficiency, quality, attention, and for the kinds of engaged professional communication that would be possible in a studio devoid of racial politics. "Overseas" represents an ethically principled order in which hierarchy evolves only out of musical excellence and professional role. It is a vision of how things could be, if the local material conditions of music production and creativity were not contaminated by apartheid politics. These factors intensify the reach for "overseas" and heighten its idealization.

Acknowledgments

I gratefully acknowledge the financial assistance and endorsement of the National Research Foundation (South Africa), National Science Foundation (USA), Wenner-Gren Foundation for Anthropological Research (USA), and Charlotte W.

Newcombe Foundation (USA). I am also grateful to the executives and employees of Gallo Africa, especially of Downtown Studios, who facilitated the research for this paper. Any opinions, findings, and conclusions expressed herein are my own and do not necessarily reflect the views of these agencies, nor of Gallo Africa.

Tolerating superfluous bodies and inquisitive ears within the confined space and intense work conditions of the studio control room is a particularly generous act. For this, as well as for sharing their views with me, I thank the sound engineers whose voices I reproduce in the text. I hope my representations have been faithful to the nuances of each individual as well as to the complexity of the sociopolitical positions from within which they speak, aspire, struggle, imagine, and create.

Thank you to Angela Impey, Marc Perlmann, and Tom Porcello for their critical editorial eyes.

Humphrey Mabote, Downtown Studio's first black engineer, fell ill and passed away on 15 May 2002. Rest in peace there amongst the big guys.

Notes

1. A tape operator, or "tape op," is an apprentice engineer who does most of the manual work of setting up and running a session for the engineer, leaving the latter free to concentrate on the console. In analog studios, the tape op literally operated the tape machine (at least in the larger studios "overseas").

2. Richard Austen worked in South Africa from the mid-1980s to the mid-1990s. Excerpt taken from a 1992 interview with me in Johannesburg.

3. Darryl Heilbrunn, interview, 19 November 1992, Johannesburg.

4. Lance Longley, interview, 8 January 1992, Johannesburg.

5. Humphrey Mabote, interview, 23 February 1991, Johannesburg.

6. Solid State Logic studio mixing console.

7. Mabote interview, 1991.

8. Longley interview, 1992.

9. As Tim Taylor has noted, the flow of forms, signs, sounds, and commodities through "developed" countries is escalating in the digital age in both frequency and quantity (Taylor 2001: 119). This flow through major centers of consolidated power and high consumption underlies the engineers' construction of "overseas." For sound engineers working in South Africa, "overseas" sometimes includes Australia.

10. Downtown Studios is owned by Gallo Africa, which is the most powerful domestic conglomerate in the South African music industry. There is a host of studios of varying sizes and capacities in Johannesburg, but Downtown is the biggest and most prominent. In the early 1990s it was abuzz with activity. Gallo Music Productions, one of Gallo Africa's wholesale subsidiaries, salaried six in-house producers, all of whom booked their sessions at Gallo's Downtown Studios. Freelancers and producers contracted to other companies also used the state-of-the-art three-studio facility. A large in-house sound processing staff comprising five engineers, a programmer who also engineered, and a trainee-programmer/tape operator served the clients. Freelancing engineers also used the studios. Most of the engineers whose perspectives I consider here worked at Downtown before or at the time I interviewed them, between 1989 and 1992.

11. I use the post-apartheid state designation "KwaZulu-Natal" for a region that at the time had not yet been amalgamated, namely the KwaZulu "homeland" and the Natal province.

12. On the role of the cultural boycott in the South African liberation struggle, see Masekela 1987 and Campschreur and Divendal 1989. With its massive market success, Paul Simon's collaboration with South African musicians (*Graceland*, Simon 1986) raised debate about the significance and problems of the boycott.

13. Occasionally women apprenticed at the South African Broadcasting Corporation and worked as sound engineers there; none, however, had moved into commercial recording by the early 1990s.

14. It was only after engineers had complained to Gallo about the discrepancy between their creative contribution to productions and the lack of acknowledgment of their input that they became part of the biennial Gallo Gold Awards. Engineers were recognized alongside producers and artists at the 1992 Gallo Awards for the first time.

15. Lee Short, interview, 19 December 1991, Johannesburg.

16. There are eleven official languages in South Africa. Many African citizens speak a few of these. Zulu, Xhosa, and Pedi have the highest numbers of speakers.

17. This dialogue is transcribed from a field recording, Downtown Studios, November 1991.

18. Amongst producers and musicians who specialize in township pop styles there are more people with better technological skills. Through the 1990s the number of people with skills and their levels of competence steadily increased, particularly as a new generation enters the studio. Of course it is not only South African engineers who struggle with their performers' inexperience with studio technology. Engineers elsewhere certainly also criticize musicians who work in studios but lack studio know-how. But the social terms (that is, the combination of race, class, ethnicity, gender, generation, and so forth) underlying their criticism are not necessarily configured in the same way as in the South African traditional music recording context.

19. Heilbrunn interview, 1992.

20. A musician from the north of the country, Thomas Chauke records Tsongan traditional music, also catalogued as "Shangaan disco." At this time he was by far the most popular artist in this style. Lee Short did the engineering on a number of his massive hits.

21. Short interview, 1991.

22. Tom Mayberry, interview, July 1989, Johannesburg. Also quoted in Meintjes 2003.

23. The assumption behind being from a place like Swaziland in the context of Darryl's talk is that the musician is rurally located, therefore more "tribal" and "traditional" than he or she would be if based in Johannesburg.

24. Heilbrunn interview, 1992. This and the subsequent excerpt also appear in Meintjes 2003.

25. DX7 refers to a widely used electronic Yamaha keyboard.

26. He is referring to the mbira or kalimba, various versions of which are played across the continent. It is also known by other names (see Berliner 1978). It is not an instrument traditional to the Zulu, however.

27. In areas of rural KwaZulu-Natal where many households live without electricity, domestic sound systems are often hooked up to car batteries for high-volume listening. In most studios even the sound of high-end productions is tested through small speakers, anticipating that there will be a range in the quality of playback equipment amongst consumers. However, the reverse is not always the case. For run-of-the-mill productions targeting the domestic traditional market, high-end consumption would not be an issue. It is the sound of low-end playback equipment that counts.

28. Austen interview, 1992. This excerpt also appears in Meintjes 2003.

29. Neil Kuny, interview, 6 January 1993, Johannesburg.

30. Peter Pearlson, interview, 15 April 1991, Johannesburg.

31. Until 1991, Downtown Studios was named RPM Studios.

32. Dave Segal, interview, 26 November 1991, Johannesburg.

33. See Hayward 1998 for discussions suggesting that Australians and Pacific Islanders could also view their local music production context as impeded by a colonial history and racially based discourses.

34. Pearlson interview, 1991.

35. The sense that international recognition and an opportunity to break from South Africa is impeded by local struggles, whether over technological experience, knowledge of cultural specificities, or communicative skills, is also shared by producers and artists, who similarly explain its origin in racialized systemic terms.

36. "Toilet" stories comprise a set within a genre of lo-fi studio narratives more widely. They entice further analysis.

References

BOOKS AND ARTICLES

Allingham, Rob. 1992. *1992 Gallo Gold Awards: 65 Years.* CD sleeve notes. Johannesburg: Gallo (Africa).

———. 1999. "South Africa: The Nation of Voice." In *World Music: The Rough Guide: An A–Z of the Music, Musicians, and Discs; Africa, Europe, and the Middle East,* eds. S. Broughton, M. Ellingham, and R. Trillo. London: Rough Guides, 638–657.

Berliner, Paul. 1978. *Soul of the Mbira.* Evanston, Il.: Northwestern University Press.

Buskin, Richard. 1991. *Inside Tracks: A First-Hand History of Popular Music from the World's Greatest Record Producers and Engineers.* New York: Avon Books.

Campschreur, Willem, and Joost Divendal, eds. 1989. *Culture in Another South Africa.* London: Zed Books.

Cunningham, Mark. 1998. *Good Vibrations: A History of Record Production.* 2nd ed. London: Sanctuary Publishing.

Daniel, Eric D., C. Denis Mee, and Mark H. Clark. 1999. *Magnetic Recording: The First Hundred Years.* New York: Institute of Electrical and Electronics Engineers Press.

Gray, Herman. 1988. *Producing Jazz: The Experience of an Independent Record Company.* Philadelphia: Temple University Press.

Greene, Paul. 2001. "Mixed Messages: Unsettled Cosmopolitanisms in Nepali Pop." *Popular Music* 20(2): 169–188.

Hayward, Philip, ed. 1998. *Sound Alliances: Indigenous Peoples, Cultural Politics, and Popular Music in the Pacific.* New York: Cassell.

Hennion, Antoine. 1989. "An Intermediary between Production and Consumption: The Producer of Popular Music." *Science, Technology, and Human Values* 14 (autumn): 400–424.

Kealy, Edward. 1979. "From Craft to Art: The Case of Sound Mixers and Popular Music." *Sociology of Work and Occupations* 6(1): 3–29.

Martin, George, and Jeremy Hornsby. 1979. *All You Need Is Ears.* London: Macmillan.

Masekela, Barbara. 1987. "The ANC and the Cultural Boycott." *Africa Report* 32(4): 19–25.

Meintjes, Louise. 2003. *Sound of Africa! Making Music Zulu in a South African Studio.* Durham, N.C.: Duke University Press.

Millard, Andre. 1995. *America on Record: A History of Recorded Sound.* London: Cambridge University Press.

Porcello, Thomas. 1996. "Sonic Artistry: Music, Discourse, and Technology in the Sound Recording Studio." Ph.D. dissertation: The University of Texas at Austin.

———. 1998. "Tails Out": Social Phenomenology and the Ethnographic Representation of Technology in Music-Making." *Ethnomusicology* 42(3): 485–510.

Sandstrom, Boden. 2000. "Women Mix Engineers and the Power of Sound." In *Music and Gender,* ed. P. Moisala and B. Diamond. Urbana: University of Illinois Press, 289–305.
Stolzhoff, Norman C. 2000. *Wake the Town and Tell the People: Dancehall Culture in Jamaica.* Durham, N.C.: Duke University Press.
Stone, Terri. 1992. *Music Producers: Conversations with Today's Top Record Makers,* ed. D. Schwartz. Emeryville, Calif.: MixBooks.
Taussig, Michael. 1993. *Mimesis and Alterity: A Particular History of the Senses.* New York: Routledge.
Taylor, Timothy. 2001. *Strange Sounds: Music, Technology, and Culture:* New York: Routledge.
Théberge, Paul. 1997. *Any Sound You Can Imagine: Making Music/Consuming Technology.* Hanover, N.H.: Wesleyan University Press/University Press of New England.

RECORDINGS
Elite Swingsters, featuring Dolly Rathebe. 1992. *Woza!,* producer H. Nzimande; executive producer West Nkosi. Cassette. GMP, MCBL 751.
Simon, Paul. 1986. *Graceland.* Warner Brothers CD 25447.

INTERVIEWS CONDUCTED BY THE AUTHOR
Heilbrunn, Darryl. Johannesburg, 19 November 1992.
Kuny, Neil. Johannesburg, 6 January 1993.
Lindemann, John. Johannesburg, July 1989.
Longley, Lance. Johannesburg, 8 January 1992.
Mabote, Humphrey. Johannesburg, 3 February 1991.
Mayberry, Tom. Johannesburg, July 1989.
Pearlson, Peter. Johannesburg, 15 April 1991.
Segal, Dave. Johannesburg, 26 November 1991.
Short, Lee. Johannesburg, 12 December 1991.

CHAPTER THREE

"The Disc Is Not the Avenue"

Schismogenetic Mimesis in Samba Recording

Frederick J. Moehn

The central event of Rio de Janeiro's famed carnival is a four-day annual competition among enormous samba "schools" that parade up a specially built avenue popularly referred to as the sambadrome (*sambódromo*).[1] These schools are community-centered organizations based around large percussion ensembles; the bigger schools may have more than three hundred percussionists on the avenue, along with a lead singer and limited harmonic accompaniment, such as six- and seven-stringed acoustic guitar and *cavaquinho* (a ukelele-like instrument). For much of the year the samba schools rehearse and prepare for carnival in large and unpretentious concrete halls called *quadras,* situated in their individual neighborhoods. There, master percussionists from the neighborhood teach drumming to younger members of the community. On the avenue, however, a samba school procession involves numerous extramusical elements: the various tightly coordinated "wings" (*alas*) of costumed dancers and singers, for example, or the giant allegorical floats. On the avenue, the visual display is as important as the aural experience.

As they parade through the sambadrome, the members of each school play and sing a samba with lyrics that tell a story about Brazilian cultural history or about prominent national figures. The paraders' costumes and the gigantic floats that accompany them up the avenue present an allegory of this story, called an *enredo* in Portuguese. For this reason, carnival samba is referred to as *samba de enredo,* or simply *samba enredo.* Every year, each school presents a single new song, repeated continuously during the eighty-five minutes allotted for its parade. The spectators to the event know the sambas well and sing along, having heard them either on the radio or on the compact disc of samba enredo that is released annually several months before carnival.[2]

In October 1998 the owners of the recording facility Company of Technicians (Companhia dos Técnicos) in Rio de Janeiro invited me to conduct ethnography in their studios during the recording of the album *Sambas de Enredo 1999*. This monthlong project impressed me as a remarkably dense episode of collective, mediated cultural production—a perfect opportunity for "thick description" (Geertz 1973) and an event in which technology, space, power, and aesthetics in music making intersected distinctively. Because the annual recording is linked to a live and public musical celebration, the values associated with the performance of samba on "the avenue" have a profound influence on the way in which samba enredo is produced in the studio—that is, on "the disc." In 1998, however, the four producers of the album began to see these two spheres as oppositional, with certain of the performative practices of the avenue hindering the commercial marketability of the recording. Consequently, they sought to sever some of the links between the live and studio contexts of samba enredo. During recording and mixing sessions the producers repeatedly told those directors of the samba schools who were present that "the disc is not the avenue" (*"O disco não é a avenida"* in Portuguese). This simple oppositional phrase was meant to impress upon the directors of the schools—who over the years had gained some influence in the studio—that the recorded album need not necessarily be an aural representation of live carnival samba. In this dichotomization of the two spheres of music making, the producers asserted their power to control the recorded sound—the marketable and reproducible product—at the expense of the influence of those in charge of the community-centered organizations.[3]

Several other subsidiary oppositional pairs relate to this central dichotomy, although these were not always expressed in such metaphorically concise and vivid terms. For example, the producers wanted the disc to sound "clean," implying that the sound on the avenue is "dirty," "rough," or "cluttered." Similarly, they characterized the singing of the samba on the avenue largely as shouting (*gritaria*), in juxtaposition with the more melodic style of singing that they sought for the album. Parallel to this was a generalized opposition between percussion—which has a very predominant role in the sambadrome—and lead voice—which was foregrounded in the studio—as well as between the groove and the melody.[4] Other contrasts were merely implied in the nature of the project, such as a distinction between the public, open-air space of the avenue and the more restricted, acoustically designed and equalized space of the recording studio.

There is an additional contrast between, on the one hand, craftwork materials and amateur participants and, on the other hand, specialized technology and professional musicians, producers, and engineers. This contrast does not obtain specifically within the disc/avenue dichotomy; rather, it is more generalized. In their public and live manifestations (rehearsals, carnival), the samba schools emphasize the participation of many members of the communities in which they are based. Aside from the rehearsals of the drum ensembles, for example, many individuals from the community participate in the preparations of the costumes and floats to be used during carnival. Furthermore, during the parade, the spectators—or "the masses" (*povão*), as the producers of the album sometimes said—sing along. The costumes, the floats, and the instruments of the percussion ensembles are made from relatively inexpensive materials (the drums are generally manufactured in low-tech local factories) while the sound system for the sambadrome and the studio recording environment both depend on advanced electronic technology requiring specialized training for its proper use. It is true that many professionals are involved in the performance and production of carnival, but the studio environment tends to exclude amateurs entirely.

I do not mean to reduce all of the facets of samba enredo expression to a set of structural oppositions. In fact, these differentiated values, aesthetics, and practices are not necessarily always in tension with each other. For example, the sound of the "masses" of spectators in the sambadrome was approximated in the studio through the doubling of the choral parts, and by adding liberal amounts of reverb to these tracks.[5] In some cases, samples of fireworks are included on the disc to simulate the beginning of the procession in the sambadrome (for example, on the samba "O Rei e os Três Espantos de Debret" ["The King and the Three Fears of Debret"] of the school Viradouro on *Sambas de Enredo 1995*). Indeed, part of my purpose in this essay is to reveal these apparent contrasts as unsustainable. Nevertheless, when the producers decided that the disc needed to lose some of its associations with the avenue in order to achieve greater sales, they emphasized the oppositional character of these varied aspects of samba enredo.

Filtered through the lens of this polemic, these oppositions served to feed a dialectic through which the aesthetic and performative distinctiveness of a unique live musical event, on the one hand, and of a related commodified musical product, on the other, are embroiled in a dynamic of "polarizing interpretations of meaning and value" (Feld 1994: 289). This dynamic, in turn, reverberates through time in a manner similar to the escalating cycles of "distorting mutuality" that Steven Feld has identified in the world beat and world music phenomena. In Feld's conceptualization, debates over authenticity and appropriation in the spheres of world beat and world music are complementary and—as they escalate—ultimately generate greater profits for the pop stars, record companies, and media conglomerates that act as both the curators and the entrepreneurs of these genres.

On the surface the case of samba enredo recording bears little similarity to the world beat and world music phenomena. The samba enredo album, for example, circulates largely in a domestic market; its sales are seasonal, and its musical material is linked to a corresponding live carnival event that attracts great numbers of moneyed tourists to Rio each February (or March, depending on the date of Ash Wednesday). Furthermore, the dynamic in question is not between two different recorded genres but rather between a live (albeit also mediated) event and a related recording. There is an added curiosity in the disc/avenue dichotomy that results from the functional nature of the album: because the disc was originally designed to prepare the public for carnival (and even to attract greater numbers to the spectacle), it is recorded and released *before* the live event in which the sambas are first performed in public. After carnival, sales of the annual album fall dramatically. Still, the principal struggles and tendencies out of which the disc/avenue dichotomy emerged can be interpreted in relation to what Feld identifies as the processual shift in mass-mediated popular music from "schizophonia"—whereby sounds are separated from their sources via electronic mediation—to a dynamic state of "schismogenesis"—in which dissimilar but mutually appropriate actions promote each other (ibid.).[6] From this perspective, the dynamic between the spheres of the disc and of the avenue represents a unique case of schizophonically induced schismogenesis.

Murray Schafer introduced the term "schizophonia" to refer to "the split between an original sound and its electroacoustical transmission or reproduction" (Schafer 1977: 90). For Schafer, progressive schizophonia in industrialized society has led to a proliferation of noise and increasingly low-fidelity soundscapes. Schafer's concept is focused on the ever more effective means of achieving and perpetuating this schizophonic break—recording technology, radio, public address systems, sound manipulation through editing and splicing, and a concomitant imperialist territorial expansion. Although all of these elements contribute in some measure to the disc/avenue dynamic, I am, like Feld, less concerned with the accuracy of Schafer's provocative argument (or its teleology) than I am interested in the usefulness of this *schiz-* word as a way of implying the sense of "nervousness" with which music makers often confront commodified grooves and sounds (Feld 1994: 259). These sounds, Feld notes, often have diminished linkages to the social relations, practices, and histories in which the music may have developed originally, or to the forms of participation that give them meaning within local communities (ibid.). In the case of samba enredo, contextual linkages to participatory and community-based music making are, in fact, manifest and highly meaningful, but they are continually challenged and redefined through interaction with commercial and market forces. The samba enredo producers' dichotomization of the disc and the avenue in 1998 is to some extent an indicator of how such forces contribute to the mutual distortion of the two contexts.

Schafer's argument begins with the awkwardly phrased premise that "originally all sounds were originals . . . indissolubly tied to the mechanisms that produced them" (Schafer 1977: 90). Sounds were thus "uncounterfeitable," as he puts it.[7] Feld notes how this argument recalls Walter Benjamin's classic essay "The Work of Art in the Age of Mechanical Reproduction," in which the latter discussed the "aura" of the original and proposed that "the work of art reproduced becomes the work of art designed for reproducibility" (Benjamin 1969: 224, cited in Feld 1994: 259). Feld further relates his discussion to Jacques Attali's argument in *Noise* (1985) that "repeating," or the transformation from representation to reproduction in music, creates a new social order in which the individual "stockpiling" of music becomes possible. For Attali, such tendencies reveal "a new stage in the organization of capitalism, that of the repetitive mass production of all social relations" (Attali 1985: 32, cited in Feld 1994: 260). My interest here is to insert samba enredo into this discussion as a case of recorded sound that evokes many of these same problems, but with certain twists.

Insofar as carnival occurs annually, repetition is integral to the performance of "the avenue." We might say that carnival, with its ancient origins in seasonal pagan rituals, has strong roots in what Schafer terms "rhythms in the natural soundscape" (1977: 229). The disc is linked to this event and its sales are thus largely seasonal. For the producers of the album, however, this type of repetition was precisely the problem they sought to eliminate in 1998. For them, a commercially viable album cannot be tied to cyclical time; rather, it must approach more closely an ideal in which its replicability (and sales of those reproductions) can extend infinitely into the future in linear time, maximizing the profit return on the "original" labor that goes into the recording process (suggesting that from the perspectives of labor and profit—rather than "aura"—the concept of the original is in many ways still viable). In this move, the producers were attempting to have their cake and eat it too, as one of the original functions of the disc was to attract more people *to the avenue*. However, the roles of the "original" and the "copy" are obscured in samba enredo, given that the disc is released *before* carnival. Is the disc the original or the copy of the public performance of the sambas?[8] Does it matter? Finally, the role of technology in this dynamic adds a third twist, because the distinction in the disc/avenue is not simply, as one might expect, that between a live event and a mediated product; the sound on the avenue is also mediated through a complex public address system. The case of samba enredo, therefore, can agitate overly simplified conclusions about the role of music technology in changing soundscapes, especially those supposedly peripheral to the major centers of the industrialized First World.

To return to Schafer, schizophonia is thus not simply the pullulation of low-fidelity soundscapes but rather a process that engenders new and multiple contexts in which the forms and meanings of mediated and commodified sound are contested. As in the world music and world beat dynamic analyzed by Feld, discourses of authenticity and questions of control over sound and its schizophonic circulation and reproduction permeate the framework through which those involved in making and producing samba enredo evaluate the sometimes oppositional and sometimes complementary contexts of the disc and the avenue. As in world music and world beat, this dynamic is also tied to questions of the profitability of the two related spheres of music making. In contrast to the dynamic Feld identifies, however, the schismogenesis between live and recorded samba enredo involves a peculiar evolution of the relationships among space, performance, technology, and sound in this genre of music making. This evolution is, in turn, informed by changes in the representation of blacks and mulattoes in Brazilian society, by local discourses and problems of national identity, and by the progressive modernization, industrialization and urbanization of the country. In the sections that follow I will describe in greater detail the background to this dynamic, and how it then unfolded in the studio.

The Development of the Samba Schools and the Construction of the Sambadrome

The metonymic disc/avenue dichotomy reduces various complex histories to a polemically efficient opposition. There is the history of carnival itself; the history of samba as a musical genre, and of the samba schools; and the history of the urban planning of streets and avenues in Rio with the eventual construction of the sambadrome. Traversing these varied histories are questions of class, race, gender, and nation as they relate to samba enredo,[9] and the broader questions of underdevelopment in Latin America and, more recently, of processes of globalization. Given my focus on the uses of music technologies in these two spheres of samba enredo, I cannot give all of these topics the attention they merit here. Before describing these two spheres in greater detail, however, a brief sketch of the historical context of samba enredo should point to a number of additional problems pertaining to Brazilian society that are approachable from the perspective of samba enredo, even if many of these problems must remain underexplored in this essay.

The port city of Rio de Janeiro became the capital of Brazil in 1763. As such, the city attracted new immigrants from Europe and served as an entrepôt for slave traders during the nineteenth century. In the latter half of that century the coffee industry took off in the regions south and west of Rio, while the sugar, tobacco, and cocoa plantations of the Brazilian northeast began to suffer. Consequently, the city expanded rapidly. After the final abolition of the last vestiges of slavery in 1888, large numbers of Afro-Brazilian laborers from the northeast migrated to Rio. Rio is often called a "cauldron" of the varied Brazilian peoples and cultures, partly in reference to the nationalist discourse of miscegenation that holds that Brazil is a racial democracy (see Moehn 2001 for an extended discussion of this topic with respect to music). Modern samba began to develop within this cauldron at the beginning of the twentieth century, especially in the center of the city, where many poor Afro-Brazilians resided in flophouses and slums. Particularly important in the early development of samba was June 11th Square (Praça Onze de Junho), referring to the victory of Admiral Barroso in the Riachuelo Navy Battle of the Paraguay War (1865–1870) and called an "Africa in miniature"(McGowan and Pessanha 1998: 22). Also in the center of the city, near June 11th Square, was the famous house of Aunt Ciata (Tia Ciata), where many of the central figures of early samba congregated to make music.

Traditional Afro-Brazilian folk samba was performed in a ring and featured the *umbigada* movement, in which two members of the circle would dance toward the center and touch at the navel. Urban samba developed out of this folk tradition in the beginning of the nineteenth century. "The call-and-response performing style and corresponding stanza and refrain alternation cultivated in the *samba de morro* (from the poor hill areas of the city, known as *favelas*) and the *partido alto* (brought to Rio from Bahia at the beginning of the century)," writes Gerard Béhague (2001), "influenced numerous urban samba styles . . . in the 1920s." Modern urban samba is a collection of related styles that includes the two mentioned by Béhague, as well as many others, such as *samba-canção* (samba song) and *samba-exaltação* (exaltation samba, generally featuring overtly nationalist lyrics). Samba enredo, of course, is the subgenre most directly associated with carnival and with the samba schools.

Samba is generally counted or notated in duple meter with predominant sixteenth-note subdivisions and a strong emphasis on the second beat. This all-important second beat is forcefully accented on a large and loud bass drum called a *surdo* (which means "deaf"). As in African American musical styles such as ragtime or jazz, syncopation is integral to samba and polyrhythms are often implied or explicit (a subdivision of the beat that approaches an eighth-note triplet figure is common). Most sambas follow a simple stanza-refrain pattern with harmonies that vary considerably, albeit often employing characteristic cadences and modulations (sambas de enredo often have two different refrains).[10] Given my focus on samba recording, it is interesting to note that the release of the song "Pelo Telefone" ("Via the Telephone") in 1917—the first recording to be labeled a samba on the disc itself—is generally regarded as marking the moment at which samba became a distinct genre.[11]

Rio's carnival, on the other hand, developed out of several loosely related traditions. Among the oldest of these is the Portuguese *entrudo,* a ribald and disorganized street manifestation in which participants ridiculed each other, doused each other with various offensive liquids, sang comical or farcical songs, and danced, often with masks and loud instrumentation such as trumpets and pots and pans (Queiroz 1992: 30). The entrudo was already practiced in Brazil by the early seventeenth century, but it was actually outlawed in the nineteenth century and eventually lost popularity. In the first half of the nineteenth century, the cordon (*cordão*) developed in Rio de Janeiro. The cordon originated in the festival of Our Lady of the Rosary—a favorite festival among Afro-Brazilians in Rio de Janeiro—and featured Afro-Brazilian percussion accompaniment (Cabral 1996: 21). Cordons were groups of allegorically costumed characters such as old men (*velhos*), devils, kings, queens, sergeants, Bahianas (Afro-Brazilian women from Bahia), or Indians (that is, indigenous Brazilians).

Another formation was the *bloco,* which, like the cordon, was all male. While social classes sometimes mixed in the cordons, participants in the blocos were exclusively of the poorer classes. Blocos were relatively informal and spontaneous groupings with little or no stable organizational structure; they were, according to Luis Gardel, musically "unpolished" (1967: 7).[12] At the end of the nineteenth century, another carnival formation emerged: the *rancho* (which means something like "group of revelers"). The ranchos included women and more varied instrumentation such as brass (that is, not simply percussion), and they were organized around particular themes. Developing alongside these street manifestations at the end of the nineteenth century were the more exclusive parties of the elites: the masked balls and European-styled processions of the so-called "grand societies," where waltzes and polkas were popular and where allegorical floats were featured.

The samba schools began to take shape in the 1930s, combining to varying degrees many of these influences. In the late 1920s certain of the central figures in the emerging genre—such as Ismael Silva of the carnival bloco Deixa Falar—rehearsed and taught samba drumming near a grade school in the Estácio de Sá neighborhood of Rio. People began to call them "professors" of samba and their groups "schools" (see Cabral 1996: 63).[13] In the hands of Silva and other *sambistas* from the Estácio neighborhood such as Armando Marçal and Bide (Alcebíades Barcelos) samba took on characteristics that distinguished it from the popular *maxixe* and *marcha* styles. These musicians slowed down the tempos, employed longer notes in the melodies, and introduced two-bar rhythmic patterns (McGowan and Pessanha 1998: 25). In the early years of the samba schools, their downtown street manifestations were often repressed by the police, as were most public forms of Afro-Brazilian musical expression. However, under populist president Getúlio Vargas, who held dictatorial power over the country from 1930 to 1945, samba from Rio de Janeiro was promoted as Brazil's national music, and today most Brazilians still regard it as such.[14]

The first contest between the new samba schools took place in 1932 in the above-mentioned June 11th Square (known simply as Praça Onze). The display attracted enthusiastic attention from the press and the public; by 1934 a Union of Samba Schools was formed of twenty-eight schools. Although samba enredo received a powerful boost from Vargas's nationalist agenda, large numbers of Afro-Brazilians were displaced (among them many samba musicians) and their homes destroyed in 1942 to accommodate the construction of the Avenue President Vargas, one of several wide downtown avenues designed by Perreira Passos and inspired by Georges-Eugene Haussmann's work in Paris. This new avenue enveloped the old June 11th Square. In 1974 the area was again torn apart to facilitate the construction of a subway. The parades were relocated to the Avenue President Antônio Carlos, but by then it had become readily apparent that the ever-growing carnival celebrations were in need of a permanent location for the parades and spectators.

The sambadrome—more formally called the Passarela do Samba (Samba Path)—was built in 1984, and the contest among the largest, most established samba schools has taken place there ever since (some lower-division schools still parade on the streets in various neighborhoods, as do the blocos).[15] It rises along both sides of the street Marquês de Sapucaí, not far from June 11th Square. It was designed by the architect Oscar Niemeyer, architect of the modernist city Brasília, deep in the interior of the country; it has been the capital of the nation since 1960. The sambadrome is approximately seven hundred meters long (just under half a mile) with permanent concrete bleachers on either side (although much of its length on the right-hand side is devoted to private box seats for the judges and those wealthy and connected enough to rent them).[16] It seats up to ninety thousand spectators.[17] At the beginning of the sambadrome is the concentration (*con-*

centração); here the schools gather together and prepare to enter the avenue. At the other end is the Apotheosis of Samba (or Apotheosis Square), where the street opens out into a large plaza. Each school is rated on a number of criteria, among which are the samba theme, the "front commission" (a special group that parades in front of the main procession), the "harmony" (the extent to which the various parts of the parade are organized and synchronized with one another), and the drumming. Thus, on the avenue, the musical sound is merely one element in a complex audiovisual event. Chris McGowan and Ricardo Pessanha write that carnival is "like a giant popular opera, with so much happening, musically and visually, that you can't possibly take it all in at once" (1998: 38).

Although samba enredo now crosses races and classes, it is still largely rooted in the poorer neighborhoods of Rio, neighborhoods that tend to have far greater numbers of Afro-Brazilians and *mulatos* than the wealthy parts of Rio's so-called "South Zone." Thus we might say that when the sambadrome was built, some of Rio's oldest Afro-Brazilian and *mulato* communities finally earned a permanent "avenue of their own." At the same time, one can imagine a gradual confluence of two realms of music making and revelry that originally had quite different spatial and social configurations: the relatively disorganized and ribald carnival street manifestations, and the "ring" of traditional folk samba. As Rio industrialized and its streets grew wider, longer, and straighter, carnival manifestations became more organized, more formalized, and—as they grew to include more revelers—more linear in character. The Haussmann-style avenues constructed under Vargas further facilitated the lengthwise development of the enormous samba enredo parades and the eventual adaptation of Afro-Brazilian musical practice to the unidirectional space and rather arbitrary time constraints (the eighty-five minutes allowed each school) of the sambadrome.[18] While this realignment of the spatial configuration of musical practice in samba merits more research, for my purposes here I am primarily interested in how the sambadrome neatly delimits the performance of each samba to a public space in which all of the schools begin their processions on one end and spend about one and a half hours parading to the other end (the "Apotheosis"). In the following section I will describe in greater detail the dynamics of live performance in the sambadrome.

Samba Enredo Today: The Live Setting

Each samba school employs a *carnavalesco*—an artistic director who oversees all of the aspects of the visual presentation of the school. Within about three months after carnival, the carnavalesco chooses the enredo (theme) for the coming season. After the board of directors (comprised of wealthy patrons and senior members of the school) approves the theme, the carnavalesco prepares a synopsis of the story he wants the parade to present visually and distributes it among the school's composers so that they can write appropriate music. The composers then submit their sambas to the directors, who choose three pieces as finalists. At the first rehearsals of the season, beginning around August or September, these three sambas are performed, along with popular sambas from previous years. Soon thereafter, usually by late October, a special rehearsal is organized at which a single samba is chosen for the coming year (see McGowan and Pessanha 1998: 40–42). Generally, the themes treat Brazilian national history and culture, although the Independent League of Samba Schools (LIESA)-imposed mandate to do so was lifted in 1996. Yet while the themes generally continue to treat national topics, they are not always entirely celebratory. Brazilian race relations, for example, have been criticized through samba enredo, as in, for example, Mangueira's samba of 1988 commemorating the centennial of the abolition of slavery. This samba bore the title "100 Years of Freedom: Reality or Illusion," and its lyrics protested the continuing poverty of blacks in Brazil (cited in McGowan and Pessanha 1998: 41).

A representative sample of the 1999 themes (the recording that I witnessed) includes the following: "The Century of Samba" (Mangueira); the landscape paintings of Brazil by Dutch painter Johan Maurits (Imperatriz Leopoldinense, the winner that year); the musical works of modernist composer Heitor Villa-Lobos (Mocidade Independente de Padre Miguel); the natural beauty and pleasures of certain regions of Brazil such as Natal (Salgueiro), Minas Gerais (Portela), or João Pessoa (Vila Isabel); and even an homage to the famous Brazilian plastic surgeon Pintanguy (Caprichosos de Pilares). The school Império Serrano, among the oldest in Rio, chose the theme "A Street Called Brasil," which referred to 46th Street in New York City, known as "little Brazil." Interestingly, the only samba to treat a theme outside of the geographical territory of Brazil focused on the street where emigrants to the United States celebrate carnival and Brazilian Independence day.

The carnavalesco and his design team also determine what the floats and costumes will look like. The paraders of a particular school are grouped into *alas,* or wings, each with a different costume and a different role in the development of the procession. A large school like Mangueira may have up to sixty-five alas of about eighty persons each—a total of over five thousand paraders (McGowan and Pessanha 1998: 42). Most people must purchase their costumes. For many, the expense represents quite a sacrifice and must be paid in monthly installments. On the avenue, the allegorical floats are spaced between groups of alas. These floats are huge structures with sculptures that often include motorized parts and platforms for the *destaques*—men and women who, when not wearing elaborate costumes, wear next to nothing. Preceding the entire parade is the front commission (*comissão de frente*), which includes the flag-bearer (*porta-bandeira*) and the master of ceremonies (*mestre-sala*), as well as the most venerable figures of the school and, sometimes, famous personalities invited into the parade. The flag-bearer is always a woman who dances while twirling the flag around, and the master of ceremonies is a male who dances around her.

In the "concentration" the directors of harmony (*diretores de harmonia*) prepare the members of the school for the parade's entrance into the avenue. At the same time, technical crews prepare a "sound car" for the procession. Atop the car the school's lead singer, or *puxador*, begins singing the samba. Fireworks announce the beginning of each school's procession, and the "front commission" enters onto the avenue. McGowan and Pessanha's description of the beginning of the parade is illustrative:

> [The puxador] is responsible for keeping five thousand voices in time with the drum section. . . . He'll sing the same song for almost two hours and must make no mistakes. Slowly the members start singing together with him, stimulated by the harmony director, who also takes care of keeping the energy high during the parade. After the whole escola [school] has sung the samba two or three times without accompaniment, the most exciting moment in the parade preparation occurs: the musical entrance of the bateria [the percussion]. Anyone who has witnessed this moment will never forget it: some three hundred percussionists under the command of the *mestre de bateria* start playing perfectly in sync with the singing, co-ordinated by the mestre's whistle—which serves as his baton.
>
> (McGowan and Pessanha 1998: 42)

In fact, a highly elaborate system for channeling and monitoring the sound on the avenue aids the puxador and the mestre de bateria in their task of keeping the parade synchronized. I will describe this system below.

As mentioned above, a samba enredo usually consists of verses alternating with a refrain, or sometimes two different refrains. The puxador shouts cues for each line while he and the members of the procession sing the entire samba repeatedly until the tail end of the procession reaches the Apotheosis of Samba. A form of call-and-response is thus an important part of samba enredo. The cues may be the first word of a particular lyric, the name of the school, short questions that are answered in the phrase that follows ("Where?" "In Brazil!"), or simply exclamatory utterances that keep the crowd excited about the school. Harmonic accompaniment for the samba enredo is provided by *cavaquinho* (like a steel-stringed *ukulele*) and classical-style acoustic guitar (with nylon strings). Bass runs are added on a seven-stringed classical guitar. These musicians, like the puxador, perform from atop the sound car, which follows the bateria up the avenue.[19] In addition, "sweetening" such as an orchestral background is sometimes added to the live sound via electronic keyboard, which is also performed from atop the sound truck. On ground level the enormous baterias lay down a dense bed of percussion, providing a steady groove that keeps the mass of paraders moving up the avenue. Among the principal percussion instruments used are the *surdo* (the aforementioned bass drum), *repenique* (a high-pitched two-headed lead drum used for cues and helping to mark the beat), *caixa* (snare), *tamborim* (a small cymbal-less tambourine that is played with a flayed plastic beater), *cuíca* (a friction drum), *ganzá* (shaker), and *agogô* (cowbell).

The surdo part is perhaps the most important element of samba enredo percussion; without a steady, loud bass drum, the beat falls apart and the parade loses synchronization or, as it is termed in Portuguese, "harmony" (*harmonia*).[20] The surdo also represents a significant link between the aesthetics of the disc and of the avenue. The pioneering samba percussionist Alcebíades Barcelos (a.k.a. Bide) of the first samba school, Deixa Falar, introduced the instrument into samba during the late 1920s as a means of maintaining a steady pace for the paraders on the street (see Cabral 1996: 42). With its goatskin head, the surdo produces a sound that is quite different from that of a kick drum in an American-style drum kit. It emits a deep, sustained tone with a complex envelope of overtones and a fundamental frequency in the range of sixty to seventy-five Hertz. If the original function of the instrument was directly linked to the performance of samba in the street, it eventually became one of the most important markers of all styles of samba. The Company of Technicians recording facility is known for the "enormous" surdo sound the engineers create and project in the monitors. As one former employee of the facility put it, "[There] the surdo is king; they have a preoccupation with surdo."[21] Indeed, in my discussions with the engineering staff at the facility, we often focused on the importance of an impressively large surdo sound. It is one of owner/engineer Mário Jorge's specialties; his method for recording this instrument is among the information most guarded by the studio owners, and by samba producers who work there.[22] In this instance, "the avenue" has influenced the recording environment (and, hence, "the disc") in a very direct manner.

Each school has developed nuances of percussion performance that differentiate one from the other, in particular in the *caixa* (snare) and *tamborim* patterns. Over time, the bateria directors have developed increasingly complicated percussion breaks (*paradinhas*) and *viradas* — that is, "turns" in the rhythm — to mark their individual styles and attract attention during the carnival competition. Sometimes these breaks can be memorable declarations, such as the now-famous funk beat employed by the school Unidos do

Viradouro in a break for their samba enredo of 1997. McGowan and Passanha describe the drum breaks as the "musical equivalent of stopping a jumbo jet's take-off at the end of the runway, and then getting it to take off again" (1998: 43). On the avenue, then, the distinctions among the different performance practices of each school are highlighted in order to attract the attention of the judges and the public.

Samba Enredo on Disc

By the 1960s, the samba schools had consolidated their legitimacy as representatives of Brazilian culture at the center of one of the largest national spectacles in the world, and 1960 marks the year in which the first professional designer from outside of the samba communities was hired as carnavalesco—Fernando Pamplona, who was hired by the school Salgueiro. "From that point on," write McGowan and Pessanha, "the parades became increasingly theatrical and grandiose" (1998: 45). National television networks began broadcasting the entire event, with little of the broadcast profits going to the schools until 1988, when LIESA negotiated a million-dollar contract with the Globo television network. In 1973 the Union of Samba Schools (now LIESA) signed a contract with the domestic Top Tape recording label, giving that company exclusive rights to release an album of sambas de enredo. As Sérgio Cabral notes, the contract included an illegal clause that gave fifty percent of the composer's rights to the samba schools rather than the composer (1996: 199). Nevertheless, the composers earned a significant income from the annual release because it became one of the most frequently played albums on the radio as well as one of the bestselling releases in Brazil for a time (ibid: 200). During the 1980s the album consistently sold over a million copies each year. The samba schools eventually formed their own record company in 1988 to produce the lucrative annual compilation album (distributed by BMG).

Company of Technicians is the principal location for samba recording in Brazil. Located in Rio de Janeiro's famed Copacabana neighborhood, it is not too far from the birthplace of urban samba in the old city center. In the tiny canteen of this facility one can encounter the best-known figures in contemporary samba recording and production.[23] Company of Technicians comprises three separate studios and a mastering room. During October all other projects are set aside while the entire facility is devoted to the samba enredo album. Most of the tracking for this project is undertaken in the two larger rooms—Studios One and Two—while the smaller Studio Three is primarily used for mixing.

Studio One features a large tracking room with wood floors and four isolation booths. The room has a very "warm" sound, and the isolation booths are used to separate the guitars, *cavaquinho, pandeiro,* and drum kit from the rest of the percussion during the recording of the basic tracks (*base* in Portuguese), facilitating greater control over the sound of these individual instruments. Most samba producers regard it as the best room in Brazil for recording the genre. Two twenty-four-track two-inch tapes (a "master" and a "slave") are used for each samba, with a partial mix of the basic tracks recorded onto the slave so that the producers can work on a given samba in Studios One and Two simultaneously. For example, vocals may be added to basic tracks in Studio One while additional percussion such as *cuica* is added to the same samba in Studio Two. Like the coordination of the alas of paraders on the avenue, the recording process is carefully planned to maximize the limited studio time available. Analog tape is the preferred medium for recording because of its "warm" sound. The natural compression and harmonic distortion resulting from the technical limitations of the medium tend to round the peaks from the percussion signals. Pushing that limit with, for example, the surdo signal creates a very "fat" bass drum sound that is pleasing to the ears—though it is often mixed at earsplitting volumes. Digital media, however, are used in processing (reverb or delay, for example) and in tuning pitches of the vocal tracks during mixing.

For *Sambas de Enredo 1999* the production credits were shared between Zacarias Siqueira de Oliveira (executive producer), Alceu Maia (who also served as an arranger), Láila (who is also *carnavalesco* for the school Beija Flor), and Mário Jorge Bruno (also chief engineer and part owner of the recording facility). Zacarias, Laíla, and Mário Jorge had been involved in the production of the album since the 1970s, while Alceu had provided arrangements for the recording for many years.[24] Alceu's first year as a producer of the album was 1998, but he had extensive experience as an independent samba producer.

Laíla explained that in the early years of the recording, the samba schools wished to attract those members of the public who attended the elite carnival balls. The samba enredo album, he said, facilitated the learning of the theme songs. At the time, many more people attended the balls than the samba school processions. "They began to look for ways to bring these people into the processions of the samba schools, and it was through the disc [that they achieved this]," said Laíla. In 1988 the sales of the recording peaked at about 1.25 million units. This impressive number became an oft-repeated point of reference for the producers in succeeding years as sales progressively fell. About 300,000 albums were sold in 1997, and this relatively weak sales figure prompted a rethinking of the production strategy expressed in the disc/avenue dichotomy.

For several years prior to 1998, the annual album was recorded in the semi-live environment of a large circus-style tent called the Teatro de Lona (Canvas Theater) in the Barra da Tijuca neighborhood.[25] Engineer/producer Mário Jorge said that they engaged about sixty members of each school, in addition to large choirs. According to him, about 1,500 musicians in total were paid for the 1998 recording. This method of recording was quite costly, in part because of the large numbers of musicians who needed to be paid (for *Sambas de Enredo 1998,* recorded in the Teatro de Lona, the cost was 430,000 reais, which was close to $400,000 at the time). Alceu explained how the chorus used to be recorded in the semi-live environment of the tent: "It used to be all chorus, *as if it were a representation of the avenue.* . . . They had the chorus singing throughout; some of the people from the schools had more than one hundred people singing; they took three, four busloads of people to the circus and everyone singing, it was beautiful. They brought the chorus from the school, they brought the people of the neighborhood, it was great" (my emphasis).

By moving the entire process to the studio, the producers wished not only to save money but also—and more importantly—to gain greater control over the sound in order to enact the changes that formed part of the "disc is not the avenue" approach. Alceu described this decision: "One of the things that [the executive producer] Zacarias said, and that [chief sound engineer] Mário [Jorge] accepted immediately, was not to record live anymore [that is, in the Teatro de Lona], in order to arrive at a cleaner sound, and enact that idea—the disc is the disc, the music industry is the music industry, and the avenue is the parade, it's a different story. Therefore, let's change radically." The sound of samba enredo, Alceu felt, needed to be "cleaned" for the disc. Before discussing how this cleaner sound was achieved, it is useful to elaborate upon some of the basic changes facilitated by the move from the semi-live environment of the Canvas Theater to the studio.

In the studio, for example, Ubirany (of the ensemble Fundo de Quintal, or Backyard Group) was engaged to play the *repique-de-mão* (repique-of-the-hand) for the samba enredo recording, but the instrument is too quiet to have an impact on the avenue. A drum kit was also used in the studio, while it is not typically found in the carnival performance. The arrangements, too, are more elaborate for the recorded samba. For example, a cello and an accordion (*sanfona*) were used on certain tracks of *Sambas de Enredo 1999*—instruments not typically used on the avenue. The accordion was used on sambas featuring themes about the Brazilian Northeast, where the instrument is popular in genres such as *baião* and *forró,* partly in the hope that its sound would attract more buyers from those regions. The Northeast is a region that has long suffered from extreme poverty and underdevelopment. As mentioned above with regard to the origins of urban samba in Rio, one consequence of this regional poverty has been the migration of great numbers of Northeast laborers south to Rio and São Paulo. Today São Paulo has an enormous population of Northeastern migrant laborers who might potentially consume samba (but see also Moehn 2001).

Synthesized string arrangements were also added to several tracks in the recorded versions. Like the example of the surdo presented above, the way in which these synthesized strings were gradually incorporated into samba enredo well illustrates some aspects of the evolution of the disc/avenue dynamic. Here is how Alceu described it, referring to "keyboards" (*teclados* in Portuguese):

> We added keyboards [some years ago] to certain sambas. When the [people from the other schools] heard this they all wanted to have keyboards too. Four or five years ago I did seven arrangements [for the samba enredo album] and in my arrangements I only felt that four sambas needed keyboards. So, the guys from the [Independent League of Samba Schools—LIESA] called me and said, "Look, [the other arranger] Jorge Cardoso put keyboards on six [sambas], you on four, that leaves one from Jorge and three from you [that are missing keyboards]. These four schools have already come to us saying that they also want keyboards." . . . We had to call the keyboardist again to record [the remaining sambas]. This year, the same thing: one of the schools said they didn't want [keyboards] so we recorded the samba [without keyboards]. But afterwards the [other producers] called me and said, "Alceu, let's put keyboards on that samba too, because otherwise it'll be the only one [on the album] without them and it'll give the impression that we didn't give the same treatment to each school. . . . Now the keyboards have been incorporated into the disc; if you remove the keyboards . . . it'll be an album that takes us back to 1970 again, which is no longer the reality. Today, you already have keyboards on the avenue.

Alceu's description here highlights a major distinction between the disc and the avenue: on the avenue competition between the schools is the driving force; the individual creativity of the carnavalesco (who, as described above, oversees the design of the entire parade) and the drum directors is rewarded either by winning the entire competition or by scoring high enough to remain in the "Special Group." Once in the Special Group, the schools are guaranteed a song on the samba enredo album. In the studio, however, performative distinctions from the avenue are minimized for two reasons: (1) The producers must give the impression that no single school receives special treatment or is allowed to stand out too much (given the volatile politics of samba school patronage, displeasing a particular school can potentially have unpleasant consequences); (2) The producers desire a certain level of homogeneity in the overall sound of the album, because they feel it increases its commercial marketability. At the same time, Alceu's description illustrates the continued interdependence between the disc and the avenue insofar as keyboards eventually came to be used in the sambadrome in order to reproduce the sound of the album. Alceu sees this as the irreversible modernization of the samba enredo genre. He describes an evolutionary timeline in relation to the use of technology in both live and recorded forms of the genre.

Recording in sequences of sections (or *naipes*), doubling parts, and having the same musicians perform on various instruments and for multiple schools are all feasible in the studio and impossible on the avenue. With multitrack recording brief corrections of individual tracks can also be "punched in." Finally, in post-production one can highlight particular instruments, remove parts, change equalizations, and add reverb, delay, echo, compression, and various other electronic effects to make the sound more compatible with pop radio. With the use of Pro Tools software or other wave-form editing programs, various vocal "takes" can be cut and pasted together and singers can even be tuned.

Another aspect of working solely in the recording studio that appealed to the producers was the idea of engaging only "professionals." In practice, this meant hiring musicians who supposedly had no bias toward any particular school. While many do, in fact, perform with particular schools, these professionals theoretically knew the *batidas*—the characteristic grooves—of each school and performed in the studio equally well for each samba they recorded. The same samba musicians, then, recorded tracks for all of the sambas, regardless of the particular school with which they might otherwise be associated (although lead singers and percussion directors, until recently, have tended to represent one school for the majority of their careers; however, some singers now move between schools with greater frequency). Zacarias commented about how the album contrasted with the semi-live recordings of the preceding years: "This disc has a different character. There are only professionals here today." The producers and engineers asserted a similar professionalism regarding their own work, insisting that they did not privilege any individual school. At one point Zacarias said, "I succeeded in making the album I have dreamed of because no one [school] has preference."

Given the greater potential for control over the sound offered by the recording studio environment, it seems that what the producers meant by the phrase "the disc is not the avenue" was something along the lines of the following: "Having recognized the different functions of samba enredo on the avenue and on disc, why not go all the way? Why not take advantage of all that the studio has to offer and prepare a disc of pop sambas for radio airplay and general consumption, rather than a 'carnival' album?" As already noted, part of this new orientation involved "cleaning" the sound. In Alceu's words, "[Once] there was no longer any intention of recording live, we need[ed] to have a certain clarity, a clean sound."

"Cleaning" the Sound

In 1998, Alceu was brought in as an additional producer partly because of his experience in producing pop samba. Alceu met with the other producers to listen to the samba enredo recordings of the previous ten years, beginning with the million-seller, in an effort to discern what had changed in the sambas during that period. They discovered that the average tempo of the sambas ten years earlier was slower, and they assumed that this had something to do with the fall in sales over the years. The increase in tempos had resulted from the demands of the avenue. Before the 1980s, there were no time limits for the parades. However, when the schools grew to reach about 5,000 people each LIESA imposed a maximum time limit of eighty minutes for each procession (raised to eighty-five minutes for 2002, while the minimum time limit was raised from sixty-five to seventy minutes). Laíla explained how this special requirement of the live performance of samba enredo affected the production of the album over the years:

> When you make a parade such as that of a samba school, you need to keep moving. . . . You're dancing in accord with the rhythm that you're hearing; if the rhythm is slow, you'll dance slowly, and your advancement becomes slower. . . . So, what was our great mistake in the recording? When we began to realize that the schools found the necessity . . . to have sambas a bit faster, a bit more hurried, in order to finish the parade in eighty minutes, we brought this to the disc. That's when we brought in the bateria directors and allowed each to choose the tempo he thought best for his school. *We wanted thereby truly to capture the characteristic of each school, only things went a little too far.* The bateria directors began to accelerate too much and you couldn't even listen to the disc anymore. It began to be so hurried, you barely understood what the singer was singing, . . . and there were the big [percussive] "disputes" between the baterias [of the different schools] in detriment to the musicality of samba enredo.[26] (my emphasis)

In Brazil, percussionists rarely use "click tracks"—that is, the click of a metronome sent to the musicians' headphones during recording in order to maintain a steady tempo. Instead of a click track, the samba enredo producers employ the most recorded surdo player in Brazil: Antenor Marcos Filho, otherwise known as "Gordinho" (tubby little one). Gordinho is regarded as a human metronome in Rio de Janeiro—one of the "steadiest arms" in the business. Thus, while on the avenue each school will have a number of surdo players, on the disc a single professional is responsible for the basic pulse of all of the sambas. Even with Gordinho's talents at hand, however, the producers often restarted the basic tracks during recording because of slight accelerations in the tempos.

As the bateria directors gained more influence in the studio, they introduced more of the individualized drum breaks (*paradinhas*) that they had developed for the avenue. The producers felt that in addition to the problem with the tempos, this increased emphasis on the percussion had progressively taken away from the musicality of the sambas and, hence, the commercial marketability of the album. Alceu in particular argued for "cleaning" the sambas of excessive drum breaks: "Something that I fought for strongly—besides the tempos—was not to have so many percussion conventions, 'bah, bah, bah, brum tum tum'; people want to samba, [and] when you have that, the samba is over." In another instance, Laíla complained about one school wanting to include a particular accentuation in the surdo part: "They don't need this business of 'ba-boom, ba-boom,'" he said, while waving his arms in the air as a demonstration of how obtrusive he felt the bass drum part to be. Alceu told the bateria director in question that he could not include the surdo part because the album was beginning to sound like a "drum contest" (*concorrência de bateria*). Laíla complained that the previous year's album had "twenty-eight conversations of *tamborins*." The bateria directors of this particular school engaged in heated arguments with the album's producers, at times creating so much tension that I felt it best to leave the room. I also noted an instance when a bateria director was sitting behind the recording console during a session, beating a pattern for a percussion break on the table and trying to grab the attention of one of the producers. The latter remained uninterested.

Since drum breaks are characteristic of samba enredo, it was not desirable to remove them altogether from the album. Instead, Alceu in particular was adamant that paradinhas relate to the music, in particular to the lyrics. When the members of some schools complained that other schools were allowed to keep more paradinhas, Alceu had to explain, "But this one has nothing to do with the lyrics." Mário Jorge expressed the problem slightly differently when he said, "This is a paradinha of the percussion, not of the basic arrangement." He added that if they kept it, it would "create a precedent that will give us [that is, the producers] problems [with other schools]; it's a paradinha that has nothing to do with the music." In one dispute with a bateria director, executive producer Zacarias asserted, "We are making an album for commerce [*comércio*], for the tastes of the public," and he stressed that the melody was more important than the percussion.

Bringing a Pop Aesthetic to Samba Enredo Vocals

For the album, the producers wanted to bring the solo singer to the fore in the mix, like the lead singer in most commercial pop music. Laíla, again emphasizing the notion of sonic "cleanliness," said that "we proposed to make the disc clean; people today want to hear that. What was missing was having the voice of the singer out in front." To that end, the role of the chorus was limited to the refrains. Next, the producers asked the singers to limit their *gritaria,* or shouting. In one instance, a young singer who had picked up on the changed priorities said in the microphone to Laíla, "I'm preoccupied with not dirtying [the vocal]."

In addition, the producers invited two *pagode* stars to sing on the sambas for the schools Beija Flor and Mangueria, the latter one of the oldest and most traditional schools in Rio. Although the term pagode was originally used to refer to informal "backyard" gatherings of samba musicians, today the word is associated with a commercialized romantic variant of samba. In either form, pagode has little direct relation to carnival samba (see Galinsky 1996 on the "roots samba" pagode). During my fieldwork, I often heard references to the three million albums sold in 1998 by the pagode group Só Pra Contrariar (Just to Contradict). Wishing to capitalize on the popularity of the pagode genre, Alceu invited teen idol Alexandre Pires, the lead singer of Só Pra Contrariar, to sing together with the octogenarian Jamelão, the beloved samba enredo singer for the Mangueira school. In addition, he invited the vocalist Belo from the pagode group Soweto to sing together with Neguinho da Beija Flor on the samba of Neguinho's school, Beija Flor. Alceu describes how he wanted to update the sound of samba enredo to reflect the current aesthetic of pop samba (that is, pagode): "What I felt was missing was the involvement of the artists of today . . . those who are popular now, and who have something to do with samba, because Alexandre Pires has to do with samba, Soweto has to do with samba. . . . People want to identify with those who are up there . . . 'Look there, it's Alexandre Pires, look, [it's Belo,] the guy from Soweto.'" Although commercial pagode is a form of samba, it represents a very different sphere of music production from samba enredo. Neither Alexandre Pires nor Belo was from Rio de Janeiro, and they did not have roots in the local samba school communities. The meeting of the two worlds was not without some friction in the studio, and the idea was dropped for the following year's album. Ultimately, having the two stars participate in *Sambas de Enredo 1999* did not seem to increase sales of the album appreciably.

Mixing: The "Gatekeepers" in Control, Finding a Balance

Antoine Hennion has called music producers "representatives of the public" (1983). Similarly, the samba enredo producers saw themselves as gatekeepers between the public sphere and the individualized egos of the percussion directors. As executive producer Zacarias commented during recording, "Here [in the studio] one doesn't do what one wants to do; here one does what one thinks the public will want." (While what Zacarias says here is true, he does not mention the profit motive behind such a stance.) Once recording was completed and the production moved on to the mixing phase, it was easier for the producers to assert control over the sound of the album. They insisted that no one from the schools be present at the mixing sessions. When one composer asked when the mix of his samba was scheduled, a producer responded, "There's no planned time. Only we will be doing the mixing." This exclusionary statement (Porcello, personal communication) underscores the struggle for control over sound and its mediation in this project, as well as the complex hierarchies of power operating here.[27] During mixing, any cleaning that was not part of the arrangements or of the recording process could be undertaken through edits. For example, on one samba, the *gritaria*—the shouted interjections of the puxador between lines of the verses—was simply edited out until the producers were satisfied that the sound was sufficiently clean. "Take that 'crap' [*porra*] out," said one producer to the mixing engineer.

The cleaning, however, was not limited merely to taking out excessive shouting; rather, the producers sought a balance between removing shouts and maintaining some characteristics of the live sound. For example, after one cleaning session, Zacarias commented that the sound was "very clean" (*bem limpa*), referring to a particular *chamada* (call or shout) of the interpreter. Alceu, nevertheless, thought that they could substitute a call from earlier in the song that was even "lighter" (using the English word "light"). Zacarias responded "But it sounds very clean." When Alceu found the other call, however, Zacarias admitted that it was "even lighter." Thus, the cleansing was not merely a matter of removing shouts—although this was part of it—but also of choosing the least abrasive *chamadas,* that is, those least identified with the rowdiness of carnival. At one point, when Mário Jorge was mixing, Zacarias joked, "Mário, if you clean more, there won't be anything left." Here, it seems, the producers reached the limit of how much of "the avenue" could be cut before the music would no longer be identified as samba enredo.

One final adjustment to the vocals remained. As part of the effort to make the album more like commercial pop music, a computer program (Antares's Auto-Tune) was used to adjust out-of-tune pitches in the recorded vocal tracks. This was the first time in samba enredo recording that such a process had been undertaken, although it is ubiquitous in pop music today.[28] In support of this process of "cleaning," Alceu quoted his wife, who, he claims, said of one of the mixes, "Now it's a song; before it was all shouting!"

Sounding the Avenue: Deconstructing the Disc/Avenue Dichotomy

I return now to the avenue in order to describe the technology employed in the mediation of the live sound for the public of the sambadrome and for television audiences (stations Rede Globo and TV Manchete). While my focus has been on the recording process, this brief detour will underscore that the dichotomy between disc and avenue is not simply a contrast between live and mediated spheres of music making. The company responsible for the sound on the avenue is Transasom, which is based in São Paulo, Brazil's industrial capital. Eduardo Lemos, the owner of the company, observed that "the sambadrome was not built for good sound; the architect did not think about it."[29] Transasom first produced the sound in the sambadrome in 1984, when the edifice had just been constructed. His engineers were horrified with the results: "The sound bounced off the walls, returned, and caused cancellations. It was a mess." As the company mythology has it, after this experience, Transasom did not produce the live sound of the avenue for nine years, during which Eduardo Lemos searched for a solution to this problem. When Transasom did return to the sambadrome, Eduardo was armed with a scheme involving a network of speakers extending along the entire avenue, pointed at specific angles that, rather than causing cancellation of frequencies from echoes, instead generated a three-decibel increase in the volume of the sound as the signals were effectively joined.[30]

The need for a large-scale custom-designed sound system in Rio's carnival has actually helped to stimulate the domestic industry in audio equipment. Eduardo proudly asserted that Brazil "is now producing equipment as good as that made overseas, or even better," in a reference to the widespread perception among Brazilian engineers that the country is technologically underdeveloped. "Through many years of doing the sound for carnival, we knew exactly what equipment we needed and we often did not find it in foreign products." The Brazilian companies Staner and Hot Sound, for example, developed speakers, amplifiers, and other equipment for Transasom, while a company called Eros developed waterproof cables so that the speakers will function perfectly even when it rains. Using these technologies and others, Transasom has since provided the sound system for the Portuguese carnival in Lisbon. As I have analyzed elsewhere, music technologies and their usage in Brazil are closely intertwined with topics relating to national identity and industrial development in that country (Moehn 2000, 2001). Eduardo, for example, made a point of observing that he is exporting his technology and his design to Europe. "I am pleased to say that we are Brazilians, yes, with much pride. We did not ask the help of anyone from outside Brazil and foreigners [notably the BBC] came here to congratulate us."

Transasom employed 126 people for Carnival 2001, forty of them simply to set up the equipment, which included 12,700 meters of cable and 200 speakers, all tested for consistent frequency response and efficiency. The Brazilian company Hot Sound provided the amplification system. Despite the company's name, the amplifiers are kept in refrigerated containers to avoid overheating during carnival. The sound system must project both the sound of the bateria and that of the puxador and harmonic accompaniment (on the sound car) through the entire length of the avenue (and send it to the television mix). Audio technicians hold long boom microphones over key instruments in the bateria—especially the head surdo (*surdo de marcação*). These technicians, of course, must follow the bateria up the avenue. The audio signals from the singer and harmonic accompaniment (that is, the musicians playing on the sound car) are sent via a "multicable" from the sound car to a mixing station.[31] Two aspects of live carnival, however, complicate this task: first, the "stage"—that is, the sound car—moves up the avenue along with the procession, right behind the bateria (the bateria is in the middle of the procession at first, then it pauses midway up the avenue in a special space to the side and continues to play as the rest of the procession passes, after which it brings up the rear). Second, all of the members of the school (and the public) sing along with the samba, and many of these individuals are situated several hundred yards away from the bateria and the sound car. These varied spatio-temporal relations between the sound car and the speaker towers through which the samba is broadcast to the paraders and to the public create constantly changing echoes and delays in the sound.

The main priority of the entire system, according to Eduardo, is that "all of the members of the samba school hear well (and the spectators), [and] that they sing in sync." All of this is further complicated by the fact that the sound of the singer and the harmonic accompaniment from the sound car is projected via four "long-throw" horns onto the avenue below to help the bateria play in sync with the singer. While this keeps the bateria and the accompaniment together, the members of the procession who are several hundred yards in front of or behind the sound car hear this signal slightly later than those close to the car. These members, however, must also sing along; were there no public address system for the spectators, the delay would be relative and proportional at each point along the length of the avenue and would cause little auditory problem for listeners, except that the sound of the bateria, puxador, and accompaniment would be considerably quieter for those far from the sound car. There would thus be little volume impact for most of the audience, and this impact is an integral part of the samba enredo experience.

The speaker array extending along the avenue is intended to keep the volume even for the whole length. However, sound travels considerably faster through cable (to the speakers) than it does through air (from the bateria and the sound car long-throw horns). Thus, without some sort of compensating adjustment, the members of the parade and the public who are singing along would first hear the sound of the puxador and accompaniment through the speakers, then, a fraction of a second later — depending on the location of the sound car — the sound that has traveled the distance from the live bateria and the horns on the sound car. This problem can prove catastrophic for such an enormous production, in which dancing paraders and giant floats half a mile apart must be in perfect rhythm and complete their procession within a specific time constraint. In the past, delays and echoes tended to cause the schools to fall behind in tempo (in contrast to the problem in the recording studio of the tempos speeding up).

The basis of Eduardo's system, therefore, is control over the delays and echoes inherent in such a long soundscape, which he achieves via a computer program that calculates the delay needed for the signal sent to each speaker tower on the avenue. As noted, the problem is that the sound car is moving, so these delays must continually be recalculated and reprocessed as the parade moves up the avenue. A Global Positioning System (GPS) satellite service is used to monitor the location of the sound car on the avenue (with a margin of error of one meter to either side of its actual location). Some of the world's most advanced technology (and technology not designed for musical purposes) is thus used to determine a crucial variable for calculating the different delays interpolated into the signals sent to the speaker towers. There is yet a further complication, as Castor, the programmer who designed the software for the system of delays, complained on Transasom's website: "At school they taught us that the speed of sound is 340 meters per second but they neglected to mention that this holds only at 14 degrees Celsius." At 32 degrees Celsius, quite normal in Rio in February, sound travels at 356 meters per second, Castor reported. Thus, the computer program must also account for changes in temperature in calculating the delays.[32]

Another problem that Transasom needed to address relates to the direction of the sound coming from the bateria and the sound car relative to the listener at street level (the members of the parade) and the public. The idea is that the individual on the avenue or on the embankments should hear the sound emanating from the speakers from the same direction as the sound reaching his or her ears from the sound car and bateria. To facilitate this, three speakers on each speaker tower point toward the front of the parade, three toward the rear. Once the sound car passes any of these points along the avenue, the speakers that project forward are turned off "so that the public on the avenue and on the embankments at this point hears the sound as if it were returning from the sound car in the part of the parade that has already passed."

One final observation regarding the mediated sound on the avenue: the intended aesthetic is not a "dirty" sound (*som sujo*), at least not from the perspective of the audio engineers. Rather, as Victor Corrêa of Transasom asserted, the aim is that there be "not one spurious echo, aberration in timbre, or audible distortion. A clear sound (and plenty loud). . . . Walking in sector 11 of the sambadrome [near its end] the impression is that the sound is right behind us when in reality the sound car and the bateria have barely left sector 1 [the *concentração*]. There is no shadow of echoes or reverberation on the Avenue." With respect to the sound of the puxadores, although their shouting is welcome on the avenue, it does require electronic compression so that it does not exhaust the "headroom" of the amplifiers and cause distortion.[33] "They have a strong peak [when they shout things like] 'Hello people of Padre Miguel!'" recounted Victor (the town of Padre Miguel is home to the school Moçidade Independente).

Simon Frith has observed that "electrical recording (and amplification) broke the previously necessary relationship between the sound and the body; tape recording broke the previously necessary relationship between a musical object in space and a musical object in time. Recording perfection ceased to refer to a specific performance (a *faithful* sound) and came to refer . . . to a constructed performance (an *ideal* sound). The 'original,' in short, ceased to be an event and became an idea" (Frith 1996: 234). In samba enredo production, the "original" as idea is the "aura" of the avenue; in 1998 the producers of the annual album began to see this aura as an impediment to the resuscitation of the disc's commercial potential. In setting the aesthetics of "the disc" against those of "the avenue," the producers wished to liberate the recording from certain characteristics of the live performance of samba enredo during carnival. On an aesthetic level, the producers expressed this contrast as one between "clean" and "dirty" sounds. Ultimately, however, aesthetics were subordinated to contrasts in function: the producers wanted to free the album from the cyclical aspect of carnival—and from cyclical (and disappointing) sales. Upon hearing the finalized mixes of the sambas, Zacarias happily commented that it was an album "for the whole year" rather than simply a rehearsal of carnival.

It is perhaps interesting to note that the cyclical to linear shift on the temporal axis contrasts with the spatial characteristics of the two spheres of music making: the avenue, of course, is linear (while the Afro-Brazilian musical traditions from which samba derives involved a ring formation). The studio, on the other hand, more closely approximates a ring, insofar as the musicians are placed equidistant from a microphone while recording, and the audio engineer's so-called "listening sweet spot" between the monitors and behind the mixing console represents the center of an acoustic semicircle. To exploit this contrast further, the visual metaphor conjured by the disc/avenue dichotomy itself highlights the interplay between, on the one hand, cyclical or circular social formations (that is, the shape of a disc), and on the other, manifestations articulated in linear space.

I would like to suggest that this attempted shift away from the cyclical utility of the disc to a production model stressing a more linear sales potential can be interpreted as a Weberian rationalization of samba enredo production, one that, in some respects, failed to achieve its full potential. In this sense, Attali's argument about how music is deritualized seems useful, if overly polemic and teleological: "Fetishized as a commodity, music is illustrative of the evolution of our entire society: deritualize a social form, repress an activity of the body, specialize its practice, sell it as spectacle, generalize its consumption, then see to it that it is stockpiled until it loses meaning. Today music heralds—regardless of what the property mode of capital will be—the establishment of a society of repetition in which nothing will happen anymore" (1985: 5). From this perspective, the producers wanted to deritualize the disc (that is, separate it from carnival). Attali, however, underestimates the importance of ritual to an ongoing dynamic between spectacle and consumption: without the avenue, the disc, in this case, loses much of its aura.

The aspect of "repeatability" of cultural goods and their attendant social relations—as formulated by Attali—pervades both the studio and the public spheres of music making. Carnival is, of course, repeated every year at around the same time and helps to reinforce nationalist sentiment in Brazil. And while the themes and sambas change each year, critics have often complained (especially in the last ten to fifteen years) that the sambas are always the same, that they have become homogenized from season to season and from school to school. With respect to the disc, its sales potential is based on the ability to infinitely reproduce (or repeat) the master recording on digital copies. These copies themselves—the discs—can, furthermore, be replayed repeatedly by the consumer. Repetitious performances of samba enredo processions and of discs (as Paul Greene has noted, playing back recordings is also performance) are like acoustic echoes that can reinforce existing social relations. Yet perhaps we should be more precise in our use of the term "repeatability"; as described above, echoes and repetitions of sound, when uncontrolled, are the bane of the sound engineer on the avenue. If in the studio technology facilitates mechanical reproduction (or repetition), on the avenue it helps to control unwanted repetitions of sound. In both cases, technology has been adapted to the needs and desires of the human beings in charge of the circulation of sound; "technology" itself is not determining those needs and desires. In both cases, what is at issue is *control* over sound.

Scholars such as Steven Feld (1994), Charles Keil (1994), René Lysloff (1997), and R. Anderson Sutton (1996) have recognized that the uses to which music technologies may be put vary in seemingly infinite ways from region to region. One of the questions addressed by these and other scholars is whether imported technologies "colonize" soundscapes. It is clear, however, that "new technologies do not simply overpower; they do not simply 'Westernize' musical life around the globe. Rather, they provide new possibilities for a range of behaviors. It is people, after all, who use the technologies; and they do so by actively making choices and actively employing the technologies in accord with their needs and sensibilities—often resulting in what Constance Penley and Andrew Ross have called the 'popular *refunctioning* of foreign technologies.'" (Penley and Ross 1991: xi; Sutton 1996: 249). As Sutton and Paul Greene (1999) point out, in many cases these technologies can serve to reinforce preexisting indigenous values, in particular with respect to the way soundscapes are saturated with music of various local varieties.[34] To the extent that the complex technology of the sambadrome public address system is designed to keep the entire parade on the avenue synchronized—in effect negating the spatiotemporal problem caused by the linear arena and by the enormous size of the samba schools—the participatory aspect of community-oriented samba is preserved on the avenue, mirroring more closely the loud and immediate sound heard in the neighborhood *quadras* where samba enredo is rehearsed. As Paul Greene puts it, these technologies help to overcome "an ideal of scale that meets a natural limit in the scope and time-delay of air . . . so that the resulting sound sphere attains a cultural shape rather than a 'natural' one" (personal communication). In the case of samba enredo, local industry has been successful in developing new technologies that meet local needs, and even in exporting these new technologies and methodologies back to the former colonial metropolis of Lisbon.

Yet we must be wary, observes Sutton, of falling prey "to the culturalist fallacy that all can be explained with reference to a deep cultural core . . . impervious to historical forces" (1996: 265). One of the problems in such an approach is the difficulty in accounting for questions of power and individual agency. Steven Feld's theoretical framework of schismogenetic mimesis — which he applied to a very different context — addresses many of the problems present in samba enredo production and allows for the introduction of power into the dynamic. Who are the gatekeepers, the curators, and the entrepreneurs, of sound and soundscapes? If much of the debate over profitability of "Third World" musics has centered on the unequal power dynamics between First World musicians, entrepreneurs, and recording companies on the one hand, and Third World makers of the "raw" musical material on the other, questions of power and profit in samba enredo are largely local. The "raw materials" are essentially culled from local wage-laborers including the bateria directors and session musicians, "polished" into a pop production, and marketed to national audiences. The producers of the disc, the composers of the songs, the samba schools, and the state tourism agency (RioTur) stand to earn significant profits as long as the dynamic between the disc and the avenue is maintained.

We might also ask about the role of informal economies in "peripheral" countries (or anywhere they are present). For obvious reasons, I have chosen not to dwell here on the connections between samba enredo and certain illegal networks for profit-making in Rio de Janeiro. The pertinent question is how are such economies embroiled in the structural maintenance of national sentiment and the tourism industry in Brazil? On a related topic, what can samba enredo tell us about the relationship between consumption and civil society? In *Consumers and Citizens* (2001), Néstor García Canclini proposes that civil societies appear less as national communities today and more as "*interpretive communities of consumers,* that is, ensembles of people who share tastes and interpretive pacts in relation to certain commodities (e.g., gastronomy, sports, music) that provide the basis for shared identities" (159, emphasis in original). Is the disc/avenue dynamic realigning along such consumption-based interpretive communities rather than along strictly national lines? Is the repeal of the mandate for national themes in carnival samba an indication of the ascension of more transnational affinities based around patterns of consumption that may or may not intersect with ideologies of national identity? What is the role of the consumption of illegal goods and services here?

Schismogenetic dynamics, then, exhibit certain peculiarities in each individual case. Feld writes that schizophonia needs to be imagined processually:

> not as a monolithic move in the history of technology, but as varied practices located in the situations, flows, phases, and circulation patterns that characterize particular cultural objects moving in and out of short and long commodity states, transforming with the experiential and material situation of producers, exchangers, and consumers (Appardurai 1986), located in historically specific national and global positions vis-à-vis late capitalism and "development" (Castoriadis 1985), cultural domination (Schiller 1976), modernity and postmodernity (Berman 1983, Harvey 1989). (Feld 1994: 260)

The results of these processual dynamics may be unexpected, as in, for example, the stimulation to the local industry for speaker and amplification technology that resulted when the engineers of Transasom found that foreign products did not meet their local technological needs and aural priorities. Another perhaps unexpected result here is that the argument for returning to slower tempos in the studio was made both in the name of "authenticity" (traditional samba enredo being performed at slower tempos) and in the name of marketing priorities—listeners, the producers complained, could not understand the vocals or dance to the sambas at the faster tempos. I was also surprised to find that the emic dichotomy between "clean" and "dirty" sound proved more complicated than it first appeared, insofar as a clean sound is precisely the priority for the sound technicians working on the avenue, just as it is in the studio. In addition, one might expect that digital recording technology would be preferred for all phases of the recording, if a sound that was "clean" in every sense were desired (Porcello, personal communication).[35] In Company of Technicians, however, analog tape is the preferred medium for recording tracks. Porcello (1996), Gay (1998), and Meintjes (1997) have shown that we need to pay close attention to the uses of language and metaphor in the recording studio.

I have tried to stress in this essay that classifying music making—whether on the "periphery" or not—into mediated and nonmediated or traditional and commercial may not tell us much about the specific uses to which technologies are put in various music cultures. Employing the "unplugged" metaphor of MTV acoustic concerts, García Canclini skillfully shifts the question of the relationship between aesthetics and technology in the arts to a larger debate over the changing nature of civil society in Latin America:

> In the plastic arts, in music, and in any cultural creation, we necessarily swing between the plugged and the unplugged. One cannot do without international information, not only to be technologically and aesthetically up-to-date, but also to nourish symbolic production grounded in multicultural migrations, exchanges, and hybridizations. But there are moments too when we need to return [to] what is our own, to our national or ethnic peculiarity, to personal interaction in our domestic spaces or to our modest individual quests. . . . There continue to exist local needs in the midst of globalization. (2001: 154)

García Canclini cautions, however, against setting up a choice between being plugged-in or unplugged. Interested in reconceptualizing the public sphere and in suggesting new paths for public policy, he notes that the dynamic between plugged and unplugged is "neither subordinated to the state nor dissolved in civil society"; rather "it is reconstituted time and again in the tension between both." García Canclini, like Feld (albeit with a different focus), is concerned with questions of power in public culture. He cites Habermas's and Bakhtin's contributions toward conceptualizing the public sphere as a "field of competing traditions" and "a space of heteroglossia" in which "'Certain meanings and traditions are reinforced' (the role of the state), 'but, in the process, new forces can attribute different meanings or emphases to the same concepts' (the role of civil society), thus avoiding the danger of exclusivity and authoritarianism" (2001: 155, quoting from Alejandro 1993). From this perspective, it is pertinent to note that (1) samba enredo came to symbolize Brazilian national identity under dictator Getúlio Vargas during the 1930s (and this is the era during which the wide and long downtown avenues were built in Rio), and that (2) American technologies first began to enter Brazil en masse in the 1960s, when the military seized power and removed existing trade barriers. Thus, the intersections among public and private spaces; local, national, and transnational culture and technology; civil society, tourism, informal economies, center and periphery; live and mediated sound, performance, and aesthetics; and race, ethnicity, and nation are all present in the seemingly simple dichotomy between the disc and the avenue. I regret that I have only glossed over most of these various intersections here.

For *Samba Enredo 2000* (recorded, of course, in 1999), the producers undertook the entire process in the recording studio again, but they did not bring pop samba singers into the project. They had, nevertheless, succeeded in taking back a degree of control over the recorded sound from the bateria directors, and they continued the emphasis on a "cleaner" sound. I overheard one producer say in 1998 that the following year bateria directors would not be allowed in the studio at all. When I left Rio, Company of Technicians had begun extensive renovations of Studios One and Two. Studio One was to receive a seventy-six-channel Neve mixing console, both tracking rooms were completely rebuilt, and private lounges for artists were constructed alongside each control room. The idea was to attract a new type of samba and pagode star — such as Alexandre Pires or Belo — who, the studio owners reasoned, prefers more privacy while recording, and facilities that are more exclusive. Unfortunately, the renovations came to a complete halt when, after the government floated the currency (the Real) late in 1998, it suddenly became impossible for the studio owners to purchase the dollars necessary for importing equipment. With the import tariffs that were in place in 1999, the Neve would cost Company of Technicians nearly one million dollars, one of the studio's owners reported. By now, however, the hectic and intimate atmosphere I witnessed in 1998, in which bateria directors, samba composers, musicians, presidents of the schools, and some of their families were all crammed into the control room, enthusiastically singing along to the samba and vying for control over the production, is probably no longer a part of Company of Technicians.

Acknowledgments

I am indebted to Mário Jorge Bruno and his associates at the studio *Companhia dos Técnicos* for the generous access they granted me to their facility. In addition, I thank Zacarias Siqueira de Oliveira, Laíla, Alceu Maia, Jorge Cardoso, and all of the musicians, composers, and others who allowed me to observe, take notes, videotape, and ask questions while they worked. I also thank Professor Martha Ulhôa of the University of Rio de Janeiro (Uni-Rio) for her support during this project, and Philip Galinsky for commenting on an early draft of this chapter and for many informative conversations on samba. The fieldwork on which this chapter is based was made possible through a Fulbright fellowship.

Notes

1. Except where indicated, all quotations are from my fieldnotes from the period Oct. 13–Nov. 4, 1998, or from personal interviews with Laíla (Dec. 9, 1998) and Alceu Maia (Dec. 4, 1998). In instances involving sensitive information, I have chosen not to name the specific producer, musician, school, or *samba enredo* about which I am speaking.

2. The CD, entitled simply *Sambas de Enredo [Year],* is a collection of the fourteen sambas from the schools with the fourteen highest scores in the *previous* carnival; these schools enter the succeeding carnival as the so-called "Special Group" (*Grupo Especial*). Similar recordings of lower-ranking schools are sometimes also released, but with far less promotion and far fewer sales.

3. Alison Raphael (1990) argues that the community base of the schools had significantly eroded over time as more middle-class whites began to participate, and as the schools began to orient their productions toward tourism. While this is partly true, the core of the samba schools—especially the percussionists—remains rooted in the poorer black and *mulato* communities of Rio de Janeiro.

4. This is not to diminish the importance of vocals on the avenue—the lead voice is amplified and can easily be heard. In the studio recording, however, the percussion is deliberately mixed far into the background. I recall listening during the sessions when just the percussion tracks were mixed; I was amazed at the samba grooves I heard then as they blasted out of the speakers with no keyboard or other sweetening. I admit to being somewhat disappointed that so much of the groove had become ornamentation to the lead vocal in the final mixes. Although this may partly be my own exoticization of Afro-Brazilian percussion, several Brazilian musicians and engineers also complained to me that they would prefer that the percussion be more foregrounded in the mix.

5. "Doubling" refers to recording a given part a second time and adding it to the original performance to give a "larger" sound. This process was used twice with the choral parts on *Samba de Enredo 1999,* effectively "tripling" the track.

6. I thank Paul Greene and Tom Porcello for drawing my attention to the similarity of these dynamics.

7. By choosing the verb "to counterfeit" rather than "to reproduce," Schafer implies that there is something inherently valuable in the notion of the original. The more important observation, however, would be that electronic transmission and recording of sound allow for *amplification* and *repetition.*

8. One can, admittedly, argue simply that the disc is a "copy" of the "original" studio performance, not of the avenue performance, which is, in fact, essentially what the producers mean by "the disc is not the avenue." However, the connections between studio and avenue remain strong.

9. The gender dynamics of samba have been understudied and must be consid-

ered in relation to other aspects, such as race. With few exceptions the producers, engineers, directors of samba schools, composers, *carnavalescos,* and samba enredo lead singers (*puxadores*) are male. The overwhelming majority of the percussionists are male; if women are allowed to play, it is usually only the shaker (*chocalho* or *ganzá*). In the studio, the only women were members of the chorus. Women feature prominently, of course, on the avenue in the *alas,* and on the floats as nearly nude *mulatas.*

10. Other styles that have also been associated with carnival include *marcha* or *marchinha* (a fast-tempo Afro-Brazilian duple meter rhythm with a strong accent on the first beat), *marcha-rancho* (a slower and more melodic variation of the marcha), and *batucada* (a broad term for Afro-Brazilian drumming employing varied instrumentation).

11. Despite the importance of "Pelo Telefone" as the historical document that marks the definition of samba as a distinct genre, in reality it was not clear at that time what exactly characterized a samba. "Pelo Telefone," attributed to Donga (Ernesto Joaquim Maria dos Santos), is actually closer to a *maxixe* — an urban dance that emerged in the late nineteenth century in Rio, influenced by tango and habanero (see McGowan and Pessanha 1998: 23) — than it is to modern samba.

12. The term *bloco,* which translates literally as "block," is still used today to refer to relatively informal carnival organizations that parade in the streets. Like samba schools, blocos are organized around samba percussion ensembles, but they are no longer limited to the poorer classes. For example, a popular bloco today is the whimsically named Armpit of Christ (Suvaco do Cristo), which rehearses in a relatively wealthy part of Rio de Janeiro (the Botanical Garden neighborhood), beneath the Christ Redeemer statue (the Corcovado).

13. Despite the element of community pedagogy, the use of the word "school" to describe these organizations is somewhat misleading, since *escolas de samba* are really more like music-making clubs rather than formal schools. Some escolas may in fact sponsor schools or nurseries (McGowan and Pessanha 1998: 39), but this is not usually the main activity of the organization.

14. Samba was the most important cultural element of Vargas's more general exploitation of Rio's *mulato* culture as a way of promoting national integration. See Vianna 1999 and Shaw 1999 for more on the social history of samba during this era.

15. In 1997 the official name of the sambadrome was changed from Passarela do Samba to Passarela Professor Darcy Ribeiro, the latter a champion of samba.

16. Musicians often complained to me that the choice of judges and the process of rating each school's procession was corrupt and plagued with bribery. On a related topic, the history of the samba schools is intertwined with the informal economy of Rio de Janeiro; schools often depend on the patronage of individuals associated with illegal gambling (the "numbers racket") and, in some cases, the drug trade. For obvious reasons, this aspect of the history is not often discussed openly. It is thus somewhat difficult to gather specific information on these elements of the organizational infrastructure of carnival.

17. I have seen various figures for the seating capacity of the sambadrome. McGowan and Pessanha claim ninety thousand (1998: 39); a tourism web site on Rio de Janeiro (www.123-rio.com) says sixty-two thousand. My guess is that it is somewhere in between. For further details on the sambadrome see Castro 1994: 215–217.

18. It is thus worth noting that in the *quadra* rehearsals of the school Estação Primeira da Mangueira, one of Rio's oldest and most traditional schools, the counter-clockwise rotation of the procession is still a central part of the all-night rehearsals, recalling the similar circular motion integral to Afro-Brazilian *candomblé* religious ceremonies and traditional folk samba. Interestingly, the spatial and acoustical environment of the recording studio occasionally encouraged a partly circular

configuration of musicians; when multiple instrumentalists were recording the same instruments in the studio at the same time—*caixa* (snare) or *tamborim* (a small frame drum), for example—they formed a semicircle around the stereo microphone arrangement set up in the middle of the room. This practice, however, is not ritual; rather, it meets technical needs by keeping all of the performers equidistant from the microphones.

19. A cordless microphone and earpiece allow the singer to descend and sing amongst the percussionists on street level, should he desire to do so.

20. The surdos provide the pulse of the groove, articulating each downbeat of the duple meter between a "first" surdo (marking surdo, or *surdo de marcação*) and "second" surdo (answering surdo, or *surdo resposta*), generally tuned about a fifth apart. The first surdo plays the lower, accented pitch on beat two. A third surdo (the *cortador*, or cutting surdo) may improvise syncopated ornamentations between the basic downbeats.

21. From a personal interview in 1999 with Ronaldo Lima, formerly an engineer at Company of Technicians and at the time of this interview an engineer at the Mega recording studios in Rio. The mixing rooms in Company of Technicians are equalized to highlight the bass frequencies below 100 Hz because samba producers and engineers desire the physical effect of the booming bass while mixing. This equalization, however, means that Company of Technicians does not adhere to international standards in which mixing rooms are kept "flat" in terms of frequency response so that the transferral of master tapes from one studio to another does not result in sounds "colored" by the acoustic properties of the different rooms. After the *pagode* group Só Pra Contrariar, headed by singer Alexandre Pires, sold three million records made at Company of Technicians in 1998, they decided to mix their next album in the more upscale studio Mega, a facility designed to attract the elite of Brazilian pop, not samba artists. When Só Pra Contrariar's engineer began mixing there, however, he complained vociferously that there was not enough bass. This engineer had mixed for years in Company of Technicians. Ronaldo Lima, however, saw the problem as the Só Pra Contrariar engineer having grown accustomed to the overemphasis of bass frequencies at Company of Technicians—his ears were *fora do padrão*, or "out of the standard." This problem of genre, design, and ear tuning is one I plan to explore further in future publications.

22. Mário Jorge's recording methodology stresses good mics carefully placed, and good preamplifiers (vintage Neve preamplifiers), with a signal as direct to tape as possible (and it must be tape!). Mixing is shared between Mário Jorge and another veteran samba engineer, Flávio Sena, also part owner of Company of Technicians.

23. The facility was once owned by RCA, which was absorbed by BMG in the late 1980s. Brazil-based multinationals held on to their facilities until the late 1980s, but by the early 1990s they had sold or shut down all of their studios due to the pressures of independent production and the high cost of equipment purchase. The sound technicians who worked at the BMG facility banded together and purchased the studio from the label in 1990, hence the name "Company of Technicians." The studio maintains a working relationship with the BMG label.

24. Following the common practice in Brazilian writing, I refer to these individuals hereafter by their first names. Laíla, in any case, uses only his first name in professional contexts.

25. I say "semi-live" because the environment was dedicated toward recording and not toward a public performance, allowing a level of control over the sound (such as re-recording a performance in the event of errors or tempo problems) greater than that achieved on the avenue but less than that achieved in the studio proper.

26. A sampling of the tempos of several sambas from the albums *Sambas de Enredo 1995, Sambas de Enredo 1999, Sambas de Enredo 2000,* and *Sambas de Enredo Inesquecíveis* (*Unforgettable Sambas de Enredo*) revealed an apparent increase in the average tempos from 1987 to 1997, albeit a very slight one, and only a minimal decrease in the tempos beginning with the 1999 production. Most fall in the range 135–150 beats per minute. The tempos on the album *Samba de Enredo '98: Ao Vivo na Sapucaí*—the live recording from the avenue—are all around 148–150 bpm. Tempos from the 1970s were generally closer to the 135 bpm range. The sambas on the album *Sambas de Enredo 2000* are all played at 140 bpm.

27. In fact, a few of the top leaders (i.e., president, vice-president) of the older, more prestigious (and often regarded as more *authentic*) schools did have some minor influence during some of the mixing sessions, suggesting further hierarchies of power.

28. An aspect of the use of music technology in Brazil that I continue to research is the possibility that Brazilian music makers "overuse" certain technologies (compared to their use in other major centers of music production, such as New York City) because of their novelty, or, in some cases, because of their association with First World music production. I often felt, for instance, that Auto-Tune was used too often on vocals that did not really need tuning (i.e., slight pitch problems did not detract from the samba). It seemed to me that they were enjoying their experimentation with the program. While personal notions of authenticity may have informed my opinion, Brazilian sound engineers working in other spheres of music making did express similar reservations about the overuse of technologies in Brazil.

29. Most of the data regarding the sound on the avenue come from printed sources and the Internet. This and all quotations from the Transasom staff are from the company's website (www.transasom.com.br). See also *Música & Tecnologia* no. 67, March 1997, pp. 14–27.

30. The speakers are only on the left-hand side of the avenue. On the part of the avenue where there are box seats (*camarotes*), the sound bounced straight back at the speakers in the old system, canceling out much of the signal. Now the speaker arrays are angled to create a zigzagging pattern of projection, actually augmenting the total volume. On street level, the sound reaches 112 dB, according to Transasom. The speakers are pretested using the LMS (Loudspeaker Measure System) by Linear X, with the objective that all speakers have the exact same frequency response and efficiency.

31. There are two parallel outputs on the sound truck so that the multicable can be changed in the middle of the avenue (as the sound car reaches the end of the length of a particular cable) without interrupting the audio signal to the mix. The same goes for the AC current to the truck (backed up by a standby power generator). This switch must be made twice along the length of the avenue.

32. To execute the delays Transasom uses an array of Yamaha SPX900s and SPX1000s controlled from the computer via MIDI. To test the efficiency of the delay software, JBL's CAD P2 program was used to construct a "virtual avenue" in the computer and then graph the distribution of sound along its length.

33. A compression ratio between 2:1 and 3:1 with a threshold of zero dB is added to the signal of the lead vocal. A zero dB threshold results in the signal being compressed no matter how strong it is, which consistently reduces the peaks in energy that can cause sonic distortion by overdriving circuitry.

34. Scholars have found that, on the one hand, uses of music technologies in countries where they must be imported "are in many ways consonant with cultural values that are deeply rooted" (Sutton 1996: 257) or, on the other hand, that these technologies facilitate a desired modernization and change of local cultures regarded by youths as too traditional (see, for example, Greene 1999: 181). I wonder if, by

orienting our study of so-called "peripheral societies" around such questions, we are not merely arguing for or against a deep-seated Eurocentric assumption that peripheral peoples are not capable of making informed decisions with regard to their futures. It seems that a normative assumption that all members of First World societies value new technologies as vehicles for experimentation and change may be operating here—an assumption that these technologies are somehow less problematic in industrialized societies simply because they originate in them.

35. This emphasis on a clean sound, furthermore, must not be regarded as Brazilian (or American, for that matter); there is little reason to give this aesthetic a *national* label. My research into other spheres of music making in Rio de Janeiro reveals that some producers and audio engineers working outside of samba associate a clean production aesthetic with the Los Angeles sound and personally prefer what they perceive to be the "dirtier" sound of New York productions. I discuss these alternative aesthetics in Moehn 2000.

References

BOOKS AND ARTICLES

Alejandro, Robert. 1993. *Hermenentics, Citizenship, and the Public Sphere.* Albany, N.Y.: State University of New York Press.

Appadurai, Arjun. 1986. "Introduction: Commodities and the Politics of Value." In *The Social Life of Things: Commodities in Cultural Perspective,* ed. Arjun Appadurai. New York: Cambridge University Press, 3–63.

Attali, Jacques. 1985. *Noise: The Political Economy of Music,* trans. by Brian Massumi. Minneapolis: University of Minnesota Press.

Béhague, Gérard. 2001. "Brazil." In *Grove Music Online,* ed. by L. Macy. (Accessed October 12, 2002). <http://www.grovemusic.com/shared/views/article.html?from=az§ion=opera.004478> or <http://www.grovemusic.com.osiyou.cc.columbia.edu=2048>

Benjamin, Walter. 1969. *Illuminations,* ed. Hannah Arendt. New York: Schocken.

Berman, Marshall. 1983. *All That Is Solid Melts into Air: The Experience of Modernity.* London: Verso.

Cabral, Sérgio. 1996. *As Escolas de Samba do Rio de Janeiro.* Rio de Janeiro: Lumiar.

Castoriadis, Cornelius. 1985. "Reflections on 'Rationality' and 'Development.'" *Thesis Eleven* 10/11: 18–36.

Cavalcanti, Maria Laura Viveiros de Castro. 1994. *Carnaval Carioca: Dos Bastidores ao Desfile.* Rio de Janeiro: Editora UFRJ.

Feld, Steven. 1994. "From Schizophonia to Schismogenesis." In *Music Grooves,* ed. Charles Keil and Steven Feld. Chicago: University of Chicago Press, 257–289.

———. 1996. "Pygmy POP: A Genealogy of Schizophonic Mimesis." *Yearbook for Traditional Music* 28: 2–35.

Frith, Simon. 1996. *Performing Rites: On the Value of Popular Music.* Cambridge, Mass.: Harvard University Press.

Galinsky, Philip. 1996. "Co-option, Cultural Resistance, and Afro-Brazilian Identity: A History of the *Pagode* Samba Movement in Rio de Janeiro." *Latin American Music Review* 17(2): 120–149.

García Canclini, Néstor. 2001 (orig. Spanish 1995). *Consumers and Citizens: Globalization and Multicultural Conflicts,* trans. and with an introduction by George Yúdice. Minneapolis: University of Minnesota Press.

Gardel, Luís. 1967. *Escolas de Samba.* RJ: Kosmos.

Geertz, Clifford. 1973. *The Interpretation of Cultures.* New York: Basic Books.

Gay, Leslie C. Jr. 1998. "Acting Up, Talking Tech: New York Rock Musicians and Their Metaphors of Technology." *Ethnomusicology* 42(1): 81–98.

Greene, Paul. 1999. "Sound Engineering in a Tamil Village: Playing Audio Cassettes As Devotional Performance." *Ethnomusicology* 43(3): 459–489.
Hall, Stuart. 1991. "Old and New Identities: Old and New Ethnicities." In *Culture, Globalization, and the World System,* ed. Anthony King. London: Macmillan, 41–68.
Harvey, David. 1989. *The Condition of Postmodernity.* Oxford: Basil Blackwell.
Hennion, Antoine. 1983. "The Production of Success: An Antimusicology of the Pop Song." *Popular Music* 3: 159–193.
Holston, James. 1989. *The Modernist City: An Anthropological Critique of Brasília.* Chicago: University of Chicago Press.
Keil, Charles. 1994. "Music Mediated and Live in Japan." In *Music Grooves,* ed. Charles Keil and Steven Feld. Chicago: University of Chicago Press, 247–256.
Lysloff, René. 1997. "Mozart in Mirrorshades: Ethnomusicology, Technology, and the Politics of Representation." *Ethnomusicology* 41(2): 206–219.
McGowan, Chris, and Ricardo Pessanha. 1998. *The Brazilian Sound: Samba, Bossa Nova, and the Popular Music of Brazil.* Philadelphia: Temple University Press.
Meintjes, Louise. 1997. "Mediating Difference: Producing Mbaqanga Music in a South African Studio." Ph.D. dissertation: University of Texas at Austin.
Moehn, Frederick. 2000. "Big Sounds from Big Peoples: A Case-Study in the Global Political Economy of Pop Music Production Aesthetics." Paper presented at Society for Ethnomusicology (SEM) Annual Conference, Toronto, Canada.
———. 2001. "Mixing MPB: Cannibals and Cosmopolitans in Brazilian Popular Music." Ph.D. dissertation: New York University.
Penley, Constance, and Andrew Ross, eds. 1991. *Technoculture.* Minneapolis: University of Minnesota Press.
Porcello, Thomas. 1996. "Sonic Artistry: Music, Discourse, and Technology in the Sound Recording Studio." Ph.D. dissertation: University of Texas at Austin.
Quiroz, Maria Isaura Pereira de. 1992. *Carnaval Brasileiro: O Vivido e o Mito.* São Paulo: Editora Brasiliense.
Raphael, Alison. 1990. "From Popular Culture to Microenterprise: The History of the Brazilian Samba Schools." *Latin American Music Review* 11(1): 73–83.
Schelling, Vivian. 1991. *A Presença do Povo na Cultural Brasileira: Ensaio Sobre o Pensamento de Mário de Andrade e Paulo Freire.* Campinas, São Paulo: Editora da Unicamp.
Schafer, R. Murray. 1977. *The Tuning of the World.* New York: Knopf.
Schiller, Herbert. 1976. *Communication and Cultural Domination.* New York: M. E. Sharpe.
Shaw, Lisa. 1999. *The Social History of the Brazilian Samba.* Brookfield, Vermont: Ashgate.
Sutton, R. Anderson. 1996. "Interpreting Electronic Sound Technology in the Contemporary Javanese Soundscape." *Ethnomusicology* 40(2): 249–268.
Vianna, Hermano. 1999. *The Mystery of Samba: Popular Music and National Identity in Brazil.* Chapel Hill, N.C.: University of North Carolina Press.

RECORDINGS

2000. *Sambas de Enredo 2000.* BMG 7432172632-2.
1999. *Sambas de Enredo 1999.* BMG 7432164984-2.
1998. *Sambas de Enredo 1998: Ao Vivo na Sapucaí.* BMG 7432158010-2.
n/d [c. 1997]. *Sambas de Enredo Inesquecíveis.* BMG 7432153297-2.
1995. *Sambas de Enredo 1995: Grupo Especial.* BMG 7432124542-2.

CHAPTER FOUR

Nigel Pegrum, "Didjeridu-Friendly Sections," and What Constitutes an "Indigenous" CD

An Australian Case Study of Producing "World Music" Recordings

Karl Neuenfeldt

This chapter uses a case study from Australia to explore some of the dynamics and relationships embedded in the industrial and cultural production of diverse musical styles loosely grouped under the rubric "Indigenous" (Mitchell 1993),[1] which often falls within the marketing niche of "world music" (Taylor 1997: 1–37).[2] The cultural politics, ethical dilemmas, and rip-offs arising out of such recording projects have attracted considerable academic and legal attention.[3] Less attended to, however, is the studio practice of music producers and engineers (a notable exception is Meintjes 2003), specifically relating to how they address aesthetic, ethical, and economic factors when they impact upon notions of what is and is not an Indigenous recording and thus "authentic" (Erlmann 1996).

As well as being cultural producers (Bourdieu 1993) mediating people and performances,[4] music producers are "technological intermediaries" (Feld 1994: 282). They are also often de facto culture brokers, in the anthropological sense of someone acting as a bridge between different cultural groups. They work daily at the interstices of cultural politics and music and are forced by circumstances to find pragmatic solutions to what is often typified (and also often overly abstracted) in academic discourse as issues of appropriation, exploitation, and legality. They must also find a practical balance between aesthetic and economic concerns. There is an industrial logic to the cultural production of popular music (Frith 1987), and producers play a major role in finding (ideally) appropriate, nonexploitative, and legal solutions to the complex weave of creativity, commerce, and culture informing "world music," or any other kind of recording project. The purpose of this chapter is to explore how an experienced producer goes about negotiating and balancing those key components of contemporary music production.

I will focus on a body of recordings produced by Nigel Pegrum, who has been directly involved as a producer/engineer on over sixty Australian Indigenous recordings. These have been mainly based around the didjeridu (or *didj*), an Aboriginal wind instrument, and more recently the music of Torres Strait Islanders and New Zealand Maori.[5] The majority of these recordings have been marketed via interactive music kiosks in tourist, souvenir, and specialty shops; consequently, they do not appear on the sales charts of the Australian music industry. However, taken in total, Nigel's work for the Indigenous Australia recording company ("committ[ed] to world music and culture") is arguably more commercially successful than any other body of Australian recordings that claims some connection (real or imagined) to Indigenous peoples.[6] For our initial purposes here they will be considered Indigenous recordings because the main artists identify as Indigenous Australians. Whether the recordings have been as successful creatively or culturally as they have commercially is open to debate and discussed in some depth later. Nonetheless, their success as commerce indicates that consumers are buying the recordings in large numbers, and they therefore warrant description and analysis.

Born in 1949 in North Wales, Nigel Pegrum immigrated to Australia (the resort city of Cairns in tropical north Queensland) in 1991. Nigel has an impressive pop music "pedigree," having performed, produced and engineered at the upper levels of the international popular music industry for several decades. After being a member of 1970s U.K. pop groups such as Small Faces and Uriah Heep, he was a drummer for twelve years with the internationally successful British "folk-rock" band Steeleye Span, who arguably were pioneers of "world music," of course without knowing so at the time. What Steeleye Span did innovatively was contemporize "traditional" U.K. folk music through rock music instrumentation and arrangements. As a musician, producer, and engineer, Nigel learned his skills over an era (the 1960s through the 1990s) when recording/sound technologies such as multitracking, synthesizers, and computerization changed profoundly how music has produced, recorded, and distributed (Chanan 1995;

Fig. 4.1. Nigel Pegrum in his studio. Photo by Karl Neuenfeldt.

Jones 1992; Théberge 1997). Consequently, he is experienced across the spectrum of new and old recording technologies used on a day-to-day basis in a professional recording studio. Crucially, he also has developed the social (and psychological) skills not only to deal with musicians' always fragile egos (and budgets) and the vagaries of the "music biz" but also the cultural considerations informing many of his recording projects.[7]

I base my description and analysis of Nigel's work as a producer and engineer of Indigenous recordings on interviews I conducted with him.[8] The excerpts emphasize Nigel's perspectives and present his own words in extended passages. I chose this method of using data both because Nigel is very articulate and because paraphrasing can lose the nuances of an organic conversation (which the interviews were). Furthermore, Nigel made interesting connections to a whole range of issues as the interviews unfolded. Like many busy producers and engineers working in recording studios, Nigel rarely has time to reflect on the processes of cultural production that he directs. They just comprise his "job" (six days a week, twelve to fourteen hours a day, forty-eight weeks a year), and his insights highlight the complexity of those processes and also their mundaneness. Because Nigel runs a small business in a regional area of Australia, economic factors are of crucial day-to-day importance.

Below I discuss the excerpts under headings of creative aspects, commercial aspects, and cultural aspects, although these groupings overlap in practice. These excerpts reveal how a successful and prolific producer of "world music" recordings goes about working primarily as a sound specialist but also unavoidably as a culture broker. The discussion section following the excerpts will address issues raised by them. The overall goals are (1) to provide an overview of Nigel's involvement with Indigenous recordings and insights on the practicalities and aesthetics of large-scale music production of a certain genre of music; and (2) to answer two questions: "Are they Indigenous?" and "Are they successful?"

Experienced cultural producers such as Nigel have had to evolve workstyles encompassing both extramusical knowledge (such as technologies of production, reproduction, and distribution) and musical knowledge (such as arrangements, instrumentation, and performance styles). However, in this case study the recording studio can be appreciated as not only an industrial, musical, and aesthetic space. It is also the cultural space for negotiating the complex and sometimes contradictory demands of creativity, commerce, and culture common to "world music" projects (Meintjes 2003). It is where all of the cultural baggage that participants bring with them into the sessions is mediated through music and where all of the energies of producers such as Nigel are directed toward making music people want to hear and buy.

Creative Aspects of the Recording Projects

Nigel's initial involvement in Indigenous projects was through Aboriginal musician, actor, painter, and dancer David Hudson. He is from the Ewamin-Yalangi people of Cape York Peninsular, Queensland, and he grew up near Cairns. David has had a diverse career that included an extended stint with the popular, if often critically dismissed, New Age musician Yanni.[9] He was also a cofounder of the Tjapukai Dance Theatre, which has evolved into an award-winning Aboriginal tourism venue in Cairns, the Tjapukai Aboriginal Cultural Park. Nigel provided the following background:

> [David] had been asked by a Sydney-based label, Indigenous Australia, to record a new album for them.[10] And of course they were keen for him to go down to Sydney or Melbourne or wherever to record, possibly Brisbane. But he'd said he'd like to try this new studio that had opened in Cairns. He had actually come in and played didj on a couple of tracks of bands which had previously been in. So he knew the facility was reasonably serious, and he brought his record company representatives in to see me. I played them bits we'd done and chatted and name-dropped like mad and did everything I could to persuade them that we were the place to come to. And sure enough they gave us the go-ahead to record the one CD, *Didgeralia*.

Fig. 4.2. David Hudson on stage. Photo used with permission of David Hudson.

The record company was very happy with the results of the collaboration on *Didgeralia* and quickly commissioned other recordings on a scale that surprised Nigel:

That recording really was the catalyst, we both enjoyed making it very much. It was made on a minuscule budget. I mean we had to; the whole recording had to be over and done within about eight or nine days. The record company . . . loved the result, the distributors loved the result, and a week later I got a call from the record company saying, "Right, well that's really good, now can you make me thirty more please?" So that was quite a blow; it was impossible to imagine just launching on a project and then of continuing with thirty more didj albums, apart from the fact that the studio was flat out with other work anyway. But we broke it down into sets of twelve and in fact we did another twelve with David within maybe five or six months from that date. I know the whole last part of the second year of the studio's existence was entirely didj albums, and really following the same basic pattern.

Although Nigel was an experienced engineer, he had to learn how to record the didjeridu effectively:

Now I had never recorded the didj, other than the couple of times that David had been in [with bands] . . . But it was obvious to me through my experience of having recorded [many] folk instruments over the last twenty-odd years that it would be good to try one or two miking techniques that David told me he had never applied to his didj before. We also applied a couple of basic reflection theories of the sound from the didj being beamed back as it were to the microphones, which were placed around the end of the didj. I'm not going to go into great details 'cause it's a little bit of a secret.

The notion of there being "secret" aspects to recording processes points out that although recording technology may be standardized worldwide (given the relatively limited number of large manufacturers and formats), individual producers or engineers may still have particular ways of recording or mixing. These arise from their particular aesthetic vision, sometimes identified as a particular "sound," such as that connected to a producer (for example, Phil Spector or George Martin) or a place (for example, Nashville or Berlin). The sounds Nigel gets from didjeridus comprise an example of the intentional sonic construction of David Hudson's recordings. In general terms, such a sonic strategy is a crucial although often subconscious aspect of why consumers may like or dislike a recording. Given the centrality of the didjeridu to the recordings, it is the sonic element of greatest importance to them.

The initial collaboration between Nigel and David was exploratory but set the pattern used for the numerous recordings that followed:

David claimed it was the best didj sound he'd ever come across [or] had, so I think that obviously spurred him to recommend to his label that he'd like to continue recording with us. We produced that first album [*Didgeralia*] [but] as a Pommie [British migrant] in Australia (and also working with somebody of the status of David), I really was very careful about putting forward any opinions. But it soon become clear to me that David liked to be produced . . . I found myself almost talking David through some of the tracks [using a combination of visual and musical cues, a technique David has always used]. [He recreates on his didjeridu] a journey he might be taking through the bush or down a mountainside to the sea . . . he seemed to be wanting that direction so I leapt in and gave it and he wasn't offended. And the end result, of course, was a very successful album.

Initially, Nigel's productions for Indigenous Australia were guided by his own preferences and experiences:

All through my musical career, even in my young esoteric days, I never saw the point in producing or playing on music that nobody wanted to hear. And of course that's continued and as I get older and mellower, I guess I want more and more people to enjoy my music without being blatantly commercial. Not because I disagree with blatantly commercial music, it's just that personally I actually can't produce it. I can't produce Top 10–sounding dance hits; it's not within my musical sphere of understanding. So I've always been, in England the term is, a catalogue producer. Somebody that produces the stock, the filler stuff. You know, the *Orchestral Hits of TV Themes* and the sound-alikes of that such as *Blah Blah Blah and His Orchestra Play Famous Classical Tunes,* but with rhythm section. And they've always been solid sellers and they've always been solidly musical albums but never the kind of supersheen pop hits. And I just applied those principles to the production work with David.

Nigel's experience as a catalogue producer was crucial to helping strike an aesthetic balance between musically unobtrusive and musically irrelevant:

[Producing the didj music] is very similar to producing underscore music, which is the music used in the film world to sit under dialogue. [But] it's a very fine line between underscore and elevator music. They're a world apart, and much of that is the musicianship involved and the originality of the performance. Elevator music daren't move out of its totally clichéd genre and the "Mantovani Strings sound" and so on and so on. Underscoring similarly has to [adhere to expectations], or I mean it daren't have any sharp edges in the overall produced finished sound. And we were producing for a market who would take these things back to the Midwest of the U.S.A. or Tokyo and play them. We were careful not to produce musical wallpaper, but basically they'd be playing them at dinner parties and so on. And [they might say] "We've just been for a holiday [to Australia] and here's the pictures or here's the video or whatever. And this is some music we bought and isn't this wonderful, the great sound of the didjeridu?" Those kind of people wouldn't want to [buy something too traditional] although we did do some very traditionally sounding albums . . . which would be bought by the slightly more serious eco-tourist who only wanted, as far as we can tell, the purer form of the didj. But that in itself is a totally other argument because who knows what the didj sounded like five hundred years ago. They didn't have digital recorders in the Northern Territory five hundred years ago so it's [unknown], like all traditional music where nobody knows what it was like one hundred years ago really.

There were other aesthetic and sound-based considerations that Nigel had to appraise when producing on the large scale of the didj projects. An important element relates to creating an "authentic" sonic ambience; that is, one where the "reality" of the didjeridu (and its essentialistic, earth-connected connotations) is juxtaposed with "unreal" synthesized sounds (and their connotations of unauthenticity). The two kinds of sounds are not necessarily antithetical, but they must be blended in a way that does not result in a jarring juxtaposition. A skilled engineer such as Nigel can create the illusion that they are concomitant and not conflicting sounds:

I get the feeling that this market that we're talking about do know the difference between everything being produced on a computer and people playing. And so 90 percent of everything we do is people playing, albeit some of it [is] people playing synthesizers; We never pretend that they're not synthesizers; they're there to create [certain sounds]. And synthesizers have a wonderful ability to create a kind of backdrop or landscape on which we then place our stronger [sound] colors, for example the didj or whatever lead instruments may be involved . . . If you want to get into the technicalities of it, as you say, from the bass drum on up [through the whole sound spectrum], we just don't engineer in a totally "in-your-face" way. Not only that the sounds themselves being put on tape are generally rounder and more mellow, but also then in the final mixing where everything is placed, for me anyway, in a more natural dynamic. [It's] as if one were in a perfect concert hall listening to a beautifully balanced jazz quartet or small string ensemble or whatever. [That is] unlike the typical rock band mixing, where the vocals and the bass drum take preference. [They are mixed] right up in-your-face and blasting the speakers and thumping you in the stomach even when you're two hundred yards back from the stage . . . it's all just this big mélange of in-your-face sound. I've actually worked to the opposite of that [aesthetic].

Nigel's preference for creating the antithesis of an "in-your-face" sound was epitomized by what he called being sonically "transparent." The term is interesting because it suggests that a goal of his studio practice was to produce recordings where the mediating role of technology was minimized. Instruments and voices were recorded and mixed (using various electronic effects, compression, and equalization) to make the audio experience seem "real" and not at all "unauthentic." This, of course, is paradoxical, given the considerable technological mediation inherent in multitrack recording:

There's a word used in recording, which is transparent, which may not mean a whole lot to your average music listener but if you read a lot of the audio magazines that term is used. It sort of denotes that the high end [frequencies are] there and there's a definition, especially these days with digital recordings. There's beautiful definition with the top-end [frequencies] without in any way causing you to wince or wish that top-end wasn't quite so searing. And that's where we get this word "transparent," that you can almost see the sound, that I can see it in my mind as I'm trying to describe it to you and as I'm mixing, that's how I envisage it. It's actually a physical and a visual thing as well as an audio thing. And there's something else as well; in my mixing process I always try to create as much depth to the sound as well as width; width obviously created by literally panning as we can between the two speakers of stereo. We won't go into "5 plus 1" and all the latest surround-sound techniques, we're still working in good old stereo. What we're doing now is creating a sense of forward and behind as well and all of that is [part of] a more [transparent sound]. Unlike a lot of the dance stuff where everything is just right up in front of you and just crashing to get down into your brain, to penetrate your skull, I tend to lay things back in the perceived soundscape and allow for people to sit there and close their eyes and almost imagine they are sitting in front of a small orchestra or rhythm section.

A crucial aesthetic consideration for Nigel was that while ensuring that the didjeridu was integrated within the soundscape, he simultaneously had to emphasize its signature sound, a sound now well circulated transnationally.[11] This sound arises from its unique qualities as a musical instrument; no two are alike (unless they are made from synthetic materials rather than different pieces of wood), and only a skilled player can take the didjeridu beyond its clichéd dronelike signature sound or animal calls. It is also unique in its sonic richness across the sound spectrum, which belies its technological simplicity as an unadorned hollow tube:

> The didj generally has an incredible facility of wrapping all the other musical sounds together, it really does. When we talk in terms of "pitches" of the didjs, one of the devices of course we have to use [is different didjs]. We can't use the same-pitch didj for every piece of music we record, for obvious reasons, because we're dealing with conventional Western instruments which have pitch and we move from key to key. We discovered early on that it's not a good thing to change key, particularly through a didj piece, because it's uncharacteristic of the instrument. You don't see a [traditional] didj player suddenly swap from one didj to another and change the pitch; it's rather unnerving. What we were trying to create anyway was almost a mesmerizing, relaxing overall effect, and changing the pitch of the didj tends to disturb that. We have done it once or twice deliberately to show that it can be done, but of course it's not natural, normal, and traditional to do that.

It is also important to remember that while the didj is not a "melodic instrument," it is capable of a wide range of sounds, and presenting those idiosyncrasies was vital over a large number of recordings by the same musician:

> We're working with didjs of different pitches, and we deliberately of course work from key to key through the album to keep the listener's ear refreshed rather than just doing a whole string of tracks in the same pitch. Although we work with didjs of specific pitches, and they're tuned just by literally cutting them shorter and longer, they don't all start at the same [point] anyway because the size of the central bore [varies] because they're all natural. So every one's different but at least when you blow down the didj and you have "X" sound come out the other end you can shorten it to make it higher if you wish. It's a very careful process. There is also a certain amount of pitching can be created with the embouchure, the tightness of the lip and so on. But although we may call one didj, let's say, "C," [or] in the note of C (it might bear a relationship to say probably two octaves below middle C on a piano), there are absolutely billions of harmonics with that sound, some of which you are aware of. The lip buzzing part alone [created by the player] would have probably six or eight notes within it, but the whole didj seems to almost fill the entire audio spectrum. It picks up all these other sounds that we've already put on the track and pulls them together to within itself. So you've got this great, lovely, big, warm didj sound with all these other instruments almost appearing within it.

This integration of diverse sounds is difficult to describe, but Nigel finds it easiest to understand in visual terms:

> It's trying to see it visually rather than on an audio spectrum. [It's] very hard to describe in words [but] when you hear it you would know. Some tracks we've started to work on have sounded really quite [disconnected]; the other instruments that we used didn't connect until the didj went in the middle. I mean, that's deliberate, and that's something we've learned, because the other thing about production anyway is that [the intention is] to create a balanced audio spectrum, say from bass and bass drum through to the top end of acoustic guitars, cymbals, and strings. Certainly the way I work is to try and have an even spread of frequencies within the instruments that are used. Now of course this occurs naturally in a Western symphony orches-

tra, because it's evolved over how many years and current-day instruments have evolved and therefore the orchestra has its own internal balance. Every instrument is there for a reason: to fill in a frequency gap that needs to be filled in. [For example], when you're creating modern music and you can put a tin whistle with a tuba or a top-endy, funny little screechy synthesizer- sound with a great big waffly, blasty sound over the lot, these rules don't apply . . . You can very easily falsify a natural balance, and of course there are certain forms of music that excel in that and only exist because that is possible.

As Nigel's remarks demonstrate, creative considerations are a key component of such projects. However, they are constrained to some degree by the skills of the musicians, the available technology, and the expertise of the producer and engineer. An experienced producer such as Nigel is hired to make the most of what a project, musician, or composition has to offer and thus achieve a professional result, even if the material itself is not always outstanding or a large body of work is being recorded. In the case of the didj recordings there are other kinds of constraints, a chief one being what happens when recordings move from concerns about creativity to concerns about commerce.

Commercial Aspects of the Recording Projects

Aside from creative, essentially aesthetic concerns, the key economic consideration driving the didj projects is their commercial agenda. The didj recordings Nigel produces are not field recordings of "traditional" music.[12] They are made to make money and compete in a vast transnational recording industry with a shifting yet firmly aestheticized sense of marketable combinations of musical ingredients (Erlmann 1996). That is not to say that these recordings cannot be both creative and commercially successful, but if making money is the goal then whatever encourages that end result will understandably take precedence. As Nigel mentioned in the previous section, he has always seen no point "in producing or playing music that nobody wanted to hear" (Pegrum 2000). However, producers working for someone else must operate within the financial limits imposed by the client, unless they are willing to underwrite the project themselves. Consequently, commerce is not inherently anticreative; instead, in this case creativity operates within the boundaries imposed by commerce. Cultural considerations may be of minor importance or even sometimes irrelevant at best or inimical at worst.

Two major commercial considerations underlying these projects were to cater to a market and to respond to (rather than lead) current musical trends. Central to the success of any commercial undertaking is the identification of its market. In this instance, Nigel and the record company had a clear understanding of who might buy the recordings and thus catered to a market consisting primarily of tourists twenty years of age and up who might want a sonic souvenir of Australian Indigeneity:

We sat down with the record company, [and] we identified the market that we were going to be selling to . . . Let's say, twenties up, I suppose the word is tourist, whether they be domestic tourists coming to the north [of Queensland] and wanting to take back to their southern homes some Indigenous representations or of course a lot of overseas tourists . . . We identified that market and that's where we [specialized]. I geared the music to appeal to that market, without being blatantly commercial about it. So essentially it was the palatable side of trancy/world music going across to almost classical-sounding orchestral or orchestrated backing tracks through to, just in one case, a small, almost lounge-bar jazz trio. But this is the music that age group would enjoy to hear. I mean [music] played seriously by very accomplished musicians; we're not talking about bad cabaret here at all.

Once the market for the music was identified, it became important to use live musicians as opposed to programmed synthesized sounds and then to mix the recordings to sound "natural":

I try not to program everything. I find it very unmusical and listener unfriendly, certainly in the ambient and the more, dare I used the word, "mature" markets that we were heading for. We weren't going for the teenage bang-crash dance market. We're aiming to an age group who don't necessarily want to hear unnatural and weird balances. They want to hear [the didj natural], it's just got to feel right, [it's] that warm fuzzy feeling that's got to come off the CD.

Another part of catering to a market was presentation, which had to be very appealing and had to "grab" the intended consumer, usually someone walking along browsing in search of a memento:

[Presentation] is absolutely [crucial], because they're sold purely on being displayed in prominent positions on high [shopping traffic] streets and souvenir shops [and] in airports. That initial attraction of those covers is everything, because the [record company] doesn't TV advertise, and they don't have distribution in the way the major record companies would have in record shops (and therefore big displays in windows and so forth). So that initial attraction is everything that sells them.

As Nigel's remarks show, combining market research and appealing packaging and titles has been integral to the commercial success of the recordings. Also integral is responding to rather than leading current musical trends. Such a strategy is an intrinsic part of producing "catalogue music," so Nigel was well versed in how to obtain a musically interesting yet somewhat predictable product. An important caveat is that consumers would first have to be introduced to the use of the didj in new contexts and then, through exposure to what the instrument offered and what skilled musicians could do with it, aestheticized to differentiate between "good"/musical and "bad"/unmusical didjeridu recordings, the latter of which are numerous. Nigel stressed earlier that the recordings were not "traditional" in intent and therefore were unrestrained as to what musical combinations could be tried within them.[13] The mark of how expertly they were crafted would be considered their musical if not necessarily monetary success. A good example of this process at work is the CD Nigel produced with David Hudson based on "Nessun Dorma" from Puccini's opera *Turandot* (act 3; music: Puccini; text: Adami and Simoni). It was subtitled *Gari Wunang,* or "no sleep," which is a literal translation of the Italian into the Queensland Aboriginal language Yalangi. The CD and the process of its production illustrate Erlmann's (1996) observations about the intricate interplay and embeddedness of aesthetic and marketing concerns in the discourse of "world music":

We put the piece which everybody knows as "Nessun Dorma" [on one album], which of course is such a well-known piece of music. Now the didj doesn't work with *anything* on "Nessun Dorma," and this was one of the theories that was put to us by the record company, by the way. "Nessun Dorma" was made famous by the Three Tenors (Jose Carreras, Placido Domingo, and Luciano Pavarotti) . . . Well, the didj can't be used within the piece itself because the chord sequences don't follow any common roots at all. So in the creation of that forty-odd minutes of music, we started to use the device which we just simply call "didjeridu-friendly sections." We have a buildup, a two- or three-minute introduction which the didj is involved in, which is suggesting the melody of "Nessun Dorma" and setting the whole thing up. And then when ["Nessun Dorma"] comes in, the didj just has to take a rest. But then after that, with similar instrumentation (therefore sounding like a continuation of the "Nessun Dorma" theme), we create the chord sequences that allow the didj to sit in the music comfortably. In fact, we did quite a few [musically interesting things]. I'm very proud of [how] two-thirds of the way through we actually have a kind of "trading licks," this is a jazz term, between the didjeridu and a baritone sax, which is [in] a very similar kind of [sound] area. I think that's one of the most successful combinations of didj with essentially formal, shall we called it, Western classical music, that I've been part of. I'm very proud of that album but nobody buys it; it's one of the worse sellers. That's life!

Another means of following current trends was to record the didj in combination with a range of acoustic "folk instruments." This strategy was generated in part by the proliferation of "world music" recordings, which have helped to aestheticize consumer's ears to a wide range of instruments, and thus possible instrument combinations. One musical device that has been used successfully to reach a target audience in quest of something exotic yet quasifamiliar is what Nigel terms the "Mists of Time." It is a particular sound combination and musical ambience based on didjeridu that is especially useful for evoking the vast expanses of desert Australia so common in tourist advertising, despite the fact that the didj was historically not common in the desert:[14]

Whenever [we need a certain production ambience we say], "Let's have a Mists of Time section here." It's all film score stuff. This is another thing, this music is eminently [suitable for use with film] and is being used by documentary makers. Now hopefully [in a documentary] when we get the shot of [the large monolith of] Uluru

[Ayers Rock in Uluru National Park, Northern Territory] at sunset, instead of it [using open-tuned chords played] on the guitar [with a slide], we'll get [the drone and growling] on the didj and a bit of our music behind it. Roll in the royalties!

One means of identifying and catering to a market and then following current musical trends is the use of innovative technology. A key to the commercial success of the projects has been the use of "interactive boards." Their role is to visually and musically present the CDs to consumers, and they are a combination of advertising display and playback system, allowing consumers to hear brief excerpts of a recording by pressing a button by a photo of a CD's cover artwork. The Indigenous Australia catalogue (2000) declares, somewhat effusively: "See it, hear it, buy it! The Interactive Music Kiosk is the Pied Piper of our times. Its lure for impulse buyers is irresistible and multiple sales are a regular occurrence. Success is an everyday thing." These boards also can be used as a background music system for the retailer if set left to play excerpts from the CDs on display. Recordings are also periodically added and deleted.

The commercial agenda behind the projects has been very successful. Nigel estimates that at least 500,000 units have been sold so far of the first two series of David Hudson and Ashley Dargan's didj recordings alone, and there is a wide range of CDs advertised in Indigenous Australia's 2003 catalogue. Such success would be the envy of any Australian producer or record company. Overall, a lot of revenue is generated by the production, reproduction, and distribution of the recording projects Nigel produces, engineers, and plays on. Given that they are obviously creatively as well as commercially successful in that they appeal to so many consumers, it is in the area of their success as culture where questions can be raised as to whether they fit as "Indigenous" recordings.[15]

Cultural Aspects of the Recording Projects

What is obviously missing from the analysis thus far is an overt concern for the role of culture in the recording projects. It arises only now for two main reasons. First, as a term and a concept, culture is notoriously difficult to define and then very subjective in its application. For example, "Indigenous" culture per se in Australia is problematic because it is not monolithic (there are many ways of being Indigenous), and Indigenous peoples have a particular relationship with and role within Australian society that carries over to the reception of artistic expressions such as music. In the context of trying to categorize music as Indigenous, ongoing problems arise when we attempt to qualify and quantify what constitutes Indigenous input, control, or benefit. Many projects are collaborative, and each is unique, thus they profess varying degrees of Indigeneity. There are very few solely Indigenous record companies or producers, and some of them also depend on direct or indirect funding from non-Indigenous government bodies or arts councils.

As musical productions the didj recordings are certainly cultural in the general sense that they are part of the soundscape of contemporary Australian society, although many are bought by tourists, who then take them overseas as mementoes of their "Australian adventure." Whether they have much to do specifically with (mainly) Aboriginal culture per se is another matter. Certainly they are marketed as Indigenous, the name of the record company is Indigenous Australia, and the Internet site is <www.indig.com>, but in the majority of cases there are no Indigenous people involved directly in the making, marketing, or profits of the recordings except for the few main artist(s).[16] The iconography of the advertising clearly draws on touristic, stereotyped images of what Aboriginal culture is supposed to be, and by extension what Australia is supposed to be as a destination in the touristic imagination. The iconography does not represent the full variety of ways of being Indigenous, but few consumers would want to see pictures of fringe camps or dysfunctional communities or references to cultural or physical genocide.[17] It is also questionable whether the hardened racial attitudes and prejudices of many non-Indigenous Australians are going to be influenced at all by a didj CD even if it is skillfully integrated with the musical icons of their own cultures.

However, such an assessment could be too simplistic, because it raises the largely unanswerable question of "what is Indigenous culture?" in the context of music. If this includes music made by Indigenous Australians, then projects that feature artists such as David Hudson are technically Indigenous, although almost all of their other participants are non-Indigenous. However, the participants feel that these recording projects are collaborative in the best sense of the term. Everyone involved had something of value to add to the projects, and they could also be viewed as forms of intercultural reconciliation through art and music. If "Indigenous culture" here refers to music benefiting Indigenous people overall, then this music is only tangentially Indigenous, because aside from a few Indigenous artists and retailers there is little ongoing benefit for Indigenous Australians. Certainly some Indigenous people do benefit, but not to the extent that non-Indigenous people do. Similar to the didjeridu harvesting, manufacturing, and retailing industries; Indigenous music profits flow mostly outside Indigenous communities, then again, they are recordings of individuals, *not* communities. However, the recordings have expanded cultural boundaries, not only impinging upon what didj music can be but also upon what Indigenous people can achieve as to commercial success if given an opportunity to reach a large, transnational audience.

A second main reason that culture has been elided thus far in this analysis is because Nigel is a producer for hire, and Indigenous culture would not necessarily be something of primary concern to him, although the Aboriginal artists that he produces, such as David Hudson, certainly have a strong cultural agenda in their recordings. Furthermore, as an immigrant to Australia Nigel would have a perspective different from people born or socialized in north Queensland, with its deep-seated, ongoing racism and prejudice toward Indigenous peoples (Reynolds 1999). This area is colloquially referred to as the "Deep North" because of its parallels with the "Deep South" of the United States. That is not to say that cultural considerations (Indigenous or general) are irrelevant to Nigel, but economics largely dictates how they might interface with the commercial agenda of the clients who hire him. For example, issues of copyright concerning Indigenous songs or artists are legally the domain of a record company, not the producer or engineer who has hired out his or her services to record them, although it could be argued that there are ethical concerns that ought to take precedence over commercial ones.[18]

Realistically there are no simple answers to the first question posed at the outset about the recordings Nigel has produced: Are they Indigenous? They both are and are not, but they are definitely very successful—exportable musical products that feature user-friendly musical sounds and visual images consciously mirroring mainly touristic images of Indigenous peoples. There are easier, more quantifiable answers to the second question: Are they successful? Given that consumers buy them in large numbers, they are certainly commercially successful, and an intrinsic part of commercial success is creative success, even when one is following rather than leading musical trends. Many people like the music when they hear (and see) it, and its clever advertising and extensive market penetration have taken the Indigenous Australia record company's version of Indigenous culture (embodied in the sound of didjeridu and a few artists) into new industrial, musical, and aesthetic spaces.

And what of the role of the recording studio and Nigel Pegrum as culture brokers? The studio provides Nigel not only with technological means but also a physical place and metaphorical space in which to negotiate the varied demands of creativity, commerce, and culture that inform his "world music" projects. He regularly uses music as the medium of cultural mediation and consciously or unconsciously acts as a sound-based culture broker between some Indigenous artists, a recording company, and consumers. It is a tribute to his skills that the music keeps both selling and changing, not only artists and genres but also the perceptions of what "Indigenous music" can encompass. His collaborative (even if highly controlled) projects such as the many didj recordings illustrate how one producer in Australia works within the "world music" genre, and his insightful comments illustrate the kinds of challenges that arise and the kinds of strategies that are employed to overcome them when the economics and the ethics of recording interact with notions of what is and is not Indigenous. There are many professional and personal agendas at play in these recordings, and this chapter has highlighted how some of them intersect, mutate, and diverge within a sound-based workplace.

Notes

1. The term "Indigenous" is used here to denote Australia's two autochthonous groups, Aborigines and Torres Strait Islanders, who are approximately 2 percent of the population. They are quite different groups with diverse histories, languages, and cultures, although in recent years they have been often administered together as a particular category of citizen. Since Australia's colonization by Britain in 1788, Aboriginal peoples (and to a different degree Torres Strait Islanders) have been at the very bottom of the racial, social, and thus economic hierarchies (Reynolds 1987), especially in Queensland, which has a large number of Indigenous people. For example, David Hudson's grandmother Rosie was a member of the Stolen Generation, referring to a time when many Aboriginal children were removed from their parents and institutionalized (Kidd 1997). His CD of the same name chronicles some of those events and policies.

2. Feld (1988) differentiates between "world music" and "world beat." For an interesting argument as to why North American Indigenous music is not always considered "world music," see Schlottner 1997.

3. For useful academic discussions of the general role of music producers and engineers in recording sessions, see, for example, Feld 1996, 1994, 1992; Hayward 1998a; Kealy 1982; Lipsitz 1994; Meintjes 2003; Seeger 1996, 1992; Tankel 1990; and Zemp 1996. Both Indigenous and non-Indigenous researchers have investigated the interface of legal and cultural systems and concepts especially relevant to popular music; see, for example, Janke 1998; Miles 1996; Niles 1998; ToLiman Mogish 1997; and ToLiman Turalir 1997. For a succinct overview of the complexity of "cultural brokerage" in an Australian Indigenous context, see Johnson 2000: 471.

4. A view on cultural production particularly apropos in this instance is Bourdieu's suggestion that it is an interwoven structure of "objective relations . . . in the division of labor of production, reproduction, and diffusion of symbolic goods" (1993: 115).

5. The author has worked collaboratively with Nigel Pegrum as coproducer on several recording projects at Select Sound Digital Recording Studio in Cairns and on location in Torres Strait.

6. For data on the studio and record company of the Central Australian Aboriginal Media Association (CAAMA) in Alice Springs, see Neuenfeldt 1997b. See Crowdy and Hayward 1999 for information on Thomas Lulungan, a prolific producer of popular music in Papua New Guinea. See Hayward 1998b for a detailed description of an intercultural project between Papua New Guinean musicians and the Australian group Not Drowning Waving.

7. The high quality of Nigel Pegrum's production of Indigenous artists and

music was recently recognized in the Queensland Recording Association's 2000 Sunny Awards: Joint Overall Best CD and Best Producer, *Walkabout* by David Hudson; Best Engineer, *Storywaters* by Tjapukai Dance Theatre; plus other recognition in the Indigenous category for *Walkabout* by David Hudson, *Storywaters* by Tjapukai, and *Follow the Sun* by Seaman Dan. Seaman Dan's CD also received Screen Sound Australia's National Folk Recording Award in 2001.

8. As Cohen 1993 and Finnegan 1989 demonstrate, the use of ethnography encompassing focused interviews and direct observation is an effective and insightful way to understand more fully the cultural production of popular music. To most people working in the industry, it is not a theoretical abstraction but rather an organized, and in some cases predetermined, industrial process leading toward an end product that is entirely unpredictable as to its commercial success or failure.

9. David Hudson can be seen performing in the Yanni video *Tribute* (1997) and its accompanying documentary *No Borders, No Boundaries* (1997), both produced by George Veras. For David's views on his performances with Yanni, see Neuenfeldt 1998c.

10. Indigenous Australia's web site is <http://www.indig.com>. The main artists marketed are David Hudson (Sound of Australia Series), Ashley Dargan (Indigenous World Rhythms of Australia Series), Tjapukai, and D-Kaz Man. The CDs are distributed through Holborne Australasia Propriety Limited. The 2003 version of the web site includes a "Mixer" section so consumers can "Download and jam with our amazing Mixing Desk." Nigel provided Indigenous Australia with a cross section of samples from recordings and consumers can do abbreviated "mixes."

11. For various aspects of contemporary didjeridu use see Neuenfeldt 1997a; see Neuenfeldt 1998a and 1998b for the role of didjeridu music in New Age discourse.

12. In "traditional" didj music there is a songman and a percussionist, and the didjeridu player is very much part of an ensemble. It would be considered culturally bizarre to have solo didj in ceremony in most contexts (see Garde 1998).

13. I have speculated in the past (Neuenfeldt 1998d: 5–7) on the commercial if not cultural logic behind collaborative recordings of "old instruments in new contexts."

14. See my "The Didjeridu in the Desert: The Social Relations of an Ethnographic Object Entangled in Culture and Commerce" for Aboriginal producer Stan Satour's comments on integrating didj into desert-based Aboriginal recordings for the Central Australian Aboriginal Media Association (Neuenfeldt 1997b: 107–122).

15. This kind of commercial success could be construed as the aural equivalent of what Renato Rosaldo typifies for films as "Imperialist Nostalgia," the pining after what one has helped to destroy (intentionally or inadvertently) via the glorification and mythologizing of what no longer exists (Rosaldo 1989).

16. An important exception would be the Tjapukai Aboriginal Cultural Park music project (the *Storywaters* CD), but because it is an award-winning cultural tourism venue jointly owned by Indigenous and non-Indigenous shareholders, it operates at a level different from individual artists.

17. Indigenous Australia does market a video addressing such issues, however—Colin Jones's *A History of Aboriginal Australia*.

18. Janke's report on Indigenous Intellectual and Cultural Copyright in Australia is particularly relevant to this analysis and can be accessed at <http://www.icip.lawnet.com.au>.

References

BOOKS AND ARTICLES

Bourdieu, Pierre. 1993. *The Field of Cultural Production,* ed. Randall Johnson. New York: Columbia University Press.

Chanan, Michael. 1995. *Repeated Takes: A Short History of Recording and Its Effects on Music.* London: Verso.
Cohen, Sara. 1993. "Ethnography and Popular Music Studies." *Popular Music* 12(2): 123–138.
Crowdy, Denis, and Philip Hayward. 1999. "From the Ashes: A Case Study of the Redevelopment of Local Music Recording in Rabaul (Papua New Guinea) Following the 1994 Volcanic Eruptions." *Convergence: The Journal of Research into New Media Technologies* 5(3): 57–82.
Crowdy, Denis and Karl Neuenfeldt. 2003. "The Technology, Aesthetic, and Cultural Politics of a Collaborative, Transnational Music Recording Project: Veiga, Veiga and the Itinerant Overdubs." *Transformations* (7 September), with recorded examples: <http://www.ahs.cqu.edu.au/transformations/journal/issue7/articles/text.htm#crowdyneuenfeldt>.
Erlmann, Veit. 1996. "The Aesthetics of the Global Imagination: Reflections on World Music in the 1990s." *Public Culture* 18(1): 467–488.
Feld, Steven. 1988. "Notes on World Beat." *Public Culture Bulletin* 1(1): 31–37.
——. 1992. "Voices of the Rainforest: Politics of Music." *Arena* 99/100: 164–177.
——. 1994. "From Schizophonia to Schismogenesis: On the Discourses and Practice of World Music and World Beat." In *Music Grooves,* ed. C. Keil and S. Feld. Chicago: University of Chicago Press, 257–289.
——. 1996. "Pygmy POP: A Genealogy of Schizophonic Mimesis." *Yearbook for Traditional Music* 28: 1–35.
——. 2000. " A Sweet Lullaby for World Music." *Public Culture* 12(1): 145–171.
Finnegan, Ruth. 1989. *The Hidden Musicians: Music-Making in an English Town.* Cambridge: Cambridge University Press.
Frith, Simon. 1987. "The Industrialization of Popular Music." In *Popular Music and Communication,* ed. J. Lull. Newbury Park, Calif.: Sage, 53–77.
Garde, Murray. 1998. "From a Distance: Aboriginal Music in the Maningrida Community and on their Internet Site." *Perfect Beat* 4(1): 4–18.
Hayward, Philip. 1998a. *Sound Alliances: Indigenous Peoples, Cultural Politics, and Popular Music in the Pacific.* London: Cassell.
——. 1998b. *Music at the Borders: Not Drowning Waving and Their Engagement with Papua New Guinean Culture (1986–96).* Sydney: John Libbey.
Janke, Terri. 1998. *Our Culture, Our Future: Report on Australian Indigenous Cultural and Intellectual Property Rights.* Sydney: Michael Frankel and Company and Terri Janke.
Johnson, Vivien. 2000. "Cultural Brokerage: Commodification and Intellectual Property." In *Oxford Companion to Aboriginal Art and Culture,* ed. S. Klienert and M. Neale. South Melbourne: Oxford University Press, 471–481.
Jones, Steve. 1992. *Rock Formations: Music, Technology, and Mass Communication.* Newbury Park, Calif.: Sage.
Kealy, Edward. 1982. "Conventions and the Production of the Popular Music Aesthetic." *Journal of Popular Culture* (fall): 98–114.
Kidd, Rosalind. 1997. *The Way We Civilise: Aboriginal Affairs—The Untold Story.* St. Lucia: University of Queensland Press.
Lipsitz, George. 1994. *Dangerous Crossroads: Popular Music, Postmodernism, and the Poetics of Place.* London: Verso.
Meintjes, Louise. 1990. "Paul Simon's 'Graceland,' South Africa, and the Mediation of Musical Meaning." *Ethnomusicology* 34(1): 37–73.
——. 2003. *Sound of Africa! Making Music Zulu in a South African Studio.* Durham, N.C.: Duke University Press.
Mills, Sherylle. 1996. "Indigenous Music and the Law: An Analysis of National and International Legislation." *Yearbook for Traditional Music* 28: 57–86.

Mitchell, Tony. 1993. "World Music and the Popular Music Industry: An Australian View." *Ethnomusicology* 37(3): 309–338.
Neuenfeldt, Karl. 1997. "The Didjeridu in the Desert: The Social Relations of an Ethnographic Object Entangled in Culture and Commerce." In *The Didjeridu: From Arnhem Land to Internet,* ed. K. Neuenfeldt. Sydney: John Libbey/Perfect Beat Publications, 107–122.
Neuenfeldt, Karl, ed. 1997. *The Didjeridu: From Arnhem Land to Internet.* Sydney: John Libbey/Perfect Beat Publications.
———. 1998a. "The Quest for a 'Magical Island': The Convergence of the Didjeridu, Aboriginal Culture, Healing, and Cultural Politics in New Age Discourse." *Social Analysis* 42(2): 73–102.
———. 1998b. "Good Vibrations?: The 'Curious' Cases of the Didjeridu in Spectacle and Therapy." *The World of Music* 40(2): 29–51.
———. 1998c. "The Yanni Phenomenon: Music Exotica and the Making of Multi-Media Memories." In *Exotic Sounds: Tropicalism and Orientalism in Post War Popular Music,* ed. P. Hayward. Sydney: John Libbey/Perfect Beat Publications, 168–189.
———. 1998d. "Notes on Old Instruments in New Contexts." *World of Music* 40(2): 5–7.
Niles, Don. 1998. "Questions of Music Copyright in Papua New Guinea." In *Sound Alliances: Indigenous Peoples, Cultural Politics and Popular Music in the Pacific,* ed. P. Hayward. London: Cassell, 123–126.
Reynolds, Henry. 1987. *Frontier.* Sydney: Allen and Unwin.
———. 1999. *Why Weren't We Told?* Ringwood, Victoria: Viking.
Rosaldo, Renato. 1989. "Imperialist Nostalgia." *Representations* 26: 107–122.
Schlottner, Michael. 1997. "'World Music' and Native Americans: How Ethnic Are Indians?" *European Review of Native American Studies* 11(2): 43–46.
Seeger, Anthony. 1992 "Ethnomusicology and Music Law." *Ethnomusicology* 36(3): 345–349.
———. 1996. "Ethnomusicologists, Archives, Professional Organizations, and the Shifting Ethics of Intellectual Property." *Yearbook for Traditional Music* 28: 87–105.
Tankel, J. 1990. "The Practice of Recording Music: Remixing as Recoding." *Journal of Communication* 40(3): 34–46.
Taylor, Timothy. 1997. *Global Pop: World Music, World Markets.* London: Routledge.
Théberge, Paul. 1997. *Any Sound You Can Imagine: Making Music/Consuming Technology.* Hanover, N.H.: Wesleyan University Press/University Press of New England.
ToLiman Mogish, Pauline. 1997. "The Status of Traditional Copyright." In *Ivilikou: Papua New Guinea Music Conference and Festival,* ed. D. Niles and D. Crowdy. Port Moresby: Institute of Papua New Guinea Studies and University of Papua New Guinea, 158–168.
ToLiman Turalir, Julie. 1997. "Traditional Ownership of Tolai Music and Dance." In *Ivilikou: Papua New Guinea Music Conference and Festival,* ed. D. Niles and D. Crowdy. Port Moresby: Institute of Papua New Guinea Studies and University of Papua New Guinea, 169–172.
Zemp, Hugo. 1996. "The/An Ethnomusicologist and the Record Business." *Yearbook for Traditional Music* 28: 36–56.

INTERVIEWS CONDUCTED BY THE AUTHOR
Pegrum, Nigel. 2000. Badu Island (27 April) and Cairns, Queensland (28 June).

CHAPTER FIVE

Music Mediated as Live in Austin

Sound, Technology, and Recording Practice

Thomas Porcello

Style, sound, and place have long been intimately linked for fans of popular music. As early as the 1920s, American popular music idioms were associated in both practice and popular imagination with specific cities (for example, Dixieland jazz in New Orleans; blues in Chicago and Memphis) or even smaller, contained urban districts or neighborhoods (the jazz scene of the Harlem Renaissance). Rock, rhythm and blues, and their derivatives have traded on such associations for the past forty years; a highly selective and abbreviated list of particularly strong style/place links would include, for instance, Liverpool (the Beatles), San Francisco (Jefferson Airplane, the Grateful Dead, and other psychedelic bands of the late 1960s and 1970s), Detroit (Motown), Los Angeles (surf music in the 1960s, or skate punk and thrash in the 1980s), New York and Los Angeles (rap and hip-hop since the 1980s), and Seattle (grunge, typified by Nirvana). In some instances, these links are so entrenched—often through the influence of a limited number of highly successful bands that represent only a portion of these cities' musical practices and diversity—that fans consider the place home to a distinctive sound; for fans of rock music, there is an immediate recognizability to the terms "Liverpool sound" or "Seattle sound."[1] Though it is perhaps less well known than these examples, musicians and fans of country, roots rock, and blues readily identify a distinctive "Austin sound" as well, and this chapter is an effort not only to describe its sonic and musical characteristics but to suggest how the city of Austin, Texas, has actively traded upon this sound in promoting a civic identity and building an associated local economy.

The link that Charles Keil makes among musical structure, performance, and participation is instrumental in understanding the nature and significance of the Austin sound as I have come to understand it.[2] In particular, I argue that processual and textural participatory discrepancies—microvariations in the temporal and intonational dimensions of musical performance—have special significance in the Austin sound, and that, consequently, Austin recording sessions are characterized by technological and social practices designed to foreground their presence. Further, these textural participatory discrepancies take on a particular ideological weight, signifying the authenticity of the local music scene and a valuation of live performance that Austin musicians often explicitly oppose to that of Nashville, the other U.S. city commonly associated with country and country-rock music.

The "Austin Sound"

The Austin sound exists both at the level of musical genre and at the juncture of the performance practices and sonic characteristics of the music. More than an aesthetic, however, it is also a deeply political stance toward the value of local musical practices in the face of an increasingly mediated and global music industry. For most musicians in the Austin country, blues, and roots rock scenes—the scenes most closely associated with the Austin sound—live performance is the hallmark of this valuation of localness.

Contextualizing the Austin punk rock scene of the 1980s, Barry Shank describes a local music history in which "even up to the mid-1980s, Austin's rock'n'roll scene was supported by a honky-tonk economy that reinforced a local set of traditional cultural meanings and established a flexible yet consistent musical aesthetic. Beneath the tonalities, rhythms, and lyrics that generically distinguished the musical styles performed in the clubs lay an emphasis on personal sincerity . . ." (1994: 15). This emphasis on sincerity draws upon larger ideologies of individualism and populism long characteristic of Texans' sense of self-identity. But sincerity is also locally embedded in the history of Austin music, from the work of John Lomax and J. Frank Dobie in bringing cowboy ballads to popular consciousness and establishing print and recording archives at the University of Texas, to the importance of honky-tonk bars in the leisure economy of the city in the 1940s and 1950s, to the blossoming link in the 1960s between liberal university students and the legendary Kenneth Threadgill's (then) rural ice-house and performance space (the most notorious member of which remains Janis Joplin), to the emergence of the Cosmic Cowboy scene (of Willie Nelson, Jerry Jeff Walker, Doug Sahm, and others) and the Armadillo World Headquarters in the late 1960s and through the 1970s.

Beyond country singer Willie Nelson (and, to a lesser extent, late blues guitarist Stevie Ray Vaughan), the ambassador most responsible for bringing Austin music to wider national recognition is undoubtedly the PBS concert series *Austin City Limits*. Now a program that showcases artists from all over the country who play in a country/folk/bluegrass/rock idiom, originally it predominantly featured musicians with close ties to the eponymous city. Shank suggests that "the success of . . . *Austin City Limits,* with its ability to broadcast nationally an image of Texas musicians, contributed to the effective linkage between a geographical location, an identity associated with that location, and the cultural practice through which this identity was produced" (ibid.: 200). With its visual backdrop of the UT tower and state capitol dome, its casual staging conventions that read as a precursor to the popularity of "unplugged" rock concerts, and its preference for singer/songwriters whose music foregrounded seemingly honest, emotional immediacy, *Austin City Limits* traded upon links among sincerity, place, musical style, sound, and live performance that, taken together, form the basis of the Austin sound.[3]

Participatory Discrepancies and Recording the Austin Sound

If the Austin sound is based in large part on the link between sincerity and live performance, then Austin musicians and bands are faced with a particular challenge when making studio recordings of their music: how to maintain the sincerity/liveness link despite a recording process that rarely relies fully—or in most cases even predominantly—on live, uninterrupted ensemble performances. A country, blues, or roots rock ensemble will typically consist of one or more guitars (possibly both acoustic and electric), keyboards (piano, organ, or electronic), electric bass, drums, and a possible smattering of additional instruments including pedal steel, fiddle, and percussion, along with one or more singers. Usually, each of these is amplified. When recording such an ensemble, one can, in principle, simply hang a stereo microphone in front of the group and ask the musicians to balance their loudness in relation to one another as part of their performance. In a variant of this approach, each instrument and singer can be given a microphone that is routed to an individual channel on a recording console, and an engineer can, in the real-time performance of the song, mix those channels into a "synthesized" stereo image that creates the impression of the ensemble playing in front of a single microphone. Both of these processes are referred to as "live to two-track" recording; seldom are they used in recording popular music because rarely can they provide the clarity, definition, and sound quality that consumers have come to expect from popular music recordings.[4]

Instead, the recording process more commonly proceeds using a series of "takes": multiple performances, whether by the whole group or by individuals playing along to already recorded portions of a song, that are recorded onto individual tracks of a multitrack tape and then mixed to stereo in a separate production phase after the performances have taken place. Multitracking makes it possible for band members never to be in the studio together; the drummer may come in first to lay down basic rhythm tracks, to be followed by the bassist and then the rhythm guitarist to round out the song's basic groove and chord progression. Later yet, musicians can record solo instruments and vocal parts by playing or singing along to the already recorded tracks.[5] While most groups stop short of completely eschewing ensemble performance, most musicians will make use of the potential for multiple takes in order to rerecord portions of their individual performances that contain mistakes, and final vocal tracks are almost never recorded until the instrumental parts are completed. This "rationalized" recording process (Théberge 1997), in which each instrument and voice is recorded on its own track—often outside the context of a real-time ensemble performance—enables sound engineers to obtain fine-grained control over the placement and balance of instruments in a musical mix, a process essential to achieving the contemporary sound of popular music. Thus, a well-mixed record is usually one that is recorded in a way that devalues, and often outright discourages, live performance in the studio.

Rock critic Mark Hunter (1987) has argued that multitracking's elimination of the necessity for ensemble performance has sapped the genre's early value on spontaneity, substituting monotonous sameness for rhythmic variation and all but eliminating the music's textural interest. This criticism is not, I think, unrelated to Charles Keil's longstanding suspicion of media and technologies of mediation (1994 [1984]; 1994 [1985]; Keil and Feld 1994: 290–330), for Hunter is essentially suggesting that sound recording technologies have alienated musical performers from collective acts of music making. Further, Hunter (unknowingly) evokes the loss of both forms of discrepancies that Keil argues are fundamental to participatory consciousness: the processual and the textural. Outside of a real-time ensemble performance, for example, the drummer in a recording session generally plays to an electronic "click track" metronome in order to enhance rhythmic regularity, which in turn eliminates interaction with both the bassist and the other rhythm instruments and, consequently, the push-pull tensions, microvariations in timing, and interactive dynamism inherent in live ensemble performance. In the subsequent instruments' "playing along to" the drum tracks instead of "performing with" the drummer, sincerity (so the argument goes) is replaced by technological calculation and liveness by pastiched, multiple performances.

If engineers cannot simply hang a stereo mic and achieve acceptable sound quality, and if multitracking and overdubbing sap the processual and textural participatory discrepancies from performances, then how can one record the Austin sound — its liveness and sincerity audibly intact — without sacrificing the sonic aesthetics expected of a contemporary sound recording? My ability to address this question has been greatly facilitated by focusing on how specific decisions made over the course of a recording session by musicians, engineers, and producers ultimately impact processual and textural participatory discrepancies (PDs). Explaining the retention of processual PDs is not difficult. Rarely, in my experience, did members of the rhythm sections of Austin bands record individually; the common approach was for the ensemble to perform and record live with the intent of keeping all of the live rhythm tracks (bass, drums, possibly keyboard and rhythm guitar) for the final mix.[6] In effect, then, the rhythm tracks were generated in live performance, and significant overdubbing was reserved for lead and solo instruments and voice. And appropriately so, if one wishes to maximize the processual PDs of live performance, for as Keil emphasizes (1994 [1966]) and J. A. Prögler (1995) and Olavo Alén (1995) reiterate, the rhythm section *is* the provenance of processual PDs. In the recorded Austin sound, then, processual PDs from the rhythm section bear much of the burden of signifying liveness, of anchoring and foregrounding the live performance/sincerity link that the overdubbed leads, solos, and vocals might otherwise belie.

There is, however, no correspondingly simple approach to foregrounding textural PDs, defined by Keil as timbre, sound, and tone qualities (1994 [1987]). My experience suggests that in recording sessions they are attended to, at least by sound engineers, with even more care than are their processual counterparts. Signal processing devices can often accomplish the manipulation of textural PDs by subtly shifting frequency information to provide microvariations in pitch and tuning (and temporal variation as well).[7] Of more interest, I think, are the nontechnologized decisions made by musicians and engineers in the course of a recording session that are directed at crafting textural PDs. Among sound engineers, the quality that signifies liveness is often glossed as "roominess," sounds that carry significant amounts of echo and reverberation. In most contemporary popular music, drum sounds are the single most important source of information about roominess, and they therefore have a dramatic impact on the degree of liveness evoked in a recording. In order to highlight the importance of textural

PDs for the Austin sound, and in advance of the discussion below about how Austin differentiates itself from Nashville on the basis of liveness, I want to detail two different approaches to recording drums, the implications of these choices for textural PDs, and their relation to the Austin sound.

A typical rock or country drum kit consists of kick, snare, rack tom, and floor tom drums, along with high-hat and two or more overhead cymbals. In order to achieve the presence and definition (the ability to perceive with clarity the spatialization of the various components of the kit) that are expected of contemporary commercial recordings, each of these drums and cymbals is given its own microphone (in some cases, more than one) and often its own track on the multitrack tape. A composite kit sound is then mixed by the sound engineer, who manipulates the balance among the individual elements at the recording console. The goal of this process is to achieve maximum isolation on tape for each piece of the drum kit, so that signal processing effects can be added to any individual component without necessarily altering the others (for example, one can add reverb to the snare drum track to elongate its decay time without affecting the sound of the high-hat, the kick, and so on). In a process referred to as "close-miking," the microphones are placed very near the sound source that they are intended to record—inches away in the case of the snare drum, toms, and high-hat; inside the kick drum; and usually within a foot of the overhead cymbals.[8] Given the physical proximity of all of the components of a drum kit, microphones are chosen in part for their ability to "reject" sounds coming from the rest of the kit. A close-miked kit is often described as "tight," a term used to signify the immediacy, clarity, and crispness of the sound.

But a tight drum kit is, within a broadly realist recording aesthetic, potentially too unrealistic (or hyperrealistic) for listeners. To understand why, consider that as organs of perception our ears and brain are remarkably adapted to providing information about the hearer's distance and direction from sound sources; the basis for our perception of spatialization is information that the ear detects and the brain processes about both volume differences and reflected sound (reverberation).[9] Sound waves reach the ear not only via direct propagation from their source but also having bounced off hard surfaces in the environment surrounding the source and the listener. Because not all surfaces are equidistant from the ear, and because the shape of the human ear results in the dampening of certain frequencies depending on the angle at which they arrive at the ear, these multiple reflected waves all have slightly different sound qualities. The ear and brain form a composite image from these many waves, and in a remarkable feat of neuroprocessing use differences in both sound quality and time delay to provide instantaneous information about distance and direction from the sound source. Textural and processual PDs, then, as part of normal hearing are integral to the basic physiological and aural experience of humanness.

Close-miking, however, because it picks up sounds only inches from the source and effectively blocks out most ambient sounds, cannot in and of itself provide the kinds of reverberant information that is part of the normal experience of hearing. Subjective evaluations of close-miked sounds often elicit descriptions such as "sterile," "dry," "produced," or "canned." These terms suggest that sounds not carrying the reverberation information that is part of one's normal listening experience are judged as artificial; working with ambience, then, is crucial to the psychoacoustic perception of liveness.

In order to record live-sounding, ambience-rich ("roomy") drums, one can technologically induce liveness simply by running the close-miked drum tracks through a reverb machine (a signal processor that creates or simulates reverberation). But in my studio work in Austin, such technologically facilitated solutions were often viewed with skepticism; engineers strongly preferred to record the real reverberation of the drum kit as it was performed in the studio's cutting room (a process glossed as "recording the room"). In order not to sacrifice the sonic control afforded by close-miking, drums were usually recorded with a series of close mics as described above, as well as with one or more pairs of stereo "room mics," which were placed at a greater distance from the kit in order to pick up reverberant, ambient sound. Whereas one might expect that putting up a pair of room mics would be a fairly unproblematic process, instead engineers regularly took as much care in selecting and positioning room mics as they did in close-miking the kit.

The link between reverberant sound, textural PDs, and the value placed on liveness in the Austin music scene became clear to me in the wake of two recording sessions that I worked on over the span of six weeks near the end of my field research. The first involved a rock/blues guitarist who was a technically accomplished performer but was not well known in the local music scene. In coming to the studio to record a short demo tape, he hired three members of one of the most prominent rock/blues bands in the area (a band that has received quite a bit of national attention and is held up as an icon of Austin music) to lay down the drum, bass, and keyboard tracks. The drum sounds received particular attention in this session, as all of the individuals involved in the project wanted to evoke the big, roomy sounds usually associated with this trio's band but found themselves working on a smaller budget, in a less well-equipped studio, and with less time than was possible with their major-label sessions. Initially, the drums were close-miked and two sets of stereo room mics were positioned (one set approximately four feet from the kit, and the other set another eight feet away). During sound checks in which the drummer played alone for well over two hours, we experimented with various signal processing effects such as equalization (to change the sound color), noise gating (to increase the definition of the drums), and reverberation.[10] We made trial mixes of the drums, trying different balances of close and room mics. But no one was satisfied, feeling that the sound lacked impact and was "too thin." Eventually, someone figured out that since the room the drums were in was two stories high, we could mount a third set of room mics high above the kit in order to capture room reflections in the vertical space; duct-taped to a boom stand tied to the metal support of a spiral staircase just behind the drummer's head, this third set of mics rounded out the ambient sound significantly. In the final mix of this session, all three sets of room mics are prominently featured, so that one hears not just the drums but three layers of textural PDs created by the reverberant character of the studio's cavernous recording room.

The second session could not have been more different. In this case, the group involved was an offshoot of the supporting band for a prominent Nashville recording artist, themselves in pursuit of a Nashville contract. Long associated with a clean, crisp, "neotraditionalist" country sound, the band wished to retain this sonic identity while recording their own songs. The studio in Austin was only used to record the basic tracks; all the mixing was done in Nashville at a later time. The "clean, crisp" sound they aspired for is, in many ways, the antithesis of the Austin sound, yet the starting point for attaining it was once again the drums. The initial plan was to close-mic the kit and put up one pair of room mics that could be subtly added to the mix if desired. Again during soundcheck, the reaction to the initial sound of the kit was negative, only this time the assessment was that the sound was too "diffuse," "hollow," and "flabby." We worked on a number of strategies that engineers commonly use to make the sound more crisp: completely eliminating the room mics from the mix; changing to microphone models that more strongly emphasize higher frequencies; adding upper-frequency equalization; enhancing the "click" of the kick drum pedal and dampening the decay resonance; heavily noise-gating the snare. Still dissatisfied, the drummer eventually brought in a set of "triggers," electronic sensors that he attached to the head of each drum in his kit, and cymbal "pads," small plastic boxes positioned where his cymbals normally would be. With such a setup, when each drum or pad is struck, a sensor picks up the impact and "plays" a digital sample of the corresponding drum or cymbal. Triggers thus allowed the drummer to select a digitized percussion sound "right" for the music yet also allowed him to play the drums in real time, without having to worry about whether microphones and room ambience were affecting the sounds going to tape. In this session, the drummer selected samples that foregrounded sharp attack and short decay times, along with a fairly high degree of high-frequency information—the prototypical "crisp" sound of Nashville country.

Lost in this process, from the standpoint of the Austin sound, is any sense of liveness created out of textural participatory discrepancies. Because the drummer played the triggers in real time, *processual* PDs resulting from human performance were still present (note that he did *not* select a programmable electronic drum machine to "play" his parts for him). However, at least two layers of textural PDs were lost by his switch to triggers. First, a drum emits different sounds depending on where it is struck on the head (the closer to the edge, the greater the proportion of high frequency sounds; the closer to the middle, the greater the proportion of low frequency sounds). With triggers, the same sound is emitted no matter where the head is struck; in other words, normal timbral variation induced by the fact that one cannot strike a drum in exactly the same place or manner twice in a row in performance disappears into the sonic sameness of an electronic circuit. Second, the layers of information from room reverberation are lost; the ear's sense of locating itself in a *space* of performance, in the presence of a human performer, is compromised. In this process, then, the elimination of textural PDs precipitates the loss of the link among liveness, performance, and authenticity forged in the Austin sound.

"The Live Music Capital of the World"

Nashville is reputed to have the highest number of churches and recording studios per capita in the United States (Daley 1996), while Austin boasts among the highest number of live, original music venues per capita. The relationship between the two cities, as experienced from Austin, is a curious mixture of jealousy and moral superiority. Yet the battle lines are starkly articulated in local discourse; Austin signifies live performance, while Nashville signifies the global record industry and recorded music. This distinction is formally coded into Austin's official city slogan, "The Live Music Capital of the World," which pointedly marks a musical identity based in performance that Nashville's "Music City, U.S.A." does not. Out of this basic dichotomy has evolved an ideology that, as expressed in Austin, ties liveness to musical authenticity (which is fundamentally linked to sincerity and personal expression) and recording to alienated, calculated corporate profiteering schemes that rely on star-making and pandering to the lowest common denominators of popular taste.[11]

In the 1980s, at about the same time that Austin entered an economic bust cycle following the bottoming out of the energy industry, Austin Convention and Visitors Bureau head David Lord began to link the success of *Austin City Limits* and the vibrancy of the local music scene to strategies for making Austin music a primary selling point for tourism to the city. He also reasoned that selling Austin's musical identity would require a set of associated businesses "devoted to the production and sale of commodified representations of that identity" (Shank 1994: 200), ranging from more clubs to hotels, recording studios, production houses, instrument stores, print shops, and so on. In essence, Lord saw the Austin sound as a possible source for the city's economic development and diversification.

While the rise of Austin-based semiconductor manufacturing and software development during the 1990s has clearly been the engine driving (and, recently, stalling) the local economy, the city has continued to aggressively market the local music scene on the basis of liveness and the Austin sound. Promotional materials directed at out-of-town visitors unfailingly highlight the live local music scene as Austin's strongest cultural asset, and one of its principal economic strengths as well. For instance, the cover of the spring 1996 issue of *Experience Austin,* a joint publication of the Austin Convention and Visitors Bureau and the city's main newspaper, the *Austin American-Statesman,* shows a live shot of blues guitarist Jimmie Vaughan sweating and grimacing while picking away at a riff on his guitar. To his left appears the salutation "Welcome to the Live Music Capital of the World." The first feature in the magazine is entitled "Hot Sounds"; in it Robert Patterson immediately creates an association among economics, local identity, and musical style as constructed and symbolized in live performance: "Like the chile [sic] peppers Austinites like in much of their food, Austin music is a red-hot commodity that offers something for just about any musical palate. In Austin, music is more than just entertainment; it's part and parcel of the community's very essence. Although the city boasts more than 100 venues—hence the moniker Live Music Capital of the World—Austin music is more than its wealth of nightclubs and concert halls." (Patterson 1996). After briefly sketching the annual South by Southwest Music Festival, which brings hundreds of musical acts from around the world into the city every March, Patterson continues:

> If Austin seems rather proud of its music scene, there's a good reason why. In a city known for its longtime bohemian leanings, the musicians here tend to be motivated as much by their sheer love for music as by any notions of stardom. In the same spirit, Austin audiences have an adventurous appetite, supporting musicians who sometimes push the artistic envelope and celebrate venerable traditions (sometimes in the very same act). Perhaps that's why you can hear rising country acts like Don Walser and Wayne Hancock at intimate weekly shows at a homey cantina like Jovita's when they're not on tour, or Country Album of the Year Grammy nominee Junior Brown at the Continental Club every Sunday when he's in town.

Three pictures accompany the article, depicting a local blues singer, an alternative rock band, and a folk-rock-blues artist and his ensemble; this visual slice of Austin's live music scene presents groups that would not require visitors to stray into territory far from Austin's main musical or geographic thoroughfares (or into its minority or working-class neighborhoods). The article individually mentions thirty-one live music venues that regularly feature local talent, then briefly touches on other music-related businesses such as record shops and retail stores. A picture emerges of a city populated by musicians who play publicly out of a love for their music and their audiences, and of a vibrant live music scene whose participants feel comfortable celebrating their unique musical assets locally.

Despite this confident presentation of a local music identity, the complexity of Austin's love/hate relationship with Nashville—and all that the latter represents as a "global" center of the international music industry—is easily detected in both the local media's accounts of Austin's music scene and the discourse from Austin's industry practitioners. Consider the following quotes from a single article that appeared in the University of Texas student paper *The Daily Texan* in late 1992:[12]

> Part of the problem [with developing the potential of the Austin music scene] has been getting people to distinguish the business side of the music industry. It's not just going out and playing for fun—it's really the bands that take it seriously and get good management that stay focused on longer-range goals [rather] than just having a gig every week.
>
> (Martin Theophilus, Austin Music Business Association, and instructor in the Austin Community College music business degree program)

> What we need to do is embrace the idea that we live in a land of plenty instead of thinking that there's not enough. Austin is an ocean of imaginative ideas and great thought systems—that's the most important thing.
>
> (Larry Seyer, producer for Asleep at the Wheel, Darden Smith, and Lyle Lovett)

> The live scene [in Los Angeles] isn't as healthy. There's always the threat that an A&R guy will be there. Everyone tries so hard to be signed they're not paying attention to the *soul* of the music like they do in Austin. It's great the way it is here—we can be more efficient, because it's music for the sake of music.
>
> (Local producer Mark Hallman, emphasis in original)

> In my experience, cities with big businesses have shitty live music scenes. In a way, we can only promote non-mainstream music here because Austin is what it is—if it was a big music city, everyone would be doing mainstream.
>
> (Heinz Geissler, co-owner of local indie label Watermelon Records)

> [Austin has] a mystique, a creativity, a spirit that Nashville only wishes it had.
>
> (Nancy Coplin, Austin Music Commission)

The relevant issues raised by these Austin figures all center upon the desirability (or lack thereof) of developing a local music business infrastructure that will increase the city's direct communication with and visibility to the major musical centers of the United States. At risk, it would seem, is the very musical style so closely associated with Austin, a style that inextricably links mystique, creativity, spirit, and soul into a complex anticorporate web of authentic personal expression — of "substance" over "style."

Austin musicians cannot, of course, control the extent to which the city draws itself into the mainstream music industry, as other individuals with far more economic and political clout certainly have their own agendas. Throughout the 1990s, as the city increasingly tried to develop more industry presence (aggressively seeking to house a regional office of the National Academy of Recording Arts and Sciences, for instance, and courting a Texas subsidiary of Arista Records), many local musicians looked to the Austin sound as a means to voice an anti-industry stance, its roughness and liveness standing in stark opposition to Nashville's slick recorded sound. Clearly, a segment of the Austin city government believes that liveness — as a form of social action and as the hallmark of the Austin sound — helps to create local business and jobs and fill hotel rooms; for a segment of the local music industry, however, it is used to symbolize resistance to the corporate hegemony of recorded music.

Those familiar with Charles Keil's career will have noticed a deliberate evocation of his essay "Music Mediated and Live in Japan" in the title of this chapter. In his title, liveness and mediatedness appear conceptually separable (though his illustration of karaoke performance demonstrates how experientially embedded they can be); in the process of recording the Austin sound, the mediations — be they the technological mediations of microphones, recording consoles, and tape machines, or the social mediations of sound engineers and record producers — vigorously guard the social value of liveness, in ways that often render the boundary between "mediated" and "live" indistinct. Perhaps it is Charlie's self-acknowledged ambivalence toward technology (mixed with his outright hostility toward its "tricknological" manifestations) that makes this conceptual boundary so crucial in his thinking about music. But for the Austin musicians and engineers I have worked with, mediation and liveness are not so mutually contradictory; both can be used to mark a local musical identity resistant to the hegemony of the record industry.

Those *extremely* familiar with Keil's career may also have noticed that the original ending of "Participatory Discrepancies and the Power of Music" (1987) is not the same as that of the reprinted version that appears in *Music Grooves* (1994). The original ends with the observation that those in the techno-vanguard of music have already "technologized participatory discrepancies" in order to make "millions buy and move, move and buy" (1987). And, he concludes, "As usual, there's nothing bold or new for us academics to do; we just have to get down to the recording studio or dance floor and ask people about what has been happening" (ibid.). When it comes to the Austin sound, remember that the textural PDs that create a roomy drum sound *can* be made by digital technologies but tend to be created with room mics; that ensemble performances by the rhythm section that preserve processual PDs are the norm; and that liveness and participation by performers (and their audiences) are the hallmark of the local music scene. When considering the Austin sound, one finds that there is resistance to fully technologizing the PDs, and while buying surely is not irrelevant, moving and participating appear far more important.

Acknowledgments

This chapter originally appeared in *City & Society* 14(2): 69–86, and it is reprinted with the permission of the American Anthropological Association. Many thanks to Roger Sanjek and Charles Keil for comments on an early version of the paper.

Notes

1. For a discussion of the "Liverpool sound" see Cohen 1994.

2. My assessment of the Austin sound is based on several factors: living in Austin from 1987 to 1996; performing individually and with bands in Austin clubs for several of those years; buying recordings and listening extensively to local music as a consumer and a fan; and working as an assistant sound engineer in an Austin recording studio while doing doctoral research for fourteen months in 1993 and 1994.

3. It is important to emphasize that country, blues, and roots rock represent only a slice of the local music activity in Austin. The "Austin sound" is therefore an exclusionary concept that legitimizes certain musics at the expense of others and creates a highly selective picture of historical and contemporary local musical activity. (The Austin hip-hop and techno scenes, for example, are thriving but clearly do not configure these links the same way.) The country, blues, and rock scenes are, however, the musics most closely associated—in both popular and official discourses—with the city. This reality will be addressed more fully below.

4. Two notable exceptions by prominent recording artists include the Cowboy Junkies' *The Trinity Sessions* (BMG, 1988) and Bruce Springsteen's *Nebraska* (Columbia, 1982). A concise account of the decision not to record *Nebraska* on multitrack can be found in Zak 2001: 139–140.

5. Popular music histories commonly suggest that the Beatles recorded much of their final work without ever seeing each other.

6. The sole exception in my primary fieldwork involved an attempt to rerecord all of the electric bass parts for an album while keeping the original drum tracks, which necessitated that the bassist play along to the recorded drum part. This decision was made because of technical problems with the bass track in the original ensemble recording and economic constraints that prevented the drummer from coming back to the studio to rerecord his part along with the bassist.

7. Artificial double-tracking (ADT) machines are a prime example. "Double-tracking" refers to the process in which a musician rerecords his performance one or

more times, with the resulting takes mixed together. The effect is that of a singer or instrumentalist performing in unison with herself, and the resultant sound is psychoacoustically more "full" than a single part. Both Brian Wilson of the Beach Boys and Beatles' producer George Martin utilized double-tracking to fill out lead vocal lines. George Martin writes that while he never fully understood the source of the "difference" that double-tracking makes, "It may be something to do with the canceling-out of vibratos. It may be something to do with being in and out of tune, since nobody actually sings the same song twice in exactly the same way" (quoted in Julien 1999). ADT provided the basis for such common effects as phasing, flanging, and chorusing; once a mechanical process involving synching multiple tracks, it is now easily (and instantaneously) accomplishable with digital effects processors.

8. There are two logistical reasons for the greater distance involved in miking overhead cymbals. First, because of the nature of plate vibration, in which very different frequencies are sounded at different points on the vibrating surface, a more accurately complex sound wave is captured when the mic is not too closely focused on only one region of the vibrating cymbal. Second, one must place the mic far enough away that it is not hit either by a cymbal swinging after impact or by the drummer's sticks.

9. For introductory but comprehensive descriptions of the physiology and neurology of hearing and of the role of reverberation in spatial awareness, see Ashmore 2000 and Taylor 2000 respectively.

10. "Noise gates" are electronic circuits that function analogous to an on/off switch. They are usually used so that sounds falling below a certain volume are not allowed to pass through the circuit (i.e., they are silenced).

11. Lexically, Austin musicians refer to themselves and their local compatriots as "musicians," "artists," "bands," or "groups," while those from Nashville are routinely referred to by the Austin music community as "acts." The ideological distinction between art and commerce is thus explicitly coded in local discourse.

12. All of the following passages are marked in the article as direct quotes from the individuals named in the corresponding parentheses. The article was written by Steve Crabtree (*The Daily Texan,* October 29, 1992, p. 11).

References

BOOKS AND ARTICLES

Alén, Olavo. 1995. "Rhythm As Duration of Sounds in Tumba Francesa." *Ethnomusicology* 39(1): 55–71.

Ashmore, Jonathan. 2000. "Hearing." In *Sound,* ed. Patricia Kruth and Henry Stobardt. Cambridge: Cambridge University Press, 65–88.

Cohen, Sara. 1994. "Identity, Place, and the 'Liverpool Sound.'" In *Ethnicity, Identity, and Music: The Musical Construction of Place,* ed. Martin Stokes. Providence, R.I.: Berg, 117–134.

Crabtree, Steven. 1992. "If You Build It, They Will Come . . . : Austin Music Industry Split over Ways to Increase Prominence, Spread of Local Recording Scene." *Daily Texan* (October 19), 11.

Daley, D. 1996. "Nashville Recording at the Crossroads." *Mix* 20(7): 84–90.

Hunter, Mark. 1987. "The Beat Goes Off: How Technology Has Gummed Up Rock's Grooves." *Harpers* (May), 53–57.

Julien, Olivier. 1999. "The Diverting of Musical Technology by Rock Musicians: The Example of Double-Tracking." *Popular Music* 18(3): 357–365.

Keil, Charles. 1987. "Participatory Discrepancies and the Power of Music." *Cultural Anthropology* 2(3): 275–283.

——. 1994 [1966]. "Motion and Feeling through Music." In *Music Grooves,* ed. Charles Keil and Steven Feld. Chicago: University of Chicago Press, 53–76.
——. 1994 [1984]. "Music Mediated and Live in Japan." In *Music Grooves,* ed. Charles Keil and Steven Feld. Chicago: University of Chicago Press, pp. 247–256.
——. 1994 [1985]. "People's Music Comparatively: Style and Stereotype, Class and Hegemony." In *Music Grooves,* ed. Charles Keil and Steven Feld. Chicago: University of Chicago Press, 197–217.
——. 1994 [1987]. "Participatory Discrepancies and the Power of Music." In *Music Grooves,* ed. Charles Keil and Steven Feld. Chicago: University of Chicago Press, 96–108.
Keil, Charles, and Steven Feld. 1994. "Commodified Grooves." In *Music Grooves,* ed. Charles Keil and Steven Feld. Chicago: University of Chicago Press, 290–330.
Patterson, Robert. 1996. "Hot Sounds." In *Experience Austin* (spring). Austin: Austin Convention and Visitors Bureau and *Austin American-Statesman.*
Prögler, J. A. 1995. "Searching for Swing: Participatory Discrepancies in the Jazz Rhythm Section." *Ethnomusicology* 39(1): 21–54.
Shank, Barry. 1994. *Dissonant Identities: The Rock 'n' Roll Scene in Austin, Texas.* Hanover, N.H.: Wesleyan University Press/University Press of New England.
Taylor, Charles. 2000. "The Physics of Sound." In *Sound,* ed. Patricia Kruth and Henry Stobardt. Cambridge: Cambridge University Press, 34–64.
Théberge, Paul. 1997. *Any Sound You Can Imagine: Making Music, Making Meaning.* Hanover, N.H.: Wesleyan University Press/University Press of New England.
Zak, Albin. 2001. *The Poetics of Rock: Cutting Tracks, Making Records.* Berkeley: University of California Press.

RECORDINGS

Cowboy Junkies. 1988. *The Trinity Sessions.* BMG/RCA.
Springsteen, Bruce. 1982. *Nebraska.* Columbia Records.

CHAPTER SIX

Media as Social Action

Native American Musicians in the Recording Studio

Beverley Diamond

Native American Audio Recordings: A Booming Niche in the Industry

A number of congruent technological, economic, and sociopolitical developments have contributed to a surge in Native American popular music production, particularly since the 1990s. These developments include the advent of technologies that reduced the isolation of remote areas by enabling satellite broadcasting and Internet marketing; the expansion of world music as a major industry niche; and the creation of new systems of legitimation, such as the Canadian Juno awards for the Best Music of Aboriginal Canada (established in 1994), the Canadian Aboriginal Music Awards (begun in 1999), and the Native American Music Awards (launched in 1997). The categories of both the CAMAs and NAMAs (or "NAMMY" awards, as they have been called) further indicate the generic diversity of contemporary Native American music.[1] By 2003 broadcaster and discographer Brian Wright-McLeod had compiled a mammoth discography of the work of over fifteen hundred Aboriginal artists, as well as names and addresses of Native radio stations (116 in Canada alone) and forty-one record companies (Wright-McLeod 2003). His music categories are equally diverse but different from those of the award organizations: Contemporary Music, Compilations, Soundtracks, Spoken Word, Chicken Scratch, Pow Wow, Flute Music, Traditional/Archival, Peyote Ritual Music, and Arctic/

Circumpolar (contemporary, spoken word, and traditional/archival). Clearly, the Native scene has become a "niche" of considerable dimension.

For women artists, a significant locus of energy and exchange was the Aboriginal Women's Voices program at the Banff Centre for the Arts, which was directed by Sadie Buck from 1995 to 2001. Here, twelve applicants would be selected each year to teach one another music from their nation or community and to undertake the creation of new, often collaborative work. The program enabled women by funding them and providing a supportive and quiet environment for them to work, and it has been widely recognized as a model for cultural alliance that offers respect for traditional knowledge while encouraging innovation. Another important landmark for women artists were two recordings by the Smithsonian Institution, entitled *Heartbeat* and *Heartbeat II,* that demonstrated the wide range of their musical practices. While statistically women have not garnered as many awards as men, and they frequently downplay the importance of such recognition (see, for example, Diamond 2002), their work is clearly respected by their peers. The Canadian Junos have had two female nominees out of five (for all but two years) in the Best Music of Aboriginal Canada category, and winners have included Susan Aglukark, Mishi Donovan, and Buffy Sainte-Marie. In addition to a significant number of female nominations in country, folk, and new age categories, Fara Palmer, Sandy Scofield, and Leela Gilday have all won the prestigious Best Song category at the CAMAs and Mishi Donovan was awarded the Best Songwriter award in 2000. Joanne Shenandoah and Mary Youngblood are among the repeat winners at the NAMMYs.

This extensive production of Native American recordings, however, has not equated with an equivalent surge in visibility. Native American musicians are positioned ambiguously between traditional, world, and popular music genres. In this essay I want to explore how contemporary Native American recording artists reflect upon and inflect this ambiguity of positioning in the process of making their CDs. Following a brief exploration of systems of circulation, I present four case studies that examine the social relationships of the recording studio as well as production/post-production techniques. In each case, a provocative question emerges: what exactly is a recording as a form of communication? This question then implicates other issues: what work does a recording do? For what social action might it be intended? Are there unintended implications when indigenous music circulates in commodified forms? When I refer to a recording as a sort of "social action," I am extending work that anthropologist Julie Cruikshank (1998) has done with Yukon First People in exploring how live performance functions as social action. I think that commodities can be considered in a similar way to live performance in this regard.[2] Hence, I will ask how exactly CDs are being defined and redefined by a number of forward-thinking Native American artists.

Negotiating the Systems of Circulation

Recently, I discovered that a large HMV store in Toronto had removed First Nations, Inuit, and Métis artists from their "World Music" section and placed them in the bin labeled "Collections." Only a few weeks earlier, in Vancouver's Virgin Records superstore, I found locally acclaimed Métis singer Fara Palmer's latest album *Pretty Brown* (comprising styles that are primarily folk and rhythm and blues) categorized in the company computer under House and Dance music.[3] If, as it seemed on those occasions, Native American music was increasingly hard to locate physically in the record store, what did this imply about the music's symbolic currency and its social location vis à vis so-called "mainstream" music? Well aware that the labeling of popular musics is a fluid practice, I wondered what exactly this ambiguity of positioning meant. In particular, how is its meaning shifting if the uncertainty about where to locate the products of First Nations, Inuit, and Métis artists is more pronounced than it was a few years ago? Are we seeing a systemic and rather violent challenge to the accessibility of this music, or does the current moment afford an opportunity for Native American artists to define themselves differently?

One answer to my questions could be that I am simply looking in the wrong physical locations. At the beginning of the twenty-first century, different ethnocultural communities may well be privileging different locations for their music. While Latin American and African-derived music CDs fill increasingly larger proportions of those same record stores, indigenous products have, to some extent at least, migrated to the web.[4] As Karl Neuenfeldt (2002) began to demonstrate in a brief look at websites for Native music, the proliferation of such sites implies a range of cultural, commercial, and creative advantages for Native American artists while also presenting certain problems.[5] Neuenfeldt does point out that the web offers a range of possibilities—teaching, for instance—in addition to commercial enterprise.[6]

A second and widely discussed reason for the relative invisibility of Native American music is that the wide range of its work in mainstream styles renders it indistinguishable from other popular music, as Michael Schlottner (1997) and others have argued. Many Native American artists choose not to present sonic markers of Aboriginality in order to argue that their music is not one but many styles and genres. The very diversity of production in mainstream styles, then, has been argued as a counter to narrow stereotypes.[7] To some extent, this strategy differs from those of other indigenous artists, particularly Saami and some Australian Aboriginal artists.[8]

A third factor relates to the distinctive and atypical practices whereby Native American music is marketed.[9] The national head of distribution for Festival Records, a distributor that not only has individual musicians such as Elizabeth Hill, Anita Issaluk, Laura Vinson, Jerry Alfred, and Chester Knight on its roster but also has exclusive rights for the Canadian distribution of recordings by Canyon and Silver Wave, explained that, vis à vis their non-Aboriginal artists, a distributor such as Festival had a smaller role, since the circulation of recordings by Native American artists operates via a fragmented and diffuse array of venues. Relative to their non-Aboriginal signees, a much larger proportion of Aboriginal artist sales occur at live events.[10] Particularly for niche genres such as powwow music, local intertribal events such as powwows and gatherings are major sales outlets. Venues associated with ecotourism (wilderness resorts and mountain lodges, for instance), the multinational gift shop, and new age sales distribution networks also play a significant role. Some artists work as emissaries for provincial or federal governments. One distributor estimated that her company probably handled 50 percent of the sales for the Native American artists on their roster. But my one attempt to cross-check the sales record of one of their artists suggested that her company probably handled only about 10 percent of the sales.[11] To some extent, then, Inuit, Métis, and First Nations artists are outside any single corporate marketing strategy, instead being dependent on several.

These factors may affect the choices that artists make about affiliating with a record company, although none of the musicians I have interviewed link either record company choice or album concept to market factors. The same factors arguably encourage album concepts that are more heterogeneous. Native American recording artists have signed with transnational companies (for example, Susan Aglukark with EMI, Kashtin with Sony), middle-sized companies specializing in indigenous music (Canyon, Sunshine, Sound of America), or smaller indigenous music specialists (Silver Wave, Sweetgrass, Inukshuk Productions, Makoche, Turtle Island) who produce their own albums. The majority of artists, however, remain with the most intimate options — independents or small companies. The reasons most provide for their choices are neither unexpected nor specific to indigenous artists — they seek collaborators whom they trust, processes in which they have input at different stages, and the option to do diverse material rather than music oriented toward a specific genre market. One artist stated, "We have to be sure of the recording process before we allow the sound" (Buck); another said, "The atmosphere in which we're creating our work has to be a good environment or I won't sing. I'll just shut right down" (Donovan); still another pointed out, "[I only work with someone who is] a good musician with the right attitude and a good heart" (Harjo). While these may seem like the rationalizations of relatively young artists who have not yet had the opportunity to sign with larger companies, it is noteworthy that several mature artists have actually rejected larger corporate opportunities to move to smaller ones. In a 1995 interview with E. K. Caldwell, the Cherokee rapper Litefoot described the experience that motivated his choice: "After an RCA record executive offered him a 'deal' on the condition that his lyrics not be 'Indian . . . because Indians don't buy tapes—they buy alcohol,'" he established his own label, Red Vinyl Records (Caldwell 1999: 63). Joanne Shenandoah moved from Canyon to the much smaller company Silver Wave; she then convinced Mary Youngblood, who reported five offers of contracts following her collaboration with Shenandoah on *All Spirits Sing,* also to sign with Silver Wave, telling her: "They really treat you right, a really heartfelt, good record company." Laura Vinson found a producer she could trust with Homestead Records. The other CDs that are discussed in the case studies below were produced independently, though in the case of the album from the Aboriginal Women's Voices project, it was produced in conjunction with the Banff Centre for the Arts in Alberta.

Several artists made contract decisions because they wanted the freedom to produce more diverse material on a single album. This begs the question of what sorts of diversity are encompassed within current "genre cultures" (to use Keith Negus's term [1999: 28–29] for the means by which the music industry organizes the culture of production), particularly the genre culture of "world music." While I can't deal adequately with this enormous question here, I will observe several ways of moving across genres that are arguably outside of the conventions of world music. One way is the extensive use of spoken word—in place of sung text, as in John Trudell[12] or Joy Harjo's work, as commentary, or as storied interludes.[13] Another way is the frequent juxtaposition, rather than fusion, of traditional and pop styles (a traditional song stands next to rap in the case of Wayquay, for instance, or a country ballad in the case of Elizabeth Hill). Related to this is the incorporation of non-Aboriginal artists or styles, but on only one or two songs on a CD. The result of this admixture is, on one hand, the disruption of the album's coherence, but on the other, a more pointed emphasis on the sociopolitical alliance at hand. That these sorts of musical diversity facilitate important social and political statements is clear in the decisions of several artists to accept a reduction in earnings in order to do the work they want. Albertan Métis singer-songwriter Laura Vinson, whose success as a country music artist ranked her (in the mid-1990s) among the top ten in Canada, abandoned this more lucrative niche on her last two albums in order to incorporate First Nations lyrical themes, musical elements, and didjeridu (a gesture that allied her work to that of Australian Aboriginal people). She and her producer/husband Dave Martineau may be typical when they report that they are "not working as much as we were when we were in the country market." But Vinson explains that a turn toward Aboriginal issues and sounds on her CDs since *Voice of the Wind* is "something I had to do." Award-winning Saulteaux-Dutch singer Fara Palmer recently opted for self-management so that she could record a more eclectic range of material, rejecting industry pressures for album coherence. At the time of the interviews presented here, other individuals or groups were contemplating independent productions after negative experiences with larger companies.

But a stlll more fundamental issue emerges in conversations about album concept, that is, what the very idea of a CD is. Here I was struck by the frequency with which artists and First Nations producers described CDs not as aesthetic objects but as the "documentation of a process," a phrase that Haudenosaunee clan mother Sadie Buck used explicitly. The rest of this essay, then, looks at various processes that four specific CDs were said to document and the effects of their participants' objectives on production decisions.

Case Study #1. The first case study relates to the CD *Tzo'kam* (Vancouver: Red Planet Records, 2000).[14] The producer, Russell Wallace from the Salish First Nation in British Columbia, described the purpose of the recording as a means of honoring his mother, Stlalimx elder Flora Wallace. The performances involved Flora, her daughters, and Russell, the youngest son. He emphasized that his mother grew to like the harmonies of Christian hymns when living in Washington State before the youngest of her children was born; the family later moved to Vancouver, where she maintained her devotion to Christianity while remaining available to do traditional repertoire when the community needed her knowledge. As her children acquired musical abilities, she liked their harmonized arrangements of songs, regarding them as a union of traditional and Christian elements. The repertoire they sing, then, generally begins monophonically and adds triadic harmonizations, often with innovative chord progressions, in later stanzas.

Case Study #2. The second case study concerns *Hearts of the Nation* (Banff: Aboriginal Women's Voices, 1997) from the Aboriginal Women's Voices Project (1995–2001) at the Banff Centre in Alberta, which was mentioned near the beginning of this essay. Under the direction of Sadie Buck, twelve women from different First Nations came together for six weeks a year, initially sharing the songs they brought from their own nation and then creating new collaborative work. Russell Wallace was CD producer and sound engineer. The album occasionally includes a traditional genre, such as the *eskanye* led by Buck, but more often the pieces defy generic categorization because of their innovative combinations of elements from a variety of traditional and popular music styles. Furthermore, the naming practices of these pieces may cross boundaries, as in the case of Jani Lauzon's "Symphony in E," a song with pop, folk, and spoken word elements.

Case Study #3. The third case study is *Point of the Arrow* (Spirit Song Productions, 1999), an album coproduced by Laura Vinson and her husband, Dave Martineau. This second album in Vinson's Aboriginal music period includes folk ballads such as "P'tit Marie," dedicated to the memory of the indigenous women (including Vinson's grandmother) who were "country wives" of European settlers, rock-oriented songs such as "Ghost Dancer," the participation of a powwow dancer, and two notable arrangements with didjeridu, that reflect a friendship that had developed between Vinson's band and an Australian yidaki player who had shared the stage with them at a pan-indigenous festival.

Case Study #4. In the Newfoundland Mi'kmaq community of Conne River, non-indigenous producer Pamela Morgan made field recordings that led to the production of a community-based album, *Miawpukek* (Conne River: Miawpukek Nation, 2000). Morgan is well known as an eclectic singer-songwriter from Newfoundland who was first acclaimed as a member of the highly successful folk revival band Figgy Duff. Featured on the CD are groups that have provided leadership in the noteworthy cultural and economic renewal in the community since the 1970s:[15] the Se't A'newey Singers, a youth choir inaugurated and conducted by Brenda Jeddore, and the male drum group the Spiu'ji'j Drummers, among others. They perform a number of traditional songs that have become widely known in Mi'kmaq communities in Atlantic Canada during the past twenty-five years, as well as a translation of "Amazing Grace" and pieces from the powwow repertoire. Traditional Chief Mise'l Joe regards the CD as a "major accomplishment in preserving and promoting our language, customs, and traditions."[16]

Issues Relating to Social Relations in the Recording Studio

Many Native American singer-songwriters are quite comfortable with the standard pop practices of recording: the laying down of bed tracks, the multitracking of individual parts, the mixing, and often the further layering of sonic elements. Of course, these practices assume that the music consists of isolatable parts and that social interaction among musicians is not a structural requirement of the performance. These assumptions are inappropriate and even unworkable for various types of traditional music, or for new practices that rely on traditional performance formats or cueing devices. Additionally, where traditional and contemporary styles are juxtaposed, the appropriate location or mode of recording may be highly variable. A wide array of production practices is thus beginning to emerge.[17]

I have written elsewhere (Diamond 2001) about the way in which Northern Tutchone musician Jerry Alfred records with his band the Medicine Beat. Since he formerly performed his music solo, accompanying himself on hand drum or acoustic guitar, interaction with band members represented a relatively recent shift in his practice. His recording process has at times involved multiple studio takes in which the band improvises an accompaniment for Jerry, but it has also required a lot of syntactical rearrangement by the producer without Jerry's involvement. At times, he records on his own and leaves spaces that the other musicians later fill in. Musicians in the Medicine Beat are very aware that the process differs from that of other bands with whom the same individuals record. The unique way in which Jerry and his friend and producer, Bob Hamilton, have found to work together thus simultaneously enables and marginalizes Jerry.

Chris Scales has done valuable work on the practices and ideologies of recording Native American artists, particularly powwow drummers. He contrasts the normal practices of recording powwow groups without multitracking, as if they are live, but reports some experimental recordings that now layer individual parts. In one paper (2002) he contrasts powwow recordings with a CD of Cree singer-songwriter Mishi Donovan, who was not involved in the process beyond the initial recording of her vocals. Scales raises important questions about the agency of Aboriginal participants, though he does not consider the perspective of Donovan herself. In an interview with me, she emphasized the importance of trust rather than sonic control, explaining how carefully she chooses the participants with whom she works. The choice of collaborators was emphasized by virtually every artist with whom I spoke. One emphasized that in her band "nobody showboats." Another stated that it had taken a long time to find a producer who was trustworthy. Still another emphasized a path of sobriety as a prerequisite for playing in the band. Women artists, in particular, regarded the choice of collaborators to be part of the production process, a part that is as significant as the more tangible techniques of production.

Beyond North America, in other Aboriginal contexts, the literature about alternative studio practices is also building. Karl Neuenfeldt's account of the production of *Strike Em!,* a CD of Torres Strait Islanders, makes clear the importance of field recording, not as an exclusive sound source but as a means of soliciting immediate input from the musicians involved (Neuenfeldt 2001). In effect, a portable studio is moved to the locale of the musicians for most (though not all) of the recording. As is often the case in other contexts, the sites of recording are multiple. Neuenfeldt's assertion that recording is one of the most collaborative of artistic enterprises is important, and it often underlies other studies of the increasingly globalized production of indigeneity. In the following paragraphs, I revisit the four case studies with an eye toward examining social relationships.

Case Study #1. The most unusual range of recording practices was encountered by the Wallace family in their production of *Tzo'kam*. They worked in not one but four different Vancouver recording studios, partly because, after each experience, they sought a greater comfort level with what Russell describes as the "performance" arrangements (the social space of the studio). At the first studio, Russell explained, he played the drum in one room while the rest of the family was in another room singing. At the second, the melody and harmony singers were in separate rooms, and overdubs were done on each group. The overdubbed options were not satisfactory from either Russell's or his mother's perspective: as one musician put it, "I think [that given] the way we sing, we have to see each other. That's one of the things I realize about traditional music . . . the close proximity and having eye contact with each other. That has a lot to do with the music." At the third studio, then, all of the performers were in a circle in one room, with individual mics facing out, while in the fourth, all of them were again in a circle ("the way we do in a live performance," as Russell explained) but with one overhead mic. Particularly in recordings made at the fourth studio, the lead voice is within the group, not in front of it, and the ensemble is noticeably improved by eye contact. What is interesting, however, is that they did not decide on one of the options but rather recorded the whole journey from one studio to the next by including cuts from each on the CD. The reasons for this will be explored in the final section of this chapter.

Case Study #2. The production of *Hearts of the Nation* was easier since, as Sadie Buck observed, the performers regarded their producer, Russell Wallace, as a trustworthy collaborator. It is clear that he returned their respect by asking their opinion. In his subsequent CD, *Chinook Winds,* which featured his own electronic compositions prepared in most cases for the Banff Centre's Aboriginal Dance project, he used samples of the pieces on *Hearts of the Nation* and manipulated them rather extensively. He first asked each composer, however, to listen to his work and judge whether he had disrespected the sound source in any way. The songs on *Hearts* were recorded in different ways, with some multitracking, particularly in the case of the more pop-styled songs, and some in a single take. Performers and producer were all aware of the intense style of interaction through which some of the collaborative songs were made. Sadie spoke, in particular, about the genesis of the final song on the album, the "Travelling Song": she described a circle in which they began vocalizing with a single vocable. Then, someone would leave that vocable to offer a song or a fragment. She continued:

> And what happens is they start to blend together. Not only the lyrics but also the melodies, they blend together. And because all of these individuals come with their own sense of music and their own sense of sound from their land, then all of those things become intertwined and very intrinsic to the actual song that does come out. . . . So . . . we learned those songs [that each woman brought] and got each other used to knowing those sounds, their sound that they have from their region, like what is contained in those sounds. . . . We jumped out of the context of those songs themselves to a traditional context of learning and being involved and sharing . . . It's a song that . . . has the voices of all those people in it.

Her story is a rare description of the way in which an arrangement came about. Furthermore, the emphasis on knowing the sounds of each region impacted production and mixing decisions.

Case Study #3. *Point of the Arrow* was produced like a pop CD. The group laid down bed tracks and overdubbed solos, having first worked out most of the arrangements in their eight-track home studio. Laura Vinson described her studio role as more conceptual than technical, taking credit for the song order and emphasizing the complementary roles of band members and the contribution of her ancestors. She described "After the Ball Is Over" as a "gift" from her grandfather and explained that her grandmother "dictated" the experiences of "P'tite Marie." She modestly said, "If I wrote all the songs, they'd all sound like [the folk ballad] 'P'tite Marie.' The other band members add the necessary instrumental variety to the project." Her guitarist, coproducer, and husband, Dave Martineau, was also casual about his contribution, suggesting that if you "burn a little sweetgrass, it always works out."

Case Study #4. As mentioned earlier, Pamela Morgan, with the technical assistance of Sandy Morris, a St. John's musician and producer, recorded the tracks for *Miawpukek* in the Bay d'Espoir community on the south coast of Newfoundland. Morgan encountered some resistance to the idea of a female producer, particularly among the male musicians. Indeed, she had to offer her opinion through her male assistant as a spokesperson, giving instructions to him that he then relayed to the drummers. As we chatted about this, sharing a concern that women still face barriers when they enter the world of audio production, she voiced her pragmatic approach: "You do what you need to do to get the job done." The women artists in the community, on the other hand, described an immediate rapport with Morgan that led to entirely different, gendered approaches to the production of their music, as described later in this essay. Like Vinson, Morgan felt that she controlled the direction and concept of the project and implicitly challenged a definition of production that would focus narrowly on its technological aspects.

Issues of Production and Post-Production

In the rapidly emerging literature on the ideologies of sound production, studio discourse is proving to be a rich area of exploration. Paul Théberge (1997) has observed that the language of the studio relies heavily on binary oppositions: fat/thin, warm/cold, wet/dry, clean/dirty, organic/processed, and so on. When people use such vocabulary, they assume, as Serge Lacasse has observed, that sound "manipulation can give rise to a range of connotations and effects whose 'emergence' in the listener's mind is not arbitrary but rather coherent" (2000a: 3). A number of producers and sound engineers have spoken about such coherences.

In some cases, the reference points for styles of sound production are regional or national sound ideals. The Nashville sound, the L.A. sound, the Abbey Road sound, and others have all been claimed as distinctive "identities" (see Porcello, this volume). The British and American approaches to sound production are often contrasted, although the characteristics described for each are not always consistent. Howard Massey's important compilation of interviews with record producers, *Behind the Glass* (2000), reinforces American and British distinctions and presents a panel of East and West Coast producers that further articulates a dichotomy within the United States. Ethnomusicologists such as Louise Meintjes (2003) and Paul Greene (2001) have explored the discursive mediation of sound production in extended ethnographic studies and non-Western contexts.

In other cases, the reference points for the discourse of sound production are generic. Wayne Wadhams, for instance, offers occasional advice about the norms of genres in his influential book *Sound Advice.* He distinguishes such things as the close-miked, highly compressed sound of rock drummers, as compared to the less punchy and more blended sound ideal of jazz (1995: 135–136). While folk music producers may position a solo voice to sound as if it is in the middle of fellow participants, a pop singer is more often placed out front. Wadhams advises, "In a slow ballad, another dramatic imaging technique involves generating the feeling that the singer is alone in a vast emotional abyss" (ibid.: 313). Still other explanations of the codes of production are gendered or related to the emotion in the lyrics.

The explanations of producers, however, generally assume that listeners understand their codes and respond uniformly. Lacasse is one of the few scholars who has done an extensive reception study to test the uniformity of listener responses. He has done groundbreaking work on the production of the voice, coining the term "vocal staging" to indicate "any deliberate practice whose aim is to enhance a vocal sound, alter its timbre, or present it in a given spatial and/or temporal configuration with the help of any mechanical or electrical process, presumably in order to produce some effect on potential or actual listeners" (2000a: 4). As Lacasse acknowledges, it is difficult to interpret respondents' comments, however, since (1) it is hard to know exactly what listeners are responding to—the style of the music, any one of several production techniques, and so on; (2) recorded music sounds different on different stereos, in different physical spaces, and so on; and (3) people's responses are likely variable from one listening to another.[18]

In line with the difficulties Lacasse (2000a, 2000b) observes, Meintjes (2003), Neuenfeldt (2002), Greene (2001), and Porcello (1996), among others, have demonstrated that the rationale for production decisions is rarely a uniform one but rather a complex mix of factors relating to identity constructs that accrue to genre and gender, age and ethnicity, region and nationality, concepts of modernity or tradition, and simply intertextuality (the desire to sound like a popular recording or a much-admired musician). Furthermore, in crosscultural contexts there may be contention about the production and post-production when economic constraints are in play or different identity factors are referenced by different participants. In small studios run by indigenous musicians, for instance, I have encountered one with only one microphone and another where the majority of the money available was spent on a variety of high-end mics rather than elaborate digital post-production technology. In the final section of this paper, I will argue that the differences in the conception of production/post-production often give rise to new narratives about sound and the work that commodified products such as CDs might do in the public sphere. In the paragraphs that follow, I return to the case studies with an eye toward the issues of production and post-production.

Case Study #1. The varied social relations in the studios where *Tzo'kam* was recorded led to different sonic results. Where multitracking was used, the lead voice was predictably forward and center but the ensemble playing was arguably less tight. In post-production, ample reverb was added, enhancing the solo quality of the lead singer. In the studio where a live performance format and a single microphone were used, on the other hand, the lead voice was less imposing but the choral responses sounded more confident. Russell

Wallace reported that Flora felt most comfortable in the latter context. Her opinion was respected: a song where she felt the most comfortable was selected as the first track on the CD even though her voice sounds more distant than on some of the later tracks.

Case Study #2. To get the trueness of the vocal and drum sounds in the production of *Hearts of the Nation,* Wallace preferred a complex recording layout featuring many microphones, some to capture each voice relatively close-miked, others to capture ambient sound from reflective surfaces. He found that post-production reverb, "an overused gimmick," was particularly problematic with these voices and preferred repeated takes, from which he selected one performance, to a lot of overdubbing, although some of the popular songs were created in overdubbed layers.

Knowing those sounds and the distinctiveness Sadie heard in the different regional repertoires is important in production and post-production processes, and minimal compression and equalization were used. Sadie contrasted this plainer sound with the production of the first CD featuring her group, the Six Nations Women Singers, where she disliked the excessive reverberation and post-production mixing, which rendered the high, clearly pitched Iroquoian water drum too low and therefore untrue to the specific sound of the region.[19]

Case Study #3. As in many low-budget projects, Laura's band worked out arrangements in an eight-track home studio prior to going to the twenty-four-track analog facility with its "expensive tube mics" and preamps that "warm up the bottom end and take the harshness out of the top." Dave spoke ardently about musical innovations in terms of shared histories of oppression of different cultures—an ethereal pedal steel solo, an Irish-sounding flute—because, he confidently asserted, there are "so many connections between Irish and Métis" or the didjerdidu (which was incorporated after a collaboration with Australians on tour), whose "sound was a killer." Dave detailed the careful mixing of the instrumental sounds, but both he and Laura claimed that little was done to the voice beyond the choice of the right mic: record it dry and add a very little bit of compression, they advised. They didn't mention such things as "vocal staging" (see Lacasse 1996), about which I was curious. When I asked why the accordion sound was far forward in the mix and the voice was back in the gentle ballad "P'tite Marie," Dave said the accordion was "all that's there," focusing so much on the instrumental sound that he seemed to forget the voice. Remarkably, in this piece, however, which Laura had the major role in arranging, he had actually manipulated the voice rather extensively, with a lot of reverberation ("because we worked it as sparsely as we could," he said). The acoustic guitar and accordion sound close to the voice, suggesting a typical folk music aesthetic where the listener is made to feel in the middle, a participant, not a voyeur. Paradoxically, the European release of *Point of an Arrow* was altered when Laura and Dave were asked to capture more "liveness." Their response to this request was to layer a narrative over each song, as if the addition of words gave the performances more of a live quality.

Case Study #4. In the case of *Miawpukek,* both producer and choir director told me about gendered differences in community opinions about musical arrangements for the CD. The male drumming group, doing both powwow songs and traditional Mi'kmaq chants that they had previously recorded with the hand drum, instructed Morgan to make no changes to their songs; any arrangement or audible changes in the mixing process were regarded as a violation of the music's authenticity. The women's ensemble, on the other hand, recognized her success as a recording artist by asking her to arrange their material. They trusted her artistic sense and felt that they had a more intimate relationship with her. While feminism has taught us that women are more often cast as the preservers of tradition and men as the innovators, here that pattern was reversed.

It is interesting to compare Morgan's arrangements with other recordings of the same songs. An early 1990s cassette of the song "I'ko," featuring elder Sarah Denny singing in a strong but gentle style with nuance in her phrase shaping and subtle vocal ornaments, contrasts with the version produced by Morgan. In the later recording a more intense, powwow-influenced vocal style has a much busier accompaniment, not the light Mi'kmaq hand drum but a heavier powwow drum, which is combined with faster and lighter djembe drum rhythms, and elements that suggest New Age conventions: bells,[20] open-fifth harmonies on a synthesizer, occasional flute entries, and birds—both cries and wing flapping. The text of this song refers to the peace between Mohawk and Mi'kmaq nations and is currently used as a "grand entry" song for school gatherings.

Paradoxically, it was the recording of the men's group that was eventually manipulated extensively in post-production. Morgan close-miked the powwow group, capturing a vocal liveness that had not been achieved in earlier recordings. But the limiter on her tape recorder cut in with every loud drum beat, causing a drop in the intensity of the voices. The mastering engineer explained that he tried to accommodate the drop out of vocal sound by digitally cutting the songs drum beat by drum beat and then manipulating the levels of voice and drum on each sound fragment. The result is not perceptible as an "arrangement" but rather as an alteration of the acoustic space (voices are much more immediate) and energy flow, especially at the accented drum "honor" beats.[21]

The Case Studies as Mediations of Identity

The clarity and accuracy of voice and drum sounds as factors essential for the identification of a region, nation, and individual musician emerged in the case studies as well as in other interview contexts. Two groups, for instance, were so concerned about the accuracy of the drum sound produced by the initial studios with which they worked that they changed studios as a result of dissatisfaction. Reverberation proved even more contentious. While Wallace and Buck disliked the excessive use of reverberation, other performers appreciated the spaciousness that reverb implies. One was quite comfortable with the New Age targeting that seems to be implicit in heavy reverb, especially when combined with flute or slow song tempos. Audience surveys soliciting information about the meaning of reverberation have also shown that it is tied to the mystical and the spiritual (see Lacasse 1996) It is likely that many listeners outside of First Nations contexts hear extensive reverb as part of the casting of Aboriginal music as "spiritual," but it is significant that none of the musicians I have interviewed mentioned such an association. Producers including Dave Martineau related the use of reverb to sparsely textured songs where the artists prefer a relatively simple arrangement. They argue that reverb is then necessary to fill the spaces. This application, however, often has other connotations, as noted in relation to Laura Vinson's albums, where the sparse, reverberant arrangements map out a certain nostalgia.

The point here, however, is that artists rarely seem to dislike market niches such as New Age or resent potential stereotyping (sounds echoing across vast open spaces) when they express concerns about reverberation or about inaccurate drum and voice sounds. Processes that destroy the specificity of the timbral information about place and nation instead seemed to them to prevent the successful documentation of processes of intertribal collaboration. Furthermore, most of the artists were open to a variety of musical arrangements provided there was trust among the collaborators.

It is significant that Aboriginal women in particular insisted on defining music production in a broad manner that included the choice of collaborators and the album concept. Male interviewees tended instead to focus more narrowly on the uses of technology. Paradoxically, even in the relatively rare instances where women have been coproducers, as in the case of Vinson, the actual manipulation of technology has remained in the control of their male collaborators. In this regard, the gendered stereotype of masculinized technology is reinforced in the Native American sphere, though it is challenged by the insistence on a definition of production that extends beyond machines to include social dimensions.

CDs As Different Forms of Social Action

Conne River choir director Brenda Jeddore spoke proudly about the role of music in Mi'kmaq community revitalization: "We are now the pace setters because of our music." Her vision resembled that of Sadie Buck and Russell Wallace, both of whom have thought deeply and clearly about the work that audio recordings do in society. Sadie was particularly articulate about the *Hearts of the Nation* CD, describing its importance as "a documentation of our process [of working together] . . . so that other people could hear it and realize that this is an opportunity and a way that they can also work." She insisted that the CD was not so much a new context as a "redirect[ion]," since "a powerful song and a good song are all essences of original contexts, specific contexts to a nation." Here she suggests continuity with past practices, like other artists mentioned earlier.[22] She explained, "We have to use the recording to grab that essence of commitment and dedication" of the participants. Wallace concurred, describing his initial fears about the act of production as related to his understanding that "it is a very important CD for Aboriginal people but also for Canadian/American music. I'd say it's a landmark because it's Aboriginal women but also it is traditional and also contemporary."

Buck's description of the CD as a "documentation of our process" seemed to fit the Wallace family's CD as well. They kept the record of their journey of encounters with different recording studios by including cuts from each one on the final CD. Similarly, the didjeridu on Vinson's album references a friendship, for instance, and the remixes of certain songs on subsequent albums again establish a series of "encounters." I began to recall other interviews where metaphors of "journeys" or "pathways" had emerged. I thought of Pura Fe's recounting of a trip to visit brothers and sisters in prison and then to an East Coast museum, an experiential juxtaposition that inspired her song "Museum Cases," or Jani Lauzon's story of a song that "went through quite a journey" as it was rearranged and remixed, a journey she recorded by including two mixes on her first CD. Such stories also extended across CDs. Describing her road of recovery from abuse and childhood trauma, Mishi Donovan explained, "All you have to do is listen to my albums and you know exactly what I went through and where I'm heading." She narrates each of her three albums to date as a stage on this healing journey, a process of change involving a shift from surface issues to "writing that goes deeper" and is really raw. Sadie Buck described her response to Robbie Robertson's recent work in collaboration with various Native American performers (herself among them) as "listening to his journey."[23]

The documentation of the process sometimes related to the artist's personal growth, as evident over a series of albums, or to the development of collaborative relationships in the preparation of a recording, or to the production processes themselves. Furthermore, in light of the fact that Native American recordings fit variably within the industry-defined concept of "genre cultures" including "world music," and that they encounter unusually diffuse modes of circulation that are shaped both by local imperatives and by not one but several corporate strategies, the importance of documenting this process for at least certain recordings becomes a more obvious issue about access and control.

The case studies presented here indicate that the concept of the CD itself should never be assumed a priori, since it may vary from being an aesthetic object to being a documentation of social processes of several types. I originally thought of myself as an ethnomusicologist to be the documenter of this process but have begun to rethink this in light of the substantial number of CDs that are described as having that role in and of themselves. This realization led to a different set of research questions. For those CDs that seem related to processes of individual development, how can ethnomusicologists look to lyrics and arrangements as indicators of different levels of personal exploration, as different stages of relationships, as signs of struggle, as indicators of patience or courage? For those CDs that seek to explore how individuals or social collectives come to relate to one another through music production itself, how can ethnography best attend to sound production as an index of the building or breaking of respect and trust among participants? These are perhaps some of the questions to address to musicians, producers, sound mixers, and so on, if we are to understand better the important artistic and political work that Native American musicians are doing in the recording studio.

It is not surprising that Native Americans are vigilant about the process of audio recording. After all, they have been recorded since the very beginning of audio recording history and are quite aware of the ways in which indigenous music has been shaped by the constraints of technology. While Frances Densmore's advice to ethnographers — that is, to allow no witnesses at a recording session, to record only one singer at a time, to avoid the use of drums and rattles since they didn't record well, and to strictly forbid all yells and talking (quoted in Brady 1999: 90–91) — may seem a quaintly offensive distortion of "authentic" performance, this essay has suggested that contemporary recordings are no less manipulative. There are still political consequences to producing a CD that has "documentary realism" (to use Feld's term for allegedly unmanipulated recordings of traditional music) or, on the other hand, to producing a recording that captures something of the pleasure of the moment or the desires of the musicians for diverse affiliations with mainstream genre worlds, ensembles, and sounds. Like those early recordings, contemporary ones document a process of intercultural communication and demonstrate the limitations and the potentials when values and aesthetics intersect.

Notes

1. The CAMAs, for instance, include awards for Best Traditional Album—Historical, Best Traditional Album—Contemporary, Best Pow Wow Album—Traditional, Best Pow Wow Album—Contemporary, Best Song, Best Songwriter, Best Producer, Best Album Cover Design, Best Group or Duo, Best Music Video, Best Rock Album, Best Country or Folk Album, Best Blues, Jazz, or Gospel Album, Best Male Artist, Best Female Artist, and a Music Industry Award; they also honor female and male elders with annual Keeper of Traditions and Lifetime Contributions awards.

2. Genres have also been regarded as forms of social action (see Miller 1984).

3. Similarly, Michael Schlottner (1997: 44) notes that John Trudell's spoken recitations are often placed with African American rap in record stores.

4. Keith Secola suggests as much when he says: "There's three elements to independence [from the record industry]—live performance, merchandising/marketing, and publishing" (quoted in *Native Peoples,* May/June 2002: 35).

5. The web's mediation of Aboriginality, of course, extends beyond music sales. Marjorie D. Kibby (1999) analyzed one hundred didjeridu websites, observing features that appropriate aspects of Aboriginal culture by non-Aboriginal urban primitivists, as well as the "articulation of new cultural meanings through the sharing of Aboriginal musical practices" (1999: 59). Further, Ter Ellingson (2002) has written about the web as a contemporary mediation of the concept of the noble savage.

6. Furthermore, as a generation under age 30 relies increasingly on the internet for its music, the whole issue of record stores and categories may become an antiquarian concern.

7. See artists quoted in Diamond 2001: 404.

8. In Norway, for instance, Saami artists are eligible for heritage funding if their recordings include joiking, but not if they choose to make a mainstream pop or rock CD. Note, however, that Saami artists, like Native Americans, have often chosen or adapted popular music genres, believing that "this course of action is the most effective way to provoke and control change" (Jones-Bamman 2001: 191).

9. Other indigenous musics are similar in many regards. Richard Jones-Bamman, for instance, observes that distribution networks for Saami LPs, tapes, and CDs "are more dependent on local Saami organizations and handicraft businesses, rather than on music shops and department stores" (ibid.: 191).

10. The producer of one artist claimed that over 50 percent of their audiences purchased CDs, particularly on European tours. Such data is hard to verify, of course.

11. This case study was Caribou Records in Whitehorse, Yukon. I am grateful to Executive Director David Petkovich for discussing sales and providing some figures.

12. Trudell has addressed the issue of "genre cultures" in relation to the fact that his work doesn't fit the industry concept of rap: "Now the suits have stepped in, the insiders in the suits, and now they say, 'You've all got to sound like this and be like this.' So it's a way of trapping it and limiting it within the context. There are more realities going on in the communities of young people than what the rappers sing about. But because they want to 'make it,' now they have to stay within the confines

of the realities that have been defined for them. And that programs them in a way that's not good for anybody" (1993 interview in Caldwell 1999: 11).

13. See note 3 regarding the confusion that spoken word causes in marketing networks.

14. The album title is a Stlalimx word meaning "chickadee" but implying that visitors are coming since, as the liner notes explain, "when you hear the chickadees singing outside your home you know that someone is coming to visit." The metaphor is, in itself, a lovely indicator of the role of commodified recordings as indicators that visiting listeners are at hand.

15. In addition to language and music programs, the Conne River community has developed a successful aquaculture program, fishing lodge, and logging operation.

16. Part of the "Welcome" message printed in the liner notes.

17. Audio recording is not the only context in which this is true. In films such as the award-winning Inuit film *Atanarjuat,* in which professional actors were joined by actors who had no "professional" training, innovative ways of working have also evolved. These are described on the website <www.atanarjuat.com/production_diary>.

18. He controls for the variable of response to production technique by taking one phrase of music and isolating each of about twelve production techniques in repeated playings.

19. *We Will All Sing,* SOAR Records, 1996.

20. Bells are a marker of "liveness" in powwow recordings (see Scales 2002).

21. The beats that are accented by the lead drummer.

22. Other instances of producing an indigenous recording that reflects continuity with live, community-based uses or aesthetic values have been documented. Michelle Bigenno, for instance, reports how Bolivian musicians belonging to the group Música de Maestros turned up the bass line in the recording studio, arguing that the music had to make people want to dance, a factor that depended on the bass and guitar lines, unknown to their producer (2002: 53).

23. These references are described in Diamond 2002.

References

Bigenno, Michelle. 2002. *Sounding Indigenous: Authenticity in Bolivian Music Performance.* New York: Palgrave.

Brady, Erika. 1999. *A Spiral Way: How the Phonograph Changed Ethnography.* Jackson, Miss.: University of Mississippi Press.

Caldwell, E. K. 1999. *Dreaming the Dawn: Conversations with Native Artists and Activists.* Lincoln: University of Nebraska Press.

Cruikshank, Julie. 1998. "Negotiating with Narrative: Establishing Cultural Identity at the Yukon International Storytelling Festival." In *The Social Life of Stories: Narrative and Knowledge in the Yukon Territory,* by Julie Cruikshank, Lincoln: University of Nebraska Press, 138–160.

Diamond, Beverley. 1999–2000. "First Nations Popular Music in Canada: From Practice to Theory." In the special topics issue of *Repercussions,* eds. J. Shepherd, J. Guilbault, and M. Dineen, vol. 8–9 (double issue), 397–431.

——. 2001. "Re-placing Performance: A Case Study of the Yukon Music Scene in the Canadian North." *Journal of Intercultural Studies* 22(2): 211–224.

——. 2002. "Native American Contemporary Music: The Women." *Worlds of Music* 44(1): 9–35.

Ellingson, Ter. 2001. *The Myth of the Noble Savage.* Berkeley: University of California Press.

Greene, Paul. 1999. "Sound Engineering in a Tamil Village: Playing Audio Cassettes as Devotional Performance," *Ethnomusicology* 43(3): 459–489.
——. 2001. "Mixed Messages: Unsettled Cosmopolitanism in Nepali Pop." *Popular Music* 20(2): 169–188.
Hayward, Philip. 1998a. *Music at the Borders: Not Drowning, Waving and Their Engagement with Papua New Guinean Culture* (1986–96). Sydney: John Libbey.
Hayward, Philip, ed. 1998. *Sound Alliances: Indigenous Peoples, Cultural Politics, and Popular Music in the Pacific*. London: Cassell.
Jones-Bamman, Richard. 2001. "From 'I'm a Lapp' to 'I Am Saami': Popular Music and Changing Images of Indigenous Ethnicity in Scandinavia." *Journal of Intercultural Studies* 22(2): 189–210.
Kibby, Marjorie D. 1999. "The Didj and the Web: Networks of Articulation and Appropriation." *Convergence* 5(1): 59–75.
Lacasse, Serge. 2000a. "'Listen to My Voice': The Evocative Power of Vocal Staging in Recorded Rock Music and Other Forms of Vocal Expression." Ph.D. thesis. University of Liverpool.
——. 2000b. "Voice and Sound Processing: Examples of *Mise en Scene* of Voice in Recorded Rock Music." *Popular Musicology Online*. <www.cyberstudia.com/popular_musicology_online/>.
Massey, Howard. 2000. *Behind the Glass: Top Record Producers Tell How They Craft the Hits*. San Francisco: Miller Freeman Books.
Means, Andrew. 2002. "Canyon Strikes Gold with Native Recordings." *Native People* (May/June): 32–37.
Meintjes, Louise. 2003. *Sound of Africa! Making Music Zulu in a South African Studio*. Durham, N.C.: Duke University Press.
Miller, Carolyn R. 1984. "Genre As Social Action." *Quarterly Journal of Speech* 70: 151–167.
Negus, Keith. 1999. *Music Genres and Corporate Cultures*. New York: Routledge.
Neuenfeldt, Karl. 2001. "Cultural Politics and a Music Recording Project: Producing *Strike Em!: Contemporary Voices from the Torres Strait*." *Journal of Intercultural Studies* 22(3): 133–146.
——. 2002. "Marketing Recordings in an Interconnected World." *Worlds of Music* 44(1): 93–102.
Porcello, Thomas. 1996. "Sonic Artistry: Music, Discourse, and Technology in the Sound Recording Studio." Ph.D. thesis: University of Texas at Austin.
Scales, Christopher. 2002. "The Politics and Aesthetics of Recording: A Comparative Canadian Case Study of Powwow and Contemporary Native American Music." *Worlds of Music* 44(1): 36–51.
Schlottner, Michael. 1997. "'World Music' and Native Americans: How Ethnic Are Indians?" *European Review of Native American Studies* 11(2): 43–46.
Théberge, Paul. 1997. *Any Sound You Can Imagine. Making Music/Consuming Technology*. Hanover, N.H.: Wesleyan University Press/University Press of New England.
Wadhams, Wayne. 1995. *Sound Advice: The Musician's Guide to the Recording Studio*. New York: Schirmer.
Wright-McLeod, Brian. 2003. *The Encyclopedia of Native Music: More Than a Century of Recordings from Wax Cylinder to the Internet, North America*. Unpublished manuscript.

CHAPTER SEVEN

Engineering Techno-Hybrid Grooves in Two Indonesian Sound Studios

Jeremy Wallach

The sources of Indonesian popular music are extraordinarily diverse.[1] Middle Eastern pop, American hip-hop, Ambonese church hymns, Sundanese *degung,* British heavy metal, Indian filmsong, Chinese folk music, and Javanese *gendhing* are but a few of the influences one might detect on a single cassette. Despite this complexity, the question of where the music on an Indonesian popular music cassette "came from" has in almost all cases one simple, straightforward answer: it was produced in a recording studio, which most likely was located in Jakarta or another large city.

The multitrack recording studio is arguably the most important musical instrument of the last half-century, and its diffusion around the globe has transformed the nature of musical practice and experience for much of the world's population. By "multitrack recording studio" I mean a facility that enables the recording of several discrete musical parts successively or simultaneously. These parts can then be manipulated, edited, and combined (mixed), to create a final musical composition in which the presence of each part in the whole is carefully calibrated to achieve maximum aesthetic impact. By materializing sound the multitrack recording studio has transformed definitions of music itself and given rise to competing discourses of sonic aesthetics, musical authenticity, and creativity (Théberge 1997: 215–222; Jones 1992).

But exactly how has multitrack studio technology transformed music? Has its impact been the same all over the world? How does this new cultural layer of technomusical practices interact with the cultural elements that preceded it in particular locales, and how have music makers taken advantage of the numerous possibilities opened up by this technology? These are important questions to anyone interested in assessing the state of world popular music, and ethnographic inquiry is an effective method for addressing them. But it is not enough for researchers to simply document creative uses of recording technology in particular locales. Each innovation is a productive intervention in social life that impacts upon the ubiquitous struggles over meaning and power that characterize popular music phenomena in general.

What follows is a brief tour through two very different recording studio facilities in Indonesia: a commercial recording studio complex located in Jakarta and an "underground" recording facility in Denpasar, Bali. I will focus on practices of what Paul Greene calls "sound engineering," the technological manipulation of sound for social strategic ends (1999), paying particular attention to strategies of what I call music "techno-hybridization": that is, using studio technologies to create novel combinations of music elements derived from different genres. I will suggest that the new music hybrids produced in Indonesian sound studios matter because their introduction creates social consequences, both intended and unforeseen. To demonstrate this claim I will discuss some of the responses I encountered to the introduction of new "techno-hybrid" musics in the course of my ethnographic research among Indonesian popular music fans.

Remixing and Reimagining Indonesian Modernity: 601 Studio Lab

The first studio we will visit is the 601 Studio Lab, a multipurpose commercial recording complex used to record a variety of popular musics. Our tour will focus on one of the most central and lucrative of these: *dangdut* remixes. But first, some background information is in order. Dangdut, an amalgamation of Indian film music, Middle Eastern pop, western hard rock, and disco, is the quintessential Indonesian pop genre. Its two most distinctive music features are a propulsive dance rhythm and a mournful, melismatic vocal style that avoids the leaps and histrionics of western pop balladry. Though often a source of laughter and derision among members of Indonesia's educated elite, who dismiss it as *kampungan* (characteristic of backward village life), dangdut remains by far the most popular music genre in Indonesia, with a large and ethnically diverse audience of ordinary Indonesians young and old. Moreover, a number of Indonesians with whom I spoke insisted that members of the middle and upper classes secretly enjoyed dangdut music but were unwilling to admit it. In the words of one professional dangdut singer, "They say they don't like dangdut, but when they hear it they always sway to the music!" My research suggests such claims are correct, at least in some cases.[2]

Though it is considered backward and provincial by its detractors, dangdut music is actually quite cosmopolitan in its borrowings from other styles. I have heard dangdut songs that incorporated musical elements from Javanese gamelan, Kenny G–type "jazz" fusion, the Balinese *kecak* dance, heavy metal, Latin pop, Mandarin pop, and Hindustani light classical music. And if this were not sufficiently eclectic, in recent years musicians and record producers seeking to engineer profitable new music hybrids have created a number of novel dangdut offshoots, which the Indonesian recording industry has grouped together under the label *dangdut trendy.* These styles include *cha cha dhut, dangdut reggae, house dangdut, dangdut disco,* and the style discussed here, *dangdut remix.* Most of these music "mixtures" (*campuran*) involve adding new rhythms and rhythm instruments, such as electronic drum machines, to familiar dangdut songs. For example, cha cha dhut is exactly what one would expect from the name: dangdut with a "one two cha-cha-cha, three four cha-cha-cha" rhythmic feel.

These self-consciously hybrid music forms are not created by an artistic elite for a limited audience of postcolonial intellectuals or even for international "world beat" consumers. They are instead aimed directly at the Indonesian mass audience, with successful recordings selling hundreds of thousands of legitimate copies—impressive in a national music market where the ratio of pirated to legitimate versions sold is roughly six to one and perhaps as much as eight to one.[3]

The Studio

The 601 Studio Lab is one site where such lucrative hybrid music forms are created. The facility is located on the far outskirts of East Jakarta in a new, upper-income housing development. It occupies a two-story house that has been converted into a sophisticated recording complex, though until recently one had to enter the vocal booth through the kitchen. I was told that the studio had been located far from the city center so as to discourage musicians and their entourages from spending all of their leisure time there. Such people have a tendency to *nongkrong,* hang out, in recording studios at all hours, even (and especially) when there is no recording that needs to be done.

The studio offers a very impressive array of recording technologies. On the first floor is a twenty-four-track analog studio used for recording dangdut, rock, and pop music, while upstairs is a thirty-two-track digital studio (with over one hundred virtual tracks) used for electronic dance music and creating dance remixes of dangdut songs. The studio also houses state-of-the-art computers used for mastering, sequencing, and graphic design, as well as samplers, synthesizers, guitar amplifiers, and racks full of electronic effects.

All of this technology is not neutral, and the origin of most of the equipment in the "developed" world is of some consequence as well. Raymond, the head engineer of the second-floor digital studio at the time of my first visit, told me of his struggles to learn English so that he could understand the technical manuals for the studio's equipment. After spending countless hours with an English-Indonesian dictionary, he proudly reported that he could understand about 40 percent of the vocabulary in these manuals, and our conversations (in Indonesian) contained an abundance of English technical terms: "frequency response," "gain," "panpot," "distortion," and so on. In the words of chief downstairs engineer Pak Cecep, the 601 studio personnel learned by "direct practical knowledge, without education." Pak Cecep described dangdut as "left behind" (*ketinggalan*); for instance, while Indonesian pop producers had been using MIDI sequencers for over a decade, the practice began to be used in dangdut recordings only three years ago.

Dangdut's producers and fans often use the Indonesian verbs *merakyat*, "to be close to the people," and *memasyarakat*, "to be close to society," to describe dangdut music. Populist rhetoric aside, however, dangdut cassette production is highly centralized and high tech, not unlike commercial country music production in Nashville. A mere handful of session musicians play on almost all of the commercial releases, and to my surprise I found out that the parts not played by these highly skilled professionals were often played by a MIDI sequencer: on recordings produced by younger arrangers, all of the keyboards and percussion parts other than the *gendang* (tambourines, maracas, trap drums, and so on) were programmed in this fashion. These technological advances have not dramatically changed the sound of the music, however. New cassette releases are easily adapted to live instrumentation by local performing ensembles, and while the sound quality on dangdut recordings has improved and the performances they contain have become more polished and technically precise, the overall dangdut "sound" has remained fairly unchanged for the past two decades. Given the music's extraordinary and continuing cross-generational popularity, it seems unlikely that so-called "pure dangdut" (*dangdut murni*) will lose its relative stylistic conservatism.

Part of this conservatism is the insistence that dangdut be recorded on analog tape. The division of labor between analog and digital recording at

601 Studio Lab seems to suggest that Indonesians have adopted the natural/synthetic and "dirty"/"clean" sonic distinctions often employed by popular music producers and consumers in the West (see Théberge 1997: 207–208). Dangdut, like rock 'n' roll, has to have a warm, rough, and unpolished sound. To record it digitally would be unthinkable: "not dangdut." Furthermore, everyone I spoke to agreed that the *gendang* drum—the central rhythm instrument in dangdut—sounds too thin and "clicky" if recorded digitally. Remixes of dangdut songs, which rerecord the analog tracks of the original and import them into the digital domain, are another matter, however.

Remixing/Reimagining Dangdut

Edy Singh, an ambitious thirty-one-year-old record producer who speaks fluent English (he learned it in private school), frequently compared his studio unfavorably to its counterparts in America, even though the facility was actually quite well equipped by American standards. He also criticized dangdut musicians for their backwardness and reluctance to embrace new music technologies, even while admitting that dangdut had to sound *kasar* (coarse, unrefined, rough) in order to be authentic and that the audience demanded that dangdut recordings stay faithful to the classic dangdut sounds of the late 1970s and early 1980s.[4] Indeed, a striking feature of contemporary dangdut is that its performers are strongly attached to pre-sampler, 1980s digital keyboard timbres. Edy maintains that if the dangdut genre was permitted to "develop," it would one day become a recognized global pop genre like reggae and rap music (which resemble dangdut in their non-elite, populist origins) and even have a market in the United States. At least this is what he hopes will happen—his "dream," as he put it.

Edy is justifiably proud of his disco, house, and rap remixes of dangdut hits. In the early 1990s, he was one of the originators of a true remix technique, using tracks from the original analog tape of a song rather than simply recording a cover version in an electronic dance style. In Edy's remixes, selected tracks on the original analog tape are transferred to a digital medium, usually minus the rhythm instruments (*gendang*, tambourine, and bass guitar). Electronic drums and samples are then added, which transform the song's rhythmic feel and create a cyborg-like fusion of the machine rhythms of electronic dance music and the warm, organic sounds of dangdut.

In his cultural history of music technology, Paul Théberge writes, "Digital instruments have become the means for both the production of new sounds and the reproduction of old ones—the perfect vehicle for a music industry based simultaneously in fashion and nostalgia" (1997: 213). This claim is well supported by the phenomenon of dangdut remixes in Indonesia, which use samplers, effects processors, drum machines, and other digital sound devices to insert novel sonic material into already familiar songs. Perhaps most striking to American listeners is the insertion of samples of spoken Black English Vernacular characteristic of the remix sound. Such samples, which include James Brown's musical exclamations and all manner of voices exhorting the listener to "clap your hands," "get funky," and so on, are available commercially to Indonesian sound engineers on CDs and vinyl records designed especially for sampling, and their frequent use has become a trademark of the dangdut remix genre. Often these samples are used percussively, in a way that makes their text unintelligible to the listener, which suggests that the sound of spoken (black) English is more important in this genre than the exact linguistic content of the utterance. Considering both the ubiquity of English speech in the mass media and the limited English ability of much of dangdut's audience, this is perhaps not surprising. Often the same sample will appear in a number of different songs, creating intertextual references to other cassettes released contemporaneously. Another characteristic sonic feature of remixes is the insertion of interlocking rhythmic vocables called *senggak,* which are found in many genres of Sundanese and Javanese music. These energetic, rhythmic shouts, either sampled or recorded "live" in the studio, add a distinctive Indonesian flavor to an already hybrid and complex sonic texture.[5] Often the samples of English utterances are organized into interlocking, senggak-like patterns as well.

Edy's first album of remixes, released in 1993, was recorded with surprisingly basic equipment: a turntable, a DJ's mixing console containing a rudimentary sampler, and a reel-to-reel tape containing the original tracks. A sampled backbeat had to be synchronized with the rest of the song by manually adjusting the speed on a reel-to-reel tape recorder in real time, which proved difficult and time-consuming. The album was then completed at considerable cost in a damp, scorpion-infested sixteen-track studio where various instruments and effects were painstakingly added to the mix. In the end, Edy's expensive gamble paid off, and the album went on to sell over 380,000 copies, still his biggest hit to date. Edy's follow-up album of remixes contained another first: accompanying the usual vocal samples of American rappers were some raps in Indonesian by Jakarta rap group Papa Weewee, their voices providing yet another sonic ingredient to be manipulated and incorporated into the final mix.

These days, with the facilities of the 601 Studio Lab at his disposal, Edy can create new dangdut remixes with far more sophisticated equipment. It is now possible to remove all of the instruments in a recording except the vocals and completely reconstruct the music using electronic instruments.[6] This is the technique used with "house" dangdut remixes, which are backed by rather austere electronic beats. Edy admits, however, that many house remixes are less than successful because melismatic dangdut vocals often do not "sit" (*duduk*) well on top of rapid, metronomic house rhythms. In these instances, the original singer is sometimes asked to rerecord the vocals at a faster, more even tempo. One major advantage to having access to sophisticated digital technology, according to Edy, is that it eliminates the need for actual club DJs to work on remixes. While the playback and mixing techniques used by DJs in club performances, such as *fading, scratching,* and *backspin,* form the foundation for the remix genre, according to Edy DJs tend to be "*egoistik*" and unreliable, and it is far easier for a producer to simulate their performance techniques with multitracked digital samples. One of Edy's collaborators, Risky, laughed when he described the "*old school*" techniques of the early dangdut mixes, which were now obsolete in Jakarta club culture even as they continued to be digitally reproduced in dangdut remixes.

Remixing Rhoma

One of Edy's most challenging remix projects was creating disco remixes of classic songs by the undisputed "King of Dangdut," Rhoma Irama. He was able to secure Rhoma's permission to use some of his old recordings as source material, but these recordings presented a challenge to Edy and his remix production team. Alone among dangdut artists, Rhoma records his music without overdubs and without a "click track" (the electronic metronome used to guide musicians in the studio). Rhoma is able to produce recordings in this way because he owns his own large studio, Soneta, and works with a complete ensemble of musicians (who are highly discouraged from working with anyone else). By recording all of the musicians playing together directly into a multitrack recorder, Rhoma claims to preserve the "heart" of the music. Without a click track, Rhoma's recordings do not precisely conform to a steady rhythmic pulse, and when producing remixes of his songs Edy had to have a live drummer play electronic drum pads in real time over the original recording, since electronically programmed drums could not be synchronized with the original rhythm.

Unfortunately, in the end Rhoma forbade any promotion for the release of Edy's remix album because a video clip for one of the songs offended him. The video featured comic sequences involving traditional Sundanese wooden puppets (*wayang golek*), one of whom bore a suspicious likeness to Rhoma. (Sadly, the only existing copies of the video were destroyed in a fire during the 1998 Jakarta riots.) The clip was only aired twice on Indonesian television, and without any promotion the cassette, the product of eight months of painstaking work in the studio, flopped.

More recently, Edy successfully obtained permission to produce a rap remake of Rhoma's song "*Santai*" (Relaxed), to be recorded by Papa Weewee. It has been less easy, however, to convince the rappers to cover a dangdut song, and the project has yet to go forward.

The Dangdut Trendy *Debate: Cultural Ramifications of a Techno-Hybrid Subgenre*

Dangdut remixes of newer recordings are usually released three to four months after the original dangdut song is released—in other words, toward the end of the first recording's commercial shelf life. Often the remix version does better commercially than the original, sometimes selling three times as many copies. The hit single from Edy's first remix album, a remix of singer Ine Synthia's "*Lima Menit Lagi*" (Five More Minutes), not only outsold the original song but led to a significant increase in sales for the original recording, from 80,000 to 120,000 legitimate copies sold. Edy explained to me that one reason for the popularity of remixes is that many young cassette buyers prefer the newer styles, and purchasing the dance remixes allows them to simultaneously maintain a nostalgic attachment to the classic dangdut sound and embrace "modern," more contemporary dance grooves.

Though undeniably popular with particular audience segments, dangdut remixes, and the dangdut trendy category in general, were also a source of controversy and faced condemnation from many sides. Given the social context into which the subgenre was introduced, it is not hard to fathom why mixing dangdut and electronic dance music was so provocative. Throughout the 1990s, "house" music, also known as *musik tripping-tripping,* was considered the height of trendiness by a sophisticated middle- and upper-class Indonesian youth subculture. The ever-changing array of discothèques and clubs where this music was played (and where the subculturally appropriate intoxicants were readily available) were exclusive hangouts for those in the know—part of a lifestyle that represented the very pinnacle of modernity and cosmopolitanism for a self-conscious urban elite seeking to distance itself as much as possible from the ways of "the village." Combining the most backward and unhip popular music genre (dangdut) with *musik tripping* would therefore constitute a grievous affront to the self-consciously fashionable, as well as an undeniable indication that non-elites were beginning to infiltrate their club culture of Ecstasy and energetic dancing (which was visibly the case in Jakarta in the late 1990s).

Elites were not the only ones troubled by the ability of recording studio products to flaunt and transgress ideological boundaries between traditional and modern, old and new. Many fans of "original" (*asli*) and "pure" (*murni*) dangdut, particularly older ones, found the new style objectionable, a corruption of the pure dangdut style. Many middle-class commentators pointed to the rise of dangdut trendy as evidence not of progress but of creative stagnation in dangdut—as though the incorporation of disco and electronic dance elements was an act of desperation hoping to inject some artificial vitality into the genre. An ironic corollary to the dangdut trendy controversy is that this subgenre still represents a minority of new dangdut releases, most of which follow the pattern of classic dangdut rather closely. I estimate that dangdut trendy music (a category including *house dangdut, dangdut disco, dangdut remix, dangdut reggae, cha cha dut,* and other styles) accounted for less than a third of the new dangdut releases between 1997 and 2000, even though dangdut trendy cassettes are less expensive to produce because they don't involve many live musicians. Dangdut trendy cassettes usually take up less than one-fourth of the space in the "dangdut" sections of record stores, which of course also contain many older dangdut recordings spanning the genre's decades-long history.

"Reformasi Cinta" (Love Reformation): Dangdut Hybrids in the Post-Soeharto Era

Much has changed in the four years since my first visit to Edy's studio in the fall of 1997. During the riots of May 1998, which specifically targeted Chinese citizens and Chinese-owned businesses, the offices of Edy's music company in North Jakarta were burned down and looted. The studio itself was almost ransacked by a mob that had just destroyed a nearby shopping complex. The army arrived just in time to prevent the rioters from reaching the studio's residential location.

Edy's spirit remains unbroken. Since the riots, the company has opened new offices and entered a rebuilding phase. Though economic recovery under President Abdurrahman Wahid and Vice-President Megawati Soekarnoputri's administration remains elusive, Edy is looking forward to a new expansion of dangdut music and its related offshoots. While disco and house remixes appear to have become passé after sales peaked in the mid-1990s, a newer dangdut hybrid called *combination ethnic*—dangdut songs played with modified traditional Javanese or Sundanese rhythms—has generated some major hits for Edy's company. Edy explains this new interest in traditional music as resulting from the new spirit of *Reformasi* (reform, reformation) in Indonesia. Edy played me a song entitled "*Reformasi Cinta*" (Love Reformation) by an artist named Lilis Karlina. In addition to exemplifying the tendency of dangdut songs to incorporate widely circulating words of the times, this recording featured the English-language sound bites and interlocking vocal interjections typical of dangdut remixes layered atop a conventional dangdut arrangement played by studio musicians. Thus the recording appeared to fuse together conventional dangdut with elements of dangdut remix in a quasi-Hegelian synthesis of "pure" and "trendy"—a hybrid recording reincorporating a previous hybrid.

Edy also informed me that new hybrid styles combining dangdut with bossa nova and drum & bass are currently in the works, and by the time the period of my field research ended in mid-2000, albums of *dangdut salsa* and *ska dhut* were available in cassette stalls.

Comparative Engineering: Dangdut and Nepali Remixes

A truly rewarding aspect of research into sound-engineering practices is that there appears to be no limit to the creative uses to which sound technologies can be put. What is striking in the case of dangdut remixes is both their commercial success and their accessibility to a large mainstream audience in Indonesia. It is instructive in this regard to compare the dangdut remix phenomenon with the Nepali remix culture described by Paul Greene (2001). While Greene found that the primary audience for Nepali remix albums was upwardly mobile university students, the Indonesian university students I spoke to considered dangdut remixes if anything even *more* low class and backward than classic dangdut. (Their disdain is countered by the enthusiasm of the vast majority of Indonesians for whom postsecondary education was never a possibility.)

Accompanying the class difference separating Indonesian and Nepali remixes is a significant difference in cultural aesthetics.[7] While Greene finds that Nepali remixes sonically emphasize disjuncture and discontinuity between different musical genres, I would argue that the intricate layering of sonically diverse materials found in dangdut remixes emphasize *copresence without synthesis*. Such an aesthetic of additive layering, to which multitrack technology is extremely well suited, bears a striking resemblance to the syncretic, resilient, and cacophonous texture of everyday life in contemporary urban Indonesia, where Hindu-Javanese mysticism exists side by side with orthodox Muslim piety, American fast-food consumerism, and, in recent years, activist democratic politics. In the midst of this boisterous, bewildering array of cultural alternatives, remix artists like Edy Singh take sonic elements from global popular culture, Indonesian traditional musics, and classic dangdut (itself a highly syncretic genre) and engineer hybrid grooves designed expressly for the purpose of moving equally hybrid Indonesian bodies. And in doing so they produce a pluralistic version of Indonesian musical modernity that is populist, creative, and compelling, not to mention danceable.[8]

Techno-Hybridity Goes Underground: Eternal Madness and Underdog State

Our second case study for what we might call "techno-hybridity" offers a perspective different from that provided by 601 Studio Lab. The Underdog State recording facility is located in a quiet residential neighborhood in Denpasar, Bali. It is rather low tech in comparison to Edy's studio—much of its recorded output is assembled on a Tascam 424 cassette four-track recorder—yet the production strategies of its owner, Sabdo Mulyo (Moel), are no less adventurous. Moel is the bassist, vocalist, and main songwriter of Eternal Madness, a Denpasar-based underground metal band that holds the distinction of being one of the few Indonesian groups that attempts to combine traditional (in this case, Balinese) music with the modern noise of underground rock.[9]

Like 601, Underdog State is a favorite hangout spot. In addition to a recording facility, there is a rehearsal space, a silk-screening workshop (for creating band tee shirts, stickers, and cassette covers), and a billiards table. The house occupied by Underdog State acts as a base camp for many members of Bali's underground music scene, which is known for its strong punk, black metal, and hardcore contingents. Eternal Madness plays death metal, a style more popular in the Jakarta and Surabaya scenes, but they play it with a definite twist. The group, which currently consists of Moel on bass and vocals, Putu Pradnya Pramana Astawa (Didot) on guitar, and a drum machine, calls their music "*lunatic ethnic death grind metal.*" In an Indonesian press release, they claim their new album *Bongkar Batas* (Dismantle Boundaries) "is a work of art that responds to the blindness and deafness of Indonesian musicians toward exploiting their own identities in the concept and style of metal music." This album, most of which was recorded at Underdog State, contains some definite "Balinese" elements: pentatonic melodies, a Balinese funerary chant, and abrupt rhythmic transitions strongly reminiscent of *gamelan gong kebyar,* the flashiest and most aggressive Balinese gamelan style. Yet Eternal Madness uses no traditional instruments, and the distorted, metallic onslaught of their music, complete with the raspy, growling vocals characteristic of the death metal genre, often seems to overwhelm its other elements.

Yet even in the most conventional passages on *Bongkar Batas* there is an audible difference that, while subtle, appears foreign to the conventions of death metal music. This sonic difference is located in the unusual rhythmic relationships that exist between the drum machine, the guitar, and the bass, which evoke those existing between instruments in a traditional Balinese ensemble. Balinese traditional music is organized around points of rhythmic convergence at the end of phrase units. Until those points are reached, however, the different metallophones in an ensemble are rarely struck at the same time. Instead of playing together in unison, each musician's instrument occupies a distinct place in the measure, filling up the sonic space with an interlocking, overlapping web of sound, "a dynamic intertwining of rhythms and tones" (Herbst 1997: 112). Moel revealed that this effect of "playing against" (*main kontra*) was achieved in Eternal Madness's music through the unique way that the songs on the album were recorded.

Moel explained that when recording a song he starts out with a rhythm guitar part that plays the basic riffs (in gamelan terminology, the "nuclear melody") of the piece. Next, lead guitar parts are added over the riffs that resemble the decorative melodic phrases that ornament the nuclear melody in Balinese gamelan music. The original guitar track is then erased. *Then* the programmed drums are added. Rather than the guitar following the beat of the drums, then, the drums play *around* the guitar, providing accents, filling in empty space, and marking transitions the way the *kendang* (a Balinese traditional barrel drum, different from the *gendang* used in dangdut) player would in a gamelan performance.

While he only uses samples of a standard western trap drum kit, Moel intentionally programs the drum machine to evoke Balinese drumming styles. He told me he often uses the machine's sampled China crash cymbal to play the part of the *gecrek,* loud crashing cymbals played in traditional Balinese ensembles that punctuate the core melody. Many of the drum parts Moel programs would be extremely difficult or impossible for an actual drummer to play; so far Eternal Madness has not found a drummer capable of replacing their drum machine.

After the drums are programmed and recorded, Moel adds the bass. He claims that the bass is like the *gong* in a gamelan ensemble. In my view, the bass lines in Eternal Madness songs more often play the role of the *bonang* (tuned rows of kettle gongs)—like the bonang, Moel's bass plays countermelodies "underneath" the nuclear melody, while the purpose of the gong is to mark the end of musical phrases. Moel's vocals are recorded last.

The method for recording Eternal Madness songs (first guitar, then drums, then bass, then vocals) is unlike the standard technique for recording rock music employed by both Indonesian and western producers: drum tracks first, then bass, then guitars, keyboards, etc., then vocals. The latter method guarantees that all of the instruments follow the same rhythm (dictated by the drums) with minimal deviation. In contrast, Eternal Madness creates hybrid music through an unorthodox use of music technology that reflects Balinese more than rock aesthetics, allowing a greater degree of rhythmic independence for each instrument.

Reception Issues: From the Village to the World

Studio-based sound engineering practices tend to facilitate a certain level of reflexivity. The nature of the recording process lends itself to a particular kind of critical engagement with the work that is taking shape through it, which then encourages thoughts about the music's origins, meanings, and potential audiences. Moel has many such thoughts regarding his music. Eternal Madness's two albums, *Offerings to Rangda* (1996) and *Bongkar Batas* (2000), both released on small independent record labels, target an Indonesian underground audience, but again with a twist. Moel doesn't think death metal fans in Jakarta and other large cities like his music much—for them it is too "ethnic" and therefore low-class and backward (*kampungan*), similar to the way that middle-class Indonesians view dangdut and dangdut remixes. But Moel believes an international audience would find his music interesting and unique; Eternal Madness received positive responses to their music during a visit to Australia, and Moel hopes his music will one day reach an international underground audience, perhaps even a world music/world beat audience.

Moel claims that he does not want to be an American, that his goal is "to be a Balinese who plays death metal music" *(jadi orang Bali yang main musik death metal)*. He does not want to copy an American sound, and if that is not good enough for the America-obsessed kids in Jakarta, so be it. Instead of focusing exclusively on the urban centers of the underground music movement in Indonesia, Moel has taken his music directly to rural areas all over Java and Bali, taking ferries, buses, trains, and motorcycles to smaller villages and hamlets. Moel claims that this promotional strategy has allowed him to sell 15,000 copies of *Bongkar Batas,* which is more than most major-label Indonesian rock cassettes sell unless they score a big hit. He criticizes members of large urban scenes like Jakarta and Bandung for having what he called a "racial" (*rasial*) view of rural listeners, that is, a prejudice bordering on racism. Moel, on the other hand, finds that this rural audience appreciates the traditional elements in the music of Eternal Madness as well as the band's occult and mythological imagery, which resembles that found in the most popular underground genre in rural areas—black metal. In this sense, the techno-hybrid music of Eternal Madness creates social consequences among rural audiences by joining together local folklore, village music traditions, and a generation-specific musical style with national and global dimensions. This combination has most likely had a lesser impact on urban areas. While city-based underground scene members with whom I spoke seemed to respect Eternal Madness's music, they were generally not interested in following the group's lead and creating their own ethnic hybrids.

Moel has not lost sight of the international market. He plans to rerecord four songs from *Bongkar Batas* with an actual Balinese gamelan, part of an EP intended "for export." He is collaborating on this project with Yudena, an avant-garde Balinese composer, who will use computer software to adjust the tuning of the gamelan ensemble in order to make its contribution compatible with the preexisting instruments on the recording. This project, then, is yet another "remix" and, like the addition of Sundanese and Javanese music elements in dangdut remixes, represents a retraditionalization of popular sounds. In this case, the objective appears to be making the "ethnic" component in Eternal Madness's music more intelligible to an international underground/world beat audience. Whether or not this remix reaches an audience outside of Indonesia is difficult to predict—no less so than the impact of such a recording on the national music scene.

While the dramatic sonic juxtapositions found in dangdut remixes can be said to be symptomatic of a characteristically Indonesian mode of coping with the heterogeneity and fragmentation of modern life, the techno-hybrid, ethnic grooves of Eternal Madness suggest fusion more than they do juxtaposition. The decentered self of dance music is replaced by the heroic individual of metal mythology, with its demands for authenticity and self-integrity. Rather than evoking coexistence without synthesis, Eternal Madness uses multitrack technology to create recordings that meld together "ethnic" and "underground," such that it is often quite difficult to detect where one begins and the other leaves off. This of course appears to be the point. The powerful music of Eternal Madness expresses the triumph of the willful individual over the pitfalls of the postcolonial condition, in which modernity on the one hand and pride in one's traditional cultural heritage on the other are often viewed as mutually exclusive alternatives. Eternal Madness "dismantles the boundaries" between these two poles, which otherwise might prevent postcolonial subjects from achieving a unified subjectivity.

Conclusions: Technology, Hybridity, Cultural In(ter)vention

What have we learned from this brief tour through two studios that produce techno-hybrid grooves? While ethnomusicologists have become increasingly interested in processes of music performance, recording studios (and popular music industries in general) remain highly *product*-oriented, for obvious reasons. Expediency rather than creativity is the primary reason behind the expansion of studio technologies, yet these can also be valuable creative tools when they become part of particular sound-engineering projects. Indeed, since the very beginning of recorded popular musics, few major musical innovations have *not* depended in some way upon new technology, from the microphone to the electric guitar to the digital sampler. Sampling technologies in particular helped bring about a completely studio-based genre: the remix. Remixes can act as metacommentaries on the nature of recorded sound; they encourage a listener to reflect upon the diverse histories and meanings of juxtaposed sonic material, such that the experience of listening can be pleasurable, disorienting, humorous, or even offensive depending on the listener's allegiances to particular entities and to the maintenance of certain cultural/class/national boundaries that, with the help of multitrack technology, can be crossed with greater ease than ever before.

Perhaps the greatest lesson that this ethnographic glimpse at two recording studios affords us is that in an era of multitrack recording technology in which "any sound you can imagine" (Théberge 1997) can become source material for the creation of new musical compositions, *no style of music is incommensurable with another* to the extent that it can be reduced to a set of malleable electronic signals by the recording process. The recording studio is thus the quintessential transcultural instrument. Once a sound becomes an electronically encoded sound print, there are virtually no limits to its possible circulation, assuming the presence of playback equipment. Thus, rap breakbeats and James Brown's yelps can turn up on a dangdut remix, and gamelan sounds can be imported into death metal compositions.

While Indonesia has always been a land of varied music hybrids, the techno-hybrids described in this chapter are part of a whole range of new music blends and juxtapositions developed in Indonesian recording studios, the result of self-conscious sonic experiments enabled by multitrack recording, sampling, and other technologies. In the commercial environment of a recording studio like the 601 Studio Lab, such experimentation is rarely carried out for its own sake; rather it is a kind of sound-engineering practice that seeks to create inspired hybrids capable of attracting new and lucrative audience formations. The success of these hybrids is based on commercial viability, not on whether their provocative juxtapositions add up to a coherent resolution of the identity issues they raise. In contrast, underground artists like Eternal Madness experiment with techno-hybrid forms to express an artistic vision that refuses to acknowledge a contradiction between ethnic/traditional and global/modern in a utopian quest for an undivided, self-authentic subjectivity.

The sounds of Indonesian traditional music can easily be sampled and stored and mixed into a pop or dangdut recording, but this capability does not suffice to explain why this practice occurs, nor does the fact that a drum machine can be programmed in an infinite number of ways necessarily lead to the creation of programs that mimic traditional Balinese drumming. Why are these hybrids being produced, and why do some of them become successful commercially? Perhaps, I would argue, because they capture the deep yearning of Indonesians who desire global modernity but want fervently to hold on to their traditional and national culture. The nineteenth-century European bourgeoisie managed such conflicting desires by creating the preservationist-motivated discipline of national folklore. But simply preserving traditional music culture in Indonesia (while it may please tourists and anthropologists) fails to achieve what so many ordinary Indonesians yearn for: a "sign of recognition" (Keane 1997) from the distant centers of power, glamour, and wealth that assures Indonesians that their "ethnic" sensibilities can be made intelligible to a modern subjectivity—that it is not necessary to abandon the culture of the *kampung* (village) in order to not be *kampungan*. By treating "ethnic" music as sonic source material for new recordings, producers like Edy and Moel "prove" that Indonesian music can fit within the multitracked syntax of global popular music.[10] The techno-hybrid grooves they produce do not just dramatize the encounter between western "modernity" and Indonesian "tradition," they offer Indonesians the freedom of not having to choose between these twin reifications.

Acknowledgments

I would like to thank Edy Singh, the entire 601 Studio Crew, and Sabdo Mulyo for their patience, hospitality, and willingness to help me with this project. Thanks also to Paul Greene and Matthew Tomlinson for their comments on earlier drafts of this essay.

Notes

1. Useful historical and stylistic overviews of Indonesian popular music published in English include Hatch 1989, Lockard 1998, Lysloff 1998, Manuel 1988, and Piper and Jabo 1987.

2. For example, upscale cabaret bands in Jakarta play a handful of dangdut songs to appreciative middle-class audiences, who often show more enthusiasm for these songs than for the usual covers of contemporary western pop hits. University student bands that play dangdut have attracted large campus-based followings throughout Java, and many middle-class Indonesians did admit to me that they liked *some* of it.

3. This is an unofficial estimate I heard from people in the Indonesian music industry, but these numbers are consistent with my observations of hundreds of roadside vendors throughout the country selling cheap, pirated cassettes out in the open and apparently without fear of reprisal.

4. See Frederick's article on the music and films of Rhoma Irama (1982) for an excellent description of dangdut music in this now-classic phase of its development.

5. In his programmatic essay calling for a new "ethnomusicology of technoculture," René T. A. Lysloff mentions Indonesian "disco-dangdut" and the subgenre's inventive use of interlocking vocal samples. He writes, "In this case, technology has provided local artists with the means for redeploying traditional ideas in new musical contexts" (1997: 215). Lysloff concludes the article with this statement: "It will be the work of the ethnomusicologist to analyze and explain the cultural negotiations involved with the global intersections of traditional musics, popular desires, and technological possibilities" (218). This essay you are reading represents my humble attempt to do precisely that.

6. The melodic, rhythmic, and sonic features of a dangdut song ideally derive from a sung melody that constitutes its most essential component. The centrality of the vocals in dangdut music may explain why it is possible to import (and subtract) so many musical elements into a dangdut song without diluting it beyond recognition: the genre identity of the song inheres in the singing, not primarily in the sound of the arrangement. Paul Greene (n.d.) has argued that the singing voice in South Indian popular music recordings acts as the point of identification for listeners and invites them to position themselves in relation to the hybrid musical textures that surround the voice. Thus the listener is encouraged to "think through" the song their own issues of identity, subjectivity, and loyalty to superindividual entities. Dangdut vocals may work in a similar fashion, inviting the listener to identify not only with the singer's emotions but also with the complicated positionality of her/his voice vis à vis the other instruments in the mix. While the eclectic sounds of the typical dangdut ensemble (distorted guitar, bamboo flute, gendang, synthesizer, etc.) have become more or less naturalized, I would suggest that novel sounds and musical settings (remixes being the most dramatic example) reopen these identity questions, encouraging listeners' reflections on the traditional, modern, national, and global consumer cultures indexed by various sounds in the mix.

7. When a version of this paper was presented at the 1999 annual meeting of the Society of Ethnomusicology, Kai Fikentscher commented that another difference between Indonesian and Nepali remixes is the debt the former owes to DJ performance practices, while the latter is purely a multitrack studio creation. Jakarta has long had an extensive dance club network, while Kathmandu's is far more recent and modest in scale (Greene 2001: 170).

8. The phenomenon of dangdut remixes is in many ways analogous to sound engineering developments in other places, where music makers have used studio technology to hybridize certain ethnic and national genres with the rhythms, sounds, and/or production techniques of electronic dance music. Examples include South Asian *bhangra*, Mexican *nortec* (*norte\nno* + techno; see Strauss 2001), and contemporary, "electrified" *raï* in Algeria and Europe (Schade-Poulsen 1999: 35, 68–70). Marc Schade-Poulsen writes that starting in the early 1980s the musical features of acoustic raï were "re-elaborated with electric instruments representing a Western Other" (70) on commercial recordings. I suspect this statement could be applied to many other techno-hybrid musics around the world.

9. Since the early 1990s the term "underground" in Indonesia has been used to describe a cluster of continuously evolving rock music subgenres (hardcore, death metal, black metal, punk, industrial, grunge, grindcore, and others) characterized by distorted guitars and raspy, unpitched vocals. Underground albums are usually produced and distributed outside conventional music industry channels, relying instead on small independent labels and grassroots promotional methods. By the end of the decade, nearly every major urban area in Indonesia was home to an underground "scene," with the most prominent located in Jakarta, Yogyakarta, Surabaya, Malang,

Bandung, Medan, and Denpasar. The most active members of underground scenes are usually middle-class university and high school students, but in recent years the popularity of underground music has spread to a larger audience of young people. Kremush, a trio from Purwokerto, Central Java, is another underground metal band whose music incorporates traditional melodic and rhythmic sensibilities, a style they call *brutal etnik*. Their independently produced cassette *Deadly Consience* [sic] was released in 1997.

10. After reading an early draft of this article, Edy Singh expressed concern that my account overemphasized his role in the production process and did not adequately address the collaborative nature of creating remixes. While I still believe Edy's role as patron and creative facilitator is crucial, there is no question that the musical hybrids discussed in this article are the result of intense social interaction between all of those involved in their production: performers, producers, arrangers, engineers, even hangers-on in the studio who are occasionally consulted on musical matters. Compared to the West, there is very little emphasis or value placed on solitary creation in Indonesia, and recording studios are nearly always exuberantly interactive settings. Music making in all of its forms is considered an irreducibly social activity, even when recording technology renders superfluous many of the social interactions involved in live performance.

References

Frederick, William. 1982. "Rhoma Irama and the Dangdut Style: Aspects of Contemporary Indonesian Popular Culture." *Indonesia* 32: 103–130.

Green, Paul. 1999. "Sound Engineering in a Tamil Village: Playing Audiocassettes as Devotional Performance." *Ethnomusicology* 43(3): 459–489.

———. 2001. "Mixed Messages: Unsettled Cosmopolitanisms in Nepali Pop." *Popular Music* 20(2): 169–188.

———. N.d. "Playback as Theatre: Performance Effects and Traditions of Distance." Unpublished manuscript.

Hatch, Martin. 1989. "Popular Music in Indonesia." In *World Music, Politics, and Social Change*, ed. Simon Frith. New York: Manchester University Press, 47–68.

Herbst, Edward. 1997. *Voices in Bali: Energies and Perceptions in Vocal Music and Dance Theater.* Hanover, N.H.: University Press of New England.

Jones, Steve. 1992. *Rock Formation: Music, Technology, and Mass Communication.* Newbury Park, Cal.: Sage Publications.

Keane, Webb. 1997. *Signs of Recognition.* Berkeley: University of California Press.

Lockard, Craig. 1998. *Dance of Life: Popular Music and Politics in Southeast Asia.* Honolulu: University of Hawai'i Press.

Lysloff, René T. A. 1997. "Mozart in Mirrorshades: Ethnomusicology, Technology, and the Politics of Representation." *Ethnomusicology* (41)2: 206–219.

———. 1998. "Popular Music and the Mass Media in Indonesia." In *The Garland Encyclopedia of World Music, Volume 4: Southeast Asia*, ed. T. Miller and S. Williams. New York: Garland, 101–111.

Manuel, Peter. 1988. *Popular Musics of the Non-Western World: An Introductory Survey.* New York: Oxford University Press.

Piper, Susan, and Sawung Jabo. 1987. "Indonesian Music from the 50's to the 80's." *Prisma* 43 (March): 25–37.

Schade-Poulsen, Marc. 1999. *Men and Popular Music in Algeria: The Social Significance of Raï.* Austin: University of Texas Press.

Strauss, Neil. 2001. "The Pop Life: On the Mexican Border, Crossing Genres." *New York Times* (March 8).

Théberge, Paul. 1997. *Any Sound You Can Imagine: Making Music/Consuming Technology.* Hanover, N.H.: Wesleyan University Press/University Press of New England.

CHAPTER EIGHT

Short-Circuiting Perceptual Systems
Timbre in Ambient and Techno Music

Cornelia Fales

In 1716, Philippe de la Hire tried to dissect the phenomenon of sound into sensations for which he had clear experiential evidence but no descriptive vocabulary: "One must distinguish the sound which is formed by the encounter of two sonorous bodies which clash from the pitch that it (the sound) has in comparison to another pitch of the same nature."[1] This less than lucid distinction between parameters of sound represents one of a very few attempts of the period to describe the phenomenon of timbre, a term that is absent from French dictionaries until the end of the eighteenth century and from English dictionaries until the century following. Perhaps not coincidentally, the nineteenth century saw both the first systematic exploration into the perception of timbre (by Hermann Helmholtz) and the first efforts to make timbre a deliberate compositional dimension in western classical music. Since that time, timbre has occupied a position of increasing importance in the western sensory experience of classical and popular music. At present, digital and sampling technology has made manipulation of timbre as flexible as pitch and dynamic variation in mediated sound of all kinds.

In 1999 a fan of Richard James attempted a close description of the first nameless track of Aphex Twin's *Selected Ambient Works, Vol. II.* The section he referred to contains a great swelling of timbre as two disparate sounds blend harmonics, like colors merging together, to create a third timbre richer than either of the original two. I know this description to be at least acoustically accurate because I have applied sound analysis to the section and seen a visual representation of the merging timbres. But the speaker below has only his ear to register the phenomenon: "then it goes up kind of like a scale—no, not a scale exactly . . . well there're two kinds of going up, right? This one just rises in sound. There's a difference between rising in sound like maybe with some frequencies coming out (but I don't mean louder, the amp stays the same) and going up like a scale, like a singer doing 'Ahhh' up a scale . . ."[2] Though several centuries later, this likewise belabored description of timbre shows sufficient similarities to the earlier description to suggest something about how listeners, historically and presently, conceptualize a parameter of sound they cannot describe directly. Both descriptions circle around the subject of timbre in an effort to capture it by exclusion, as the quality that is neither pitch nor loudness. And both employ the evasive tactic of sliding rhetorically between what I will call the three domains of sound: production, acoustics, and perception. The *productive domain* focuses on the sound source and the physical motion that produces the sound; the *acoustic domain* concerns primarily the spectral composition and transmission of sound; and the *perceptual domain* consists of the perceived sensation resulting from acoustic sound.[3]

Properly speaking, these domains are stages in the transmission of sound from source to listener, but they are also ideational abstractions that both reflect and shape habits of thinking and talking about sound. Any feature of sound can be described from the perspective of any of these conceptual domains, but an observable truth is that careful descriptions of timbre seem to need the vocabulary of all three domains to capture the reality of tone quality. Thus, de la Hire speaks of "pitch," which is *perceptual,* the clashing of sonorous bodies, which is *productive,* and the resultant "sound," which is *acoustic;* similarly, the Aphex fan *perceives* the sound "going up," *produced* by something like "a singer singing 'Ahhh' up a scale" and resulting in what he imagines to be the *acoustic* phenomenon of "some frequencies coming out." It is not difficult to find other historical passsages that parallel contemporary attempts to describe the substance of sound. Among English and French speakers, at least, it seems we have a limited repertoire of strategies to talk about the unnamable parameter of timbre. For now, the important point is that in spite of its intense foregrounding in electronic sound, the parameter of timbre still seems as elusive in percept to many general listeners today as it was to de la Hire in 1716.[4] Even regular consumers of popular electronic music, which includes genres whose entire structures are built on shifting tone color, often lack precise awareness of timbre as a distinct, dynamic feature of music, even as they are powerfully affected by it.

I will argue in this essay that the cognitive mechanisms that allowed nearly two and a half millennia of documented western history to pass before the word "timbre" was devised to designate a discretely covariant parameter of sound remain in operation, though they face a sonic environment substantially different from the one in which they evolved. In particular, I will address the technological creativity that is the subject of this volume in proposing that the sampled and synthetic sounds that comprise popular electronic music — sounds that modern listeners have grown to accept as part of the world's repertoire of noises — are slowly effecting a profound shift in our orientation to the auditory world, as mediated by the principles by which we perceive timbre. I begin from a distinctly cognitive perspective, focusing most closely on the experience of the listener.

Since at least the mid-1950s and the publication of Leonard Meyer's *Emotion and Meaning in Music* (1956), listener-centered approaches to music have been present with more or less prominence. These approaches have evolved under various names (reception theory, audience response theory, anthropology of listening), have defined their objects of attention with variable specificity, and have developed techniques and terminology appropriate to their respective goals. At their broadest, these approaches transform listeners into "consumers," and their patterns of behavior are subsumed under theories of consumption. At the opposite extreme lie narrow studies of higher-level auditory cognition, applied to one or more specific genres as they are performed in their customary contexts. It is at this end of the continuum that Steven Feld might find the approaches to listening that he targets with "as many cultural monkey wrenches as possible" (Keil and Feld 1994: 164), launched by his theory of "interpretive moves."

According to Feld, the experience of music actually comprises two interlocking processes. One dialectically arranges a sound object between musical and extramusical markers, engaging it in space, history, attention, and memory. The other entails a series of interpretive moves through which listeners traverse the dialectic of their musical/extramusical realities while shaping a particular musical experience according to the dimensions of their social and historical environments. Thus interpretive moves resolve the dialectic of engagement, render musical experience intelligible, and entwine it with listeners' social history, both current and past. The combination of these processes induces the creation of a "frame," which Feld defines as "a conceptual sensing of organizational premises and a foregrounding of the operational dynamics of a situation" (Feld 1994 [1984]: 90). An important aspect of frames is that they work to shape their specific contents — in this case, a particular musical experience — but may endure beyond the singular object that provoked their construction, as abstracting mechanisms to be used to reflect on the experience just passed, to interpret a future experience, or to think generally about musical engagement.

The result is an inventory of frames applicable to new and repeated musical experiences; framing also functions as a discursive device, a medium for the communication of musical experience between listeners. Feld is eloquent and insightful as to the position of listeners "caught in a moment of interpretive time, trying to force awareness to words" (Feld 1994 [1984]: 92–93). And I agree that there's no "necessity for a level of verbal articulation to go with each level of perceptual reality" (Keil and Feld 1994: 162); indeed, there are a great many levels of perceptual reality that preclude awareness, and hence description, altogether. But occasionally a listener struggles to find a mode of expression that is intelligible across subjectivities, resorting inevitably to "linguistic shorthands" whose hazy and undefined referents are consensually understood to convey meanings "feelingfully ingrained in affective time and space" (Feld 1994 [1988]: 112). Feld also points to the metaphoric tendency of thought and expression as a manifestation of associational, categorical, reflective, and other interpretive moves that ideally provides "a particular language for thinking about the necessarily vague, general and nebulous dimensions of the experience of music" (Keil and Feld 1994: 165).

Perhaps because of its format and phrasing, Feld's theory and especially its social, interactive nature seem crafted intentionally to counter Meyer's theory of syntactic expectations, which Feld feels neglects the sociocultural aspects of musical experience. Because, he says, Meyer's musical expectations are "hooked . . . to the physiological apparatus of musical perception" (Keil and Feld 1994: 164), they are inevitable given a certain musical configuration and thus might as well be contained in the music itself. For Feld, musical meaning is negotiated among all of the social, subjective, and cultural forces of a listener's world and cannot possibly be adequately represented by "the invariable laws of human cognition" (Meyer quoted in Feld 1994 [1988]: 148). One cannot help wondering if the substantial developments in cognitive psychology and neuropsychology during the eight years since the publication of *Music Grooves* might not inspire Feld to reconsider some of his criticism of a cognitive view of musical experience. For example, it is widely accepted at present that there are no dedicated cortical mechanisms that function autonomously from an individual's bodily experience of the environment; the brain itself, in fact, has proven to be much more physically malleable when subjected to environmental, cultural, and social influences than was ever suspected previously. Further, there are levels of cognition, and on lower levels, cognitive processes that—rather than precluding the activities prescribed by Feld's theory—actually prepare the listener to undertake precisely the interpretive moves necessary for musical engagement. Many of the interpretative processes enacted on higher levels of cognitive activity are remarkably similar to those that occur on lower levels: we will see, for instance, that the source-orientation of auditory processing functions effectively to transform the simple perception of sound into a robust metaphor maker.

Techno

Though the observations to be made here apply to many varieties of popular electronic music, I will be drawing examples from only a few genres, whose emphasis on timbre allows extra clarity of example. Like many terms in current popular use, "techno" has a certain ambiguity of meaning. Originally the term designated a specific form of dance music; with the proliferation of numerous subgenres in a remarkably short time, it has now become a generic term that on the one hand covers most popular music that includes a substantial electronic component, and on the other hand continues to distinguish electronic dance music from nondance music, most notably various genres of ambient music. Early techno was a synthesis of latter-day disco, hip-hop, and the first attempts by European groups to use the electronic techniques of the classical avant-garde in popular music. Among the early explorers of this electronica were Cybotron, with its roots in the dance clubs of Detroit, Afrika Bambaata, representing a hip-hop aesthetic, and the German group Kraftwerk, of which David Toop has said: "Kraftwerk: the original power station, the conductors, the operatives, the sound fetishists. . . . Kraftwerk: sexual, pure concentration, edible. Constraint with humour. Camp. Boys in uniform. Expression through proportion. Emotion through detachment. Inspiration through work" (Toop 2001: 202–203).

A simultaneous genre related to techno was Chicago house; however, whether house is a subcategory of techno or techno a subcategory of house depends on who is telling the story. The original Detroit techno was dry, sparse, and minimalist in character, whereas early Chicago house was deliberately and defiantly disco-derived, with a strong funk influence and futuristic sounds. By the late 1980s and early 1990s, a conjunction of techno and house gave rise to the rave movement, which centered around mass-attended all-night dance parties fuelled by the consumption of Ecstacy and related drugs. At its height, the rave movement was a cohesive subculture with a well-delineated ethos that has been compared to the youth movement of the 1960s.

At about the same time, house and techno on either side of the Atlantic were beginning the regressive splintering that has resulted in countless subgenres and subsubgenres. Among the better known of these are acid house, whose sound is dominated by the distinctive Roland TB 303–produced bass; trip-hop, which is known for virtuosic displays of rap techniques as well as other techniques unique to the genre; and hardcore techno, which emerged from the home-based, nonprofessional studios that arose in the early 1990s with the advent of affordable, more accessible technology. As a term, "hardcore" generally refers to both specific genre(s) and a quality accrued by existing genres as they have been developed particularly by British and other European musicians. Out of the hardcore movement emerged drum 'n' bass techno, which incorporated elements of hip-hop and Jamaican dub and in turn fostered subgenres defined by variations of the bassline for which the genre is known. One of the examples to be examined later represents the subgenre drill 'n' bass as developed by Squarepusher, which is characterized by a driving bassline that is so rapid and irregularly syncopated that it prohibits dancing. Another example we will look at comes from a movie soundtrack composed by Eric Serra; it occurs at a point where the music closely matches the physical action of the plot and thus falls into no particular category, though it demonstrates characteristics from several genres of techno. The evolution of generic variation in techno music in the last twenty years has reflected changes in the social/cultural conditions of musicians and listeners as well as the sophistication of accessible technology. My interest here, however, is in the new sounds that characterize the digital era, their use in music, and their consumption by technologically literate listeners who have most likely spent some portion of their lives in the presence of electronically altered sound. In order to remain within the constraints of a single chapter, I will say very little about their production or their significance to the subcultures where they are most familiar.

Preattentive Timbre and the Fallibility of Listening

It has become almost commonplace to point out that most languages have little domain-specific terminology to describe timbre; or that, out of all of the parameters of sound, timbre is the most difficult to abstract into a describable system because it does not vary in a perceived order of increments; or that perceptually timbre is often tricky to separate from other parameters of sound. But these observations are also supported by experimental research suggesting that a considerable amount of auditory information, perhaps more than other sensory data, is subliminally interpreted and responded to by listeners. Unattended processing in any sensory domain, of course, is important for cognitive efficiency. Timbral details in particular, it seems, are often preattentively processed for use in other cognitive operations, but not for direct examination, though it is clear that with deliberate effort and/or instruction as to how to listen, listeners can be made conscious of qualities of sound. More often, though, they appear inclined to leave the phenomenon of timbre comfortably subsurface, where it provides information while avoiding explicit attention.

In his otherwise insightful book *Rhythm and Noise* (1996), Theodore Gracyk discusses our limited memory for timbre in a way that seems to reflect his awareness of the preattentiveness of timbre, but in his eagerness to bolster his intuitions with more authoritative evidence, Gracyk misrepresents Robert Crowder's findings concerning human abilities to image sound. In particular, he quotes Crowder as saying that "memory of timbre [is] 'a modest human ability, once it is separated from semantic connotations,'" when actually Crowder finds that memory for timbre is considerable, and Gracyk's choice of quotes actually refers specifically and very clearly to vocal quality rather than instrumental timbre. Unlike Crowder, for whom relevant terms are precisely defined, Gracyk appears to confuse the ability to *image* timbre with the ability to *remember* it. The test of timbre's memorability is in our ability to recognize a timbred tone heard previously (a relatively achievable task), not our ability to hold a timbre in mind as an image. Indeed, the fact that the imaging of timbre is more transient than the memory for timbre is completely consistent with a salient feature of preattentive phenomena: that the information they contain are fully and efficiently useable even as they are inaccessible to direct inspection or recall (Mandler 1991).

Research shows that timbre is crucially important to the interaction between hearing beings and their environment, and that—in spite of evidence to the contrary—listeners are not at all unaware of timbre, though as noted above their awareness may not be totally conscious.[5] Human auditory acuity for timbre perception has been demonstrated to be at least as sharp as the ability to discriminate pitch; and on a subliminal level our sensitivity seems even greater for the discrimination of timbre than pitch.[6] Nevertheless, contrasts in pitch and loudness register on a conscious level more immediately and starkly than timbre contrasts of equal magnitude. I have presented a theory of preattentive timbre elsewhere (Fales 2002), beginning with the goals of unconscious processing and showing that musicians regularly succeed in thwarting those goals in music.[7] Since the point of this essay is to show that the auditory processing of electronic music confronts a different configuration of timbres than one finds in acoustic music, I will only summarize the theory and its implications here. The theory proposes that the preattentiveness of timbre originates with the fallible nature of auditory processing in general, a fallibility that can be inferred from three related characteristics of the operations that turn acoustic signals into the perception of sound.

First, auditory perception is source oriented. Human interpretation of complex sound stimuli has been shown to be precisely geared to source identification. Lower-level processing, in particular, is based on what appears to be hardwired information about sound sources, much of which determines the raw components of timbre. The auditory world of a normal listener, it seems, is founded on a canonical knowledge of sound and its sources. *Second, auditory perception is heuristic in nature* (Bregman 1990). Since sound is a moving phenomenon, its processing is necessarily interpretative and time dependent, comprising the best of several hypotheses in light of current information. To compensate for incomplete information, the auditory system[8] has developed methods to restore missing parts of an auditory gestalt or to make backward revisions when incoming information shows an earlier interpretation to have been faulty.[9] *Third, sound processing is profoundly tautological.* Before identifying a sound, the auditory cortex must group into individual percepts the ongoing flow of simultaneous elements arriving from a complex soundscape of sources. It is in this organizing process that the innate knowledge of sound sources is visible, as the brain groups together elements constitutive of characteristics "typically" found in source emissions.[10] In discerning sources, then, auditory processing operates on circular reasoning, analyzing percepts for the same source characteristics that it has used to construct the percept to begin with.

Together, these three features ensure the success of auditory source characterization, but a success that is preordained by our procedural assumption of the evidence we are seeking and by our ability to retroactively correct a percept in light of incoming evidence.[11] Whatever its apparent success, auditory processing as described above is clearly less than foolproof. Indeed, it is theoretically capable of massive inaccuracies, though it operates with enough artifice to conceal its mistakes from the listener. Of all of the parameters of sound, timbre is the one most directly affected by the stratagems of the auditory system, since it is a product of the processes that organize the mass of simultaneous acoustic elements into source groupings.[12] In fact, the grouping of components by source *is* the creation of timbre, and it is in this process that the system's tautology begins. Whether or not the auditory system makes actual "mistakes" in processing acoustic information, there is clear evidence that it shapes a percept beyond the actual features of the signal according to priorities of its own. The very sensation of timbre itself is an example of perceptual modification of an acoustic signal, in that it relies on processes of perceptual fusion applied by the auditory cortex to a signal's individually pitched harmonics, transforming them into the unitary sense of tone quality. In a very real sense, timbre exists only in the mind of the listener.

Auditory fallibility arises because the productive, acoustic, and perceptual domains described earlier are interactive but discrete in function. The perceptual domain, enclosed in the mind of the listener, can only know the productive and acoustic domains via its own processes. To gain access to these two domains, it must first make assumptions about them—about sources in the productive domain and sound behavior in the acoustic domain. The confidence with which listeners describe perceived sound from the point of view of production or acoustics is testimony to a causal faith in their auditory mechanisms—*since* they hear certain features, the source *must* be acting in a corresponding fashion.

One of the most profound differences between acoustic and electronically produced sound is the capability of the latter to invalidate the causal logic that has bound together productive, acoustic, and perceptual domains since the beginning of auditory time. Electronic sound requires a redefinition of "source" and "production," it conflates the productive and acoustic domains, it boggles assumptions of canonical sound possibilities, and in a sense to be elaborated later it deprives the perceptual domain of at least part of its traditional role in processing musical timbre. And yet, as suggested in the beginning of this chapter, the auditory systems of modern listeners seem to roll along as usual, fully unaware of an occasional incongruity.

Perceptual Equilibrium

If accurate and efficient source characterization is important to the welfare of listeners, the infallibility of the system—whether real or imagined—is vital to their perceptual equilibrium; that is, to their ongoing confidence in the evidence of their senses and their sense of a stable, perceivable external world. Though most of the perceptual modification of acoustic signals seems to aim at increasing perceptual efficiency—removing inconsistencies, filling in degraded signals, deciding what in a chaos of ambient sound to eliminate as unworthy of attention—it appears that the auditory system also expends some amount of energy camouflaging its own contribution to perception (Merikle and Daneman 1998; Fales 2002). In particular, the auditory system works to promote the perceptual confidence that signals from the acoustic world literally *are* the percepts they provoke, thereby concealing the fact of an *acoustic world* of which listeners' *perceptual worlds* are only "best guess" versions.

I suggest that the preattentive nature of timbre constitutes a backgrounding of the very parameter where evidence of the acoustic world is most visible. In this sense, it is the first line of defense in the ongoing efforts of the auditory system to maintain a listener's perceptual equilibrium. Since the cognitive economy of the nervous system often functions by attending to events only when they offer new information, the deliberate nonattention to timbre may work with inverse logic to emphasize it as a static parameter, a permanent and faithful representation of an immutably physical world. The need to maintain this illusion is so strong that listeners project the fundamental premise of their perceptual logic onto the data it is meant to interpret, propelling subjective auditory sensation onto a world of sources, conflating productive, acoustic, and perceptual domains until sound equals source. We say "I hear a *cricket*" not "I hear a *sound* that may indicate the presence of a cricket." Or, as though to colonize the acoustic world, we transfer even our *reactions* to a sound onto its imputed source; we say "I hear a sad violin" when it is a *sound* we hear, and *we* who are sad. Our entire auditory world, it seems, is based on a substitution of the indexed for the indexical and the effect for the cause.

Music

In comparison to environmental sound, musical sound seems to promote more flexible auditory processing. Research indicates that a distinctive characteristic of music listening is the degree to which *source characteristics may be ignored* during the grouping process (Peretz 1988) in favor of other organizational priorities. The inclination to hear sources in sound constitutes a perceptual schema—a template by which to organize discrete acoustic elements—and because it is the default system of the auditory mechanism, listeners must be strongly motivated to relinquish it. Nevertheless, a skillful musician can incite listeners to forego default source-ridden perception for the sake of special effects that foreground timbre and momentarily disrupt a listener's perceptual equilibrium. Since listeners cannot form a sensation without some organizing system, part of their motivation must include an alternate perceptual schema for exchange with the default schema they have renounced.

The implications of an exchange of perceptual schemata are best understood by considering an example in the visual domain. In a reversible figure-ground image like the well-known "Rubin's Goblet," viewers establish a visual schema specifying two conceptual fields, one meant to be background for the other. With reversal, the opposite schema is invoked and the two fields, figure and ground, exchange places. Whether one sees the profiles or the goblet as figure depends on which perceptual schema is used to organize the optic elements of the picture: are the curving segments in the middle of each line the protruding noses of the profiles into the ground, or indentations of the goblet stem? This process of organization is directly analo-

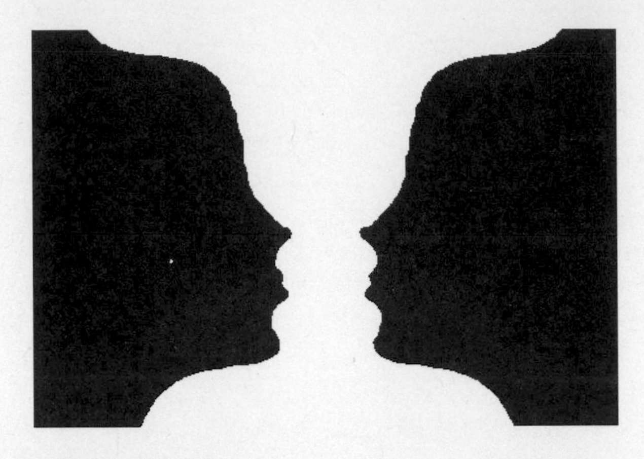

Fig. 8.1. Rubin's goblet.

gous to the organization of acoustic elements in the auditory cortex, where the default schema is the one based on source characteristics.

But, of course, there is a difference between a reversible figure-ground like Rubin's Goblet and the experience of perception in the physical world. Figure-ground images are *artifacts,* artificially constructed to promote alternative organizations of elements. In Rubin's Goblet, there is no perceptual default schema; neither the profiles nor the goblet is a "correct" interpretation of the configuration, and both are equally possible. In the physical world, on the other hand, stimuli reaching our eyes and ears have an inherent organization imposed by the fact that they originate with real, discrete sources. The creation of a real-world version of Rubin's Goblet would entail positioning identical twins face to face, erecting a white backdrop behind them, painting their faces black to disguise the colors and three-dimensional quality of their profiles, and so on. The point of all of these extra effects would be to *artifactualize* the real world, to visually obscure the fact that the optic elements of this view have an inherent organization based on their origin in or "belonging" to a coherent unit in the real world. In music, artifactualization often takes the form of a softening of a listener's awareness of multiple sound sources.

One of the profound differences between electronic and acoustic music is that, depending on how one views the synthesizer as a musical instrument, purely electronic music can be said to be either sourceless or monosourced. In terms of perceptual schemata, therefore, electronic sound is as much an artifact as Rubin's Goblet—it is, in fact, an exact auditory analogue. Not only is a synthesizer physically a single source, but the sounds that it creates evoke no immediate perceptual schema as do sounds in the acoustic, source-ruled world. If synthesized sounds are sufficiently ambiguous, they can be grouped in more than one way, resulting in auditory illusions offering two percepts that can be switched back and forth like a reversible figure-ground image, neither percept more correct that the other. The potential disorientation of listeners from such effects has been described by Simon Reynolds as a kind of "schizophrenic consciousness," a "deconstruction of subjectivity" intended to "delocalise the perception apparatus," even "allowing forms of perception to emerge that one had previously attributed to lunatics or schizophrenics" (Reynolds 1996b).

The spectrogram in figure 8.2 demonstrates the acoustic construction of the kind of effect Reynolds describes, one of a multitude of tiny timbre tricks that flood the listener in Squarepusher's "Port Rhombus" (*Big Loada*, track 8), passing by too quickly for analysis but functioning as a collection to shape the piece. To the spectrogram of the Squarepusher segment, I have attached a tone (at 6.2 seconds) of 400 Hz (with two overtones) to help locate the same harmonics in the music represented. While it is absurd to describe verbally an auditory illusion—by definition, a sound that must be heard—one can see at least that the ongoing tone of approximately 400 Hz (with its harmonics at 800 and 1200 Hz) in the Squarepusher segment is

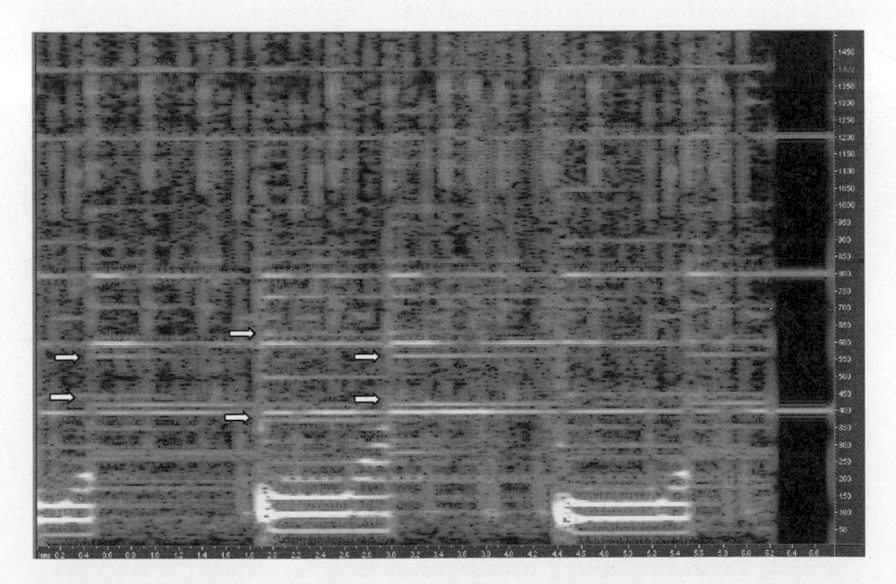

Fig. 8.2. Squarepusher, track 8: "Port Rhombus," 0–6.2 secs. Spectrogram of the first 6.2 seconds with added 0.5 seconds of a single tone at 400 Hz (three harmonics). Arrows indicate double harmonics that provoke alternate percept of constant harmonics. Vertical axis is frequency, horizontal axis is time; brightness indicates a frequency intensity.

joined by extra harmonics (marked with white arrows) above and below the ongoing harmonics, with the result that the extra harmonics offer an alternative to the perceptual schema with which listeners have organized the sounds thus far; a listener can, in other words, allow the temporary harmonics to dictate an organization that includes them, capturing certain components from the original percept while leaving the remainder to be heard as a separate percept.

The fact that musicians like Squarepusher often construct sounds to include source characteristics does not change the status of the sounds as artifacts—even if these sounds occur as part of an unaltered sample. Rather, the presence of source characteristics in a synthesized sound creates an auditory metaphor that *contextualizes* the sound in the acoustic world. Contextualization can be dense and compact or slight and sporadic, making the sound more or less divergent from the real-world sound it imitates. But however faithful the resemblance between an auditory metaphor and its acoustic referent, it is still the case that the sound is an artifact and that its perception as metaphor is no more "correct" or veridical than the percept resulting from any other organization of its elements.

The process of sonic contextualization, in fact, is comparable to altering a Rubin's Goblet figure, undermining its reversibility by adding facial features to the profiles in imitation of real-world twins. In this sense, contextualization is the direct opposite of artifactualization: artifactualization camouflages the distinctive features of real, acoustic sound that betray its origin in a sourceful soundscape; contextualization attaches to an artifact features that are typical of acoustically produced sound, thus locating the sound in the acoustic world.[13] Artifactualization loosens the constraints of source-ridden perception; contextualization intensifies the auditory inclination of listeners toward source-based perception.

What is the point of timbre manipulation in music? Is it simply to provoke a kind of auditory seasickness that begins with schizophonia and ends with the total perceptual breakdown that Reynolds and others depict so vividly?[14] The theory presented here proposes that when music timbre is handled in specific ways, it works against the ongoing efforts of the auditory system to maintain a seamless perceived world where the ability to listen depends on belief in the success of the system. If the auditory system cannot show us the gross discrepancies between the perceived and acoustic worlds by presenting us with timbral anomalies and fictional sources, then timbre manipulation forces us to acknowledge evidence that the same acoustic signal yields different percepts from one moment to the next. Shaped by a skillful musician, the borders of a timbral unit become fluid, changing from one context to another—a phenomenon all the more alarming when the sounds come from the real acoustic world. Techniques such as these disrupt perceptual complacency, fracturing the carefully constructed blind between the perceptual and the acoustic worlds. Listeners begin forceably to acknowledge, if not to approach, the acoustic world, a world that they would otherwise never know to exist.

It would be foolish, of course, to suggest that every time listeners experience the right combination of timbres in music, they suddenly understand all the principles of acoustics. Like many auditory phenomena—the Squarepusher excerpt above, for example—timbre effects pass swiftly and with a subterranean impact. If indeed timbre is a parameter of sound that is unconsciously processed and experienced, then listeners exposed to timbre-manipulated music will not be conscious of each perceptual tremor delivered through their ears. Rather, I suggest that the very subliminality of these sensations is a clue to their power. Given the tendency of timbre to escape direct examination, it is not surprising that listeners might feel the power of music without ever considering its timbral basis. Instead, the cumulative effect of a musical experience of variable timbre manipulation—the flashing into view of the acoustic world—may move listeners within a range of specificity and emotion: from a more or less vague sense of perceiving something normally imperceivable, to a general notion that music is an imperfect translation of something, to a numbing anxiety at electronic sounds with no correlation at all in the real world, which incite listeners to feel not simply aware of but drowning in the acoustic world.

Categories of Sound

The idea of variability in listeners' reactions to timbre manipulation leads to a rough taxonomy of sounds common to ambient music. I propose these to fall into four categories that, like many musical phenomena, actually form a continuum, here defined by decreasing contextualization. The first category, at one end of the continuum, consists of exact copies of real-world sounds, derived perhaps from unaltered sampled sounds. These might be acoustic instruments, environmental noises, or other sounds that demonstrate maximum contextualization and the tightest metaphoric connection to some acoustic referent. Between that category and the next, the level of contextualization attenuates gradually and sounds maintain their metaphoric quality but diverge by increments from a known acoustic referent, until by category two, sounds are unfamiliar but possible or imaginable in some musical universe. While not pointing to a specific referent, that is, these sounds indicate sources that follow the rules of the acoustic world, and they conform to our canonical sense of how sound works in the world; these are not shocking sounds, they are simply ones we have never heard before.

The third category contains in some ways the most affectively provocative sounds; here, sounds are neither familiar nor imaginable, their metaphoric connection to acoustic referents tenuous. In particular, these sounds play with the listener, carefully conforming to our canonical sense in some qualities while radically violating that sense in other qualities in the same sound. Sounds in this category acknowledge the rules of the acoustic world in their infraction of them, and we recognize the sounds they diverge from; these are sounds that are impossible, that could never exist in the perceptual world in which we believe so wholeheartedly. In effect, these sounds tempt listeners with the security of contextualization, only to pull it away with some incongruous feature that is so fleeting that we know only that something strange has happened. Such sounds might combine characteristics typical of mutually exclusive categories of instruments: for example, a tone might consist of the abrupt, noisy attack of an impulsive sound, followed by the long steady state typical of sustained instruments rather than the decay we would expect. Or a sound might undergo a slow, deliberate morphing from one familiar instrumental sound toward another, never quite reaching the second sound and thus leaving us dangling between sources. Or a sound might jump to a distant pitch without the slight noise that is inevitable whenever a nongliding pitch change occurs.[15]

The fourth category of ambient sounds is a kind of catch-all bin, leaving the continuum of contextualization open-ended at one extreme, as though extending into some domain of yet-to-be-imagined sounds. This category contains sounds that lack any vestige of contextualization. If they present themselves as either conforming or incongruous and disobedient to the rules of a familiar soundscape, it is by accident, for they inhabit a sort of forsaken universe where the very notion of a humanly bounded soundscape is meaningless. Sounds in this category exist in total autonomy from any canon of sounds we might favor. A deluge of these sounds makes us anxious for a foothold, for something familiar to direct our auditory efforts; to try to describe them in words would be a barren undertaking, because they are so diverse, formless, and unstable that they deprive us of anything to describe, even if we had the vocabulary. More than the sounds of other categories, these must be experienced, since they exist only in the hearing, refusing the abstraction of description. Often, these sounds are some kind of noise, unpitched and purely timbral. If they have pitch, it is backgrounded as a parameter and rarely develops into any kind of melody.

Since the scope of this essay precludes the presentation of examples for each of the four categories, I have chosen a single example of a sound typical of the third category. The excerpt below is taken from the soundtrack of the film *The Fifth Element,* in which it follows a performance of the "madness aria" from *Lucia di Lammermoor,* sung by a flagrantly extraterrestrial diva with an operatic and distinctly terrestrial style. Abruptly, the music changes into the harsh techno of the "Diva's Dance," and we begin to suspect that the Donizetti performance has used the diva's talents only modestly. The style of the "Dance" is so radically different from that of the aria, where we have so absorbed the diva's thoroughly human vocal characteristics, that we do not notice the peculiarities of her vocal techniques right away: consistent with the uptempo energetic movement of the music, the diva executes a series of vocal leaps from high to low that are unusual but not alarming—after all, this is galactic music.

In particular, we do not notice that with each rotation, the diva reveals a bit more of what turns out to be an impossibly expansive vocal range. By the end of the series, she has covered a range between 100 and 1550 Hz, or from G/G#2 to G6, about five octaves. Something of this range is illustrated in the figure below, as the diva slides up a scale of almost three octaves (an arrow marks the beginning of her ascent). Prior to that feat, the diva demonstrates leaps in pitch at a rapid tempo; suddenly, a string of notes speeds by, and almost in retrospect we realize, or think we realize, that a reedy brittleness was present in the highest few notes (marked with double arrows) that was inconsistent with the diva's voice as we knew it, or any voice at all, for that matter. For a brief moment, her voice becomes aberrant, something that ought not to exist, a timbral anomaly. It is a subtle

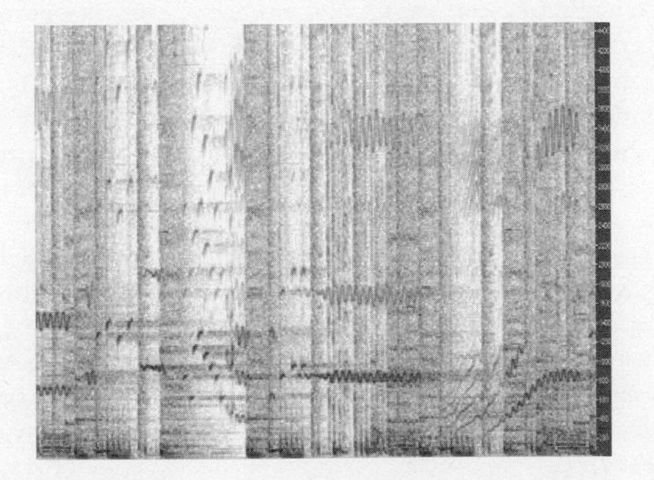

Fig. 8.3. Fifth Element "madness aria."

effect, and listeners not attending to those few notes — especially if they are distracted by the screen visuals — may be left with a vague sense of disorientation without ever knowing why.

Together, the two alterations, the reedy top notes and the extended range, convert the diva's voice into a timbral anomaly. Our experience and innate knowledge of sound builds categories by defining their limits and characterizing their members. In the diva's voice, the composer attacks in both directions. The extended range pushes her already exceptional voice beyond the believable pitch limits of the category, and the reedy notes introduce a timbre that violates the permissable variations in vocal quality. Each technique varies one parameter while maintaining the trajectory of the rest of the voice. At the lowest point in the diva's range, the artificial sound presents a timbre that is typical of a low-register voice and — more impressively still — is consistent with the low-register timbre she has demonstrated in her natural range up to that point. The reedy notes are also so spectrally consistent with her true treble notes that it is a mystery as to why the phenomenal distinction between them is so clear. A comparison of spectral analyses of the diva's natural treble voice with the synthetic sounds reveals a nearly identical harmonic structure and attack; the only real differences between the real and synthetic sounds are the amount of noise in the real tone and the precise harmonicity of the synthetic tone.

These are obviously effects that would be impossible with acoustic instruments. Though the principles behind timbre manipulation in acoustic and electronic music appear to be the same, the means are clearly different, as is the sometimes blatant prominence of effect. A major difference lies in the position of the listener relative to the music. In earlier papers on timbre manipulation in traditional acoustic instruments, I have identified several techniques of manipulation, two of which involve the same kind of reshuffling of acoustic elements between percepts that we saw in the Squarepusher example. These techniques I called respectively "timbral anomaly by extraction" and "timbral anomaly by redistribution." In the extraction technique — a defining feature of genres like overtone singing or didjeridu music — one or a group of harmonics are emphasized — made louder — until they actually break perceptually from their original timbre to form an independent timbre. The redistribution technique — central to Burundi whispered singing, for example, as well as other genres implicating distinct noise elements — involves a general regrouping of elements so that those emitted by one source fuse perceptually with those emitted by another source; in Burundi whispered singing, several frequencies from a pitched instrument are perceived as part of the simultaneous noise of the whispered text, lending it a pitched quality that it actually lacks acoustically (Fales 1995).

Both extraction and redistribution techniques create timbral anomalies that have the same effectiveness as the diva's voice. But these two methods for reshuffling harmonics differ in the degree to which they use acoustic factors to incite perceptual reorganization—or, from another point of view, in the respective roles of the musician and the listener. If one conceives of perception as shared responsibility, the result of contributions from the acoustic world and the perceiver's own mind, then the extraction and redistribution techniques differ in the relative degrees of contribution required from the listener and the acoustic signal. The extraction technique works in the acoustic world, altering the acoustic signal until parts of it stand out in relief as a separate percept against the remainder of the tone. The redistribution technique works in the perceived world, with little or no change at all to the acoustic sound; any change that occurs is only in the mind of the listener. From the point of view of musicians, the creation of a timbral anomaly in overtone singing, for example, requires that they change the sound; the creation of a timbral anomaly in Burundi whispered *inanga* requires that they change the listeners, inducing them to alter their mode of perception. Thus a performer's control over the effect of a timbral anomaly is correspondingly greater with the extraction than with the redistribution technique; the extraction of relevant harmonics is largely a matter of musical skill, while the redistribution of acoustic elements is a matter of musical persuasion.

Another difference between acoustically and perceptually driven effects is the relationship between the musician and the audience. A musician can successfully execute the extraction technique all by him/herself; the effect is in the music, with or without listeners. But the same is not true of the redistribution technique: the listener's role constitutes fully half of the actual performance; without a cooperative listener, the effect is unsuccessful. A musician who uses the redistribution technique must therefore possess a talent for indirection, for working at one remove from the effect he creates.[16] He intends his music to introduce a timbral anomaly into the perceived world of his listeners, but whether by design or necessity he cannot productively change the acoustic world of his sounds, and he cannot enter the perceived world of his listeners. Instead, he carves out from their shared acoustic world a smaller performative world where perhaps listeners find it safe to relinquish their source-ridden perception without risk. Often the artifactualization required for an exchange of perceptual schemata is built directly into whatever genre is congenial to the desired effect. Following the generic rules of the music, the musician creates an atmosphere conducive to perceptual flexibility, a place that promises reward for a simple change in perceptual subjectivity; from that place, he beckons to the audience with all of his skill, but finally listeners enter or not as they will.

In the visual domain, an analogy to the distinction between perceptually and acoustically driven timbre effects is illustrated in figure 8.4. Compare the phenomenon of Rubin's Goblet with this image, commonly called an illusory contour. Whereas Rubin's Goblet presents a viewer with a set of components that can be viewed with various organizations, an illusory contour presents a set of components with an implied organization that is so compelling that we experience the percept it defines though we must fill in missing elements to do so.

The illusory contour is, again, an artifact. In music, where acoustic sources generate nonartifactual sound, performers of acoustic instruments are limited to a productive control of timbre—for the extraction technique, for example—by altering the source vibration[17] or, less frequently, the resonator of the instrument.[18] With the right combination of musical elements, they can also provoke a perceptual modification of timbre—for the redistribution technique, for example—on the part of listeners who are amenable. Electronic musicians, on the other hand, have substantial control over the

Fig. 8.4. Illusory contour.

acoustic composition of the sound itself. If they wish, and if they have the appropriate equipment, they can bypass the productive stage altogether, ignoring the intricate mechanics of performance to modify the signal directly,[19] changing single frequencies or the relative amplitudes of entire spectra of components by adding or removing noise or extra harmonics, by prolonging or curtailing the resonance of a tone, by applying preprogrammed effects, and so on. The important point is that in acoustic music, timbral anomaly by extraction occurs in the *productive* domain and anomaly by redistribution occurs in the *perceptual* domain, while in electronic music both timbre effects occur primarily in the *acoustic* domain.

This difference gives electronic music enormous timbre capabilities—in theory, the potential to use all of the techniques available to acoustic musicians as well as an entire repertoire of effects possible only with direct signal manipulation. But the ironic result of this power is that electronic music often constrains the perceptual domain of listeners, even while freeing them from the confines of source-based perception. Even electronic musicians who derive creative strategies from the experience of timbre in acoustic music seem to retain no awareness (if ever they possessed it) that some part of the acoustic effects that inspired them may have occurred in their minds, not in the music. Or perhaps these musicians recognize the role of the perceptual domain in creating timbre but do not always trust listeners to yield to their persuasion. Whatever the reason, timbre manipulation, at least in ambient and some other genres of techno music, often seems to begin and end in the acoustic domain. The strategic indirectness of acoustic musicians who must work at one remove from the effect they intend is unnecessary in electronic music, whose effects can be controlled through the direct manipulation of the signal, bypassing its source altogether. Instead of creating the perceptual means to experience a timbral anomaly, electronic musicians often create the anomaly itself; instead of artifactualizing sounds to prepare listeners for an exchange of perceptual schemata, electronic musicians either contextualize sounds until only one source-based schema will fit them or relieve them of all contextualization until *no* schema will fit them.

The exercise of absolute control over timbre effects through the modification of the signal in the acoustic domain is comparable to the creation of an illusory contour figure by filling in the missing elements, effectively depriving listeners of the opportunity to contribute to the effect perceptually. The difference between a musician who creates timbre effects totally in the acoustic domain and a musician who counts on listeners to complete the effect perceptually is the difference between showing listeners something and inciting them to see. The range of possible timbres in acoustic music is shaped by the constraints of material instruments, while the range of possible timbres in electronic music is shaped—theoretically, at least—by the imagination of the producer or composer. And while the constraints of material instruments are based in the external acoustic world, the constraints of the imagination are based in the subjective perceived world. Composers of acoustic music juggle the material constraints of their instruments with listeners' preattentive proclivities to offer a glimpse of the acoustic world in breach of perceptual constancy. Electronic musicians take what would ordinarily be the workings of an actively subjective perceptual world and externalize the result into the outside world, territory previously reserved for acoustic objects. Whereas, in other words, acoustic musicians enforce the divide between the acoustic and perceived worlds by temporarily crossing it, electronic musicians extend their subjectivity beyond the borders of the perceived world, intrepidly denying the acoustic world altogether.

When listeners find the contents of their auditory imaginations turned out into the external world, they are faced with something like Baudrillard's notion of the simulacrum that imitates a nonexistent original (1988). Without indulging in elaborate postmodern analyses, I will conclude by pointing out a parallel between, on one hand, the four stages proposed by Baudrillard to constitute the progress of a representational image toward full simulacrum and, on the other hand, the four kinds of sounds that occur in ambient and other electronic music. According to Baudrillard, it is the nature of idols and other representational symbols to covertly subsume the authority of the symbolized, to subvert their intended role as conduits to the symbolized by blocking the channel, so to speak, absorbing transmissions destined for the originals that they represent. The transformation of a simple representational image into a simulacrum proceeds through the following stages:

1. It is the reflection of a basic reality.
2. It masks and perverts a basic reality.
3. It masks the absence of a basic reality.
4. It bears no relation to any reality whatever: it is its own pure simulacrum. (1988: 170)

Thus, says Baudrillard, an image begins with a faithful represention of its referent, develops into a misrepresentation of its referent, then uses its misrepresentation to hide the fact that there is nothing to correctly represent ("just as prisons are there to conceal the fact that it is the social in its entirety, in its banal omnipresence, which is carceral" [1988: 172]), finally existing blatantly and willfully with no external justification whatsoever, without claim to representation, altogether unconnected to any existing referent.

Similarly, the first category of sound in ambient music reflects precisely its acoustic referent. The second category of sound follows canonical rules of sound to distort or lie about a nonexistent source. The third category, by transgressing the same rules, deceives by showing itself to be the exception that proves the rule–that is, since it is a sound that defies the rules of source-emitted sound, then there must be sounds that obey these rules. And the fourth category contains sounds autonomous from a world of acoustic referents altogether. Each of these four categories provokes a realization on the part of listeners about the nature of the auditory world and of perception in general. The first category reassures listeners that auditory perception is a precise reflection of sound sources in the acoustic world. The second category alerts listeners to the fact that auditory perception is rule-governed and very likely an inexact copy, one of several possible versions of the world. The third category uses listeners' realization of a possible disjuncture between the acoustic and perceived worlds to hide the fact that there may not be an acoustic world from which the perceived world is disjunct. And the fourth category suggests more directly that perception is caused by nothing in the external world but is rather a hallucination, a product entirely of the listeners' minds.

The alignment of kinds of sounds with perceptual realization leads to a final difference between acoustic and electronic music. Though acoustic music can imitate the first three categories of sound with more or less ease, it cannot produce a true metaphor by virtue of the fact that its sounds are the referent that a sonic metaphor is meant to represent. And it cannot imitate sounds of the fourth category at all, since acoustic sounds are the referent whose absence defines the category. Nonelectronic music, that is, can produce sounds that fracture listeners' comfortable nescience of the acoustic-perceptual disjuncture, and it can force them to acknowledge that some part of their perceptual world is self-created, but it cannot cause the listener to doubt that there is an external world at all from which their perceived world diverges. Only electronic music can so externalize the subjective consciousness of sound on the part of listeners that they begin to suspect that their collected percepts and reactions to auditory experience are nothing more than their ears listening to their minds—in the words of Baudrillard, "perfect simulacra forever radiant with their own fascination" (1988: 169).

Notes

1. "On doit distinguer le Son que se forme par la rencontre de deux corps sonores qui se choquent d'avec le ton qu'il a en le comparant à un autre ton de la même nature." In fact, the translation in the text obscures the true ambiguity of language about sound in the seventeenth and eighteenth centuries, since it renders the word "ton" by "pitch," when in actuality "ton" seems to designate both pitch and tone indiscriminately during this period.
2. Interview with Steve Anglin, December 1999.

3. Thus, perceptual: "Your sound is much too loud"; acoustic: "Your sound is so strong it's bouncing off the walls"; and productive: "You're really banging the hell out of that drum."

4. By "general listener," I mean one who is a relatively naïve—i.e., musically untrained—and/or one who listens unreflectively.

5. For example, though listeners can easily determine that an unfamiliar instrumental sound is an impulsive (e.g., struck or plucked) rather than a sustained (e.g., bowed or blown) tone, listeners must often be prodded for this information with questions as to the actions (plucking, bowing, blowing, etc.) that the musician might be making to play the instrument. They can, in other words, more easily describe the production of the sound than the perceived features of the sound that allow them knowledge of its production.

6. Recent Mismatch negativity (MNN) experiments show listeners able to preattentively detect timbral changes in sound segments so short in duration that a pitch determination is impossible.

7. I will use the terms "unconscious" and "preattentive" synonomously in accord with current usage, though the conflation of the two terms is problematic in some ways.

8. By "auditory system" I mean any part of the neural or cognitive processing necessary to convert physical acoustic stimuli into the subjective sensation of sound.

9. Such corrective strategems are routinely applied by the listening brain without exciting any conscious awareness whatsoever in the listener.

10. For example, the cortex assumes that since sources generally emit signals with characteristics X, Y, and Z, all acoustic elements constitutive of those characteristics are grouped together as having originated from the same source.

11. It is important to note that the guarantee is for source characterization, not source identification. Though one frequently hears a sound whose source is unfamiliar, it is usually possible to derive a good deal of information about the source nevertheless. This is because the organization of acoustic elements into source groupings occurs at least in part from the bottom up, so that though this organization process may present us with an unfamiliar source, it has constructed that source from characteristics it knows to be typical of likely sources in our environment. This is the nature of the tautological processing of sound.

12. In theory, all of the information needed to determine the pitch and loudness of a natural sound is available before it has even left the inner ear

13. My argument does not change even though sampled sound—like recorded sound—occurs already contextualized, or does not need contextualization (depending on how one configures these ideas); the fact remains that for an artifactual sound, source characteristics, however obtained, locate it in the real world, though it has lost its literal source.

14. "Schizophonia" is term coined by R. Murray Schaefer (1997) to capture the unbalanced feelings on the part of listeners in the presence of sourceless sound.

15. This effect relies on the fact that there are two ways that an instrument can move from one pitch to another. Either it has a number of devices (keys on a piano, holes on a recorder, strings on a harp), each of which initiates one pitch, or it has a single device (a single stringed instrument, the slide on a trombone, human vocal chords) that is responsible for producing the entire pitch range of the instrument. If pitch is changed on a guitar by plucking several strings, it belongs to the first category; if pitch is changed on a guitar by sliding a finger along a single string, it belongs to the second category. If a multidevice instrument changes to a higher pitch, it must initiate another wave of higher frequency, whereas a single-device instrument can simply slide up to the new pitch, thus increasing the frequency of the existing waveform. In either case, a disjunct move to a higher pitch requires a new

waveform, which by definition cannot occur without the slight noise that accompanies the initiation of any vibration.

16. In Burundi this is especially true, as musicians agree uniformly that while playing, they cannot hear the effect—the melodicized whisper—that they are creating. One suspects that this might often be the case with perceptually driven effects, since the performer must actively resist the illusion fostered by artifactualization in order to continue to create it.

17. For example, the plucking technique on a string.

18. Alteration of the resonator is most easily accomplished when the resonator is the human mouth in singing or mouth harps; such a flexible resonator is difficult to construct otherwise, though gourdlike resonators sometimes are modifiable. In theory, acoustic musicians can also can work in the acoustic domain through their choice of performance environment, thus controlling the architectural acoustics that influence the sound.

19. If some part of an electronic sound is sampled or if the actual production of a raw signal precedes acoustic modification, then one can speak of productive domains; otherwise, the creation of electronic music constitutes a collapsing of the productive and acoustic domains.

References

Aphex Twin. 1994. Nameless track, *Selected Ambient Works. Vol. II.* New York: Warner Brothers Records.

Baudrillard, Jean. 1988. *Selected Writings,* ed. Mark Poster. Stanford: Stanford University Press.

Bregman, Albert. 1990. *Auditory Scene Analysis.* Boston: MIT Press.

Crowder, Robert G. 1993. "Auditory Memory." In *Thinking in Sound,* Stephen McAdams and Emmanuel Bigand, eds., New York: Oxford University Press.

De la Hire, Philippe. 1716. *Experience sur le Son.* Memoires de l'Academie Royale des Sciences.

Fales, Cornelia. 1995. "Auditory Illusion and Cognitive Patterns in Whispered Inanga of Burundi." *Systematic Musicology* 3(1): 125–154.

——. 2002. "The Paradox of Timbre." *Ethnomusicology* 46(1): 56–95.

Feld, Steven. 1994 [1984]. "Communication, Music, and Speech about Music." In *Music Grooves,* by Charles Keil and Steven Feld. Chicago: University of Chicago Press, 77–95.

——. 1994 [1988]. "Aesthetics as Iconicity of style, or, Lift-Up-Over Sounding. In *Music Grooves,* by Charles Keil and Steven Feld. Chicago: University of Chicago Press, 109–150.

Gracyk, Theodore. 1996. *Rhythm and Noise: An Aesthetic of Rock.* Durham, N.C.: Duke University Press.

Keil, Charles, and Steven Feld. 1994. *Music Grooves.* Chicago: University of Chicago Press.

Mandler, G. 1991. "The Processing of Information Is Not Conscious, but Its Products Often Are." *Behavioral and Brain Sciences* 14(4): 688–689.

Merikle, P. M., and M. Daneman. 1998. "Psychological Investigations of Unconscious Perception." *Journal of Consciousness Studies* 5(1): 5–18.

Meyer, Leonard. 1956. *Emotion and Meaning in Music.* Chicago: University of Chicago Press.

Meyer, Leonard. 1987. "Toward a Theory of Style." In *The Concept of Style,* ed. Berel Lang. Ithaca: Cornell University Press, 21–71.

Peretz, Isabelle, and José Morais. 1988. "Determinants of Laterality for Music:

Towards an Information Processing Account." *Handbook of Dichotic Listening: Theory, Methods and Research,* Kenneth Hugdahl, ed. New York: Wiley, 323–358.
Reynolds, Simon. 1996a. *Generation Ecstasy: Into the World of Techno and Rave Culture.* Boston: Little, Brown.
———. 1996b. "Low Theories." *The Wire* issue 146, No. 4. <http://www.mille-plateau.net/theory/download/reynolds- thewire.pdf>.
Schafer, R. Murray. 1977. *The Tuning of the World.* New York: Knopf.
Serra, Eric. 1997. "Diva Dance." *The Fifth Element.* New York: Virgin Records.
Squarepusher. 1997. "Port Rhombus." *Big Loada.* New York: Warp Records.
Toop, David. 2001. *Ocean of Sound, Aether Talk, Ambient Sound, and Imaginary Worlds.* London: Serpent's Tail.

CHAPTER NINE

"Heaviness" in the Perception of Heavy Metal Guitar Timbres

The Match of Perceptual and Acoustic Features over Time

Harris M. Berger and Cornelia Fales

Introduction and Methodology

Studies in timbre perception have historically proceeded in one of two directions: either they have attempted to identify the salient features of an acoustic signal that translate into the perception of a specific instrumental tone quality; or they have attempted to connect verbal descriptions of instrumental timbre with some feature(s) of the acoustic signal. Both approaches have yielded results indicating that the phenomenon of timbre—in both perception and description—is multidimensional, with a number of factors interacting to produce the exact tone quality that is perceived or described by a listener. The standard definition of timbre in books of auditory perception, in fact, generally describes the phenomenon by negative exclusion, specifying timbre to be all of the qualities of a tone—with the exception of pitch and loudness—that differentiate one tone from another (ANSI 1973).

This report describes a project that has two objectives. First, it explores the electric guitar timbres of a genre of popular music known as heavy metal. The concept of "heaviness" is applied by members of the heavy metal subculture to a range of instrumental timbres (drum timbres, vocal timbres, bass timbres) and compositional elements (melodic motifs, harmonic approaches) in their music, and heaviness is the defining feature of the genre.

While the term "heavy" functions in a variety of ways, it is most commonly used to describe guitar timbres (Berger 1999; Walser 1993), and all of the other uses of the term are metaphoric extensions of this primary use. The project's first goal is to understand some of the acoustic features that correlate with the perception of heaviness in heavy metal guitar timbres.

The project's second goal is to demonstrate a new methodology for studying timbre. In particular, this methodology expands upon the second approach to timbre research identified above, the linking of a verbal description of tone quality with acoustic features. Previous efforts have proceeded from a consensus by listeners as to the adjectives appropriate to a particular timbre. The methodology demonstrated in this project, however, begins with agreement by heavy metal subculturalists, known as "metalheads," that a particular timbral quality in the music has changed in a specific way over time. In other words, rather than searching for agreement among listeners that a specific sound is characterized by descriptor X, to which the acoustic elements A, B, and C can be correlated, this project takes a historical perspective. It is commonly held among metalheads that the characteristic guitar timbres associated with this genre have changed since the genre's inception in the early 1970s, becoming heavier and heavier over time (Berger 1999); as a result, prototypical songs from these periods can be analyzed for some acoustic property, or constellation of properties, that changes in the same direction and increments specified by the listeners.

The theory informing this methodology is as follows. There are two major problems in the effort to correlate adjectives describing timbre with acoustic qualities that elicit those adjectives. One has already been mentioned—the acoustic multidimensionality of timbre. Unlike the sensation of pitch (which can be more or less directly correlated with the acoustic property of frequency) or the sensation of loudness (which correlates to the acoustic property of amplitude), the sensation of timbre is the result of multiple interacting acoustic factors, making correlations complex. The second problem is that, unlike pitch or loudness, there is no relative scale for timbre. That is, while changing pitch moves by regular intervals through an octave and shifts in dynamic move continuously from soft to loud, timbre does not progress in regular perceptual increments with all possible timbres arranged along a single trajectory. However, in a given context—a single piece or genre of music—a listener can distinguish greater or lesser degrees of a given timbre (here, the tone quality is darker than there; now, the tone quality is brighter than before).

While some features of heavy metal have remained the same over time, what listeners specify as the quality of "heaviness" in distorted guitar timbres has been observed to increase incrementally over the genre's history. As

Berger notes (1999: 58–60), metalheads almost universally assert that the distorted guitar timbres of 1970s heavy metal were heavy, those of the 1980s reached new levels of heaviness, and those of the 1990s were heavier still. Such a trajectory affords a unique opportunity for timbre research and allows for a new method for study. This broad agreement among metalheads not only provides a consensual description of a timbral quality in a genre for which timbre is primary but also specifies that this quality heightens or intensifies in a regular manner. If one were to apply previous approaches to the study of timbre, a researcher interested in "heaviness" might proceed as follows: (1) given the adjective "heavy," identify one or more acoustic elements tentatively responsible for the sensation of heaviness; (2) present listeners with representative sounds from the genre but with the identified acoustic elements artificially reduced; (3) ask listeners if they find the resulting sound to be more or less heavy than the original sound. If listeners find the altered sound less heavy than the unaltered sound, then the elements removed from the altered sound can be considered to have contributed to the sensation of heaviness. The problems with this procedure are many and complex, especially its artificial context, which many ethnomusicologists find to be fiercely disturbing. What we have done instead is selected songs commonly associated with this well-known pattern of perceptual change, the increase in heaviness, and analyzed the guitar timbres for acoustic changes that correspond to the perceptual change independently agreed upon by listeners.

Context: Distorted Guitar Sounds and Heavy Metal History

To clarify these issues, it will be helpful to briefly discuss the phenomenon of acoustic noise, the underlying sound technology involved in producing electric guitar distortion, and the role of distorted guitars timbres in the history of heavy metal. Generally speaking, periodic sound waves are experienced as tones of discernible pitch, while aperiodic sound waves—those that do not repeat in a regular fashion—are experienced as unpitched noise. Traditional music in many parts of the world makes skillful use of both tone and noise, and these elements often occur in combination. Produced by sound waves comprised of periodic and nonperiodic elements, such sounds may be created by attaching foreign objects over tone-producing instruments (for example, to the strings of a piano for certain prepared piano sounds, or to the resonators of instruments like the African mbira or xylophone), by increasing the breathiness of a blown instrument, or simply by reducing the tension of the vibrating device until it responds with a pronounced buzzing quality. Such modifications will produce combinations of tone and noise in one of two perceptual configurations: listeners hear the combination either as two distinct sounds occurring at the same time (noise layered on top of a distinct tone; a tone in the presence of noise) or as a noisy tone, in which the two sounds are fused together into the percept of a single sound. Acoustically, the difference lies partly in the degree to which the noise conforms to the spectral structure of the tone: if the noise and tone are layered, then the tone's spectrum is obscured by a band of noise that covers the entire range of the tone's harmonics; if the noise and tone are fused, each harmonic of the tone is individually surrounded by a band of noise (Fales and McAdams 1994). The noise produced by heavy metal distortion is predominantly of the latter kind and results in guitar sounds that are buzzy or hazy with extra frequencies.

In electric guitar music, distortion refers to any situation in which a component of acoustic noise is added to the electric guitar's signal. Such additions can be achieved at any point in the instrument's signal path: the strings themselves, the magnetic pickups that translate the energy of the vibrating string into the changing voltage of an electronic signal, the cable or radio transmitter that sends the signal to the amplifier, the amp itself, or its speakers. In fact, the signal chain may be far more complex than this. One or more processing devices may be placed between the guitar and the amp to change its sound; in live music, the amp itself may be miked, and that signal may be processed, amplified, and sent to a PA system; in recorded music, the guitar signal may be sent to an amp and miked, or it may be fed directly to a mixing console and recorder, where additional processing may be applied.

While electric guitar strings themselves may produce distortion in a manner analogous to those of the prepared piano, it is usually the amp or signal processor, and occasionally the speakers, that are used to create an intentionally distorted timbre. More than just adding a noise component, distortion tends to modify the electric guitar's sound by increasing sustain, boosting upper harmonics, flattening the dynamic envelope, and changing the textural blend when two or more guitar strings are played simultaneously. In a history of electric guitar distortion, Michael Hicks (1999) reports that manufacturers of early guitar amps treated such modification of the electric guitar's sound as a sonic flaw, and only those guitarists using inexpensive amps or those pushing their equipment to their loudest sound levels would play with a distorted timbre. He observes, however, that in the late 1940s, blues guitarists began to actively seek distorted sounds, either by turning their amps up to high levels, modifying the internal components of those amps, or intentionally damaging their speakers (Hicks 1999: 14). Manufacturers eventually began to design their amps to produce desirable forms of distortion, and beginning in the early 1960s special signal processors were constructed to add noise to the signal.

In guitar amps, distortion is primarily achieved at two different stages of the amplification process — the preamp, which boosts the weak signal coming from the pickups and is primarily responsible for shaping the guitar's timbre, and the power amp, which boosts the signal to concert levels and sends it to the speakers. While distortion can occur at either stage, the preamp is the component that the guitarist often focuses on to shape his/her instrument's distorted timbre. For example, full distortion sounds at low levels can be achieved by turning the preamp volume to its highest level, thus producing distortion, and cranking down the master volume. The type of electronic components in the amp also play a key role in the achievement of distortion. While transistor-based amps make for rugged and reliable gear, many performers feel that the distortion they produce tends be less "warm" and "rich" than that of the more fragile vacuum tube–based amps. Experienced technicians can distinguish between the types of distorted timbres produce by different models, manufacturers, and vintages of vacuum tubes, and the adjectives technicians and guitarists use to describe those timbres is astounding in its variety. The smooth, full distortion of a tube amp pressed to its limits is usually referred to as "overdrive," and this timbre can be heard in a range of musics, especially the electric blues of the 1950s and 1960s. While manufacturers have had some success in imitating overdrive sounds with transistor-based signal processors, such devices can also be used to produce their own unique variety of distortion, called fuzz. Often brighter and more nasal than overdrive, fuzz was a staple of many 1960s rock distortion sounds; as Hicks observes, the buzzing, raspy guitar tone of The Venture's tune "2,000 Pound Bee, Part 1" nicely illustrates the fuzz timbres of the early 1960s. The 1970s and 1980s saw the development of an ever-wider range of amps and processors, and many of the emergent subgenres of popular music have been identified by their characteristic distortion timbres. The mid-1990s saw the development of modeling processors and amps — devices that digitize the guitar sound, use complex mathematical formulas to model the physical components of different amps, convert the signal back into analog form, and feed it to an amp in real time. Emulating the electronic components of different types of gear, such equipment allows guitarists to instantly switch between the characteristic distortion sounds of different types of equipment, musical genres, or performers.

Even more than other styles of popular music, heavy metal is defined by its guitar sounds, and the history of the music is intertwined with the history of these timbres. Most scholars agree that the exact origin of the style is open to question, but it is generally understood that metal first began to emerge in the late 1960s or early 1970s during a period of substantial fragmentation in rock music (Weinstein 2000; Berger 1999; Walser 1993). As Weinstein and Walser both observe, early heavy metal's two immediate influences were the guitar-based rock bands of the late 1960s and psychedelia. From guitar heroes like Eric Clapton and Jeff Beck, metal bands took their blues-based harmonic vocabulary, their reliance on long, elaborate guitar solos, and their instrumentation (guitar, bass, drums, lead male vocals); at the same time they drew their thick ensemble textures, extreme volume levels, and densely distorted guitar sounds from psychedelic bands like Iron Butterfly. Jimi Hendrix, perhaps rock's greatest "guitar hero" and one of the pioneers of psychedelia, provided a key influence. To this mix, seminal metal bands like Black Sabbath and Judas Priest added new elements—keening, high-pitched vocals, an emphasis on minor keys and grimmer emotions, and the use of occult themes. Though most scholars agree on the broad outlines of this historical narrative, such a listing of musical influences and stylistic features gives an unrealistically rigid picture of 1970s metal. As Weinstein argues, the dividing line between heavy metal and hard rock was a blurry one in this decade, and nowhere is the fact more evident than in the question of Led Zeppelin's generic status. While neither scholars nor fans doubt that Zeppelin cast a long musical shadow, there is often disagreement about whether the group was a founder of heavy metal or a hard rock group that informed metal's style. However that issue is decided, it is clear that while some of the bands of this period where unquestionably on the metal side of the line (Black Sabbath, Judas Priest, Motörhead), the hard rock/heavy metal boundary was a fluid one until the late 1970s and early 1980s.

What changed during this new period was an explosion of U.K. groups commonly referred to as the New Wave of British Metal. The huge audiences garnered by bands in this movement, including Iron Maiden, Def Leppard, Venom, and Saxon, allowed metal to distinguish itself from hard rock. Stylistically diverse, each of these groups developed the generic features of 1970s metal in different ways, and, after several years of growth, these differences became so great that metal began to split into a wide variety of subgenres. Weinstein argues that these subgenres can be grouped into two more or less discrete camps, lite metal and speed/thrash metal, each of which focused on a different set of themes explored by the 1970s-era founders (2000: 35–52). Lite metal bands like Quiet Riot and Twisted Sister, she suggests, focused on Dionysian themes and the ecstatic release that comes from the sensual pleasures of sex, drugs, and rock 'n' roll; bands in the speed/thrash tradition like Slayer or Anthrax examined the theme of chaos and emphasized imagery of the occult, fantasy, madness, violence, oppression, and war. These differences were also expressed in a band's musical style and its relationship with the mainstream music industry. Lite metal highlighted the vocal melody and employed lighter ensemble textures and shorter songs, while groups on the speed/thrash side tended toward thicker ensemble textures, extremes of tempo, longer instrumental sections, and compositions oriented more toward rhythm than melody. With songs that fit into rock radio formats, lite metal embraced the mainstream music industry and developed as a more or less coherent style. Often referred to as "the metal underground" by its adherents, the speed/thrash camp instead consisted of a wide variety of styles united by its participants' opposition to lite metal and the mainstream music industry.[1] In the 1980s and early 1990s, underground metal styles included thrash metal (a hybrid of metal and punk), death metal (characterized by growled vocals and grim themes), doom metal (with extremely slow tempi), and black metal (with its satanic imagery). Additional stylistic changes emerged throughout the late 1990s and continue to the present.

While distorted guitar sounds are important for all types of metal, these timbres are particularly crucial for the speed/thrash side. Musicians and listeners in this camp tend to view lite metal as an offshoot of the "true" metal tradition and construct the music's history as a linear narrative that starts with Black Sabbath and Judas Priest, continues through the heavier of the New Wave of British Metal bands, and culminates in the present underground. In such a view, metal history has unfolded in a *progressive* fashion, with the music getting heavier and heavier, and better and better, over time. While, as we have suggested above, the term "heaviness" can be used to refer to a wide range of instrumental timbres and compositional elements, first and foremost the term "heaviness" refers to distorted guitar timbres (Berger 1999: 58–59). Though some traditionalists may hold that the 1970s compositions of Black Sabbath and Judas Priest are just as heavy as those of today's bands, it is widely agreed among underground metal fans that guitar sounds have gotten heavier over time, and the development of the genre as a whole is seen as having been driven by the guitarist's achievement of ever heavier timbres. It is worth noting that while lite metal adherents are generally uninterested in underground metal and its pursuit of heavier tones, almost all would agree that underground guitar timbres have gotten heavier over time.

Choice of Samples

The present research is intended as a pilot, a preliminary test of the relevance of the consensual perception of timbre change to similarly changing acoustic patterns. For this test, we sought musical examples from 1970s bands that were unambiguously considered to be in the heavy metal style (rather than hard rock) and 1990s bands from the underground (rather than lite) tradition. Several factors limited our selection of recorded samples. Our methodology dictated that we use prerecorded samples rather than ones recorded in the laboratory, but this constraint introduced a difficulty. Digital sound-analysis tools such as spectrum analyzers and spectrograms work best when applied to sounds from single instruments, while most recordings involve an entire band playing simultaneously. Thus, we were forced to find samples of solo guitar in metal's recorded corpus. In the end, this stricture and other practical considerations limited us to four main samples and two additional samples, each an example of isolated guitar playing in a similar pitch range of the instrument. While the sample size was constrained by various factors, the bands were selected to provide unequivocally typical timbres of their periods and subgenres. Obviously, the sample size is sufficient only for a pilot study such as this. Additional samples from the 1970s and 1990s, as well as samples from the middle period (the 1980s) would be needed in order to verify the preliminary conclusions that we have drawn from our limited corpus.

Introductory passages from Black Sabbath's "Paranoid" (1971) and Judas Priest's "Tyrant" (1976) were chosen as representative samples of 1970s-era metal. "In Love" by Grave (1991), a death metal band, and "Wages of Sin" by Winters Bane (1993), a progressive metal outfit, were selected as examples of the 1990s underground sound. The main samples used were all examples of what rock and metal musicians call "power chords"—chords that most frequently are composed of a root, a fifth, and the octave in the lowest octave of the guitar's range. The power chord comprises the most common harmonic material used in metal and the typical vehicle for displays of timbral heaviness. Two additional samples of unmuted, single-note runs were also used to examine dynamic envelope; a short passage from "Tyrant" was employed to represent the earlier period, while another from "Wages of Sin" was used to illustrate the later period.

Results

Location of Energy. Characteristic of heavy metal music across the thirty years of its history is an immense amount of acoustic noise contributing to its overall timbre. However, an examination of spectrograms of these samples reveals that the frequency range of both harmonics and noise cuts off at a lower point for samples from the 1970s era than for samples from the 1990s era. For the early period, the Black Sabbath example (figure 9.1) shows an abrupt reduction of energy above 4.5 kHz, with a small amount

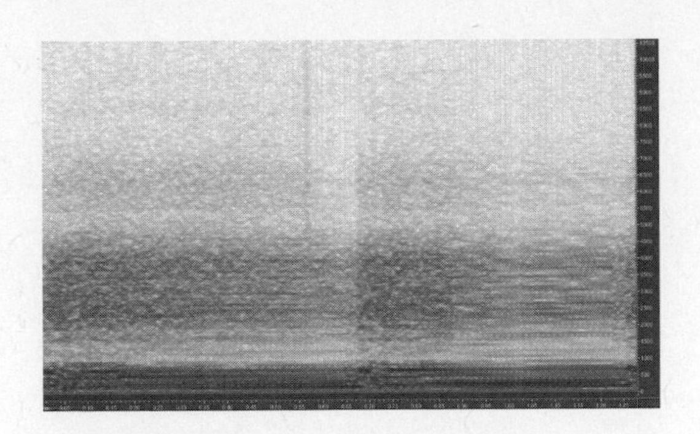

Fig. 9.1. Black Sabbath.

of additional energy around 6.3 kHz; in the Judas Priest example (figure 9.2) the energy stops abruptly around 5.8 kHz. From the late period, the Grave example (figure 9.3) shows energy through 7.5 kHz and the Winters Bane example (figure 9.4) significant energy up to 14 kHz, a range beyond the capabilities of most acoustic instruments. Further, both the periodic and aperiodic contents of the earlier examples stop abruptly at their end points, while all of the energy in the later examples seems to fade into softer and softer formant-like bands.

Perhaps more important is a band of energy with high noise-to-harmonic content in the low range or midrange of the spectra of all samples; this formant occurs lower in the earlier examples than in the later examples. In the Black Sabbath example (figure 9.1) the formant runs from nearly the bottom of the spectrum to 800 Hz and is terminated by a sharp notch from 800 to 1500 Hz. In the Judas Priest example (figure 9.2) the formant runs from nearly the bottom of the spectrum to 900 Hz and is terminated by a notch from 900 to 1700 Hz. The later examples show a rather different pattern. The Grave and Winters Bane examples (figures 9.3 and 9.4) show far less energy below 1000 Hz relative to the rest of their spectra than do the early

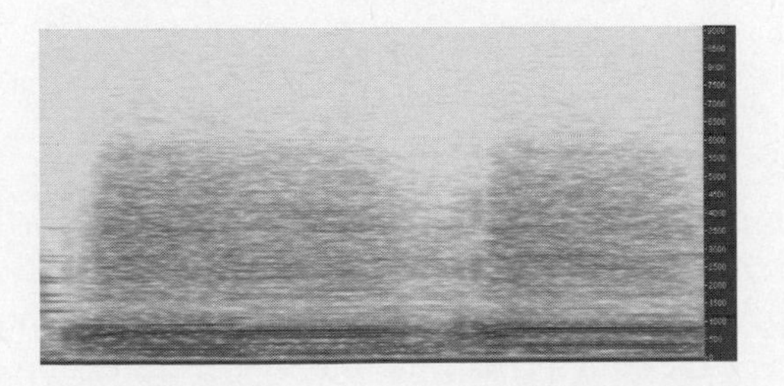

Fig. 9.2. Judas Priest.

Fig. 9.3. Grave.

period examples. In the Grave example, a noise formant exists from about 1.7 to 4 kHz; a notch terminates this noise formant at its top end, from 4 to 4.5 kHz. In the Winters Bane example, a noise formant is located from 2 to 6 kHz; a notch terminates this formant at its *bottom* end, from 1.5 to 2 kHz. In sum, the earlier examples have a noise formant below 1.5 kHz, and the later examples have a noise formant above 1.5 kHz.

Dynamic-Temporal Envelope. The dynamic-temporal envelope demonstrates a signal's amplitude change over time. To examine the difference in the envelopes of early and late guitar timbres, we sampled isolated examples of unmuted, single-note runs. Guitars (and other impulsive instruments; see below) show a characteristic amplitude spike during the initial attack of a note and a characteristic decrease in amplitude at the decay end of a note. These features are greatly lessened in both the early period examples (Judas Priest) and the later period examples (Winters Bane), with attacks still partially visible in the Judas Priest and virtually nonexistent in the Winters Bane example. Figure 9.5 shows a spectrogram of three separate attacks in

Fig. 9.4. Winters Bane.

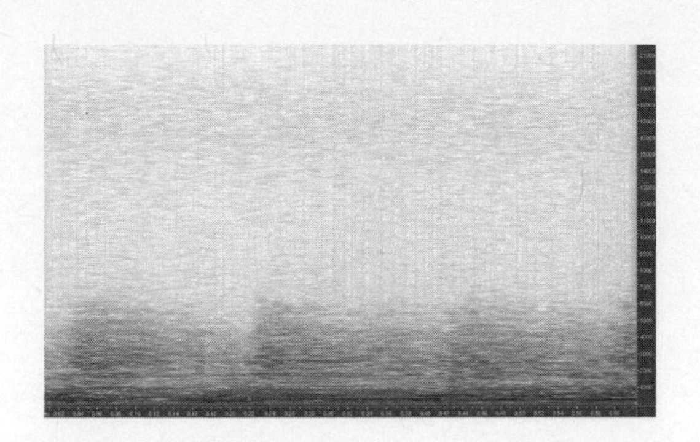

Fig. 9.5. Judas Priest: spectrogram of three separate attacks.

the Judas Priest song. While much less evident than the attack of an undistorted guitar, the attacks are still slightly visible at .22 and .42 seconds. Figure 9.6 plots amplitude (measured in volts) against time for the same sample and illustrates the same attacks. Figure 9.7 illustrates the transition from one note to the next in the Winters Bane sample; the transition occurs at .25 seconds, but the occurrence of a new note is noticeably *un*marked by an visible attack; the voltage plot in figure 9.8 illustrates the same information at 120 milliseconds. In sum, both examples have a flatter dynamic envelope than one would expect in an undistorted guitar, but the later example is far flatter.

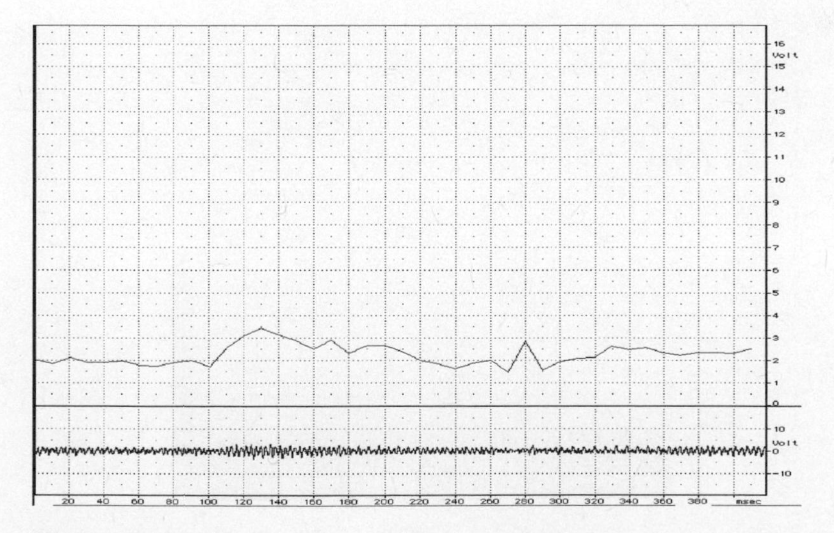

Fig. 9.6. Amplitude plotted against time for the same three attacks.

Fig. 9.7. Winters Bane: note-to-note transitions.

Discussion

Energy Placement and Noise. The results of our analysis provide insight into specific qualities of heavy guitar timbres as well as the general connection between acoustic and perceived events. Our search for acoustic elements in the target examples that changed over time identified the prominent noise component of the timbre to be key in provoking the sense of "heaviness" for which the genre is named; this result is consistent with the belief of metalheads themselves that noisy textures are heavier. More interesting, however, in regard to the relationship between the acoustic and the per-

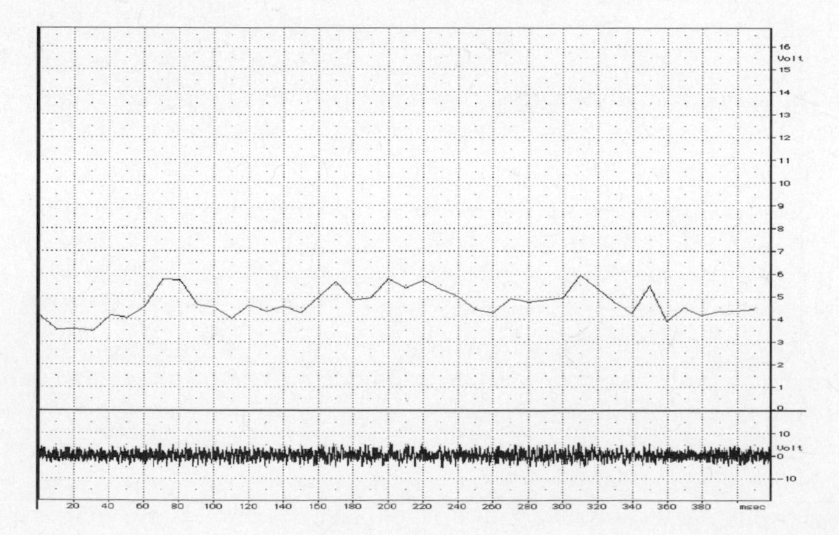

Fig. 9.8. Winters Bane: voltage plot.

ceived worlds is the fact that the quality described by informants as becoming "heavier and heavier" over time translated acoustically into a frequential difference as well as an intensity difference.

The puzzle, in other words, is this: metalheads affirm that they hear a quality X, heaviness, that defines the genre that contains it, a genre that must demonstrate greater X—that must increase in Xness—over time. If X were "brightness" (presumably a timbral quality), then over time the music's timbre would become brighter; if X were "syncopation" (presumably a rhythmic quality), then over time the music's rhythm would become more syncopated; the nature of the *pattern,* the kind of augmentation described by "increased X," depends entirely on the identity of X. Thus, if the intention is to discover an acoustic correlate to a perceived quality by applying listeners' descriptions of a *change* in that quality, not only is the quality unknown but the nature of its change is unknown as well. The researcher must therefore isolate acoustic features that (1) together provoke some perceived quality and that (2) intensify together according to the various parameters implicated in their configuration.

Since metalheads described the perceived quality of heaviness as increasing, we expected to find an acoustic conglomerate of features whose particular timbral distinctiveness would be emphasized—made more distinctive—over time. If the quality of "heavy" translates into the presence of acoustic noise, then heavier must translate into *more* noise. But what is more noise? Is it louder noise? Is it broader-band noise? Rather than a simple increase in the noise-to-harmonic ratio of the sound—that is, rather than the noise becoming louder relative to the non-noise elements of the sound over time—the noise in heavy guitar timbres changed frequency location as well. Acoustic noise provokes a sensation that is called "heaviness" by listeners, but an increase in that sensation is not simply *more* noise or *louder* noise but—perhaps more prominently—noise that is *different* in location relative to other elements.

The correlation of an intensified sensation of a timbral quality with a frequency change is significant in regard to efforts to connect listener descriptions with acoustic structures. Robert Walser (1993; 1991) has observed that one of the main effects of distortion in power chords is the expansion of the guitar's perceived frequency spectrum. Walser reports that, on the one hand, the distortion in power chords produces "resultant tones," the perceived impression of energy below the acoustic fundamental of the vibrating strings; on the other hand, the distortion strengthens the upper harmonics of the signal. With respect to the upper range of the frequency spectrum, our research confirms that distortion strengthens the upper harmonics of the guitar's frequency range; further, we observed that timbres perceived as heavier have greatly increased upper harmonics compared to those perceived as lighter. The situation with respect to the lower part of the frequency range is more complex. Resultant tones are a perceptual—rather than acoustic—feature that would not be depicted in the spectrograms of the guitar samples. While resultant tones are not clearly audible in the samples we have examined, our data show that the perceptual quality of heaviness is related to a change in the location of energy in the frequency spectrum. The correlation of the simple linear gradation of perceptual heaviness with the complex change in size and location of the noise formants is one important result of this research; investigation of this correlation is clearly not exhausted by this study and requires further examination.

Dynamic Envelope. Sharp attacks and marked decays are associated with tones from impulsively stimulated instruments, whereas tones from instruments excited by a constant source of energy to their main vibrating element, usually through bowing or blowing, are characterized by much flatter dynamic envelopes. Guitarists in heavy metal and other kinds of popular music prize distortion for its ability to add not just noise but sustain to the instruments' timbre. Distortion allows the guitar player to let notes ring almost indefinitely, a feature only achievable without distortion through devices called compressors. But the added sustain that distortion provides has other consequences as well; attacks are flattened, and the final release of the note is foreshortened considerably. In sum, distortion simulates the conversion of the guitar from an impulsive to a sustained or driven instrument, and this transformation may be part of the acoustic correlate to the perceptual experience of heaviness. Walser has observed that the seemingly infinite sustain that distortion provides serves as an icon of "extreme power and intense expression" (1993: 42), two values critical to heavy metal's aesthetic. Our research confirms Walser's conclusions and shows not only that the flattened dynamic envelope is correlated with the perceptual quality of heaviness but also that increases in the perceptual quality of heaviness are correlated with flatter and flatter envelopes.

These results speak to broad themes in the analysis of heavy metal in particular and auditory cognition in general. Discussing metal instrumental timbres, Walser cautions researchers to avoid over-reading the iconic relationship between the distortion of the sound (increased sustain, increased spectral range) and its meanings for metalheads (power and strength). The meanings of distortion are certainly tied to this iconicity, but, as Walser correctly asserts, they are not determined by it, and distorted timbres have been given meaning in different ways at different historical moments. Building on these ideas, we observe that hard rock, lite metal, and underground metal all employ distortion to signify "extreme power and intense expres-

TABLE 9.1 Tabular Summary of Results

Feature	Early	Late	Results: heavier timbres correlate with
Energy cuts off	BS: above 4.5 kHz (fig. 9.1)	G: above 8 kHz (fig. 9.3)	More high frequency energy
	JP: above 5.5 kHz (fig. 9.2)	WB: above 8.5 kHz (fig. 9.4)	
High-End energy	Ends abruptly (figs. 9.1 and 9.2)	Fades off in weaker formant bands (figs. 9.3 and 9.4)	A gradual fading of high end energy
Noise Formant Location	BS: Formant, 0–.8 kHz; notch, .8–1.5 kHz	G: Formant, 1.7–4 kHz; notch, 4–4.5 kHz	Formant of noise and harmonics above, rather than below, 1.5kHz
	JP: Formant, 0–.9 kHz; notch, .9–1.7 kHz	WB: Formant, 2–6 kHz; notch, 1.5–2 kHz	
Type of energy below 2kHz	Harmonics (fig. 9.1)	Noise (figs. 9.3 and 9.4)	More noise
Dynamic envelope	Weakened but still visible attacks (figs. 9.7 and 9.8)	WB: No attack is visible (figs. 9.5 and 9.6)	Flatter dynamic envelope

Key: BS = Black Sabbath
JP = Judas Priest
G = Grave
WB = Winters Bane

sion"; however, the quest for a maximally heavy distortion is specific to the speed/thrash tradition, and such "heaviness" signifies a range of meanings and qualities in addition to, or beyond, power and intensity. In English, the word "heavy" literally denotes great physical weight and can be used to connote a range of affective or valuative qualities dear to the speed/thrash tradition—seriousness, gravitas, grimness, threat, implacability, and durability. Of the five acoustic features that we see varying in a regular fashion between the 1970s and the 1990s, four correspond with Walser's observations about distortion in general rather than heaviness in particular. Our data on high-frequency energy and the gradual fading of that energy in the upper frequencies confirm Walser's assertions about distortion and increased spectral range. Our data on the flattening of the dynamic envelope confirm Walser's assertion about distortion's ability to increase sustain, and our data on the increase in the overall amount of acoustic noise confirm the general expectation that distortion leads to an increased noise-to-harmonic ratio. The shift of the formant of noise and harmonics above 1.5 kHz, however, corresponds neither to anything in Walser's work nor to the guitarist's common understanding of the acoustic effects of increasing distortion. For this reason, we suspect that these shifted formants, in concert with the other features, may be at least partially responsible for the quality of heaviness per se rather than distortion in general.

This result is surprising for two reasons. First, the shifted formant is unlike the other acoustic features in that there is no obvious iconic relationship between it and the qualities of heaviness that it evokes. Second, heavy metal guitarists often describe the heavy distortion sound of the 1990s as the "scooped-mids death tone" (Berger 1999: 58); the expression refers to the fact that some guitar players produce this characteristic sound by setting the tone controls on their amp or equalizer to increase the extreme high and low frequencies and decrease (or "scoop" out) the mid-range. It is possible that such filtering, in combination with other elements of the signal chain (the guitar's initial signal itself, the tone-shaping effects of signal processors, the amp and the speakers) would produce this formant—although not all underground guitarists adjust their equipment in this way, and such a result would be counter to many of the musician's own expectations about the overtone structure of his/her guitar tones. Future research is needed to confirm that this formant does indeed contribute to heaviness per se and to understand why this feature is heard as "heavy" by metalheads.

This discussion impacts upon larger issues in auditory perception. As we have suggested above, studies of timbre have traditionally relied upon researcher-modified sound samples and highly artificial experimental contexts to find correlations between acoustic and perceptual phenomena. This study has relied upon a unique feature of one music community (the consensus about the incremental changes of a timbral quality) to avoid problems of decontextualization associated with traditional research methods. We believe that fruitful inquiry in a variety of areas can be achieved by putting ethnographic evidence, either from published sources or original research, to the service of discovering culture-specific perceptual phenomena. Researchers in the area of cognitive ethnomusicology have begun to explore the cultural dimensions of sound perception, and we hope to contribute to this growing effort by illustrating how historical change, change in a music culture across time, can play a role in the processes of perception. Heaviness is a comparative term, and in any given listening act, the quality of heaviness experienced by a metalhead is informed by his/her past experiences with distorted guitar sounds. Our research emphasizes the significance not just of cultural context or immediate situated context but of the lived context of past musical forms for present perceptual processes. Understanding auditory phenomena as historically emergent within specific music cultures can help us to gain richer perspectives on perception and cognition more generally.

Acknowledgments

The authors would like to thank Art Thompson of *Guitar Player Magazine,* who provided information on distortion in guitar technology for a related project.

Note

1. While there is no question that lite metal is a product of the mainstream music industry, the relationship between underground metal and that industry is a complex one. Weinstein observes that in the early 1980s, speed/thrash was largely recorded by independent record labels and aired on college radio stations (2000: 48). While the music has almost never achieved significant commercial radio airplay, a number of important thrash bands signed major-label contracts in the late 1980s (Walser 1993:14), and independent labels have often signed distribution deals with majors labels. This said, much activity in underground metal does occur at the local level, and the actual relationship between the metal underground and the mainstream industry is neither one of simple opposition nor of simple identity.

References

BOOKS AND ARTICLES

American National Standards Institute (ANSI). 1973. *Psychoacoustical Terminology.* S3.20. New York: American National Standards Institute.

Berger, Harris M. 1999. *Metal, Rock, and Jazz: Perception and the Phenomenology of Musical Experience.* Hanover, N.H.: Wesleyan University Press/University Press of New England.

Fales, Cornelia, and Stephen McAdams. 1994. "Fusion and Layering of Noise and Tone: Implications for Timbre in African Instruments." *Leonardo Music Journal,* vol. 4: 69–77.

Hicks, Michael. 1999. *Sixties Rock: Garage, Psychedelic, and Other Satisfactions.* Urbana: University of Illinois Press.

Walser, Robert. 1991. "The Body in the Music: Epistemology and Musical Semiotics." *College Music Symposium* 31: 117–124.

———. 1993. *Running with the Devil: Power, Gender and Madness in Heavy Metal Music.* Hanover, N.H.: Wesleyan University Press/University Press of New England.

Weinstein, Deena. 2000. *Heavy Metal: A Cultural Sociology.* Rev. ed. New York: Da Capo Press.

RECORDINGS

Black Sabbath. 1971. "Paranoid." *Paranoid.* Warner Brothers 3104–2.

Grave. 1991. "In Love." *Into the Grave.* Century Media CM 7721–4.

Judas Priest. 1976. "Tyrant." *Sad Wings of Destiny.* RCA AYK 1–4747.

Judas Priest. 1976. "Victim of Changes." *Sad Wings of Destiny.* RCA AYK 1–4747.

Winters Bane. 1993. "Wages of Sin." *Heart of a Killer.* Massacre Records MASS CD 013.

CHAPTER TEN

Mixed Messages

Unsettled Cosmopolitanisms in Nepali Pop

Paul D. Greene

> This is an age of jazz. This is an age of having long, tangled hair, and of [young men] wearing an earring, and of wearing caps backwards [with the visor in the back]. And it is also a period of rap. Some raps are known as *bhatti* rap and some are known as party rap. And some are meaningless raps. But at this moment, it is a time of *deusee* rap. Deusee rap!!
> Opening rap in "Deusee Rey Extended Mix," by Brazesh Khanal (in Nepali)[1]

Throughout Asia, the English word "mix" (or variants thereof) is being used today to characterize a new mode of musical borrowing and syncretism distinctive of several pop musics that have emerged in the 1990s. Earlier modes of pop music borrowing typically involved timbral, rhythmic, and melodic adaptations of both indigenous and foreign materials, in which contrasts between different musical elements were smoothed over so that they could be integrated into unified musical expressions. In contrast, the new "mix" music of India (Greene 2000: 545–546), Nepal (Greene 1999a; Henderson 1999), Japan (Condry 1999), Indonesia (Wallach 1999), and the South Asian diasporic communities (Manuel 1995) employs the latest sound-studio technologies to reproduce the precise timbres, rhythms, and tunings of sound bites of both foreign pop and indigenous music more precisely than ever before. Yet as these foreign and indigenous sounds come more sharply into focus in Asian soundscapes, their meanings and histories seem to be going *out* of focus. For one thing, a "mix" commonly takes the form of a sonic montage: abruptly juxtaposed musical styles heard in rapid succession that project only a weak sense of overarching form. In this "mix" configuration, foreign and indigenous sounds sometimes present themselves as inscrutable sound bites — snippets detached from their original musical and cultural contexts. Mixes typically celebrate sonic contrasts rather than attempting to reach or move the listener within any single musical idiom. Moreover, foreign sounds travel to Asia so quickly through radio, music television, recordings, and the Internet that they are detached from their histories and original cultural contexts and often present themselves as suggestive, intriguing, but ultimately underdetermined cultural indexes. This point is taken up below in the analysis of Nepali heavy metal, one of the elements in the mix. Both western pop and indigenous sounds become perspectival constructs, taking on a range of meanings and affective forces in different listener experiences. Mix music embodies new, understudied, and essentially postmodern musical aesthetics (in the sense of Manuel 1995) that have taken root in Asian and other world communities.

A leading genre of the new sound is the *remix,* which may be defined as a studio-produced reworking of a familiar song, often intended for dancing, in which a vocalist is heard before a shifting backdrop commonly involving several musical styles. In many cases remixes grow out of live DJ practices (see Fikentscher 2000). Remixes have become very popular in late 1990s Nepali pop, as has the general mix aesthetic. The urban valleys of the Himalayas have become echo chambers in which the precisely reproduced sounds of Nepali folk music, Tibetan *dung chen* sounds, Hindi and Nepali filmsongs, *Hindusthani* classical, heavy metal, rhythm and blues, jazz, reggae, disco, and other musical styles from both Nepal and abroad reverberate and are juxtaposed in studio-produced mixes. For example, the remix quoted above combines passages of rap, hard rock guitar, *lok git* (a Nepali folk-popular music), and folksongs from the Nepali Tihar festival in which young men seek the elders' blessings. "As people today like to eat mixed *chamal,* so I must offer a mixed sound," one studio musician told me.[2] Mix music breaks with the three older popular music traditions in Nepal—*adhunik git* ("modern song"; see Grandin 1989: 116–119), *lok git* (Grandin 1989: 123–129), and Nepali filmsong (Grandin 1989: 113–115), genres that also integrate many diverse styles but are designed to be organic, smooth integrations.

What does this new "mixed sound" mean? How does it function in the lives of young, urban, middle- and upper-class Nepali students, the primary fans of the music? What do young people think about as they listen to sounds that are unmoored from their histories? I will explore these questions ethnographically through listener experiences in the Kathmandu Valley and find that Nepali pop mixes reflect a specifically Nepali condition, one having to do with the new circumstances in which young urban Nepalis find themselves today. As they journey toward professional identities, they contemplate the many contradictory worlds—both traditional and highly westernized—in which they are expected to live and work in the new urban

Nepal. "Remix" characterizes not only their music and their soundscapes but also their imagination of contemporary Nepali urban society.

In Nepal the mix sound emerged from sound studios rather than through live disc jockeying. Mix music first became prevalent around 1993, and dance halls ("discotheques") employing live DJs did not become popular in Nepal until late 1996. The more traditional dance practices (such as *banbhoj* and *rodi*) have only recently incorporated pop music.[3] In 1992, Alesis began to market the ADAT, an affordable eight-track recorder (see Théberge 1997: 248–250) that brought the cost of multitrack recording technology on the global market below a threshold of affordability. According to Nepali sound engineers, recorders with at least eight tracks are the essential technology to manipulate and combine the many sounds that comprise mix music. Within a year there was an explosion of multitrack recording studios in the Kathmandu Valley, and studio production costs began to fall within the budgets of middle- and upper-class students in their teens and twenties. In large numbers, they began to produce mix music using now-affordable synthesizers, drum machines, ambient effects processors, and sound distortion devices. The new, high-tech mix sound became popular, and the leading record companies in the Valley also began to include remixes as a substantial portion of their output.

Part of the meaning of the mix sound therefore has to do with its high-tech nature. To an extent, the mixing *is* the message: the new music involves technologies and sound qualities that are new and intriguing in the Kathmandu Valley. Thus, studios are often pictured on album sleeves, and some studios have become familiar "brand names," which help their albums to sell. But the draw of technology alone does not explain the particular form that contemporary high-tech pop has taken, with its abrupt stylistic juxtapositions of traditional and western sound bites.

Although the new mix sound is self-consciously western influenced, it is not accurate to conclude that young Nepalis are trying to recreate a western society in Nepal. For one thing, listeners voice strong reservations about western societies, which they associate with crime, drugs, and family problems. Further, Nepali pop mixes are eclectic in the western styles that they borrow. In the mixed sound are heavy metal, rap, disco, blues guitar, reggae, and Latin dance music but not vocal blues, swing, punk, gospel, or country western, although Nepalis are quite familiar with these sounds through MTV and FM radio. Nepali pop is therefore different from contemporary Chinese popular music, in which one hears more of a rock 'n' roll sound with gritty rhythm and blues vocals, or Indonesian pop, in which one hears jazz or death metal (Wallach 1999).

At first glance, mix music may seem to be a musical compromise—a crossover marketing strategy to capture the interests of diverse listeners. But there is more to it than that. For one thing, mix music heightens musical contrasts rather than smoothing them over, thus reversing the usual strategy for making a crossover sound. Mix music does not gloss over musical difference; if anything, it *clarifies* the differences and contrasts between the many music genres Nepalis now listen to. Also, as Yubakar Raj Rajkarnikar, editor of Kathmandu's leading pop magazine *Wave,* told me, "Everyone listens to everything" that becomes popular there: heavy metal, rap, disco, *lok git, adhunik git,* Nepali folksongs, and Hindi pop songs. My own findings corroborate his: mix music cannot be called a musical crossover, because the youth market, although culturally diverse, seems not to be comprised of distinct music taste groups.[4]

Since Nepali pop mixes, like American rap music, involve deliberate musical discontinuities, the analytic work of Tricia Rose (1994) is a useful starting model. She proposes that Americans listening to moments of musical discontinuity, or "ruptures," in rap music respond by "dancing through adversity"—treating rupture as an opportunity for pleasure, self-expression, and prowess in breakdancing. But young middle- and upper-class urban Nepalis do not share the same general social conditions as the African and Latin Americans of Rose's study, whose communities and social lives have been ruptured through racist policies and actions. Rather, the Nepali listeners are members of a privileged class, most with strong ties to their home communities. Moreover, the pop dance craze is quite new in Nepal. My data suggest that Nepali mix music is more drawn into practices of meditative listening than dancing. The music functions as a thought-provoking backdrop for identity exploration in a changing, cosmopolitan Nepal.

In this chapter I explore the meanings of the new mix sound ethnographically through listener experiences. This is a study of "imagination as social practice" (Appadurai 1996), in which technology-facilitated imagining is analyzed not only as an escapist vehicle of class domination, or the coalescing of non-face-to-face communities like nations (Anderson 1983), or a strategy of creative resistance, but also as a general, everyday practice, in which a young person continuously constructs and reconstructs the self in an ever-changing plurality of social worlds. Exemplary of the analytic approach I take are the ethnographies of Sara Dickey (1989) and Mark Liechty (1995), poststructural anthropologists who have also studied large urban South Asian groups.

My method is to play pop songs for listeners and then follow the conversations as they move from musical topics into topics of identity, tradition, youth culture, and contemporary Nepal. By using music as an entry point into such discussions, I hope to trace out some of the common processes by which listeners, mostly young people, contemplate, find, or construct meanings in the music. I have conducted approximately 120 interviews, with an emphasis on students from three schools in the Kathmandu Valley.[5] I have also interviewed musicians, engineers, and record company executives, read pop culture magazines, and visited restaurants and shopping centers that young people frequent. Young Nepalis are very articulate and interested in describing their reasons for listening. I conclude that young listeners contemplate new Nepali cosmopolitanisms in the western sounds they reinterpret, as well as in other sounds, which in turn resist definitive interpretation by them. Although audibly quite distinct from earlier musics, the new mix music, as experienced by young Nepalis, reinvokes a trope from traditional folklore—the journey or trek—as a means of grappling with new, shifting social conditions.

Kathmandu Youth Culture

The fan base of Nepali pop is comprised of urban young people, mostly in high school or college, a group that shares certain social and cultural conditions that increasingly separate them from other groups in Nepal today. Nepali pop and Nepali urban youth culture both became distinct formations in the late 1980s and early 1990s, at a time when a disjuncture also emerged between flows of knowledge, technology, and music to and from different spheres of cultural life in Nepal (Appadurai 1990). State development programs have been accelerating (Pigg 1990), as has transnational commerce generally. With the advent of satellite television, MTV and other western music programs enter many Nepali homes. There has also been a spurt in education, including an especially strong dose of western culture and technology. As a result, young students today find themselves in a more western-influenced, technological world than their elders did (Liechty 1995). A similar disjuncture has also emerged between the upper and middle classes on the one hand and the lower classes on the other, since lower-class people generally do not attend these schools. As new technologies of sound production take root in cities, they are immediately drawn into the lucrative urban youth cultures but not into rural music production. In many ways, then, rapid cultural changes starting in and radiating outward from cities and urban schools have transformed the lives of upper- and middle-class young people, had less effect on their parents, and have hardly affected rural communities or the working class. Western popular music finds more resonance in some segments of Nepali society than others because of these different rates of cultural transformation.

At the same time, wealthy parents in Nepal's alpine villages have begun to send their children to urban schools in unprecedented numbers. The cultural diversity of urban campuses has increased, and young Nepalis, unlike their parents, increasingly find themselves interacting not only with members of their own ethnic and caste communities but also with people from Tamang, Gurung, Sherpa, Tibetan, Rai, and many other ethnic and caste communities. Nepal, a Hindu caste-based society with significant internal geographical barriers, has long maintained boundaries between people of different castes and ethnic groups. This has been changing rapidly in urban schools, and young Nepalis increasingly find themselves in a plurality of social worlds.

To be sure, ethnomusicologists are finding that similar disjunctures and broad social processes are emerging in urban youth cultures around the world. But as Appadurai argues, disjunctures take different forms in different cultural settings (1990). Nepali mix music is best understood in relation to a distinctively *Nepali* condition, which emerges as the country's traditional cultures encounter new global circumstances. It is beyond the scope of this article to thoroughly describe this contemporary Nepali condition. Instead, I will use music as an entry point into the concerns and issues facing young Nepalis today and in this way illuminate both the social functions of mix music and the contemporary Nepali youth culture.

Refunctioning Western Sounds: Heavy Metal in Nepali Pop

Although Nepali soundscapes are filled with western sounds, these sounds have taken on quite different meanings and associations, because they have become detached from their original western interpretive frameworks and histories. Two short anecdotes from my field experience should suffice to show this. I spent Christmas Eve of 1998 in the Thamel district of Kathmandu and found that Nepali merchants observed Christmas by playing back recordings of western rock and pop very loudly into the evening of Christmas Eve and all through Christmas Day. The most prominent sounds were the Beatles, Bob Marley, and Metallica. If what I would call Christmas music was conspicuous in its absence during a Thamel Christmas, it was perhaps equally remarkable in its presence in other contexts. I heard the melody of "Jingle Bells" used as filler music at a hotel telephone switchboard, played over the phone line until a connection is established. No one operating the switchboard knew the origin of the melody or its original words. In both cases, sounds were detached from their original cultural contexts and frameworks, such that both Christmas and a Christmas melody can be reconstructed quite differently in Nepal and given new meanings. Appadurai (1990) offers the insight that in the complex currents and crosscurrents of today's global cultural flows, some elements travel around the world at faster rates than others. Sounds travel especially quickly through electronic media, and since 1993 sound studios have allowed Nepalis to immediately and accurately reproduce these sounds in their mix music. But the original meanings, histories, and cultural frameworks of these sounds do not travel as quickly. Through this disjuncture, new meanings emerge.

As an American ethnomusicologist working in Kathmandu, I found myself continuously struck by new meanings of musical sounds that I felt I already understood. In most Nepali listeners' experiences, reggae does not bring to mind Jamaican Rastafarianism, nor is it heard as rebellious or countercultural. Instead, reggae is most commonly used as a persuasive musical setting for seductive love songs. My informants immediately identified rap in Nepali pop, but few were aware that rap was developed in American inner cities or that it originally served as a vehicle of social protest. Many were surprised to learn that rap originated in African American culture, of which they have various understandings. Remarkably, *all* were surprised to learn that it originated in working-class or lower-class communities. In Nepal, rap is a cosmopolitan, happy dance music that is never, to my knowledge, a vehicle of protest.[6] Although rap and reggae have been adopted by many disenfranchized subcultures (Lipsitz 1994), in Nepal they are generally associated with Western culture, technology, and freedom, and specifically with upscale Nepali weddings, discotheques, and picnics of middle- and upper-class youths.

Heavy metal is also a relatively new and underdetermined, yet now common, element of the Kathmandu soundscape. Nepali youths have listened to western heavy metal avidly since the mid-1980s.[7] They soon began to form heavy metal cover bands, such as Wrathchild, and perform at school functions and public festivities. This performance scene began to dry up in the 1990s, but young electric guitarists continued to practice heavy metal, and starting in 1994, with the band Cobweb, they brought heavy metal guitar sounds into Nepali pop. Although the sounds and imagery of heavy metal are quite accurately reproduced, I find that the music is taking on quite different connotations. In an advertisement for their first album (figure 10.1), Cobweb included imagery typical of western heavy metal but departed from the western model by describing themselves as "devoted musicians out to conquer your heart" with "heart winning music." This ad, which marks the emergence of what is today Nepal's leading heavy metal

Fig. 10.1. Advertisement for Cobweb album, *Anjaan* (Wave 1994).

band, suggests that heavy metal has taken on nuanced meanings in Nepal. In this case, heavy metal is promoted in much the same manner as sentimental songs or *adhunik git*.

The heavy metal sound functions as a prestige marker, as do many elements of western cultures, especially those involving technology. It is a lifestyle component that marks one as sophisticated and cosmopolitan, much like using English words or wearing western fashions. But there is more to it than that. I decided to study the meaning of heavy metal sounds in Nepali listeners' experiences. By comparing my findings to those of Weinstein (1991), Walser (1993), and Berger (1999)—who study heavy metal generally, and guitar distortion specifically—I set out to determine to what extent heavy metal sounds occupy semantic spaces in Nepal that are similar to those in western musical cultures. I found that heavy metal in Nepal occupies a much broader, less clearly specified space, and it is a vehicle for some markedly different affective experiences. In general, it is about catharsis but not transgression.

Since, as Walser says, "the most important aural sign of heavy metal is the sound of an extremely distorted electric guitar" (1993: 41), a first step was to determine whether the distorted guitar in Nepali pop is also recognizable as a musical sign to Nepali listeners. I designed a series of listening tests that I conducted on over sixty listeners: I played segments of Nepali remix music, asked listeners to identify shifts in musical style, and then asked them to name the musical styles of the segments they heard. I found that heavy metal was indeed easily recognized by most Nepalis, usually by name.[8]

Interviews revealed that heavy metal in Nepal is a music of the upper and middle classes; it is rarely heard as an aggressive sound; and it is almost never heard as a transgressive or "dangerous" sound. This contrasts with the fact that heavy metal originated in the western working classes (Walser 1993: x) and continues to speak to working-class frustrations (Berger 1999: 66–67), although it has also achieved a wider fan base.[9] Further, much of the performative and listening pleasure in western heavy metal seems to lie in the fact that it offers aggressive experiences of power (Walser 1993: 41–42). Western heavy metal affirms "identity via opposition" (Berger 1999: 265) and, in its exploration of the darker sides of life, can become a rebellious or "transgressive" voice, challenging dominant identities and institutions (Walser 1993: xvi–xvii). Western guitarists shock the established aesthetics by deliberately using heavy distortion, insisting that sounds that had always been heard as "noise" be reinterpreted as music. As heavy metal appropriates chords, figuration, and virtuosity from classical music, it crosses what many listeners feel are the "sacrosanct boundaries" (Walser 1993: xv) of classical music, "reworking what is now the most prestigious of musical discourses to serve the interests of what is now the least prestigious of musical communities" (ibid.).[10] Further, guitar soloists frequently break out of earlier conventions of style, playing at dazzlingly fast speeds and offering louder performances of pitched sounds with broader bandwidths than ever before heard. The power that many western fans experience in heavy metal is the capacity to break out of confining musical expectations and limitations—constraints that may be similar to those that they must face in their own social lives. To be sure, in the last decade heavy metal has been fused with more and more musical styles and has acquired some new meanings and functions. But the heavy metal sound has a history as a dangerous, transgressive, and empowering music, and this history has not yet been erased.

In Nepal there is no history of hearing heavy metal as transgressive or dangerous. For the most part, listeners laughed when I asked if the distorted guitar made the musicians sound dangerous. For one thing, although talented Nepali pop guitarists reproduce western classical elements of heavy metal music fairly accurately, Nepali listeners generally do not recognize the western classical style in the music.[11] Therefore, heavy metal in Nepali pop *cannot* be heard as transgressively appropriating western classical music. Further, young Nepalis do not constitute a disempowered group seeking the thrill of transgressive empowerment. Instead, they are members of a stable, privileged class, and they already have access to the prestige of high culture. As students, they are on professional tracks, seeking empowerment through the approved channels of certification, study, and the respect of their social betters. Their dreams, as students, are not to overcome insurmountable barriers but rather to climb the social ladders that are open to them. It is hardly surprising, then, that heavy metal in Nepal has no history of association with Satanism (or any other evil spirit).[12] Conversations with young listeners moved fairly quickly from topics of music to critiques of the traditional culture of their families, but I found that these critiques were, for the most part, not countercultural or transgressive but progressive: "Nepali culture is not good for us. It is old now. We have to change our minds, to develop the country, to fit into the world community. To some extent, traditional Nepal does not fit into the world community. In our way, we are trying to change Nepal to make it better" (a young man interviewed with his friends at home). These young people are not rebelling against disempowering social structures. Instead, they generally say that Nepali culture, family structures, or gender relations should undergo some kind of change, in order that Nepal be "more modern" and "more technological" to "fit into the world community." (Compare this to Berger's [1999: 261–275] portrait of an Ohio metalhead and musician.)

Whereas determining some of the meanings of heavy metal that have *not* traveled to Nepal is fairly easy, determining what the sounds *do* mean there is more difficult.[13] I found that heavy metal is experienced as intense emotional expression, but it invokes a wider range of emotional responses in Nepal than in western cultures. In Nepali pop as a whole, one hears the heavy metal guitar employed successfully to express or intensify the expression of a wide range of emotions, including sorrow, grief, anger, and joy.[14]

PG: How does the electric guitar help the singer to give the listener a certain feeling?
It makes the song[15] more melodious. It is a tragedy song. The guitar tries to express more than the words. Like "Why did she depart from you?": more meaning to the song. Some emotion: very tragedy song.

PG: Is it angry?
Not angry *(laughs)*. We should listen to that song when we depart from our girlfriend.

PG: Does the guitar make him sound more dangerous?
(Laughs) The singer does not sound so dangerous. Just his heart is paining.

A teenage boy at the Pacific Academy

PG: Does your "destruction" patch make you sound angry?[16]
When I'm very angry I like to play the "destruction" sound. When I am relaxed, I use just delay and equalizer; phaser delay is very nice . . . I used to play "destruction" when I was fed up, . . . like when you're angry you speak loudly.

Professional session guitarist hired chiefly for Nepali pop production

Heavy metal gives many different kinds of moods. When you enjoy this kind of music you forget who you are. You think about wild things. If you are depressed by anything, then when you play that heavy metal, it gives you a different feeling in the mind. A feeling that is not angry. You can stop thinking about your own things [concerns]. People have different ways of enjoying heavy metal. Somebody [one person] feels no worry about things. He forgets everything. Somebody [else] feels very [much] joy. Or maybe crying of the heart, tragedy feelings. Just like crying, he misses some lady, whom he likes very much. Can be missing mother or father.

PG: So, is the heavy metal sound always about missing something?
Actually there are different types of feelings in the heart. Sometimes when I feel very bored, I want to go crazy [he shakes head and hands in the air] and that's the different feeling. A let-loose expression. You feel like Tarzan: aaaah! A remix singer

PG: How does the electric guitar help the singer to give the listener a certain feeling?
The song is tragic. . . . The guitar also brings the listener to a good mood—the purpose is to express sad feelings so you feel better later. An older male listener

Catharsis is a recurring theme in listener interviews about heavy metal. Perhaps the channel overflow and unflagging sustain that Walser (1993) foregrounds in his heavy metal analysis signifies to Nepalis a more general sense of emotional excess and release. In Nepali experience, therefore, heavy metal embodies catharsis without transgression.

This explains something I initially found quite puzzling in my personal listening experiences of Nepali heavy metal, especially of Cobweb guitarist Dipesh Mulmi's solos. Although he is quite talented and possessed of a strong rhythmic sense and creativity in improvisation, I began to feel that his solos lacked a kind of "edge" that I experienced in western metal solos. When multiple solos appeared in a single song, he often repeated entire passages verbatim. Often I found that the performative energy increased very little, if at all, from one solo to the next in a song. Although Dipesh's solos are rhythmic and angular, they often do not feel very climactic. This is partly because Dipesh frequently performs his more unusual, "noisy" sounds and angular fragments not in his solos but instead in his brief interjections in the vocal line. The song "Chahera," on the album *Cobweb,* comes to what I experience as a "sudden" end precisely at the point in an alternating pattern where a guitar solo would otherwise begin: Dipesh passes up an obvious opportunity to end the song with what in western heavy metal would most likely be the song's most intense, energetic section. I concluded that, in Nepali heavy metal, the guitar solo is no longer the site of the greatest buildup of performative energy, and, by design, it is not quite as aggressive. This also explains why Nepali sound engineers say that a primary concern in producing heavy metal is to make sure that the guitar does not obscure (that is, acoustically transgress upon) the other parts, especially the vocals. Their solution is to avoid the extremes of distortion found in western heavy metal, limiting the guitar timbre to a conservative, relatively narrow bandwidth that emphasizes the higher partials without producing the many lower resultant tones that would make the sound more muddy (cf. Walser 1993: 43).[17]

Inscrutability and Cosmopolitanism

Many of the musical styles that make up mix music are even less familiar or semantically determined than heavy metal. Further, because an overarching form is at best weakly projected in most mix music, clues about any fragment's meaning are usually not forthcoming from its musical context. It follows, therefore, that many of the sound fragments in a mix may present themselves to the listener as inscrutable sound bites. By "inscrutable" I do not mean "meaningless" but rather "difficult to fathom, obscure, and mysterious." I found that the inscrutable nature of borrowed sounds was one important new aspect of the experience of late 1990s Nepali pop. Again and again, I encountered sounds that in listeners' accounts had very unclear meanings.

It is not just western sounds that are inscrutable; some traditional Nepali sounds are as well. "Unbho Unbho," a song concerning a journey into Sherpa territory by the Nepali pop group Mongolian Hearts, starts out with twenty seconds of music from a Sherpa or Tibetan devotional ritual, in which one can hear the distinctive *dung chen* trumpet and cymbals. (Although Sherpas are culturally distinct from Tibetans in many ways, they share a strong heritage with Tibetans, and it was unclear to most of my informants whether the sounds heard in this passage were actually Sherpa or Tibetan in origin.) The sound bite then fades into a pop music texture featuring guitar, synthesizer, flute, and vocalist. (This passage is included as an online sound file in Greene and Yubakar 2000.) To be sure, it is not new to borrow Tibetan or Sherpa elements into Nepali popular music. For several decades, Sherpa and Tibetan rhythms such as *bhote selo* have been incorporated into Nepali popular musics such as *lok git*. But these elements have always been subtly reworked to fit their new musical settings and seamlessly integrated into the music. In "Unbho Unbho," the musical contrast is quite patent, and the Sherpa/Tibetan sounds, although recognized as such, are experienced by most listeners merely as exotic sound. In fact, it is not at all clear to most Nepali listeners what the sounds, although precisely reproduced, might mean in Sherpa/Tibetan culture. The passage does not open the listener up to share an experience of Tibetan or Sherpa culture, nor does it clarify what it is to *be* Sherpa or Tibetan. The passage is inscrutable. Even two Tibetan listeners found it hard to feel really connected to the passage: "Yes, we can hear the Tibetan sounds, and they have put in a few Tibetan words. It feels like the musicians are interested in Tibetan culture and sound. It makes us feel that Tibetans are included in Nepali pop, sort of. This is just an introduction to Tibetan culture, but it is better than nothing."

Although it is difficult to generalize about inscrutable sounds, I found that their presence in Nepali pop reinforced a spirit of *cosmopolitanism* that is especially strong in Kathmandu youth culture: young Nepalis are aware and very inclusive of the many ethnic groups in Nepal, but these groups retain their cultural distinctiveness and sometimes remain inscrutable. As mentioned above, because more young people have been coming down from rural villages to the cities for education, Nepali students today encounter more culturally diverse people than any other group in Nepal. Moreover, young Nepalis encounter students who have studied in Europe and the United States and are preparing themselves for jobs in increasingly multicultural settings. I played this song for many listeners and took notes as our conversation moved toward broader social concerns:

[One] must socialize more: make more friends, interact with many different people. Don't just sit at home. Get confidence, socialize, face the world! There is so much competition nowadays. Socializing is essential to face the competitive world.

PG: What are the dangers of staying at home too much?
The danger of not socializing: we won't be able to interact with other people. There may be a fear of going out. These days we have to be able to interact with other people. Ten years ago it didn't matter much because people [young women] thought of marriage only, and having kids. Today, we believe you should know the person [you will marry]. Avoid the dangers of arranged marriage.

A young woman

We want to learn about foreign cultures. Older people are not so interested. They are very conservative. It would be better if older people were more interested in foreign cultures. A group of young men interviewed at home

The "mix" quality of "Unbho Unbho" seems to suggest to listeners that, in Nepal, young people of quite different cultures *do* belong together and must find ways to interact despite patent cultural differences. But the song itself does not suggest a cultural merging. If anything, "Unbho Unbho" makes different cultures seem even more different because of the sharp musical contrast between Sherpa/Tibetan sounds and the ensuing Nepali pop texture. "Unbho Unbho" reflects on the diversity of Nepal and in this sense breaks with the longstanding popular music genre of *lok git* ("folk song") in which elements of Nepal's diverse traditional musics are organically fused together, bringing to mind the unified nation of Nepal. (In fact, *lok git* was initially cultivated at the state-run Radio Nepal in the 1950s.)

"Unbho Unbho" and other songs like it suggest that cultural syncretism in Nepali pop mixes sometimes functions not as a logical *and* but as a logical *or.* For some time urban ethnomusicologists, following Bruno Nettl's trailblazing anthology (1978), have analyzed syncretic music that combines, for example, traditional African polyrhythms with electric guitar, allowing the music to draw together two or more cultural worlds in the construction of a new urban identity: in this case, African *and* modern (Waterman 1989). In contrast, syncretism in "Unbho Unbho" brings to mind at least two different cultural identities: urban Nepali *or* traditional Sherpa. To be sure, one could argue that the Sherpa/Tibetan sound bite, although inscrutable to urban listeners right now, may be a first step toward a future merging of the two Nepali cultures. But for the time being, "Unbho Unbho" *clarifies* cultural differences. In the shift from the *lok git* typical of the 1980s to mixes like "Unbho Unbho" in the 1990s, Nepali music and culture have generally moved away from an urban model of syncretic fusion toward one of greater multiculturalism and cosmopolitanism, reflecting the new condition young urban Nepalis now experience.

As mentioned above, the differences between musical styles were coming more sharply into focus while it seemed that the meaning of each style was, in a sense going *out* of focus. A remix engineer offered the following insights:

PG: Remixes typically draw together many different musical styles. Why so many styles? Does this confuse the listeners?
It is not confusing. The response depends on what category the listener is in. If the listener is a fan of folksong, then he hears remix as a folksong. He doesn't realize the western influence in it. Those who are more involved in western lifestyle listen but don't bother about the wordings. They keep their curiosity on the music, and recognize it as a western music.

PG: Like a pun? Like a word that can be heard correctly to mean more than one thing?
Yes, exactly.

If this sound engineer is correct, then it seems that *misunderstanding music, not understanding music*, or *understanding music differently* are important modes of cultural experience in Nepal today. In a related vein, Manuel finds that "the sound of the folk drum or the quaint plinking of the Punjabi *tumbi* lute become at once quirky simulacra as well as symbols of ethnic identity" in South Asian diasporic communities (1995: 237). In the pop music of Kathmandu as well as South Asia's diaspora, traditional sounds are taking on multiple, complex, sometimes even contradictory layers of meaning, as young listeners today contemplate new, sometimes shifting relationships between their urban, westernized, cosmopolitan lifeways and their own traditions.

Musical Discontinuity and Journeys toward Professional Identities in "Deusee Rey Extended Mix"

In the remix ["Deusee Rey Extended Mix"] one can find thousands of different kinds of songs . . . joined in the one song. That is why such songs are very popular everywhere. If one finds any bad impact by such remix, I am the very first wrong maker or fool for that; after that Brazesh has done even more.

Kumar Basnet, in an email message to the author about his participation in "Deusee Rey Extended Mix" (1999)

Today in Nepal, the melody is lost in a flashy world. To appreciate the beauty of Nepali music you must meditate on the melody. The new generation has no patience to listen to music while sitting quietly . . . Modern living is also responsible:

less time to listen for enjoyment, more for listening to flashy moments, no sustained thought. The population explosion also means people have less time, must work more and be more interrupted, so they can't meditate on the old culture. They need patience to sit and listen. Today, if you do that you can't feed your children. The Walkman is also to blame. People hear music only in interrupted flashes while driving through the city. Prakash Thapa, pioneer producer of Nepali films (1998)

"Deusee Rey Extended Mix," as mentioned at the beginning of this article, is a remix produced at Music Nepal that combines rap, distorted electric guitar licks, folksongs, and Nepali *lok git*. The original "Deusee Rey" folksongs are part of the Nepali festival of Tihar, on the fourth day of which young men gather together in groups and go from door to door. They sing and call out the words "Deusee Rey," begging for blessings from their elders (Ghimire 1975). In the remix version, a young man travels around and pursues a blessing in the form of a reply to a love letter he has written earlier. (Excerpts from this song are included as sound files in Greene and Yubakar 2000).

In the two quotes above, two prominent figures in the popular arts of Nepal offer their opinions about the meaning and value of the song, or of mix music generally. I choose these two quotes because they articulate quite eloquently the discursive positions that young Nepalis take as they discuss mix music with me. Often, listeners move back and forth between positions that are close to the two articulated here.

Kumar Basnet, the leading *lok git* singer of the past few decades (Grandin 1989: 124) and also a pioneer of Nepali remixes[18] sees mix music as an appropriate continuation and adaptation of Nepal's musical traditions to the contemporary, westernized, cosmopolitan world. One listener articulated this position as she explained a passage of "Deusee Rey Extended Mix" to me. I asked her to explain why, in a single passage, one hears the "sweet," polite, *lok git*–styled singing voice of Kumar Basnet juxtaposed with distorted hard rock guitar fragments. She explained,

Because this is a modern song. It is modern, quite soothing, entertainment. It is modern culture.

So what is the modern Nepal?
Modern Nepal has technology and western influence, but also tradition.

This general discursive position seems to be strengthened by the fact that reworked versions of Nepali folksongs such as "Deusee Rey Extended Mix" are now selling better than either pure folksongs or completely western-fashioned pop songs (Yubakar interview, 1999).

In contrast, Prakash Thapa argues that the loss of musical continuity in remixes constitutes a fundamental breakdown of an essential meditative quality in the Nepali musical experience. Young Nepalis, articulating this position, do not frame the concern in the discourse of South Asian high arts (as Prakash Thapa does) but instead frequently invoke the concept of *mahasus:*[19]

> *Mahasus* means "realization" and "being convinced." After you are convinced you feel it. For example, we have realized it is the right thing to focus on one melody . . . You are convinced of happiness, or convinced of a decision . . . Music can convince people: to divert from the worriness, or to stop ruining your life. Sometime when I have a big worry, I think, I have to give up and die. But a friend may come and say this Sanskrit *sloka* says this, or a song says this and that. I think of these things . . . If music is played in a disorderly way, it won't work.
>
> An urban listener in his thirties

An important purpose of music, in many listeners' experiences, is to achieve a target emotion or experience a comforting realization by meditating on words or melodies that "convince." Although *mahasus* comes up often in discussions of other musics, listeners, even the most avid fans, rarely use the term to describe mix music. Remarkably, 83 percent of my informants (primarily urban students in their teens and early twenties, representing both genders and several social classes, ethnic groups, and caste communities) disagree with Kumar Basnet's claim that remixes are unified expressions (many musics "joined in the one song"). Further, listeners say remixes do not really continue folk traditions, and 76 percent say that remixes are influencing Nepal in bad ways. Remixes draw attention away from the country's real folk heritage and if anything are part of a splintering of Nepal's diverse cultures.[20] Ironically, young Nepalis are typically quick to critique the very mix sound in which they find much pleasure, and with which they now saturate their lifeways and soundscapes.

Playing "Deusee Rey Extended Mix" for young Nepalis quickly brought up issues of musical continuity, cultural tradition, technology, and westernization. Listeners typically offered ambivalent opinions on these subjects, sometimes shifting back and forth between positions, as did this business student:

> *PG: Is this remix a good or bad thing?*
> Remix is change. We need change, that's all. Westerners [tourists] come to Nepal for a cultural change. Maybe they adopt something good from Nepali culture. We're doing the same thing. Change can be good or bad. We are tired of our culture. It is very traditional, very Buddhist. Change is good. Not that we completely adopt your culture [i.e., western culture], but we like it. Change is good.

His apparently contradictory remarks ("change is good," "change can be good or bad") suggest that he is searching, as he speaks, for a position, a stance in relation to the confusing, contradictory, and continuously changing expectations of the traditional and the westernized worlds he finds himself in. Western cultural influence, technology, and heightened multiculturalism have clearly brought about positive changes, but in their wake have come drug problems, family problems, and even gang warfare in the late 1980s (*Wave* 1997). He likens himself, and young Nepalis generally, to the soul-searching western tourists who, since the 1960s, have come to Nepal to explore and carefully select elements from another culture to incorporate into their own lives. Listeners like this business student are not finding the sort of *mahasus* described above. Nor are they seeking unified musical statements such as those of *lok git,* which more smoothly integrate diverse musical elements from traditional Nepal and the West, and which may come to constitute a national sound (a charter goal of *lok git* as it was initially cultivated at the state-run Radio Nepal). Rather, the new discontinuous music inspires practices of free association, in which individual listeners contemplate the concerns and conditions facing young Nepalis today. Listeners are not so much fashioning a culturally unified Nepal; instead they are contemplating multifaceted, cosmopolitan selves—selves that can function in a new, "translocal" Kathmandu (Liechty 1996).

"Deusee Rey Extended Mix" is an exceptionally thought-provoking backdrop for identity contemplation because it is remarkably heteroglossic. Like the western novel as analyzed by Bakhtin, the mix presents the listener with a series of performed personae to consider and to possibly identify with. Whereas most *lok git* or *adhunik git* songs typically feature a single performer, and filmsongs involve at most two lead singers, "Deusee Rey" involves four lead vocal soloists, each performing a distinct persona, and several other voices as well. Furthermore, the remix leaves unspecified how the different personae are interrelated. For example, the rapper (Brazesh), the *lok git* singer (Kumar Basnet), and a third voice, Madan Singh, although clearly quite different, all seem to perform the persona of a love-stricken protagonist seeking a reply to his love letter. And since part of the reply he seeks is the blessing of her father, the recurring passages from the original *deusee* folksongs, as well as the group of young men one hears calling out "deusee rey!" can also be interpreted as performances of the protagonist's voice.

As sonic embodiments of the protagonist, each voice is a likely candidate for a listener to identify with, yet each brings to mind a different genre of music, and each embodies a different affective position with regard to the shared narrative of pursuing a young woman/blessing. The rapper persona is assertive, even demanding ("I traveled from Omugle to Sailung and Kuleshwar to Bhashmeshwar, from Baneshwar to Tripureshwar and from Dharahara to Ghantaghar. Where else haven't I been, to receive the reply of my love letter?"); the *lok git* persona is polite, sweet, even imploring ("Queen of the earth and your youthfulness, I will give this life to you. After making both hearts beat as one, please don't leave from me now on");

folksong choruses frame the request in traditional Nepali imagery and concepts ("Let's laugh and play, gathering in the paddy dance [*rodi*]. Let's make a love with full strength and desire"). The song offers not a single affective and cultural response to an unfolding narrative but a range of responses and a range of responders. It is not designed to inspire a single *mahasus;* it involves many different acts of convincing as well as a variety of personae doing the convincing, and being convinced. Sometimes the singer tries to convince the young woman to marry him; sometimes the singer tries to convince her father to bless the union; and sometimes the protagonist seems to be convincing himself (in the folk-styled chorus "As I am a Gorkha soldier, I will definitely marry her").

Young Nepalis describe the listening experience as a journey (see also Feld 1996), thus reinvoking a metaphor and narrative structure common in Nepali folklore (see Lienhard 1992). I asked one young man why there were so many different musical styles in the remix "Deusee Rey." He invoked a metaphor of movement to explain: "People these days can't stay in one place for even half an hour. We get lost listening to the same music for some time. We can't do it—it makes us dumb. I, for example, can't sit in one place for a while. I must move to many places. . . . Teenage life is like riding a motorbike through a city." Several comments like this one lead me to interpret mix music as a kind of multifaceted urban architecture that listeners wander through, a sonic reflection of Kathmandu comprised of various ethnic and cultural spaces, each with its own distinctive soundscape. Further, many Nepali pop songs, including most of those analyzed in this article, involve or tell the story of a journey or a trek. In this vein, it is worth noting that my informants described the freedom to travel and wander around the city as one of the important new freedoms granted to young people in Nepal today:

PG: As a young person, do you have any new freedoms, which young people in the past did not have?
Yes, we can roam about everywhere we like.
We can sit with girls and talk with them.
We are more independent to make decisions. If we want to study or play we can do so.
We can roam about with girls, and wear different types of clothes.

Sixteen-year-old boys at the National View College

Moreover, mix music has actually *become* part of the urban environment that young people are wandering through. Played back in countless places, it is now a kind of expandable and retractable architecture, mapping and remapping social spaces in homes, college hostels, marketplaces, parties, and picnics. Approaches developed by Schafer (1977), Feld (1996), and others may be helpful here: to consider music not only as a code or symbol complex to interpret but also as architecture, environment, landscape, or place, perhaps with only a weak sense of temporally projected form (see also Sterne 1997 and Greene 1999b: 476–484). Nepali mixes are designed to bring to mind various generalized social spaces through particular styles of music that can be heard to index those spaces in various generalized ways. The listener is invited to contemplate identity issues before a variety of backdrops, as if on a journey.

In "Deusee Rey," for example, a listener is invited to find herself or himself in traditional folk culture (through folksongs), in "the West" as a general category (through rap), and then in one of Nepal's new discotheques (through the beat). A sense of multiple distinct spaces is reinforced through the use of digital effects processors, which help to "situate" the listener in various generalized places, such as a small room, a valley in the mountains, or a concert hall (Greene 1999a; see also Feld 1996: 98). Mark Liechty also finds that Nepalis explore and imagine Nepal in terms of various shifting places, including "nowhere places" (1995, 1996). Through music, film, and television, Nepalis both imagine themselves and find themselves in not only traditional Nepali but also imagined foreign places, including hip-hop and heavy metal cultural settings or even New York street gangs (*Wave* 1997). The shifting spaces of mix music variously limit and open up the listener's imagination, in some ways inspiring pleasurable but escapist fantasies, and in other ways inspiring constructive reflection on the new, cosmopolitan Nepal.

I found that Nepali mixes are not merely a crossover marketing strategy or a simple westernization of Nepal's music. Whereas earlier listening practices involved imagining Nepal as a unified national community, the new mix sound breaks with the "unified" aesthetic, perhaps reflecting instead Nepal's more recent slogans of progress (*bikas*), such as "unity through diversity." Mixes are not strategies of resistance, for young middle- and upper-class Nepalis instead seek empowerment through approved channels. The ever-changing quality of mix music may reflect the fact that this search for empowerment is a very active and responsive one, taking Nepalis back and forth between many cultural worlds as they respond to the shifting global flows of technologies, information, goods, sounds, images, people, and foreign capital (Appadurai 1990) on which Nepal is dependent. Mixes do not prescribe cultural identities from above, nor are they rebellious self-expressions of a youth culture from within. They are the pleasurable tools that young Nepalis use to imagine, create, and recreate the spaces in which they contemplate and construct their own identities. Mixes situate them in the several, contradictory, cultural worlds that are on their minds as they journey toward professional identities in a new Nepal.

My method—playing music for young listeners and following the conversation into subjects of youth culture and identity—naturally led me to the patterns of discourse in which Nepali pop mixes are embedded, and in which they take their meanings. But despite my emphasis on discourse analysis, I do not want to leave out one of the important new functions that mix music has taken on: providing a kind of dance music at urban parties, college picnics, and in Kathmandu's new discotheques. One evening, my guide and I paid an exorbitant fee of 300 rupees each, stepped behind a gate guarded by sentries, and spent a few hours at Kathmandu's Sun Moon Discotheque. The interior was like a western disco, with flashy images on the walls, a disco ball, a bar, and a giant mirror on one side of the dance floor. At first, no one was dancing. But at ten o'clock, two young women entered the dance floor and began to dance, incorporating standard "disco" gestures of the sort often seen in Nepal's and India's film-song-and-dance numbers. They danced side by side, facing the mirror, watching themselves move. After a few minutes, two young men entered the floor, and one of the women left. The three dancers formed a symmetrical triangle, still looking at the mirror and moving up and back together as a unit in coordinated "filmi" dance patterns. In time, more people entered the floor, and it gradually became more difficult for them to see their own reflections. But this instance of dancing before the mirror, which I suspect is not an isolated one, strengthened my impression that guiding self-reflection is an important purpose of the music. Attuning themselves to the unifying dance beat, young Nepalis reflect on themselves, and they dance. Perhaps they are doing something analogous to "dancing through adversity," as described by Rose (1994): they are dancing, thinking through, and even finding pleasure in the identity issues that arise in today's urban Nepal, and in the many contradictory and ever-shifting cultural worlds in which they now live.

Acknowledgments

This chapter originally appeared in *Popular Music* 20(2): 169–188 and is reprinted with the permission of Cambridge University Press.

This field project was funded by grants from Pennsylvania State University. I would like to thank Professor Gert-Matthias Wegner, Chair of the Kathmandu University Music Department, and research assistant Mr. Shamsher B. Nhuchhen-Pradhan, Esq., for their generous help and guidance. I also wish to thank my co-participants on the panel "Sound Engineering as Cultural Production" at the Society for Ethnomusicology's 1999 meeting in Austin, Texas: Cornelia Fales, Thomas Porcello, Boden Sandstrom, and Jeremy Wallach. Our discussions on and surrounding this panel were very stimulating and helpful.

Notes

1. Contained on New Media's *Mega Mix* album, produced at Music Nepal in 1998. Excerpts from this song, including this passage, are included as sound files in the Nepali pop magazine *Wave Online* (Greene and Yubakar 2000).

2. *Chamal* is uncooked rice. Nepalis mix together different kinds of rice, cook them, and serve them together with lentils, other vegetables, and spices.

3. *Rodi* is a traditional folk dance of the Gurung people in Nepal, in which boys and girls dance together, sometimes as a prelude to romance or marriage. A *banbhoj,* or "picnic" (literally "forest feast"), is a major social event in schools and colleges in which young people play music and dance. The *banbhoj* practice emerges out of a longstanding tradition of having a party after making an offering or animal sacrifice at a major temple. This is why many such picnics take place near devotional or pilgrimage centers. Most are out in the woods, separate from the institutions and spaces of daily cultural life, but today there are also several designated picnic centers that are not located at temples.

4. Yubakar theorizes that there may be a small, emerging subculture of fans of western heavy metal, since he finds that some young Nepalis write in with very specific biographical questions about western heavy metal artists only. But I believe that even heavy metal must be at most only a small, loosely defined subculture, because none of my informants gave any indication that they were aware of listener groups organized around this or any other music genre.

5. These are the National View College Higher Secondary School, the Padma Kanya Ladies' Campus, and the Pacific Academy. (A school that offers degrees past the tenth-grade certification level can call itself a "college.")

6. Young Nepalis do mention the explicit descriptions of sex in the western raps played back at discos. In my interviews I found that this music was heard not as a vehicle of a kind of countercultural rebellion but rather as a collection of liberal ideas about sexual freedom, which young Nepalis associate with the West. Thus, the Nepali experiences of western rap seems to reverse a process Feld identifies in western experiences of world beat: Nepali bodies are freed up by western rhythms rather than the other way around (see Feld 1988). The Nepali experience of rap undoubtedly has to do with the fact that many young people are rethinking traditional gender relations, critiquing traditional practices of arranged marriage, and marrying across caste and class boundaries. More work needs to be done in this vein.

7. The most popular metal or hard rock bands today, according to music vendors, are Metallica, Van Halen, ACDC, Led Zeppelin, Rage Against the Machine, and Def Leppard.

8. I also found that its most identifiable feature in Nepal is the distorted guitar, which, as one listener said, is "the key to recognizing heavy metal." From responses to additional questions I was also able to conclude that heavy metal is not mistaken for or even likened to any traditional Nepali or Tibetan sound. I asked listeners whether the heavy metal distorted guitar brings to mind any traditional instruments, especially Tibetan ones such as the *dung chen,* an extremely loud instrument that like the distorted guitar produces a wash of angular sound waves and overdrives the sound receivers of any human ears in close proximity to the source (Pertl 1992). The answer was an emphatic no.

9. Only two of my informants knew that heavy metal originated in western working-class communities.

10. For those western listeners who don't feel that the boundaries of classical music are "sacrosanct," the appropriation of classical music may be experienced more as a practice of conformity with tradition than a transgression. Also, as heavy metal becomes an increasingly familiar sound in western soundscapes, it may lose its "edge" as a shocking, transgressive sound.

11. Western classical music is relatively rare in the Kathmandu soundscape, and none of my informants indicated that they heard any connection between heavy metal and western classical, inasmuch as they were familiar with the latter. When I asked about specific guitar passages, several listeners volunteered that the guitar

player sounded quite talented. Heavy metal is never dismissed as untalented music, but in Nepali experience it seems not to make a claim to the prestige of art music. Although listeners are unaware of the western classical influence, some of the guitarists know about it.

12. A new heavy metal group called Dristhy included a song on their first album, "Roopa Maheswaram," that summarizes the *Mahabharata*. Singer and guitarist Iman clarified that the *Mahabharata* is a good subject for a heavy metal song because it is about "war and aggression." It does not offer an evil spiritual message, however (*Wave* 1999).

13. To explore the meaning of the electric guitar sound, my first line of inquiry was to play passages of Nepali pop featuring heavy metal guitar and then ask listeners to describe the meaning or emotional quality of the guitar sound. For the most part, I got nowhere: listeners said that it was the singer who was responsible for the meaning and emotional quality of the music, not the guitarist. So I developed a new line of inquiry: I asked how the electric guitar helps the singer to inspire feelings in the listener. Such questions were much more fruitful, and patterns begin to emerge from the responses I received.

14. My Nepali research assistant, Mr. Shamsher B. Nhuchhen-Pradhan, summarized all of the heavy metal songs we could find and identified these primary target emotions.

15. The song is "Behoshima," one of Deepak Bajracharya's rare heavy metal songs, featured on the CD *Top of the Pop* (Digital Santana Records, Kathmandu).

16. "Destruction" is a name of a dedicated distortion effects processor. Whereas a common studio practice in western popular music is to play heavy metal guitar through amps and then mic the amps, in Nepal the guitar cable is plugged into one or more effects processors or pedals, which are then patched directly into the mixing console. Many guitarists don't own their own distortion pedals or effects boxes. Since the live heavy metal performance scene is no longer active, heavy metal has become more of a studio-based practice.

17. In their promotion of their first album, Dristhy band members claimed to offer a new, more distorted heavy metal sound, in which the vocals were *deliberately* "hard to hear" (*Wave* 1999). This shocking new sound, together with their explanations of it, may in time shift Nepali experiences of heavy metal toward that of western listeners. Dristhy band members had received musical training in the United States.

18. Kumar Basnet composed and produced remixes as early as 1994, although the genre did not become popular until a few years later. There are others who claim to have produced remixes earlier.

19. The Nepali *mahasus* is a cognate of *mehsus* or *mahsus,* a term that means "perceived, felt, or known" in Hindi, Arabic, Urdu, and other languages in the region.

20. Opinions about this song are commonly aligned along gender lines: young women are generally more optimistic about "Deusee Rey Extended Mix," and young men are more pessimistic. Perhaps this is because young women have less to gain from traditional culture than young men, who may therefore be more concerned about the decline of traditions.

References

BOOKS AND ARTICLES

Anderson, Benedict. 1983. *Imagined Communities: Reflections on the Origin and Spread of Nationalism.* London: Verso.

Appadurai, Arjun. 1990. "Disjuncture and Difference in the Global Cultural Economy." *Public Culture* 2(2): 1–24.

——. 1996. "Here and Now." In his *Modernity at Large: Cultural Dimensions of Globalization.* Minneapolis: University of Minnesota Press, 1–23.

Appadurai, Arjun, and Carol Breckenridge. "Public Modernity in India." In *Consuming Modernity: Public Culture in a South Asian World,* ed. Carol Breckenridge. Minneapolis: University of Minnesota Press, 1–20.

Berger, Harris M. 1999. *Metal, Rock, and Jazz: Perception and the Phenomenology of Musical Experience.* Hanover, N.H.: Wesleyan University Press/University Press of New England.

Condry, Ian. 1999. "Japanese Rap Music: An Ethnography of Globalization in Popular Culture." Ph.D. dissertation: Yale University.

Coplan, David. 1987. "The Urbanization of African Music: Some Theoretical Observations." *Popular Music* 7: 113–129.

Dickey, Sara. 1989. *Cinema and the Urban Poor in South India.* Cambridge: Cambridge University Press.

Feld, Steven. 1988. "Notes on World Beat." *Public Culture* 1(1): 31–37.

——. 1996. "Waterfalls of Song: An Acoustemology of Place Resounding in Bosavi, Papua New Guinea." In *Senses of Place,* ed. Steven Feld and Keith Basso. Santa Fe, N.M.: School of American Research Press, 91–135.

Fikentscher, Kai. 2000. *"You Better Work": Underground Dance Music in New York City.* Hanover, N.H.: Wesleyan University Press/University Press of New England.

Ghimire, M. P. 1975. "Nepalese Folk-Songs." In *Nepal: An Introduction to Nepalese Culture,* ed. M. P. Ghimire. Kathmandu: Sahayogi Press, 15–24.

Grandin, Ingemar. 1989. *Music and Media in Local Life: Music Practice in a Newar Neighbourhood in Nepal.* Linköping: Department of Communication Studies.

Greene, Paul. 1999a. "Engineering Spaces in Nepal's Digital Stereo Remix Culture." Paper delivered at the panel "Sound Engineering as Cultural Production," Society for Ethnomusicology annual meeting (Austin), 19 November.

——. 1999b. "Sound Engineering in a Tamil Village: Playing Audio Cassettes as Devotional Performance." *Ethnomusicology* 43(3): 459–489.

——. 2000. "Film Music: Southern Area." In *Garland Encyclopedia of World Music, vol. 5: South Asia.* New York: Garland, 542–546.

Greene, Paul, and Yubakar Raj Rajkarnikar. 2000. "Echoes in the Valleys: A Social History of Nepali Pop, 1985–2000." *Wave Online* (Nepal) 50. Reprinted in *Wave* 63(2001): 16–18, 21.

Henderson, David. 1999. "The Sound of the City (Kathmandu Remix)." Paper delivered at the annual conference *Asian Studies on the Pacific Coast,* 18 June.

Kumar Basnet. 1999. Email interview, 9 March.

Liechty, Mark. 1995. "Media, Markets, and Modernization: Youth Identities and the Experience of Modernity in Kathmandu, Nepal." In *Youth Cultures: A Cross-Cultural Perspective,* ed. Vered Amit-Talai and Helena Wulff. New York: Routledge, 166–201.

——. 1996. "Kathmandu as Translocality: Multiple Places in a Nepali Space." In *Geography of Identity,* ed. Patricia Yaeger. Ann Arbor: University of Michigan Press, 98–130.

Lienhard, Siegfried. 1992. *Songs of Nepal: An Anthology of Nevar Folksongs and Hymns.* Delhi: Motilal Banarsidass.

Lipsitz, George. 1994. *Dangerous Crossroads: Popular Music, Postmodernism, and the Poetics of Place.* New York: Verso.

Manuel, Peter. 1995. "Music as Symbol, Music as Simulacrum: Postmodern, Premodern, and Modern Aesthetics in Subcultural Popular Musics." *Popular Music* 14(2): 227–239.

Nettl, Bruno, ed. 1978. *Eight Urban Musical Cultures: Tradition and Change.* Urbana: University Press of Illinois.
Pertl, Brian. 1992. "Some Observations on the *Dung Chen* of the Nechung Monastery." *Asian Music* 23(2): 89–96.
Pigg, Stacy. 1990. "Disenchanting Shamans: Representations of Modernity and the Transformation of Healing in Nepal." Ph.D. dissertation: Cornell University.
Rose, Tricia. 1994. *Black Noise: Rap Music and Black Culture in Contemporary America.* Hanover, N.H.: Wesleyan University Press/University Press of New England.
Schafer, R. Murray. 1977. *The Tuning of the World.* New York: Knopf.
Sterne, Jonathan. 1997. "Sounds Like the Mall of America: Programmed Music and the Architectonics of Commercial Space." *Ethnomusicology* 41(1): 22–50.
Théberge, Paul. 1997. *Any Sound You Can Imagine: Making Music/Consuming Technology.* Hanover, N.H.: Wesleyan University Press/University Press of New England.
Wallach, Jeremy. 1999. "Engineering Techno-Hybrid Grooves in an Indonesian Sound Studio." Paper delivered at the panel "Sound Engineering as Cultural Production," Society for Ethnomusicology annual meeting (Austin), 19 November.
Walser, Robert. 1993. *Running with the Devil: Power, Gender, and Madness in Heavy Metal Music.* Hanover, N.H.: Wesleyan University Press/University Press of New England.
Waterman, Chris. 1989. *Jújù: A Social History and Ethnography of an African Popular Music.* Chicago: University of Chicago Press.
Wave. 1994. Advertisement for Cobweb album. *Wave* 2 (Nov.–Dec.), 21.
——. 1997. "Tuff Turf: Reminisces [sic] of a Lost Childhood," part 1 and 2. *Wave* 20 (July), 11–14; *Wave* 21 (Aug.), 18–22.
——. 1998. "The Influence: It's in the Name." *Wave* 28 (April), 36.
——. 1999. "Know Your Band: Dristhy." *Wave* 41 (Aug.), 21.
Weinstein, Deena. 1991. *Heavy Metal: A Cultural Sociology.* New York: Lexington.

INTERVIEWS CONDUCTED BY THE AUTHOR
Kumar Basnet. 1999. Email interview, 9 March.
Prakash Thapa. 1998. Interview at his home in Kathmandu, 12 December.
Yubakar Raj Rajkarnikar. 1999. Editor of *Wave,* Nepal's leading popular culture magazine, interviews with the author: 18 August 1999 at Hotel Utse, Thamel, Kathmandu; 19 August 1999 at the office of *Wave* magazine.

CHAPTER ELEVEN

The Soundscape of the Radio

Engineering *Modern Songs* and Superculture in Nepal

Ingemar Grandin

I will discuss here a case of musical engineering. The direct engineering involved may seem basic enough—straightforward mono recordings fed onto broadcasting and records—but it had far-reaching consequences. The location is Nepal, and the genre is locally called *adhunik git*—literally, "modern songs." The time period is essentially the years around 1975—stretched backward to 1960 and forward to 1991 or so (consequently, I will use the past tense rather than the ethnographic present).[1]

The processes through which these modern songs evolved, grew, and were engineered were defined by a number of seemingly rather distant conditions. The "unification" of the various small polities of the Himalayan foothills into the larger entity today referred to as Nepal was one of them. The government's process of taxing, at extortionate rates, the all-important agricultural production—strangling development and keeping Nepal poor (Regmi 1978)—was another. These two conditions helped produce a third: the dichotomy between Kathmandu—where taxes flowed in and the elite resided, and which had nurtured its own version of South Asian "great tradition" for centuries—and the rest of the polity. Add to this Nepal's close but often antagonistic relationship to India, and we have the basic matrix.

Let us start with the genre. Modern Nepalese song is a genre maintained and disseminated on recordings within this format: three to four minutes in length; strophic structure with a refrain-verse form; mostly romantic lyrics; well-known, solo, "star" singers interpreting the words; an accompaniment by predominantly Western instruments (strings, guitar, bass guitar) but with some indigenous percussion and melody instruments. To a student of the world of popular music, this all seems familiar enough. The genre looks like popular music in other respects as well: it was developed in close connection to the mass media, and it was (and still is) distributed widely to a mass audience.

But there are differences too. Discs were pressed in runs of some 300 to 500 copies—a figure that suggests the print run that a Nepali publisher might give to a book of poetry rather than a commodity produced by the profit-maximizing music industry. And while modern songs were indeed saleable commodities when they were finally issued on cassettes, rather late in their development, cassette producers and market considerations had nothing to do with the development of the genre.

As we will see, certain concepts come up almost automatically in a study of engineered music—music that is recorded for a medium and engineered so as to fit that medium's requirements; notions at play here include those of "market" and "commodity," "producers" and "consumers," "mass media" and "audience." Indeed, the steps seem to be short between "media," "popular music," and "the music industry," both empirically and in terms of conceptualization (see, for instance, Wallis and Malm 1984, Manuel 1988, Feld 1994).

The understanding of engineering in relation to the prevalent conceptions of popular music/music industry/commodification, then, is one key issue in the following discussion. The other major strand in the study is the role of politics and the state in musical engineering. To address this, I have put the standard notions aside and tried instead tools borrowed from Hannerz's study of cultural complexity (1992), the notion of superculture as proposed by Slobin (1993), and a Williams-inspired approach to musical economy (1977)—tools verbalized in such terms as mode of production, organization of production, patronage, and others.[2]

The development of a cultural infrastructure opens up new conditions for a "superculture." A superculture, according to Mark Slobin, is "an umbrellalike, overarching structure" (1993: 29) upheld by the "state and its institutionalized rules and venues" as well as the (music or culture) industry. Without going further into Slobin's own discussion, I can usefully adapt this notion to the Nepali context. First, the superculture acts as an "umbrella" over the different ethnic (regional) cultures, and ethnic cultural elements may be incorporated into it. In Nepal, quite a few ethnic cultures and modern songs clearly belong to the cultural umbrella, together with folk songs collected by professional folklorists. Second, officially sanctioned "national culture" (that is, cultural elements that promote an official national consciousness) is an important component. The development of national

Nepali culture was an important undertaking in our period (1960–1991). But national culture and superculture are not one and the same: third, the superculture also channels cultural goods from the outside (anything from Hindi film songs to western development rhetoric), and fourth, it includes dissonant countervoices (in our period, notably those of the leftist and democratic opposition).

Such a cultural creature was exactly what took shape in Nepal in those years. Did this mean, then, that Hindi film songs, or leftist propagandist songs, or ethnic separatist agitation, or rock 'n' roll proceeded to spread like wildfire throughout Nepal? It is now relevant to look at sonic engineering in two related senses. In a more narrow sense, "engineering" refers to the specific process whereby a certain technology is applied. In the case of modern songs, this means recording the music onto magnetic tape, transferring these recordings to discs, transforming the discs into radio signals, and the like. In a wider sense, "sound engineering" means "to plan, manage, or direct": to use sound "to execute . . . social strategies" (Greene 1999: 460–61). In other words, sound engineering becomes cultural engineering—the "purposive manipulation of the social organization of meaning," as Hannerz (1992:17) puts it. Such engineering was evident, for instance, when the Education Act of 1962 confirmed that among all of the languages spoken in the country, only Nepali should be used in education. The development of modern songs was very much a case of cultural engineering.

What this amounted to in actual practice will be examined in this chapter, including a brief introduction to the music. However, this discussion cannot be more than a sketch and should not be seen as a presentation of the empirical materials that the discussion is based upon.[3]

A few reminders to begin. Kathmandu, the uncontested political, administrative, and cultural center of the modern nation-state of Nepal, has always supported a rich musical life, including various traditional musics (percussion groups, flute ensembles, vocal groups), raga music of current North Indian variety, Western-type brass bands, and piano bars. What was not there was the (international) "music industry." Even the Gramophone Co., the Indian giant, was conspicuously absent. And attempts at cultivating Western-style rock/pop only caught on in the 1990s, and then in the localized shape of "Nepali pop" (see further Greene and Rajkarnikar 2000; Greene 2001).

Engineering New Music in the Orient

Modern songs were born and matured in Nepal before rock/pop became the hegemonic language of global popular music. In that cornerstone of popular music research, his 1971 work on "new music in Africa, Asia and

Oceania," Wolfgang Laade gave us a fascinating overview of what was engineered onto records in that earlier era. He finds much the same developments in "the whole Orient, from Morocco to India."

Throughout this area, large orchestras were employed to play film and radio music—orchestras where the unison playing of a Western string section provided much of the color, with accents provided by indigenous lutes and wind instruments, all to the accompaniment of local and Western percussion playing simplified, traditional rhythms (Laade 1971: 228–31). Heterophony and influences from Western strophic song characterize these melodies, which are often shaped periodically and based on traditional, local modes. Modern songs were well within Laade's purview, and what happened in the Himalayan valleys (bordering on, but not included in, the area surveyed by Laade) in fact points to much more comprehensive musical developments. These are cases of music being engineered, but not in the rock/pop fashion involving small groups actually constructing their music by multiple overlays in prolonged studio sessions, with the studio work of producers and engineers a key feature of the creative process. So what did the musical engineering amount to in the pre-pop-era genre of modern songs?

Ratna Records ESR-1—a four-song disc in the EP format typical of this Nepali label—is a good starting point. It is from 1969 (temporally bordering on what Laade studied), and three of the songs were recorded in Calcutta (as Nepali artists had been doing for a couple of decades by then). Though evidently the orchestra is quite large, the recording compresses it into one compact unit in which individual instruments appear as colors rather than voices. And floating on top of all of this is the singer's voice, the only individual layer to stand out clearly in the mix. But the fourth song was recorded at the studios of Radio Nepal with Nepali musicians. (This would henceforth be the normal practice: only songs for Nepali movies would be recorded in India.) Instead of the compact wall of sound of the Indian orchestra, the single instruments of the much smaller Nepali orchestra stand out clearly in the Radio Nepal recording. While the separation is so clear that one might think that the recording is in stereo (which it is not), the instruments are not allowed to detract from the priority of the voice. The singer remains foregrounded.

Engineering for Radio Nepal: The Classical Form of Modern Songs

The sonic engineering involved here was, at least in one sense, very simple: recording the orchestra and singer simultaneously, mixing down a number of mics directly in mono; transferring this from the master tape to a cartridge; and choosing among these cartridges for direct or taped broadcasting. But the role of the studio in modern songs cannot be reduced to what actually happened within its walls or within the process of recording itself. With the studio as a dedicated facility with recording technology and skilled personnel, a focal point for the whole creative process had been established.

In the studios of Radio Nepal, musical facilities were bundled with recording technology. Certain instruments were permanently in the studio and musicians were on staff. The Radio Orchestra used for the recording of modern songs in 1980 included eight violins, one cello, two Yamaha organs, bass guitar, rhythm guitar, mandolin, flute, and "Western drums," and there were full-time musicians for all of this equipment (setting up these facilities had involved retraining army band musicians, who could read music, into violinists).[4] This group could be expanded with a pianist "from one of the hotels" (the studio had its own piano), trumpet or saxophone "from the military bands," and so on. In addition, tabla, Nepali *madal* drum, sitar, accordion, mandolin, and vibraphone (there was one in the studio) are common on the recordings.

With the studio as the focal point, most of the musical engineering was done prior to the actual work in the studio. All of this pre-studio work—composition, arrangement, and so on—was planned and devised with the studio recording in mind. That everything was recorded at once meant that neither an individual mistake from a musician nor an imbalance in the mix could be corrected without repeating the whole performance. And to start with the arrangement, everything had to be worked out, or scored, before the recording.

I witnessed this process in a series of recordings with Amber Gurung in 1986. A large ensemble was not available for these recordings, but the basic ideas about how to work out the arrangement were nevertheless realized. First came a "sketch": only harmonium and tabla here; then a fuller arrangement where the harmonium and the tabla were complemented by guitar, electronic keyboard, and sitar. For each musician, Amber Gurung made the appropriate notation: chord symbols for the guitarist, Indian syllabic notation for the sitarist, Western notation for the keyboard player. In the simpler recordings, the harmonium had much the same role as the string section in a Radio Nepal recording: heterophonic "shadowing" of the vocal melody and some interludes. The keyboard assumed the strings' part of offering countermelodies and also took some turns as a melodic soloist.

Foregrounding the Voice

The standard practice for a modern song is to compose a melody for a preexisting lyric. A great many songwriters (*gitkar*) have contributed lyrics, typically presenting the reflections of one individual person upon the beloved.

The poetic genre of songs (*git*) includes certain conventions. A song will be metrically regular and probably rhyme, and it will be organized into an opening refrain (*sthayi*) followed by two or three verses (*antara*). Composition and engineering would then convert these paper songs into real ones.

Former studio musician Peter Karthak (1997) says about Amber Gurung: "He was the first Nepalese to blend East and West in Nepalese musical compositions, from three-verse songs to cantatas and longer works. He adapted to and drew from Nepalese folk, Indian classical and contemporary Western music and other schools. He taught and trained us, through his own compositions, on melodic patterns, musical forms, harmonic norms, chordal progressions, modulations and other styles, genres and disciplines."

Ratna Records ESR 110 (from 1976) gives a good glimpse of Amber Gurung's creolizing efforts at work. The first song takes its melodic ideas from a raga, though its harmony progresses steadily, jazz fashion, along the circle of fifths.[5] The second song borrows melodic ideas from folk songs, though with its melodic phrases expanded far beyond the folk song format. The opening song on side two again relies upon sharpened leading notes. Incidentally, these three songs illustrate what Amber Gurung and other composers took to be the three general styles of composition: one based on classical raga, one based on folk song, and a contemporary one.[6]

To the singer Narayan Gopal, it was clear what was most important in the art of modern songs: melody, lyrics, and the singer. This did not rule out other aspects, however. Chords, he said, are required to put life in the music, but the chord progression is part of the arrangement, not something to base the composition of the melody on. When the melody is composed, the arranger will make the progression from the melody. Without a good arrangement, Narayan Gopal said, a song will be like a vegetable dish without salt or other spices.

To stick to Narayan Gopal's metaphor, what he talked about and what we find in Amber Gurung's work as a composer and arranger can be seen as a musical recipe (Grandin 1984). I cannot go into a detailed examination of this recipe here; a somewhat fuller account is found in Grandin 1989. In the observations above on specific songs we have already witnessed aspects of this "recipe" at work. Key characteristics include nonrepetitive melodies moving over the accompaniment in short, repeated rhythmic figures; heterophony, countermelodies, chords, and harmonic progressions; one melody for the refrain, another for the verse(s), and then—as part of the arrangement—melodies for the "music," the instrumental interludes marking off the sung sections. Variation and diversity is built into this recipe. The exact composition of the orchestra varies from song to song (here flute and sitar for melodies, there accordion and strings; here tabla and snare drum, there congas; here a piano for the chords, there an acoustic guitar) and can include, for instance, an electronic organ entering only at the end, playing a total of three notes, or subtle shifts in instrument combination and figures in the repeated rhythmic patterns. The whole way of using the various musical resources and each detail in these songs seems to underline that this is music where melody is paramount. Recording practice, with its foregrounding of the melody of the human voice, gives further emphasis to this. As Narayan Gopal said: "The most important thing for a song to become beautiful is its melody."

Technical Engineering, Cultural Engineering, and the Development of a Genre

Modern songs were not exclusively a studio product, nor were they the sole new Nepali music development. They could well be sung live—most basically to the accompaniment of harmonium and tabla, and maybe a guitar—and a variety of new musics were developed alongside them. Modern song composers wrote songs for Nepali films, "operas" (the Nepali term is *gitinatak,* literally "song-drama"), and "progressive" political songs and "patriotic" songs. They might even compose folk songs as a radio genre, though in that case only being credited with having "collected" the song. The soft, solo singing in the studio of individualist ("I" and "thou" are the preferred pronouns here) and contemplative lyrics is where modern songs stand out in the family of Nepali new musics. And this contrasts in every way with, for instance, the loud, collective singing of political texts (appealing for collective action with "we" as the most prominent pronoun) live from the stage that is typical of progressive songs (see Grandin 1996).

For modern songs, the studios of Radio Nepal were at once the technical prerequisite for the genre and the key point in a wider process. This is to say that the technical process of sound engineering is woven into the cultural process of sound engineering. The relation is dialectical: technical engineering makes cultural engineering possible, while cultural engineering determines the way technical engineering is used.

The development of the genre of modern songs was formed by this dialectic. To give a glimpse of that development, I will cite three instances. First, as the veteran artist Ratna Das Prakash related, the ruling idea when he started to sing in the 1930s was that there was no such thing as Nepali music.[7] *Thumri, ghazal, bhajan*—these light classical genres were what was respected when it came to songs. And the language used should be Hindi or Urdu, certainly not Nepali. Nepali songs were worth nothing but ridicule: "That's what the beggars sing!"

Second, modern Nepali song came into being by breaking away from Indian models. This was where Ratna Das saw his own contribution; and the composer Nati Kazi said that in the early days of radio songs (that is, the days of Ratna Das, among others!), the Indian models dominated due to a lack of knowledge of the Nepali folk traditions.

The third instance takes us back to India—or rather, to the district of Darjeeling, with its large community of Nepali-speaking people.[8] As Peter Karthak says, the composer Amber Gurung is "the undisputed source of all that is modern Nepalese music today, developed by him in Darjeeling since late 1950s" (1997).

These are partly conflicting versions of the genre's history. Hard data suggest that Kathmandu and Darjeeling were equally important as nurseries of modern song artists. Among composers, Nati Kazi and Shiva Shankar from Kathmandu and Amber Gurung and Gopal Yonjan from Darjeeling account for 56 percent of all of the modern songs brought out on EPs and LPs by the state-controlled Shree Ratna Recording Corporation until 1980.[9]

Engineering As Patronage and Sponsorship of Music

"Without the radio, there would be no modern songs"—the composer Nati Kazi was clear that Radio Nepal's role in the creation of modern songs was beyond discussion. Meeting him in his radio office in 1986, when he headed the light music department and shared a large room with his equally renowned artist-colleagues Shiva Shankar (at that time head of classical music) and Tara Devi (responsible for the radio's musical instruments), this seemed a very natural thing for him to say. These were artists who had come to Radio Nepal almost directly after the broadcasts started, and who had stayed on there for most of their professional lives.

However, this was not an unchallenged view; Narayan Gopal contested it rather bitterly. "Unproductive things like sports they have supported," he told me, referring to the Nepali government, "but the government is not involved in the development of modern music." Narayan Gopal himself had spent a period of time in government service: in the early 1980s he was general manager of the National Theater. With little money and a lot of pressure from above, he quit after a few years. "Whatever we have done, we have done by ourselves, with our individual effort and with no support from the government. We started our careers in public places; we raised funds and so on. Most of the talented singers and composers are not government employees."

So what did patronage and sponsorship from the state amount to in actual practice? Alongside Radio Nepal, the Ratna Recording Corporation brought out discs and cassettes, the National Theater staged performances of modern "operas," and the Royal Nepal Film Corporation produced films. All of these entities were operated by the state, and all produced Nepalese music, including modern songs. Musical artists could be found in top administrative positions, such as that of general manager, as well as in lower posts and as staff musicians. And the singers, composers, and songwriters who worked on an RNFC film were rather well remunerated.

But otherwise, remuneration for freelance artists was low (it would take about two hundred songs for Radio Nepal to equal what one would earn on a single film). To live as a freelance artist, Amber Gurung told me in 1981, was simply impossible. And the salaried positions were, on the whole, few. This might be what Narayan Gopal had in mind. And one might say that it was not so much the musical artists who were supported, but *music itself.* As well as the music studios and the recordings of songs by Radio Nepal, the discs and cassettes of Ratna Records, and the Nepali songs included in feature films, we had the venues for performance: the Academy Hall, the City Hall (or National Meetinghouse, in direct translation from the Nepali), the National Theatre, and the auditoriums at Tribhuvan University.

Wiring the Nation

The provision of these musical resources was part of a larger process. In terms of territorial control (essentially taxation rights), the unification of Nepal was completed in the seventy years from 1744 to 1814. In social and cultural terms, however, this unification has been a much longer process. Roads, education, communications, a public musical life—whatever aspect you choose, Nepal had almost nothing of it in 1951, when the old Rana regime fell. At that point, though, the infrastructure for national integration was greatly expanded. In 1950 there were eleven secondary schools in the whole of Nepal. Ten years later the number of such schools had increased a hundred times to 1,065. Roads barely existed at all outside the Kathmandu Valley before the mid-1950s—Kathmandu was connected to the south with a ropeway. But by 1972 a network of roads connecting major towns inside the country and connecting Nepal itself to both India and China had been completed.[10] Radio, records, and films followed the same pattern.

It was during the three decades of partyless *panchayat* democracy, from 1961 to 1990, that nation building and national integration really came into their prime (see Burghart 1994, Pfaff-Czarnecka 1997). The panchayat system of government was integrative already in itself. From the very bottom—

in all of the nooks and corners of the country—representatives were elected upward from one tier to the next all the way to the National Panchayat.

Time now to step back and listen to all of this from a more analytical point of view.

The Cultural Apparatus: Music Industry or "Extended Stage"?

Along with a cultural and physical infrastructure, we now find in Nepal what Ulf Hannerz (1992) calls a "cultural apparatus," which he, following C. Wright Mills, sees as "the organizations and milieus in which artistic, intellectual and scientific work goes on, and the means by which such work is made available to the public" (Mills 1963: 406; quoted in Hannerz 1992: 82). It is important to note the form that this cultural apparatus took in Nepal.

In the Western context, the music industry is the center of the musical part of the cultural apparatus, to which the radio is annexed in an interlocking system (Malm and Wallis 1992: 30–31, fig. 2.3). What ties this system together in an integrated whole is, above all, the market.

This was not the case in Nepal. Here, the apparatus centered upon radio broadcasting, and annexed to the radio we find concert halls, makeshift stages, films, and disc and (later) cassette production. The market is marginal; it is state patronage that fuels this system. Roads and education help tie all of this together in an integrated system: folk song collectors, artists, Kathmandu-trained teachers, as well as Kathmandu ideas were helped along to the villages (and village singers to the studios of Radio Nepal). The whole apparatus can be seen as a "stage" extending from radio broadcasting (rather than a music industry per se).

The cultural apparatus "connects one person or a relative few (creators, personified symbols, performers, players) with a greater many who are more passive (clients, spectators, audiences)," according to Hannerz (1992: 82). The music industry and the extended stage both do this, and both include the same types of organizations and milieus (disc production, radio, education, concert arenas, and so on). The differences lie elsewhere: in the structure the system assumes, in what ties it together, in the way power and control can be exercised.

This is clear from Radio Nepal's firm control over (much of) the music it broadcast. Most of it was Nepali: about 90 percent of all music programming in 1974 and 60 percent in 1986.[11] And here, Radio Nepal did not choose among available products from the industry, it used almost exclusively—Nepali film songs were the exception—its own recordings. (Indeed, it was in fact the other way around: disc and cassette production depended upon the larger stock of radio recordings.) A presumptive artist had to pass a voice test, and here was the key to cultural engineering: To control the radio, as the state did, was to control not only the technology of production and distribution but the center of a network of venues that together comprise the extended stage.

Musical Economy and the Organization of Music Production

Music is produced in certain ways, using certain technologies within a certain framework of social organization. This mode of music production is in its turn part of a music economy—and I use economy here in a comprehensive sense (Williams 1977), irrespective of the extent to which money is used. With their intimate relationship with the resources of the state-controlled cultural apparatus, modern songs were produced within the frame of sponsorship-patronage, with the state as sponsor and patron. Now, sponsorship and patronage together make up only one specific form of social relations in the production of music; another, of course, is the market, and a third form is what could be called "self-sustained community music"—a musical form of a subsistence economy. These are ways of *socially organizing* music production, and they must be kept analytically distinct from the *forces* of production, production technologies such as musical instruments or sound recording. And as table 11.1 shows us, there is no necessary connection between a certain technology and a specific organization.

The state is not the only possible patron or sponsor; one can easily think of individual or corporate sponsorship and patronage. The classical sponsors of art music were wealthy individuals. The traditional music of the Nepalese Gaine minstrels and Damai wedding musicians was provided to these patrons rather than sold on a free market (Weisethaunet 1998, Tingey 1994), and the hymn-singing groups of the Kathmandu Valley were sponsored by grants of land or the like (see Grandin 1997). Progressive artists (providing the dissonant countervoices of the superculture) such as Rayan and his old colleague Raamesh were able to find sponsors for their cassettes, videos, operas, and stage performances among non-government organizations, missionaries, the French cultural center, and a Bangkok cultural organization. Moreover, the state can use ways other than sponsorship/patronage in its efforts to engineer the superculture. Malm and Wallis (1992) suggest one obvious way: media (and cultural) policy that aims to control or tame the music industry and the forces of the market.

The three general forms of organizing music production comprise different ways in which those people who produce music—as musicians, singers, composers, radio broadcasters, or engineers—are integrated with others in the cultural economy. This is to say that they are manifestations of the division of labor in a complex culture, and this includes how the music

TABLE 11.1 Technologies and Organizations of Music Production

Organization (Relations of Production)	Forms of Music	Associated Technology (Forces of Production)
Self-sustained	Local, "ethnic" music; (partly) dapha, bhajan ensembles	(Cassette technology)
Patronage/ sponsorship: "Traditional"	(Partly) dapha, bhajan ensembles; occupational musicians: Gaine, Damai	
Patronage/ sponsorship: Supercultural	Shastriya sangit; radio genres: modern song, folk song, patriotic song; film songs (RNFC)	Radio technology, disc technology, cassette technology, film technology
Market	Film songs; Nepali pop; marketized radio music	Cassette technology; (from the 90s only) CD technology, FM radio technology

artist gets paid, as with, for example, *jagir* (government service): the classical singer Qayum Khan, recruited to the Nepali court in 1798 (Regmi 1995: 21, 30n.16), as well as the modern composer Nati Kazi can be seen as *jagirdars* (government servants), though the way *jagir* is held has shifted from a land grant to a regular salary paid out in money. This is quite distinct from a musical artist selling his music in the marketplace. It is also distinct from the nonremunerated community musicians—subsistence farmers who make music together for entertainment, traditional, or religious purposes.

The "Audience"

But the three forms of organizing production cannot be reduced simply to the forms of remuneration. The different ways of organizing music production have very different implications when it comes to the question of the "audience." In market-produced music, the audience can be seen as buyers of the musical commodity, and the system will include feedback from the audience of "consumers" to the "producers" in, essentially, monetary figures. This is where the notion of "audience" really fits; it is more problematic elsewhere. In certain forms of community music, there is quite simply no audience. The participants sing for one another and for the gods; any other audience (such as passers-by) is unintended.[12] Under patronage, the "audience" may well be the patron himself along with a circle of friends. This was most likely the situation when Qayum Khan performed, as it was for *shastriya sangit* (classical raga) musicians until (at least) the fall of the

Ranas in 1951. Here, the feedback to the artist can take any form (raising her pay, dismissing her, and so on). But to be a patron or sponsor is above all a matter of pride rather than music support, and the sponsorship can be managed in general and distant terms.

But what of the state-sponsored music of Radio Nepal? The apparently obvious audience consists of radio listeners. Communication between consumers and producers in a market organization of production is provided by the market itself. But there is no market here, and this audience is not known very well by the artist. How big is it? What does it think of the music? All this will be reduced to listeners' requests for songs in their letters to the well-liked Nepali songs programs. But there is another "audience" that is better known: the circle of colleagues and friends—people who like the artist him/herself belong to the cultural apparatus, who are colleagues, coperformers, songwriters, singers, composers, teachers, or students, and who might make or break his/her reputation.

Artists and Their Peers

There is nothing strange here, of course. Producers look to their peers rather than to their audience for feedback and evaluation in media (McQuail 1994: 209–211) and, of course, in academia. Ulf Hannerz discusses this on a more general level. Drawing upon Becker's (1963) classic study of dance/jazz musicians and research on journalists, Hannerz (1992: 159–61) sees this reliance on peer feedback as following from the "division of labor/subculture segmentation dialectic." "With such subcultural evolution, there is a tendency for the practitioners of a specialization"—modern song artists, in this case—"to turn inward toward one another in their attentions. The peculiar, perspectival experiences, beliefs, and values of the specialists find the most authentic appreciation only within their own circles. It is, therefore, tempting to give the public only as much as is necessary"—not much, considering the minimal feedback from the actual listeners—"to safeguard the flow of material resources, and otherwise to turn inward toward subcultural process, where the symbolic rewards are richer" (1992: 160). To spell out one implication: it is a subculture that produces the superculture.

Also, other genres of supercultural music—*shastriya sangit,* the radio-type folk song (*lok git*)—were maintained by a sponsored subculture. In this regard, there is a certain similarity to some forms of self-sustained community music. As long as the income from the land grant is forthcoming, a Newar *dapha* or *bhajan* ensemble can orient itself to its musical business and go on training newcomers. And as long as sponsorship is forthcoming, a raga musician, a radio folksinger, or a modern composer can go on attending to musical business and orienting herself or himself to her or his subculture—where a song or an artist can be evaluated in artistic rather than commercial terms by subcultural peers.

We find here a rather peculiar way of relating to the media and their engineering technology. Discs were signs of artistic prestige and success—"vanity records," as they are called in some American circles—rather than a way of reaching out to the audience. And the mass audience actually reached by the radio was reduced to being eavesdroppers to an internal musical conversation among the artists.

Soundscape of the Superculture

Engineering shapes the soundscape, and, therefore, attention to the soundscape can help to reveal the nature of the engineering. Indeed, one of the basic ideas underlying R. Murray Schafer's (1994) theory of the soundscape is that it can be "read"—the way things sound in a place tells us something about that place.[13]

Radio Nepal is a keynote sound in the Kathmandu Valley soundscape even today. Two decades into the cassette era, and with TV, Radio FM, and compact discs as more recent competitors, you can still follow Radio Nepal's programming quite well from the radios in homes, shops, cars, teahouses, offices, and so on. Of course, the further we proceed backward in time, the fewer radio sets were in operation. Still, I noted in 1981 that it was no problem to follow Radio Nepal continuously while walking down a street. And Robert Anderson and Edna Mitchell, who visited Kathmandu in 1974, gave a similar observation: "Even one radio in a hamlet or neighborhood reaches a large number of people since owners play the volume high" (Anderson and Mitchell 1978: 251).

The musically radio-dominated soundscape of the panchayat heydays tells us that the superculture has been successfully engineered, whereas the increasing dissonances from the cassette music of the late panchayat era could be read as a loss of this firm control. The post-panchayat soundscape, in turn, with its different languages (English in many FM broadcasts; regional languages from Radio Nepal), its larger influence from Western music (from FM radio as well as cassettes and CDs), and its generational shift from the modern song conglomerate to Nepali pop is a good sign of the consumerism and overt ethnic and political contradictions now at the forefront of the superculture.

With the radio's high content of modern songs, the melody of the individual voice was made another keynote of the soundscape. Modern songs were engineered—composed, arranged, sung, recorded—in such a way that the unique voice of the unique individual (the singer) and the words of the text were foregrounded. Wherever you were, you would hear the unique voice of an individual singer voicing a contemplation upon life and love in modern times.

Of course, there is much more to read. But keynote sounds do not give the whole story. The panchayat soundscape also indicates that what from the perspective of the modern song artists may be an essentially unknown audience is in fact active and not at all musically powerless. The rifts and fissures of the panchayat hegemony were audible in sound events such as the ethnically or politically dissident songs heard from cassettes, stages, picnics, processions, and people's homes (see Grandin 1989, 1995b).

Modern Songs as Tales People Tell about Themselves

Modern songs were an important part of the panchayat soundscape. But are they "a tale a culture tells about itself"? As Manuel (1993: 5) points out, the self-referencing built into this Geertzian notion is problematic in the context of complex cultures (*who* tells what about *whom?*). Yet music, like other aspects of the soundscape, also indicates—even indexes—things not necessarily communicated intentionally.

The obvious unit that modern songs say something about is the *nation*-state of Nepal, and they tell us that this is a *developing* (the non-ethnic, nontraditional music), indeed a *modern* (the contemplative individualism of the foregrounded voice; moreover, the instruments, the use of harmony, the arrangement and recording) nation, with its *own voice* ("Nepaliness," folksong-based melodies) and a modern *culture of its own* (the genre of modern songs), but a place that is culturally *open* and no longer isolationist (the instruments, etc.). And, above all, it is an *independent* nation. This is not India, as the language of the lyrics and the Nepaliness of the music tell us.

If this is the tale modern songs tell about Nepal, it seems uniquely well tailored to panchayat objectives. Here, various variations on the theme of Nepali nationalism—national unity, national allegiance, national independence, national dignity, national development—were key concerns, at least in the rhetoric.[14] But it is easy to make too much of this congruence. The more or less philosophical and romantic meditations of modern songs were not explicit panchayat propaganda, and the artists were hardly mouthpieces of the state. More or less opportunistically, artists adjusted to the ideological climate as much as necessary in order to gain or retain access to the resources of the cultural apparatus. Naturally, different artists steered differently between career opportunities and peer judgements of their artistic integrity.

And conversely, the genre of modern songs was not *concocted* by the panchayat state. Indeed, the genre was a rather natural development, considering how well it adheres to Laade's general observations for a large area, and also the fact that similar Indian genres also emerged (there was a genre called *adhunik* also in neighboring Bengal!).[15] Rather, we find the same pattern in music as the one Onta (1996, 1997, 1999) has shown concerning history, language, and literature: activists, both in Nepal and in "exile" in India, worked to achieve what was in effect the total reversal of relative values. In literature, Hindi, Urdu, and English were respected; Nepali was "useless" and "unsuitable."[16] In music, as we have seen, *shastriya sangit* was respectable; Nepali songs were something sung by "beggars." Modern songs, then, were an effort to create Nepali music in the same way that there was a Nepali history, language, and literature.[17] And it is somewhat ironic that the musical as well as the literary, linguistic, and historical contents of this nationalism were to a significant extent developed in Darjeeling in India.

Retrospectively, in the evaluations of an intellectual such as Abhi Subedi (1975) as well as a musical artist such as Nati Kazi, modern songs were actively developed away from Indian models. Modern songs are obviously related to many "Indian" genres.[18] In literature, given ("Indian") forms were filled with local content (language, plots). In music, into the given ("Indian") forms was similarly poured local content (melody, rhythm). The process in music thus replicates that in literature/language/history, though it took place much later and much more from scratch. Whereas panchayat nationalism could appropriate, for its own ends, the nationalist literature and history that were already there, there was not much to build upon in the case of music.

Modern songs were not the only candidates for musical nationalism. When it comes to the central value of Nepaliness, modern songs lose out to folk songs even before the race is started, and the Royal Nepal Academy, for instance, would choose folk songs to represent Nepal abroad. As Weisethaunet (1998: 133–41, 313–22) demonstrates, the "folklorized" radio genre of folk songs ties in with the national-historic concerns. Modern songs and (folklorized) folk songs can best be seen as an alliance, a two-faced conglomeration, with modern songs speaking to the internal community (predominantly in Kathmandu) and folk songs to the external community (to the Nepali villages as well as to the outside world).

As a patron of music, the panchayat state in fact adopted the same role as its predecessors. In this respect, the modern song can be seen simply as the successor to *shastriya sangit* (classical raga music) — a successor that retains the emphasis on soloist melody. There was a transition from the family-run state of the Ranas, which patronized shastriya sangit on the secluded stages inside their palaces, to the constitutional panchayat state, which patronized modern songs on the public, extended stages of the radio and elsewhere. Compared to shastriya sangit, modern songs can even be cheaper to finance (they require less practice; hence it is possible to be a modern song artist while having another job) and have no connotations to either the old Rana regime or to India. Traces of mutual hostility between modern and classical musicians can be seen in this light: scorn for the artistic pretension of modern song composers by a classical musician; Nepali classical musicians deemed "very inferior" to Indian artists by a modern singer.

So what the state's engineering of the musical superculture amounted to was one strand of its cultural engineering: to develop, preserve, and propagate the national language, literature, culture, and arts for the purposes of "national prestige" and "dignity" (to quote some key words from the National Education System Plan and the Communication Service Plan, both from 1971).[19]

But the way this was done—by means of patronage/sponsorship of music—opened up spaces that artists could use for their own purposes. One might conclude that the case of modern songs shows us how engineering technology has operated in a system based on pride—that is, national prestige and dignity, and recognition among nation-state peers, for the patrons-sponsors, and artistic honor and recognition among artist peers for the musical artists.

Pride or Profit: Engineering and Popular Music

"They had ordered a kebab and a bottle of whisky. We gathered around the radio": for the purposes of the concluding discussion, let us leave Nepal for Egypt for a moment. The quote is from *Miramar,* the novel by Nobel laureate Naguib Mahfouz (1978: 21), and in this novel a radio concert (with Umm Kulthum, of course) stands out as the central event. With these concerts, as Virginia Danielson says in her study of Umm Kulthum, "Life in the Arab world came to a stop." To sum up the role of the radio here, Danielson (1997: 85; quoting El-Shawan 1980) concludes that it was a main source of patronage for musical artists, and the major vehicle for the dissemination of music.

Though the radio appears in a more low-key manner in Nepal, providing keynote sounds rather than central events, its role as patron and vehicle for dissemination was no less important here than in Egypt. Another example can be drawn from the work of Mark Slobin (1993: 3), who "first had to elbow aside, then recognize the power of, radio music emanating from Kabul" in his study of Afghanistani music around 1970, and still another example from Wallis and Malm (1984: 260), who talk about radio Tanzania as "a remarkable music station" facilitating "a buoyant live music scene" in a country with no phonograph industry at all (see also Malm and Wallis 1992: chap. 6). Yet none of these studies seem to really have assimilated their own findings. As I said in the introduction to this chapter, it seems easy to jump very quickly from recording technology to assumptions about music production that in fact are very specific. In spite of her observation about the Egyptian radio, Danielson talks about "institutions of commercial music including the media" and about "capitalist" institutions (Danielson 1997: 13). In spite of his observation that "the penetration of mass media . . . is more extensive than the spread of consumerism, [and] capitalist values and practices," Peter Manuel (1993: 11, xvi) jumps from "the connection with the media" to "music which is produced and marketed as a mass commodity" and from "recording technology" to a "salable entity" that acquires "commodity status" and thus is subject to "mass-market pressures and incentives" (1993: 7). Moreover, he finds no problem in treating "radio" under the more comprehensive heading of the "music industry" (1993: chapter 3). In spite of their own, eloquent Tanzanian example to the contrary, Wallis and Malm jump from recording technology (or "music industry technology," as they call it!) to the "music industry." And, to give a final example, Steven Feld (1994) jumps from "schizophonia" (a term of R. Murray Schafer's indicating the split of a recorded sound from its source) to commodification.

This is to confuse a technology (a force of production) with an entire mode of production. Recording technology alone does not make a music industry or effect commodification of music. That will require a market-organized, profit-oriented social organization of the production in question. To conclude this discussion, I will sum up the observations that our

TABLE 11.2 Paradigms of Music Production

	Music industry paradigm	Extended stage paradigm
Type of cultural apparatus	Music industry	Extended stage
Central medium	Disc production	Radio broadcasting
Organization of production	Market	Patronage
Orientation	Outward: mass audience	Inward: peer audience
Audience	Pays the piper; calls the tune?	Eavesdroppers
Feedback	Monetary	Rudimentary
Motive	Profit	Pride
Music	Commodity	Art?
Technology and engineering	Electronic recording and distribution of music	Electronic recording and distribution of music

case of Nepali modern songs has actualized in two paradigms (or maybe modes) of music production. Both use sound engineering to produce supercultural music and to reach a mass audience. The cases mentioned above—Tanzania, Afghanistan, and probably Egypt—would line up with Nepal in the extended stage paradigm, as would Central Europe until 1990 (see Hammarlund 1998). What can be concluded is that the relation between engineering and popular music needs further clarification. Does the notion of "commodification" make sense outside the music industry paradigm? And the concept of popular music needs thorough rethinking, concerning the assumption of commodification as a central feature, and what, exactly, the role of the "mass audience" is supposed to be. Otherwise, popular music studies will either misrepresent or risk losing not only Nepali modern songs but the music of Afghanistan, Tanzania, possibly Umm Kulthum, and maybe the pre-pop/rock "new music" of the entire Orient.

Sponsorship/patronage as a musical organization of production opens creative spaces for musical artists. Unlike the unhappy jazz/dance musicians described by Howard Becker (1963), they have no mass audience, no "consumers" of musical "products" whose tastes and purchasing power must be taken into consideration. Given that sponsors and patrons do not meddle too much in actual production, patronage and sponsorship may open up the possibility of artists making their music for the artistically most qualified "audience" possible—their own peers—whereas the national audience becomes no more than eavesdroppers. It is fascinating to think that this might be what we find inside the most overtly mass-oriented genre, that of popular music.

Notes

1. The main research drawn upon here was done in 1985–1988, preluded by an initial field trip in 1981 and followed up in 1992–1997. The materials include conversations and taped interviews with most of the leading Nepali modern song artists as well as with people in administration and the like, field notes, and assorted discs, cassettes, small print, etc. SAREC (the Swedish Agency for Research Cooperation with developing countries) and HSFR (the Swedish Council for Research in the Humanities and Social Sciences) furnished research grants, and the Swedish Institute scholarships, that made my extended periods in Nepal possible. My special thanks to Manjul, Gujya Malakar, and Gert Wegner for their friendship, support, and constant discussion of any issue related to Nepali music throughout these years.

2. On the role of patronage and the state, I have learned much from Neuman (1985) on India; DeNora (1995) on Vienna at 1800; and Hammarlund (1998) on the changes in Central Europe around 1990.

3. Elsewhere, I have discussed the reception of modern songs (Grandin 1989) and their musical style (Grandin 1984), as well as modern songs in relation to political opposition (Grandin 1996), to the urban setting (Grandin 1994), to ethnicity

and traditional-modern linkages (Grandin 1995b), and to creolization and global cultural flow (Grandin 1995a).

4. Amber Gurung, personal communication, 1981.

5. A transcript of the melody and harmonic progressions of this song is given in Grandin 1990: 35–39. Another Amber Gurung composition on a raga base is discussed in Grandin 1995a.

6. Cf. also Anderson and Mitchell 1978: 254, although their discussion of raga- and folk-based composition seems misguided.

7. For information on the artists including biographical data, see Darnal (2038 V.S.) and Grandin (1989, 1994, 1995b).

8. See Hutt 1997.

9. Calculations are based on Ratna Records catalogues; see Grandin 1989: 118. They have the same position in retrospective evaluation: Amber Gurung, Gopal Yonjan, and Nati Kazi draw a total of 57 percent of the votes in a recent Internet poll (NHP/Kantipur 2000a). In the field of male singers, posterity has accorded Kathmandu a supreme position with Narayan Gopal (67 pecent of the votes in NHP/Kantipur 2000b, 9.5 percent of the songs on disc), whereas Darjeeling has provided the top female singer with Aruna Lama (44 percent of the votes in NHP/Kantipur 2000c, 4.7 percent of the songs on disc).

10. Schools: Ragsdale 1989: 14. Roads: Seddon, Blakie, and Cameron 1981: chap. 7.

11. Figure for 1974: Anderson and Mitchell 1978: 251. Figure for 1986: Grandin 1989: 132.

12. The *dapha* and *bhajan* ensembles of Newar neighborhoods work in this way. See Grandin 1989.

13. This is not necessarily a hermeneutic enterprise of "interpretation" or extracting "meanings" but rather a way of working with the inherent indexicality of sound.

14. There is a large literature on this subject. Some examples: Onta 1999, Pfaff-Czarnecka 1997, Krämer 1996, Burghart 1994.

15. Ray 1973.

16. Onta 1997: 80, 94.

17. As Onta (1999: 2) observes, national Nepali culture, with its promotion of the Nepali language, is too easily seen as just a mask for the vested interests of "nameless Hindu Parbatiyas" (that is, the Nepali-speaking "ethnicity") through a panchayat state that is accorded excessive agency. As a state-patronaged genre, modern songs are close to national culture, but "Hindu Parbatiyas" are not overwhelmingly present among the artists who created this music.

18. The very question of what is actually and musically "Nepali" and what is "Indian" has a bigger potential for misunderstandings than for clarification. Modern songs are best seen as a branch of a musical tree that has its roots in many South Asian traditions, both "folk" and "classical." Other branches of this tree include film songs, light classical *ghazals,* pop *ghazals,* Bengali *adhunik* (modern), Rabindra sangit, community and commercialized bhajan, etc. See Grandin 1995a; 1989.

19. From Amatya 1983, which is very much an insider's view. On the Education Plan, see Ragsdale 1989.

References

Amatya, Shaphalya. 1983. *Some Aspects of Cultural Policy in Nepal.* Paris: UNESCO.

Anderson, Robert, and Edna Mitchell. 1978. "The Politics of Music in Nepal." *Anthropological Quarterly* 51(4): 247–259.

Becker, Howard. 1963. *Outsiders.* New York: Free Press.

Burghart, Richard. 1994. "The Political Culture of Panchayat Democracy." In *Nepal in the Nineties: Versions of the Past, Visions of the Future,* ed. Michael Hutt. Delhi: Oxford University Press.

Danielson, Virginia. 1997. *The Voice of Egypt. Umm Kulthum, Arabic Song, and Egyptian Society in the Twentieth Century.* Chicago: University of Chicago Press.

Darnal, Ramsaran. 2038 V.S. *Nepali Sangit Sadhak.* Kathmandu: Nepal Rajakiya Pragya-pratishtan.

DeNora, Tia. 1995. *Beethoven and the Construction of Genius: Musical Politics in Vienna, 1792–1803.* Berkeley: University of California Press.

El-Shawan, Salwa. 1980. "Al-Musika al-'Arabiyyah: A Category of Urban Music in Cairo, Egypt, 1927–77." Ph.D. dissertation: Columbia University.

Feld, Steven. 1994. "From Schizophonia to Schismogenesis: On the Discourses and Commodification Practices of 'World Music' and 'World Beat.'" In *Music Grooves,* ed. Charles Keil and Steven Feld. Chicago: University of Chicago Press, 257–289.

Grandin, Ingemar. 1997. "Raga Basanta and the Spring Songs of the Kathmandu Valley: A Musical Great Tradition among Himalayan Farmers?" *European Bulletin of Himalayan Research* 12–13: 57–80.

Grandin, Ingemar. 1984. "Modern Songs in Nepal." Master's thesis: Institutionen för musikvetenskap, Lunds Universitet.

———. 1989. *Music and Media in Local Life: Music Practice in a Newar Neighbourhood in Nepal.* Linköping: Tema.

———. 1990. "'Varför skulle vi sjunga utländska sånger?' Om moderna sånger, medier och traditionell nevarimusik i Nepal." In *Musik och kultur,* ed. Owe Ronström. Lund: Studentlitteratur.

———. 1994. "Nepalese Urbanism: A Musical Exploration." In *Anthropology of Nepal: People, Problems, and Processes,* ed. Michael Allen. Kathmandu: Mandala Book Point, 160–175.

———. 1995a. "One Song, Five Continents, and a Thousand Years of Musical Migration." *Saragam sangitik traimasik* 1(1): 56–65.

———. 1995b. "Modernisation and Revival in a Newar Tradition: The Songs of Ram Krishna Duwal." In *Sauhrdyamangalam: Studies in Honour of Siegfried Lienhard on his 70th Birthday,* ed. M. Juntunen, W. L. Smith, and C. Suneson. Stockholm: The Association of Oriental Studies, 117–139.

———. 1996. "'To Change the Face of This Country': Nepalese Progressive Songs under Pancayat Democracy." *Journal of South Asian Literature* 29(1): 175–189.

Greene, Paul. 1999. "Sound Engineering in a Tamil Village: Playing Audio Cassettes as Devotional Performance." *Ethnomusicology* 43(3): 459–489.

———. 2001. "Mixed Messages: Unsettled Cosmopolitanisms in Nepali Pop." *Popular Music* 20(2): 169–187.

Greene, Paul, and Yubakar Raj Rajkarnikar. 2000. "Echoes in the Valleys: A Social History of Nepali Pop, 1985–2000." *Wave Online* 50. Reprinted in *Wave* 63 (2001): 16–18, 21.

Hammarlund, Anders. 1998. *Kulturbrytningar: Musik & politik i Centraleuropa.* Stockholm: Carlssons.

Hannerz, Ulf. 1992. *Cultural Complexity: Studies in the Social Organization of Meaning.* New York: Columbia University Press.

Hutt, Michael. 1997. "Being Nepali without Nepal: Reflections on a South Asian Diaspora." In *Nationalism and Ethnicity in a Hindu Kingdom: The Politics of Culture in Contemporary Nepal,* ed. David Gellner, Joanna Pfaff Czarnecka, and John Whelpton. Amsterdam: Harwood Academic Publishers.

Karthak, Peter. 1997. "Gopal Yonzon: In Memorium." *The Kathmandu Post* (May 1997).
Krämer, Karl-Heinz. 1996. *Ethnizität und nationale Integration in Nepal: Eine Untersuchung zur Politisierung der ethnischen Gruppen im modernen Nepal.* Stuttgart: Steiner.
Laade, Wolfgang. 1971. *Neue Musik in Afrika, Asien, und Ozeanien: Diskographie und historisch-stilistischer Überblick.* Heidelberg: Wolfgang Laade.
Mahfouz, Naguib. 1978. *Miramar.* Transl. Fatma Moussa-Mahmoud, ed. and rev. Maged el Kommos and John Rodenbeck. London: Heinemann.
Malm, Krister, and Roger Wallis. 1992. *Media Policy and Music Activity.* London: Routledge.
Manuel, Peter. 1988. *Popular Musics of the Non-Western World.* Oxford: Oxford University Press.
——. 1993. *Cassette Culture: Popular Music and Technology in North India.* Chicago: University of Chicago Press.
McQuail, Denis. 1994. *Mass Communication Theory: An Introduction.* 3rd ed. London: Sage.
Mills, C. Wright. 1963. *Power, Politics, and People.* New York: Ballantine.
NHP/Kantipur. 2000a. NHP/Kantipur Century Poll Results: Who was the most important musician of the past century in Nepal? <http://www.nepalhomepage.com>
——. 2000b. NHP/Kantipur Century Poll Results: Who was the most influential male singer of the past century in Nepal? <http://www.nepalhomepage.com>
——. 2000c. NHP/Kantipur Century Poll Results: Who was the most influential female singer of the past century in Nepal? <http://www.nepalhomepage.com>
Neuman, Daniel. 1985. "Indian Music as a Cultural System." *Asian Music* 17(1): 98–113.
Onta, Pratyoush. 1996. "Creating a Brave Nepali Nation in British India: The Rhetoric of *Jati* Improvement, Rediscovery of Bhanubhakta, and the Writing of *Bir* History." *Studies in Nepali History and Society* 1(1): 37–76.
——. 1997. "Activities in a 'Fossil State': Balkrishna Sama and the Improvisation of Nepali Identity." *Studies in Nepali History and Society* 2(1): 69–102.
——. 1999. "The Career of Bhanubhakta as a History of Nepali National Culture, 1940–1999." *Studies in Nepali History and Society* 4(1): 65–136.
Pfaff-Czarnecka, Joanna. 1997. "Vestiges and Visions: Cultural Change in the Process of Nation-Building in Nepal." In *Nationalism and Ethnicity in a Hindu Kingdom: The Politics of Culture in Contemporary Nepal,* ed. David Gellner, Joanna Pfaff-Czarnecka, and John Whelpton. Amsterdam: Harwood Academic Publishers.
Ragsdale, Tod. 1989. *Once a Hermit Kingdom: Ethnicity, Education, and National Integration in Nepal.* New Delhi: Manohar.
Ray, Sukumar. 1973. *Music of Eastern India: Vocal music in Bengali, Oriya, Assamese, and Manipuri, with Special Emphasis on Bengali.* Calcutta: Firma K. L. Mukhopadhyay.
Regmi, Mahesh. 1978. *Thatched Huts and Stucco Palaces: Peasants and Landlords in Nineteenth-Century Nepal.* New Delhi: Vikas.
——. 1995. *Kings and Political Leaders of the Gorkhali Empire.* Hyderabad: Orient Longman.
Schafer, R. Murray. 1994. *The Soundscape: Our Sonic Environment and the Tuning of the World.* Rochester: Destiny Books.
Seddon, D., P. Blaikie, and J. Cameron. 1981. *Peasants and Workers in Nepal.* New Delhi: Vikas.

Slobin, Mark. 1993. *Subcultural Sounds: Micromusics of the West.* Hanover, N.H.: Wesleyan University Press/University Press of New England.
Subedi, Abhi. 1975. "Nepali Songs and Their Singers." *The Rising Nepal* (Nov. 14).
Tingey, Carol. 1994. *Auspicious Music in a Changing Society: The Damai Musicians of Nepal.* New Delhi: Heritage Publishers.
Wallis, Roger, and Krister Malm. 1984. *Big Sounds from Small Peoples: The Music Industry in Small Countries.* London: Constable.
Wiesethaunet, Hans. 1998. *The Performance of Everyday Life: The Gaine of Nepal.* Oslo: Universitetsforlaget.
Williams, Raymond. 1977. *Marxism and Literature.* Oxford: Oxford University Press.

CHAPTER TWELVE

Music and the Rise of Radio in Twenties America

Technological Imperialism, Socialization, and the Transformation of Intimacy

Timothy D. Taylor

The effect of radio cannot be underestimated. It was perhaps the most important technological innovation in communications of the twentieth century, at least in the United States. It reconfigured notions of public and private, helped usher in a new form of the consumer economy, played a large role in the creation of the star system in the entertainment industry, gave the country the first mass-media superstar in popular music, Rudy Vallee, and more.

While some scholarly literature (though not much) has paid attention to the programming of music on the air, this essay considers the early days of radio and the rhetoric surrounding the period immediately following its development, and the role that music played in promoting radio. This historical moment in the rise of a technology seems to be a particularly interesting juncture, especially with respect to radio. Workers in the field of science and technology studies (STS) tend to concentrate on the development of a new technology, or its subsequent uses, but give less attention to the way that a technology in development is pushed and cajoled into social existence.

It is this long moment that is of interest here. Radio hobbyists proselytized on its behalf in countless articles. Dozens of discussions in the early radio press suggested ways of using the radio—on the beach, in the car, in the boat, camping—so that readers could learn how to integrate the new technology into their everyday lives. Since music was prominently featured on the air in the early days of radio, especially before the rise of the comedy programs, music played an important role in the championing of radio and its early uses.

Technological Imperialism

Radio was advocated, in part, by employing discourses of modernity. The rhetoric about radio in the 1920s was caught up in an ideology of modernity, a technological modernity marked not only by radio itself but by other recent technologies such as film, the phonograph, the automobile, and the airplane. "Are your new neighbors modern people?" asks an unnamed person in the *Buffalo Express* in 1922. "Modern?" replies another. "Say, they sent in last night to borrow our Radio set!" (RD 1922a). This exchange reveals as much about conceptions of modernity as it does about the importance of consumption, of owning a radio that one's neighbor doesn't have.

Don Slater identifies the 1920s as probably the first moment in which people actually believed themselves to be moderns, inhabiting modernity: a contemporary state, not one being striven toward (Slater 1997: 13). This technological modernity, marked by the dominance of machines and by an underlying ideology that promotes them, was called "technopoly" by Neil Postman, an ideology that arose in the mid-1920s (Postman 1993).[1] Whether or not one adopts Postman's term, it is clear that this ideology arose for a number of reasons. First, of course, there were the new technologies just mentioned. Also, industrial production was made more scientific, as is well known, thanks to the writings of Frederick W. Taylor and the practices of Henry Ford. Manufacturing was increasingly updated technologically. Lynn Dumenil (1995: 59) writes that 70 percent of industries were electrified in 1929, whereas only 30 percent had been a decade before. Electrification and mechanization, she writes, vastly increased productivity in this era.

There was a downside, of course, with workers' jobs becoming increasingly banal and mind-numbing. Even low-level white collar workers were not immune. Artworks of the time thematized the increasingly technocratic nature of the era and the mindlessness of work, such as King Vidor's 1928 film *The Crowd,* which depicts the utter mundanity of everyday life of a white collar worker, or Charlie Chaplin's 1936 *Modern Times.*

But the majority of the members of the middle classes, in a position to reap the benefits of this new technological era, celebrated technology.[2] They promoted radio, even proselytized for it. Susan J. Douglas (1987) has cogently written of the ways that broadcasting was socially constructed, but it is useful to discuss one important strategy employed by radio's enthusiasts that Douglas doesn't examine.[3] This tactic, also identified by Michael Taussig (1993) was simple: the technological modernity represented by radio was emphasized by juxtaposing it to peoples thought to be premodern.[4] The burgeoning publications on radio in the 1920s frequently featured radio and indigenous peoples, both as listeners and performers (see figures 1–3; figure 2 looks particularly stagy).[5] Most of these treatments of racialized others were in photographs with occasionally negatively stereotypical captions, such as a photograph published in *Radio World* in 1922 captioned "Hears White Fathers' Signal Fire." This photograph showed Chief Sherman Charging Hawk, in suit, tie, and headphones, seated at a table with a small radio set. The text under the photograph reads: "Chief Sherman Charging Hawk whose only knowledge of sending and receiving long-distance messages was that of the Indian's beacon fire placed on a high hill.

Fig. 12.1. "The Buffalo Nickel Indian Broadcasts" (PR 1925) Author's collection.

Here he is photographed, experiencing, for the first time, the receiving of messages by the white father's latest invention. A concert broadcast over distant leagues has given him his first idea of the world's greatest advancement" (RW 1922b). This copy is perhaps disingenuous, for it is difficult to believe that Chief Sherman Charging Hawk had never heard of the telegraph or the telephone. Note also the concluding phrase about radio as "the world's greatest advancement," which emphasizes the achievement of radio against the primitive mode of communication thought to have been used by the Chief in the photograph.

Photographs and articles such as this were fairly common, both in "reporting" and advertising. For example, a full-page ad in the mid-1920s placed by the Crosley Radio Corporation, a leading manufacturer, featured a picture of a Native American couple in front of a fire, the copy referring to the radio as "the Modern Signal Fire."[6]

Another photograph from 1922, captioned, in faux Native American dialect, "Little Chief Bear Hears Big Radio," depicts Little Chief Bear in traditional garb listening to a large radio. The text under the photograph reads, in full: "Little Chief Bear, son of Big Chief Bear, who was killed in Custer's Last Stand, had his first experience with radio at the National Hotel and Restaurant Show in Chicago. The chief donned the head piece while music was coming over the ether and insisted on keeping time on his tom-tom" (RW 1922c).

Fig. 12.2. "Onondaga Indians" (RB 1924). Author's collection.

Fig. 12.3. "An Eskimo Lullaby at WGY" (RB 1927a). Author's collection.

A 1926 article in *On the Air* about one Kiutus Tecumseh, great-grandson of Chief Tecumseh, began, "What a treat it is to hear an Indian musician!" But it transpires that Tecumseh wasn't performing "Indian music" but rather some undisclosed popular music, having honed his skills as a cowpuncher in Washington state and then as a sailor in the Navy during World War I (*On the Air* 1926).

There were dozens of such articles and photographs. While they were mainly representations of America's others, particularly Native Americans, foreigners appeared as well, as in figure 12.4.

Representations such as these provide evidence of a phenomenon or strategy that could be called technological imperialism, in which the West's conception of itself as technological and modern is highlighted and reinforced by juxtaposing itself and its technologies against people without those technologies. Western technology, in fact, frequently serves as a metonym for the West itself in these representations. The number of photographs and articles featuring indigenous peoples also emphasizes the reach of radio technology: radio as medium traverses space as radio as technology seems to extend across time, into the premodern world.[7]

Such representations and articles suffuse the early radio press throughout the 1920s. By the 1930s, however, the promotional campaign for radio had proved largely successful. Radio had become an integral part of most

Fig. 12.4. "The Yellow Peril via Radio" (PR 1926a). Author's collection.

American homes. But the ideology of technological modernity with technological imperialism as its agent continued with the establishment of successful comedies that put ethnicized and racialized people on display. Representations of indigenous or premodern peoples gave way as the ideology of technological imperialism became wedded to that of the melting pot.[8] Immigrants to the United States could participate in this glorious new technological modernity. Program after program—whether *The Rise of the Goldbergs,* with Mama speaking in her Yiddish accent, or *Life with Luigi,* with Luigi and his Italian accent—emphasized the modernity and shining technological future offered by radio through the juxtaposition of these people who represent the old, and literally the Old World.

Emphasizing radio's modernity through such juxtapositions in image and prose in this representational process labeled technological imperialism created an ideology of radio as not only modern but necessary. Radio's proselytizers had to represent radio as something more than a fad—as something useful, something everyday, something everybody must have. A household without radio was a household that was no better than the native peoples and other groups without radio.

Technology and Everyday Life

Radio, as an important marker of America's technological modernity, was thought to be able to accomplish almost anything. It could make the disparate peoples of the nation one; it could uplift everyone culturally by playing good music; it could provide news; it could provide crucial weather and agricultural information for farmers; it could educate.

Who, however, was listening? The original people for whom radio was of interest comprised mainly a small group of male hobbyists, some of whom had worked with radio during their service in World War I.[9] Other hobbyists were boys and young men who were fascinated by listening over long distances, trying to pull in stations from as far away as possible. By about 1920, however, the broadcast of the James Cox–Warren G. Harding presidential race generated a huge number of phone calls to Westinghouse's switchboard (Douglas 1999: 64). In 1921 the Jack Dempsey–Georges Carpentier fight was one of the most anticipated broadcasts of the day, making clear that radio was beginning to find users beyond the hardcore hobbyists and was beginning to insinuate itself into everyday life. The year 1921 saw the creation of twenty-eight new stations; by 1922, Douglas writes, "the floodgates were opened" (ibid.: 64). This was a pivotal year, remembered by Erik Barnouw as euphoric with respect to radio. The year 1922 saw the number of new stations skyrocket (Barnouw 1966: 91). Frederick Lewis Allen (1931: 137) writes that although radio broadcasting had been publicly available since 1920, it wasn't until the spring of 1922 that radio sales took off. It was a veritable craze, amounting to $60,000,000 in sales that year and climbing higher afterward. This craze was registered in American culture in many ways, some silly, some creative, some serious.

The frenzy of interest in radio did not mean that people simply went out, purchased radios, and began listening, however. Radio was still a new technology for which ways of integration into everyday life had to be found. The following stories show the many ways that radio was incorporated into everyday life, how it ceased being solely a mere technological novelty and became something that people used in their everyday lives for pleasure, information, and more. Radio hobbyists who became proselytizers extolled the virtues of radio in countless magazine articles, articles about radios being installed in hotels, in hospitals, on buses, on cable cars, in automobiles, in baby carriages for lullabies, and about how they could be used on camping trips, and more. Here are some of these stories.

An editorial in June 1922 in *Radio Digest* (RD 1922c) suggested that motorboat enthusiasts take the radio with them while boating. Later that same month, *Radio Digest* reported that "a hoopskirt has been successfully used as an antenna," which meant that "ladies will have a distinct advantage in the matter of Radio receiving if this quaint and now remodernized fashion comes back" (RD 1922d).

In June 1922, Rudolph Friml, a composer, wrote a song on a steamship bound from New York to Europe and radioed the music back to New York to be heard later that night in a Ziegfeld Follies Show. Friml wrote out the entire melody in solfège (that is, do re mi) syllables. He had the lyrics with him, as did the Ziegfeld. With this string of solfège syllables, it would be easy enough for the solfège-trained musician to translate the tune into music notation and derive the rhythm from the lyrics (RW 1922h).

In July 1922, Wallace Blood of Chicago outfitted his car with a radio for a driving trip to the Pacific coast, which Mr. Blood said was the first radio tour on record (RW 1922i).

Also in 1922, there was a suggestion that army buglers be replaced by radio (RD 1922e).

Radio World (RW 1922j) reported in September 1922 "a young man in a large red touring car equipped with loop aerial, receiving set, and loudspeaker. He dashes to and fro along the Great White Way, and—well, you ought to hear the music!" The anonymous author went on to comment on the quality of reception and tone of the radio.

Radio World (RW 1923a) featured five bathing beauties on its cover of July 7, 1923, instructing readers in the caption that "Radio Adds to the Pleasures of the Seashore"; a few weeks later, Velma Carson urged readers of *Radio World* to take their radios camping with them (RW 1923b).

In 1923, *Popular Radio* discussed a method by which Mom could be sure she could hear her programs when she wanted:

> When Mother reads in the paper that a song she especially wants to hear is to be sent out by a certain station at nine o'clock Tuesday evening she reserves that hour on the sheet. That holds the hour for that station and for her against claims of other members of the family. Sister may reserve Thursday evening for jazz from her favorite band and invite in her friends, secure in the knowledge that no one else will have pre-empted the set that evening for a missionary lecture or the report of a prize fight. (PR 1923)

Note that it is the mother and sister who are targeted here, as part of the strategy of extending radio beyond the realm of the male hobbyist and military.

In 1924 a barbershop in Washington, D.C., installed a nickel-in-the-slot radio receiver so that people getting their hair cut could listen to the radio while the barber worked (PR 1924; see also RN 1926a). The *Popular Radio* story of this phenomenon was accompanied by a photograph of a baleful young girl getting her hair cut by an African American man (see figure 12.5).

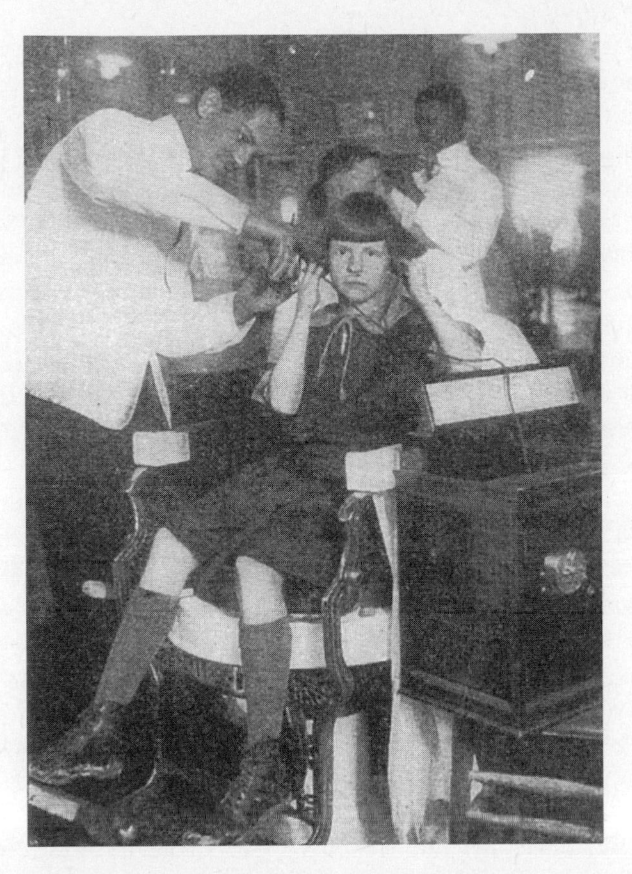

Fig. 12.5. "The Newest Radio Bob" (PR 1924). Author's collection.

In one American city in 1924, the organ grinder was replaced by the "Radio Barrel Organ" in a cart drawn by a donkey (RW 1924a).

Even some cowboys employed the radio for singing their cattle to sleep. "It sure is a big saving on the voice," Tom Blevins, a Utah cowboy, wrote in to his local radio station in 1926. "The herd don't seem to tell the difference. Don't put on any speeches, though. That'll stampede 'em sure as shootin'" (PR 1926b).

In Lancaster, Pennsylvania, in January 1927, radio opera lovers offered a $100 reward for information on a man who interrupted Giuseppe Verdi's *Il Trovatore* as it was being broadcast by the Chicago Opera company. "Good evening, folks. This is my regular concert. How do you like it?" he asked. "Lancaster people do not want opera anyway. Radio reception in Lancaster depends entirely upon me" (NYT 1927d).

Also in the mid-1920s, instruments were being modified and made anew so that they would be able to broadcast directly over the ether. So there was the "pianorad," the "tromborad," a "new radio violin" with a pickup for amplification, a "giant-tone radio violin," and a pipe organ modified for broadcasting (RN 1926a; RN 1927a; PR 1926c; RN 1927b; *Radio Amateur News* 1920; see also RW 1924b).

The foregoing are all everyday uses of radio, but this new technology found its way into life practices that occured less frequently as well. There was, for example, a spate of radio weddings in the 1920s. One such wedding, in Chicago in the spring of 1924, featured a broadcast of the wedding march from Richard Wagner's opera *Lohengrin*. The bride's brother, a radio enthusiast, arranged with the local radio station to have the work broadcast at precisely 8 P.M., while the bride and groom stood before the minister at the church (NYT 1924c). On New Year's Eve in 1926, in Belleville, New Jersey, a couple waited in the bride's parents' home for the orchestra they had hired, but it didn't appear. An enterprising bridesmaid, the bride's sister, telephoned station WAAM in Newark and requested that they play a wedding march. As soon as the bride's father turned on the radio, the ceremony proceeded (NYT 1927b). In 1928 a more spectacular musical event at a wedding occurred when the composer and conductor Ernest Schelling played Mendelssohn's "Wedding March" on the piano from his villa on Lake Geneva to his friends in Manchester, Massachusetts, at their wedding (NYT 1928).

There was also a move to include radio music at another important ritual, the funeral. In late 1929 a funeral director at a meeting of the New Jersey State Funeral Directors' Association introduced a resolution that special radio programs should be established to broadcast suitable music for funerals. "The arrangement of such a program might be fixed for a certain hour in the afternoon, so as to fit in as part of the funeral services," read the resolution, "and such services could be readily timed so as to permit the rendering of music in keeping with the solemnity of the occasion" (NYT 1929).

Not all of the stories in this era about radio were favorable, however. At a party in Brooklyn in February 1927, a young Frenchman was arrested for smashing a broadcasting microphone because he objected to the broadcasting of the "Marseillaise," shouting something about "desecration" as he wreaked his havoc (NYT 1927c).

Radio Music and Healing

Preexisting attitudes about music were newly tested with the advent of radio. Radio music, for example, was said to soothe savage beasts. At the Bronx Zoological Park in 1923, Chief Keeper John Toomey played music over the air to various animals. The lion, as evidenced by an accompanying photograph, "lacked musical appreciation," but the bears liked the music, especially the organ music, and "Grandpa," the ancient tortoise estimated to be 269 years old, seemed "decidedly pleased" with the radio music (RB 1923).

And, perhaps most curiously, radio could soothe and heal people. Well, it was *music* that was thought to have healing powers, but this belief was buttressed by the novelty of radio, so that in many contemporary writings there was a good deal of slippage from the healing ability of music to the wonder of radio itself. For example, in May 1922 a doctor in Boston put a radio receiver in his office for patients to listen to while waiting: "The patient is naturally feeling blue and sick at heart as well as body. Either the doctor or Mrs. FitzGerald [his wife] takes a seat at the radiophone and plugging in starts tuning up to catch Medford, Pittsburgh or Newark. The patient's mind is immediately taken up with the wonder of the new invention, which is explained to him while pop-eyed he hears songs sung thousands of miles away" (WA 1922a).

In June 1922 an ambulance in Fort Smith, Arkansas, was equipped with a radio, to play "soothing music" for a patient being transported to the hospital. "Music was furnished all the way from the train to the hospital," reported *Radio Digest,* which accompanied its article with a photograph of the ambulance, the radio barely visible (RD 1922f).

In August 1922, Dr. W. F. Jacobs, medical superintendent of the Cumberland Hospital in Brooklyn, said that "Radio deserves to be ranked with the best mental therapeutic agencies. In fact, for hundreds of cases the radio telephone can be prescribed as the one best treatment" (WA 1922b). Dr. Jacobs had been experimenting with radio on his patients since the previous September and had installed some sets at his own expense in the hospital. A new hospital was also being built that was completely equipped with loudspeakers and connections for headsets in all of the wards. "Think what it will mean," continued Dr. Jacobs,

> for some poor devil, friendless, homeless, laid up with a broken back, never receiving any visitors, with nothing to do from one day to another but look at the wall and think. I have put headsets over the ears of many such men, and have seen them transformed in a few minutes from creatures that were just dully existing to the intelligent, interested men they once were and now soon will be again, permanently, and much quicker because of the interest, the life, the health that radiates from radio. (WA 1922b)

The New York City Visiting Committee, whose activities mainly consisted of providing concerts in municipal hospitals and almshouses, helped solicit funds to equip Jacobs's new hospital, for it was the committee's "firm conviction that in the near future every institution will be equipped with radio apparatus. Endless vistas are opened for the bed-ridden and shut-ins generally."

No matter how excellent the medical care, nor how scrupulous the attention to material needs, the average patient in a municipal institution, where visitors are allowed only about twice a week, is apt to be discontented. He feels bored, out of touch with the world, impatient of delay. Imagine the change which a radio would make in this atmosphere! Without any tiring effect he can feel himself again a part of the world; his thoughts will be turned to something other than his own troubles and he will want more than ever to get well. There is reason to think that the period of convalescence would actually be shortened by the presence of the right sort of radio apparatus. (ibid.)[10]

Even those whom radio couldn't heal could nonetheless be touched by it. Radio's cultural force was so potent when it was new that even the deaf reported that they could "hear" radio music. In 1926, for example, some deaf listeners claimed to be able to perceive jazz:

This information has been conveyed to Paul Ash, orchestra leader and radio star of KYW in letters from several women who explain that these are the only sounds they have been able to hear and that they enjoy the jazz music although otherwise deaf. A famous ear specialist of Chicago has become interested in the subject, it is reported, and is conducting a series of tests to determine the possibilities of utilizing this means of "bone conduction" of sound so that those who have lost normal hearing may through radio have the pleasures of music. When the unique investigation has been completed the renowned specialist promises the issuance of a report and a test program over the air is to be given with deaf persons asked to "listen in" and to report what they "hear." (PR 1926d; see also RW 1924c)

More spectacular, however, was the rapturous letter to the Symphony Society of New York by Helen Keller in 1924.

I have the joy of being able to tell you that, though deaf and blind, I spent a glorious hour last night listening over the radio to Beethoven's "Ninth Symphony." I do not mean to say that I "heard" the music in the sense that other people heard it; and I do not know whether I can make you understand how it was possible for me to derive pleasure from the symphony. It was a great surprise to myself. I had been reading in my magazine for the blind of the happiness that the radio was bringing to the sightless everywhere. I was delighted to know that the blind had gained a new source of enjoyment; but I did not dream that I could have any part in the joy. Last night, when the family was listening to your wonderful rendering of the immortal symphony some one suggested that I put my hand on the receiver and see if I could get any of the vibrations. He unscrewed the top, and I lightly touched the sensitive diaphragm. What was my amazement to discover that I could feel, not only the vibrations, but also the impassioned rhythm, the throb and the urge of the music. The intertwined and intermingling vibrations from different instruments enchanted me. I could actually distinguish the cornets, the roll of the drums, deep-toned violas and violins singing in exquisite unison. How the lovely speech of the violins flowed and flowed over the deepest tones of the other instruments! When the human voices leaped up thrilling from the surge of harmony, I recognized them instantly as voices. I felt the chorus grow more exultant, more ecstatic, upcurving swift and flame-like, until my heart almost stood still. The women's voices seemed an embodiment of all the angelic voices rushing in a harmonious flood of beautiful and inspiring sound.

The great chorus throbbed against my fingers with poignant pause and flow. Then all the instruments and voices together burst forth—an ocean of heavenly vibration—and died away like winds with the atom is spent, ending in a delicate shower of sweet notes.

Of course, this was not hearing, but I do know that the tones and harmonies conveyed to me moods of great beauty and majesty. I also sensed, or thought I did, the tender sounds of nature that sing into my hand—swaying reeds and winds and the murmur of streams. I have never been so enraptured before by a multitude of tone-vibrations.

As I listened, with darkness and melody, shadow and sound filling all the room, I could not help remembering that the great composer who poured forth such a flood of sweetness into the world was deaf like myself. I marveled at the power of his quenchless spirit by which out of his pain he wrought such joy for others—and there I sat, feeling with my hand the magnificent symphony which broke like a sea upon the silent shores of his soul and mine.

Let me thank you warmly for all the delight which your beautiful music has brought to my household and to me. I want also to thank Station WEAF for the joy they are broadcasting in the world. (NYT 1924d)[11]

Keller's story is remarkable but no more so than the everyday stories. I present so many of these accounts simply to illustrate just how powerful radio had become, and how deeply it had infiltrated the sacred and the profane aspects of everyday life.

Clearly, some of these uses of radio are faddish. Fads, though, are social ways of dealing with the new and different. Once a fad is over, the object of the fad is usually normalized, if it is not forgotten altogether. Most of the stories retold above are from the early days of radio, a strategy chosen neither by design nor by accident: such stories abounded when radio was new. But by the 1930s, what excited peoples' interest was not so much radio as technological object or signifier of modernity but instead what was on the radio—the programs.

Whose Everyday Life?

All of the above stories illustrate how radio was pushed and pulled into everyday life, and by extension its uncommon cultural power. But it is important at this point to wonder just who was permitted to participate in this "everyday life." If radio in the 1920s was a sign of an American technological modernity, it had to be counterposed against those premoderns who didn't possess this technology—or understand it. In order to sustain the modern/premodern binary, uses of radio technology had to be found for every modern person—man, woman, and child.

It was this last group that posed the greatest problem, for how does an infant use a radio? Uses had to be found, for otherwise infants were dangerously unmodern, like the native peoples against whom American technological modernity was being compared. And uses weren't long in coming. In May 1921 some Union College students, members of the college Radio Club, rigged a "wireless receiving station" on an ordinary baby carriage, with a small megaphone attached (these were before the days of radios with speakers). With the baby in the carriage, a young woman back at the campus sang a lullaby, which was distinctly heard more than a mile away. The *New York Times* reported that "the baby was 'as good as could be,' soothed by the lullaby from start to finish . . ." (NYT 1921a; see also RN 1921).[12]

The question of the lullaby is particularly interesting. Since the lullaby was something normally sung by women, broadcasting lullabies was also a way of extending this new technology to women. Broadcasting lullabies seems also to have been a way for fathers to become more involved with their children. A cartoon published in *Radio World* in 1922 depicted a father in pajamas walking back and forth with his baby while the mother is seen sleeping in the bedroom. The radio loudspeaker is spouting musical notes, a song whose title, we are told, is "Go to Sleep My Radio Kid." The caption reads: "Mr. Jones says he doesn't mind walking the floor with the baby at all, now the radio is installed" (RW 1922e).

Also in 1922 the *London Opinion* published a cartoon with a baby in the cradle throwing a tantrum while Dad read the newspaper. The caption: "Harassed Parent: 'Good heavens! I suppose I must have switched the little beggar on to the political meeting at Limehouse instead of the lullaby concert at the Linoleum Hall'" (RW 1922f).

The idea of a lullaby concert wasn't unusual. In the early days of radio, several stations presented women singing lullabies and telling stories at bedtime. In Chicago in 1922 Miss Louise Forester sang thousands of babies to sleep every night (see RW 1922g). Later, Agnes Lenard told stories and sang children to sleep, accompanying herself on the ukulele on station WJZ in Newark in 1924; in Chicago, Mrs. J. Elliott Jenkins told bedtime stories and sang songs for children on WMAQ in 1925; Val McLaughlin conducted the popular children's program that was sometimes known as "Lullaby Time" on station WLS in Chicago in 1926. In New York, May Sprintz sang sleepy time songs, read poems, and told stories for children on her popular children's show. She also told many Mother Goose stories on WINS, New York City, in 1932, for fifteen minutes, Monday through Saturday, 7:00–7:15 P.M. (WA 1924; *Encyclopedia of American Radio* 2000).

Even children's nighttime programs weren't free of the stunt mentality. On September 13, 1924, Gus Carey, otherwise known as "Uncle Wip," a bedtime storyteller on station WIP, owned by Gimbel Brothers' department store in Philadelphia, donned a diving suit and jumped off the end of a pier in Atlantic City, New Jersey, shortly after 7 P.M. He had a receiver inside his helmet so he could hear his pianist, Harry Link, sitting at the piano on the end of the pier. Uncle Wip's microphone was inset in a rubber sponge and connected to a broadcasting unit on the end of the pier so that Link could hear him. Thus situated, Uncle Wip told a bedtime story first, as usual, followed by a recitation of the names of those youngsters who had written to him. Then he sang his lullaby. "The accompaniment was perfectly timed," wrote the *New York Times,* "and to listeners-in the song sounded as if it was being sung beside a piano in the usual manner" (NYT 1924b).

Radio, the Intimate Medium

The above stories were meant to demonstrate the way that radio was integrated into social lives, as well as how the "social" was in some sense defined by who wasn't in it—the racialized and ethnicized others—a juxtaposition that also highlighted the newness and technological achievement of radio compared to the supposedly backward premoderns depicted in so many photographs in the 1920s. These pictures showed how radio was thought to have conquered both space and time, from modern to premodern.

Even as radio was brought into the realm of social life, however, it was at the same time reconfiguring the nature of the private, of intimate space, being integrated into individual lives and private fantasies. As many authors have noted, radio was a crucial factor in blurring the distinction between public and private in America in the twentieth century.[13]

While it was perfectly possible before radio to hear music in the home, either music one made oneself or recordings played on the phonograph, radio was different.[14] In the 1920s, radio music, unlike the phonograph, was live. And radio, unlike most home musicking, offered the best musicians around, as sponsors never tired of telling their listeners.

It would be difficult to underestimate the impact of radio on live entertainment. A particularly vivid firsthand description of the changes wrought by radio appears in a memoir by George Burns:

> The only problem was that just as we were becoming stars, vaudeville was dying. No one could pin the rap on us, though. Everybody believes it was the movies that killed vaudeville. That's not true. Movies, vaudeville, burlesque, the local stock companies—all survived together.
>
> Then radio came in. For the first time people didn't have to leave their homes to be entertained. The performers came into their house. Gracie and I knew that vaudeville was finished when theaters began advertising that their shows would be halted for fifteen minutes so that the audience could listen to "Amos & Andy." And when the "Amos & Andy" program came on, the vaudeville would stop, they would bring a radio onstage, and the audience would sit there watching radio.

> It's impossible to explain the impact that radio had on the world to anyone who didn't live through that time. Before radio, people had to wait for the newspaper to learn what was happening in the world. Before radio, the only way to see a performer was to see a performer. And maybe most important, before radio there was no such thing as a commercial.
>
> Radio made everybody who owned one a theater manager. They could listen to whatever they wanted to. (Burns 1988: 86–87)

Listeners home alone listening to the radio were free to construct fantasies about themselves and about the people they were listening to, as Susan J. Douglas writes (1999).[15] And once again, music was one of the best vehicles with which to do this, particularly since radio ushered in a new style of performing that came to be known as "crooning." Crooning arose because other styles of singing—operatic, Broadway, and vaudeville, for example—were too loud for radio equipment in the 1920s. A softer style of singing was necessary to preserve the equipment, and it was a woman, Vaughn de Leath, who pioneered this new style. But it was quickly picked up by male singers such as Whispering Jack Smith and Gene Austin. Rudy Vallee became the first hugely popular crooner, however, and indeed the first national mass-media popular music star in America.[16]

The striking feature about crooning was that, even when it was broadcast or played back on phonograph records, it offered a greater sense of intimacy than live singing. Opera singers are specifically trained to sing loudly so that they can be heard, unamplified, in the back of the concert hall. Vaudeville and other popular singers cultivated a piercing, nasal singing style, and/or a particular mode of enunciating words that was almost barking, which rendered them audible to people sitting in the cheap seats. Preradio singing styles, therefore, were manifestly "public"—meant to be heard by many listeners.

Crooning, on the other hand, had the effect of the singer singing to only one listener. Whereas the other styles mentioned above were clearly intended for listening in public spaces, with the singers singing as loudly and/or as penetratingly as possible, crooning was just the opposite—it was as if the singer was singing only to you in your home, through the miracle of radio. Few recordings of these early programs survive, but Rudy Vallee and other crooners in the 1920s and 1930s made commercial recordings that are still easily available. Listening to them today, one is struck by the unremarkable singing style, for crooning was in effect the first of the modern singing styles, employing the microphone the way that all singers today do. And yet, the strangeness of this style then is accessible to us now. Listening to Rudy Vallee sing songs such as "I'm Just a Vagabond Lover," in which he doesn't simply croon but seems to be deliberately decreasing the volume, one is struck by the strikingly private nature and directness of this style.[17]

Crooning as a singing style thus introduced a paradox: while radio was proclaimed as uniting disparate Americans into a single culture, this singing style that had been ushered into existence by radio helped create and maintain an illusion that listeners' relationships to singers and other broadcasting individuals were unmediated and personal. Even when broadcast, crooning was a more personal mode of musical expression than those that people could have heard live.

Crooning, combined with the intimacy that was thought to be intrinsic to radio because of its placement in the home, resulted in an unprecedented intrusion into peoples' private spaces and lives. The focal point of this intimacy, however, was not all listeners, but women. Singers such as Vallee became hugely popular with women fans, though there were many male fans as well. Vallee's popularity with women and the underlying gender issues have been recently discussed by Allison McCracken and thus don't need to be considered here, except to note that her argument centers on the ways in which Vallee's supposed effeminacy resulted in his being eclipsed by Bing Crosby fairly quickly in popularity (McCracken 1999). Rather, the question of intimacy that is not central to McCracken's discussion will be addressed here.

A 1930 *Radio Revue* contest designed to elucidate the reasons for Vallee's popularity was won by a "mere man," though the second-prize letter was by a woman who addresses the intimacy issue in it. Vallee is the "eternal love," she writes. "Always breathing romance, singing the praises of love, enrapturing his phantom sweetheart with his ardent whisperings, and at the same time yearning for his own dream girl—he makes the women believe that each one is the only one—that she alone is his beloved" (*Radio Revue* 1930a).

At the same time, *Radio Revue* held a different contest for the best letters on the subject of "Who Is My Favorite Radio Artist—and Why?" Margaret H. Heinz of Buffalo won first prize for her letter about Vallee. Rudy Vallee, she says, "is a clever youngster—he knows how to use that voice. He knows that every woman likes to feel that he is singing just to her—and so he sings to every woman as an individual" (*Radio Revue* 1930b).

McCracken quotes a woman's fan letter on the same theme: "'Your voice is strangely similar to that of a friend, of whom I've lost track, that I act like one in a trance while you're singing'"(McCracken 1999: 376). "It is a real treat for me to hear the voice of an old friend each night," wrote another (ibid.: 377).

Vallee's fans weren't the only people who believed that he sang to them directly; this was the highest praise that only the best radio entertainers could receive. And musicians themselves seem to be well aware of this. Bradley Kincaid, an early country musician, wrote this in one of his song-books to his fans: "When I sing for you on the air, I always visualize you, a family group, sitting around the table of the radio, listening and commenting on my program. Some of you have written and said that I seem to be talking right to you, and I am. If I did not feel your presence, though you be a thousand miles away, the radio would be cold and unresponsive to me, and I in turn would sound the same way to you."[18]

Advertisers seemed to be aware of crooning's intimate qualities. Herman S. Hettinger, an early scholar of broadcast advertising, wrote in 1933, "The real success of crooning has been not in its musical aspects, but in the personal touch and atmosphere of romantic intimacy which the crooner has been able to build up through his distinctive delivery" (Hettinger 1933: 221).

Crooning might have been the most intimate form of singing at the time, but radio itself was thought to be intimate too, even though at the same time listeners well knew they were tuning in simultaneously with thousands or millions of others. The idea that the radio waves were entering almost directly into one's own head was powerful, as the following poem by John Webster from 1922 suggests.

The Radioman's Love Song

I am high on the breast of the swelling sea,
And your voice comes from faraway home to me;
It comes clear and true from the weird above—
And you sing of love—you sing of love.

I start—I look! But you are not near!
I wonder—I ask: Is it you I hear?
Yes—'tis you!—though your voice comes o'er leagues of sea—
For you sing to me—you sing to me!
(RW 1922d)

Though, of course, she sings to anyone who has a radio.

A cartoon from early 1923 entitled "Perfectly Satisfied" (RW 1923g) depicts a young couple on a love seat, his arm around her, each with their own headphones—separated, yet united by their connection to a radio. The dialogue reads, "'Gee, Annabelle! Ain't it nice of them to broadcast 'That Ever Lovin' Pair' for our benefit. They know us, all right.'"

This belief about intimacy and directness was so potent that there was an occasional tragedy. In February 1927, Karoline Groschek committed suicide in her bedroom. She was in her fifties, a cook for a wealthy family. She had fallen in love with a singer on the radio in Vienna and wrote him many letters, to which the only response was an autographed photo (NYT 1927a). Yet even this tragedy was reported by the unremittingly boosterish American radio press in radio terms, not human ones: "The First Suicide for Love of a Broadcast Artist" was the title of the report in *Popular Radio* (PR 1927).

Some programs were particularly adept at invoking the changing nature of the public and private, even going so far as to invoke each sphere in turn. Chase and Sanborn's enormously popular program with Eddie Cantor, *The Chase and Sanborn Hour,* for example, began with the announcer opening the program, followed by a lush orchestral introduction that could have served just as well as the musical introduction to a major Hollywood film. Then a musical transition led back to the announcer, who said: "Rubinoff and his violin." (The Russian violinist Rubinoff—who went by his first name only—was a fixture on Cantor's program.) This interjection is followed by a trumpet fanfare, then Rubinoff playing a dreamy, romantic solo accompanied by the orchestra. The intimate quality of the solo serves to move the listener from the "public" mode of the announcer and the opening music to the "private" mode of home listening, a privacy and intimacy emphasized by Cantor's opening lines and style of delivery, which is essentially crooning in speech: "Are you listenin,' folks, huh? This is your old pal Eddie Cantor just a'callin' round for a good old visit with you all. Pull yourself up an easy chair by the good old fireplace, folks, and we'll smoke a herring together."[19] Cantor's deliberate southernisms—"a'callin'" and "you all"—further heighten the sense of hominess and intimacy that listeners were supposed to receive.

Perceptions of the intimate character of radio went beyond listeners' infatuations with singers and songs. Susan J. Douglas writes of the ways that radio was seen as mysterious and even spiritual in its early history. The issue of radio's almost telepathic mode of communication, however, is arguably separate from the spiritualism that sprang up around it in some quarters. Radio, unlike any previous communications technology available to the public, was *live:* people heard it in real time and knew that others were hearing it in real time at the same time. This was a difficult concept to grasp for people still caught up in a print culture.

And radio was often understood in terms of telepathy. This is the fulcrum upon which Douglas makes her arguments about spiritualism, but it seems possible that radio as telepathy has as much or more to do with the intimacy of the medium. As we saw with respect to radio crooners, to listeners in the 1920s the radio really seemed to be speaking to them individually, particularly in the early days, when people listened to it directly with headphones.[20]

Douglas is right, however, to focus on the discourses of telepathy with respect to radio in the 1920s, for there are plenty of examples. For instance, in May 1925, Hugo Gernsback, editor and publisher of *Radio News,* wrote an intemperate column about "mental radio" in which he debunks the beliefs of people who claimed to be able to receive radio signals in their heads. Gernsback writes that he received ten to fifteen letters per week from people who "possess this affliction." Gernsback goes on to relate how he "cured" a woman of this "delusion" by suggesting she sleep with a magnet under her pillow and then suggesting later that she sleep with her ears tightly closed (RN 1925).

Now, the question is not whether or not people were actually receiving radio signals. Rather, Gernsback's column serves as one of many examples of the discourse of the era that held radio to be a personal and private mode of communication. This belief was widespread enough that telepathy was termed "mental radio" for a time, as in Upton Sinclair's book by that title published in 1930 (Sinclair conducted experiments to uncover the nature of his wife's telepathic powers). Trained scientists carried out similar experiments about radio. In March 1922 three psychology professors, from Northwestern University, Columbia University, and Antioch College, attempted to send thought waves through the radio from station WJAZ Chicago; no mention of their reception has been found (RW 1924d). Aimee Semple McPherson established her own radio station and described the antenna towers as "alive, tingling, pulsing spires of steel, mute witness that at Angelus Temple every moment of the day and night, a silent and invisible messenger awaits the command to carry, on the winged feet of the winds, the story of hope, the words of joy, of comfort, of salvation."[21] McPherson exhorted listeners to place their hands on the radio and pray with her, as if they could all be connected.[22]

Any new technology needs to be promoted; uses need to be found for it, or else it won't develop a social life or social uses. Radio was no different. But radio was never simply a technological gadget: it was a communications technology, a medium. By foregrounding the historical moment after radio's invention and before its unquestioned acceptance into everyday life, this essay has attempted to show the myriad avenues that radio's proselytizers used to push it into everyday peoples' lives.

And once people found uses for it in everyday life, from lullabies to weddings to hospitals, radio's social existence began to shape peoples' experience of music and entertainment more generally. No longer did one have to leave the home to hear professional-quality live music, for the radio brought it into the home, transforming peoples' conceptions of public and private as formerly public voices and sounds and modes of discourse were listened to in private settings. With music and voices, radio connected people from distant places, even as those people maintained a notion that radio was speaking to them alone.

With all of these innovations, all of these alterations to social life, radio in the 1920s and 1930s came to symbolize perhaps more than any other technology, with the possible exception of the automobile, Americans' sense of themselves as moderns, especially compared to peoples without radio. And yet radio allowed Americans to maintain a premodern sense of unmediated relationships, as it seemed to speak to listeners directly. While radio may seem to be a humble technology today, in many real and important ways—bureaucratically, legally, and culturally—television is but a footnote to radio.

Acknowledgments

I would like to thank Sherry B. Ortner for her always invaluable suggestions. I would also like to thank the members of my graduate seminar on music and radio at Columbia University in the fall of 2001. I would also like to thank David Cuthbert, editor of the *Historical Journal of Film, Radio and Television,* where this article first appeared, for his useful editorial suggestions. Finally, thanks are due to Tom Porcello and his colleagues at Vassar College, who heard a version of this paper and offered many penetrating comments.

Notes

1. For the earlier version of this ideology, see Jacques Ellul's conception of "technique," which he defines as "the *totality of methods rationally arrived at and having absolute efficiency* (for a given stage of development) in *every* field of human activity" (Ellul 1964: xxv; emphasis in original). Postman's work is essentially an updated version of Ellul's critique.

2. See Dumenil 1995: 148 for a similar point.

3. See especially the chapter "The Social Construction of American Broadcasting."

4. This kind of juxtaposition has been one of the central interests of much of this author's work. See, for example, Taylor 1997 and several of the chapters in Taylor 2001.

5. Figure 2 was reused in PR 1921. For just a few more examples: RD 1922b; RW 1923d; RB 1925; RW 1922a; NYT 1924a; RB 1927b; RW 1923e; RW 1923f; RN 1924a.

6. For an example of one of these ads, see *Radio News* (May 1924), p. 1613. Michael Adas (1989: 3) writes that by the middle of the eighteenth century, one of the most important ways, and sometimes *the* most important way, that Europeans judged other cultures was by their scientific and technological advancement.

7. Thanks are due to Sherry B. Ortner for help on this point.

8. For a discussion of the importance of the immigrant saga and early radio, see Hilmes 1997, especially chapter 1, "Radiating Culture."

9. See Douglas 1987 for a useful discussion of radio as a male domain in its earliest usages.

10. St. Luke's Hospital in upper Manhattan was also equipped with radio in its four wards (RW 1923c).

11. In 1916, Helen Keller was photographed with Enrico Caruso, singing into her fingers (Victor Talking Machine Company 1916, p. 6). Thanks go to David Suisman for finding this.

12. This exploit was worthy of an editorial in the *Times* the following day: NYT 1921b. Cornell students also attempted the same experiment; see RD 1922g.

13. Many scholars of radio have argued this point. For a few useful sources, see Douglas 1999; Loviglio 2002; and Marchand 1985, especially the chapter "Abandoning the Great Genteel Hope: From Sponsored Radio to the Funny Papers."

14. See Roell 1989 for a discussion of the role of the piano in the American home.

15. Especially the chapter "The Zen of Listening."

16. For lengthier histories of crooners, see Douglas 1999 and McCracken 1999.

17. This song is collected on Rudy Vallee, *Heigh-ho Everybody!* Pavilion Records PAST CD 7077, 1995.

18. Quoted by Kristine M. McCusker (1998: 179).

19. This program, probably aired on December 13, 1931, is one of the few *Chase and Sanborn Hours* recorded and is available on *The Eddie Cantor Chase & Sanborn Radio Show, 1931–1933,* Original Cast Records OC-8715, 1999.

20. The radio loudspeaker did not become commonplace until 1925.

21. Quoted in Dumenil 1995: 179.

22. Later, Oral Roberts adopted the same technique. Thanks are due to Sherry B. Ortner for sharing this memory.

References

Abbreviations: NYT: *New York Times;* WA: *Wireless Age;* PR: *Public Radio;* RB: *Radio Broadcast;* RD: *Radio Digest;* RN: *Radio News;* RW: *Radio World*

Adas, Michael. 1989. *Machines As the Measure of Men: Science, Technology, and Ideologies of Western Dominance.* Ithaca: Cornell University Press.

Allen, Frederick Lewis. 1964 [1931]. *Only Yesterday: An Informal History of the 1920's.* New York: Harper.

Barnouw, Erik. 1966. *A Tower in Babel: A History of Broadcasting in the United States to 1933.* New York: American Philological Association.

Burns, George. 1988. *Gracie: A Love Story.* New York: Viking Press.

Douglas, Susan. 1987. *Inventing American Broadcasting, 1899–1922.* Baltimore: Johns Hopkins University Press.

———. 1999. *Listening In: Radio and the American Imagination . . . from Amos 'n' Andy and Edward R. Murrow to Wolfman Jack and Howard Stern.* New York: Times Books.

Dumenil, Lynn. 1995. *The Modern Temper: American Culture and Society in the 1920s.* New York: Hill and Wang.

Ellul, Jacques. 1964. *The Technological Society,* transl. John Wilkinson. New York: Knopf.

Hettinger, Herman. 1933. *A Decade of Radio Advertising.* Chicago: University of Chicago Press.

Hilmes, Michele. 1997. *Radio Voices: American Broadcasting, 1922–1952.* Minneapolis: University of Minnesota Press.

Loviglio, Jason. 2002. "*Vox Pop:* Network Radio and the Voice of the People." In *Radio Reader: Essays in the Cultural History of Radio,* ed. Michele Hilmes and Jason Loviglio. New York: Routledge, 89–111.

McCracken, Allison. 1999. "'God's Gift to Us Girls': Crooning, Gender, and the Re-Creation of American Popular Song, 1928–1933." *American Music* 17: 365–395.

McCusker, Kristine. 1998. "'Dear Radio Friend': Listener Mail and the *National Barn Dance,* 1931–1941." *American Studies* 39: 173–195.

Marchand, Roland. 1985. *Advertising the American Dream: Making Way for Modernity, 1920–1940*. Berkeley: University of California Press.

New York Times. 1921a. "Very Latest in Wireless; Union College Students Find a 'Universal Lullaby' for Babies." (May 11): 12.

——. 1921b. "Anyhow, Baby Was Good" (editorial). (May 12): 16.

——. 1924a. "Oskenonton, a Mohawk Indian Inspecting WEAF" (photograph). (May 4): sec. 9, p. 16.

——. 1924b. "'Uncle Wip' Sings Lullaby from Ocean's Floor, Off Atlantic City Pier." (September 14): sec. 1, p. 30.

——. 1924c. "Use Radio for Wedding." (March 6): 15.

——. 1924d. "Helen Keller Gets Music by Radio." (February 10): sec. 1, part 2, p. 8.

——. 1927a. "Ends Life over Radio Love." (February 8): 3.

——. 1927b. "Wedding Has Radio Music." (January 1): 7.

——. 1927c. "Smashes Microphone As Anthem Is Played." (February 11): 44.

——. 1927d. "Reward for Air Nuisance." (January 31): 12.

——. 1928. "Schelling in Europe Plays for Bride Here." (September 2): sec. 2, p. 2.

——. 1929. "Music by Radio for Funerals Urged by Undertaker's Group." (December 5), p. 13.

On the Air. 1926. "Marvin Plotke, Radio's 'One and Only' Indian Tenor." (January): 10.

Popular Radio. 1921. "Is Radio Broadcasting Killing the Wild Savageries of JAZZ?" (February): 139–140.

——. 1923. "Advance Seat Sale for Radio Concerts." (October): 528.

——. 1924. "The Newest Radio Bob." (July): 96.

——. 1925. "The Buffalo Nickel Indian Broadcasts." (December): 588.

——. 1926a. "The Yellow Peril via Radio." (September): 494.

——. 1926b. "'Sing Down the Cattle' by Radio." (October): 615.

——. 1926c. "The New Radio Violin," by Patrick Whelan. (July): 229

——. 1926d. "Jazzing the Deaf by Radio." (March): 296.

——. 1927. "The First Suicide for Love of a Broadcast Artist." (April): 408.

Postman, Neil. 1993. *Technopoly: The Surrender of Culture to Technology*. New York: Knopf.

Radio Amateur News. 1920. "Georges Desilets, Music by Radio Spark Tones." (June): 681.

Radio Broadcast. 1923. "'Music Hath Charms—.'" (September): 415.

——. 1924. "Onondaga Indians." (October): 487.

——. 1925. "In the Village of Juan Diaz, Panama." (November): 35.

——. 1927a. "An Eskimo Lullaby at WGY." (October): 373.

——. 1927b. "Real Hawaiians at KHJ" (photograph). (June): 97.

Radio Digest. 1922a. "How about the Antenna?" (June 17): 6.

——. 1922b. "Eskimos Step to Tunes from CFCN." (December 23).

——. 1922c. "Concerts for the Motor Boat Owner" (editorial). (June 17): 6.

——. 1922d. "Hoopskirts Radio Back." (June 17): 6.

——. 1922e. "Army Reveille Is Now Sent by Radio." (May 13): 3.

——. 1922f. "Maimed and Sick Forget Pain in Model Radio Equipped Ambulance." (June 3): 2.

——. 1922g. "Now for a Radio Milk Bottle!" (April 29): 4.

Radio News. 1921. "A New Use for Radio." (June): 856.

——. 1924a. "When Broadcasting Was in Flower" (cartoons). (February): 1069.

——. 1924b. (May): 1613.

——. 1925. "Mental Radio," by Hugo Gernsback. (May): 2043.

——. 1926a. "Five Minutes of Radio for a Nickel." (April): 1433.

——. 1926b. "The 'Pianorad,'" by Hugo Gernsback. (November): 493.
——. 1927a. "Building the 'Tomborad,'" by G. B. Ashton. (April): 1237
——. 1927b. "The Giant-Tone Radio Violin," by R. F. Starzl. (April): 1236.
Radio Revue. 1930a. "Mere Man Wins First Prize in Rudy Vallee Contest." (January): 47.
——. 1930b. "Rudy Vallee and Jessica Dragonette Lauded in Prize Letters." (March): 36.
Radio World. 1922a. "Indians Hear Songs by Radio" (photograph). (June 17): 14.
——. 1922b. "Hears White Fathers' Signal Fire." (June 24): 25.
——. 1922c. "Little Chief Bear Hears Big Radio." (May 27): 30.
——. 1922d. "The Radioman's Love Song," by John Webster. (September 9): 12.
——. 1922e. "Radio Has Made It a Joy!" by Harry R. Stillman. (September 16): 19.
——. 1922f. "Radiograms." (September 2): 14.
——. 1922g. "Radio and the Woman." (April 22): 13.
——. 1922h. "First Radio Written Music Is Sung on New York Stage." (July 8): 31.
——. 1922i. "He Shall Have Music, Indeed." (July 1): 22.
——. 1922j. "Radiograms." (September 9): 14.
——. 1923a. "Radio Adds to the Pleasures of the Seashore" (photo caption). (July 7): 1.
——. 1923b. "Take Radio Camping with You," by Velma Carson. (July 28): 30.
——. 1923c. "Radiograms." (February 3): 14.
——. 1923d. "First Radio Music for an Indian Dance." (February 24): 30.
——. 1923e. "Some Original Americans Enjoy a Broadcast Program" (cover photograph). (September 1): 1.
——. 1923f. "These Romany People Appreciate Radio Broadcasting" (cover photograph). (September 22): 1.
——. 1923g. "Perfectly Satisfied" (cartoon). (February 10): 26.
——. 1924a. "Many of Our Old Institutions . . ." (April 26): 18–19.
——. 1924b. "Runs a Radio Piano." (April 12): 15.
——. 1924c. "Radiograms." (February 16): 11.
——. 1924d. "Thought-Waves by Radio?" (March 22): 11.
Roell, Craig. 1989. *The Piano in America, 1890–1940*. Chapel Hill, N.C.: University of North Carolina Press.
Sies, Luther. 2000. *Encyclopedia of American Radio, 1920–1960*. Jefferson, N.C.: McFarland Press.
Sinclair, Upton. 2001 [1930]. *Mental Radio*. Charlottesville, Va.: Hampton Roads.
Slater, Don. 1997. *Consumer Culture and Modernity*. Malden, Mass.: Polity.
Taussig, Michael. 1993. *Mimesis and Alterity: A Particular History of the Senses*. New York: Routledge.
Taylor, Timothy. 1997. *Global Pop: World Music, World Markets*. New York: Routledge.
——. 2001. *Strange Sounds: Music, Technology, and Culture*. New York: Routledge.
Victor Talking Machine Company. 1916. *New Victor Records* (July).
Wireless Age. 1922a. "Concerts for Doctor's Patients." (May): 37.
——. 1922b. "Ward Seeley, Radio Relief for the Ailing." (August): 35.
——. 1924. "Peeps into Broadcast Stations." (February): 43.

CHAPTER THIRTEEN

Afterword

Thomas Porcello

If asked, most of the contributors to this volume would likely define themselves as anthropologists or ethnomusicologists; those fields, at any rate, are the disciplinary home of the vast majority. Audio technologies and the practice of sound recording have, of course, deep histories in both disciplines, ranging from the collection of music traditions and oral narratives for the sake of posterity and/or analysis to the elicitation of linguistic data. In this volume, however, the authors suggest that audio recording technologies and practices should be, for scholars in these and in other disciplines, more than just the tools of documenting expressive culture; they should be objects of study in their own right. In many ways, then, they argue for a shift in scholarly focus from the examination of the products of sound engineering (for example, musical or other sonic texts) to the processes of engineering as a vital aspect of contemporary cultural life. These processes can be engaged in by industry professionals (see the chapters by Diamond, Meintjes, Neuenfelt, and Porcello) but just as importantly by consumers in their daily listening or reinterpreting practices (see the chapters by Berger and Fales, Fales, Greene, Taylor, and Wallach). In this approach, technology is seen not just as a tool but as a critical means of social practice.

To take such an approach is to acknowledge, implicitly or explicitly, that current anthropological and ethnomusicological approaches to technology and sonic culture inhabit an inherently multidisciplinary territory, sharing theoretical and topical ground with scholars in media studies, cultural studies, and science and technology studies. To read a bibliography in any of these disciplines is to run across a set of recurring names (Adorno, Attali, Benjamin, Castells, Horkheimer, and Raymond Williams, for example) whose imprint on the critical assessment of the relationship between technology and social practice remains indelible. But what binds the chapters of this volume together is precisely that feature that is most glaringly absent from the work of these foundational figures: a persistent focus on the everyday *uses* of technology by social actors in crafting sonic artifacts and environments. Here, the value of ethnography as the principal methodology of anthropology and ethnomusicology bears fruit by providing a window into how people deploy technology to engineer (whether by making, listening to, or circulating) their musical and sonic lives.

To "epistemology" and "acoustemology" (Feld 1996), then, these chapters suggest the utility of a third and complementary term, "techoustemology," to foreground the implication of forms of technological mediation on individuals' knowledge and interpretations of, sensations in, and consequent actions upon their acoustic environments as grounded in the specific times and places of the production and reception of sound. When someone experiences the sound of a drum kit played live as less "realistic" than what she is used to hearing on recordings, the role of sound recording practices and technologies in forming a musical techoustemology is revealed; such is also the case when fans perceive heavy metal as becoming heavier and heavier over time (Berger and Fales, this volume), or when increasing the low-end distortion of a keyboard riff produces "The sound of Africa! Africa!" (Meintjes 2003). In this volume, music is the principal object of techoustemological inquiry, but other sounds are equally open to such an analysis. When subjects report that real guns sound more "fake" than guns in the movies, for instance, they are pointing to the sonic expectations set up by the conventions of film sound mixes, as well as movie theater and home theater sound systems; such is also the case when the richly warm FM-radio announcer's voice sounds thin and flat in face-to-face conversation, absent its compression-rich and cardiod-mic proximity-effect-enhanced radio timbre. Even where technological mediation is absent from the sonic signal chain (an increasingly infrequent event in contemporary life in all parts of the globe), its absence has a ghostlike implication for our expectations, our templates, of how we expect sounds to sound.

Individuals' knowledge, interpretation, sensation, and action in relation to sound and technology as anchored in specific times and places as well as particular historical, cultural, and social contexts — this definition of techoustemology intentionally privileges (perhaps demands) empirically grounded accounts of the production and consumption of sounds. It shares with the "technoculture" concept of Constance Penley and Andrew Ross (1992) and the social construction of technology work of Wiebe Bijker, Trevor Pinch, and Thomas Hughes (1987) a recognition that "any technology is not only culturally constructed but . . . its uses are culturally defined as well" (Wong 2003). However, it simultaneously pushes these sociotechnic theories firmly back into the realm of the lived experiences and meanings derived through the techoustemological practices of social actors. It demands an accountability not only to the specifics of how technology is deployed but to a serious consideration of the resultant *sounds* of sociotechnical action, and to how individuals and groups conceptualize, rationalize, and discursively render their own techoustemological ideologies and practices. It is axiomatic that these specifics will vary from situation to situation; as such, they actively resist efforts to impose a single, unifying theoretical framework around these chapters. Such unifying efforts seem too frequently to yield categorical statements that are easily imploded with the most cursory of ethnographic studies.

Philip Auslander's otherwise thought-provoking essay on the changing meanings of live performance in rock music provides a case in point. Arguing from a framework linked to "remediation" (the practice by which new media refashion prior media forms; see Bolter and Grusin 1999: 273), Auslander claims that whereas live performance in rock music previously signified the authenticity of the performer vis-à-vis rock ideology, it now exists at one level of remove, "imitat[ing] music video imitating live performance" (1999: 92). Auslander continues: ". . . the music video occupies the place formerly held by the sound recording as the primary musical text *and* has usurped live performance's authenticating function. The function of live performance under this new arrangement is to authenticate the *video* by showing that the same events and images that occur in the video can be reproduced onstage, thus making the video the standard for what is 'real' in this performance realm" (ibid.: 93, emphasis in original). This situation arises, he argues, because "video is the primary experience of music in a mediatized culture" (ibid.: 92). In positing this relationship among sound, image, technological change, industry, and capital, Auslander has no doubt astutely recognized that to the extent that music is now consumed audiovisually, live performance does more than simply authenticate the sounds of recorded music. But as a matter of social practice around music consumption, the primacy of video as the experience of music—even in those places that can be unquestionably characterized as "mediatized cultures"—is certainly a matter of empirical inquiry; Auslander's claim is undoubtedly true for some groups of music consumers, but as a typical practice—even for live-performance-attending fans—it is doubtful.[1] Techoustemology demands an accountability for how music, technology, sound, and social practice are used and made meaningful locally, and for ethnomusicologists and anthropologists, the value of ethnography lies in its particular ability to provide just such grounded information. Writing not about technology but about recent theoretical treatments of the concepts of the global and the local (which relate, of course, to technological and musical flows), Keila Diehl articulates the value of ethnography: "What gets grabbed out of the torrent by whom, what is done with it, and what this *means* to the grabber and his or her family and friends: this is where the global and the local come together and seem to preserve a place for ethnography for a while longer" (2002:11; italics in the original). The torrent of (new) media technologies and the resultant scholarly premium on theorizing media create a parallel trajectory to what Diehl suggests for globalization theory and the importance of ethnography; ethnography is offered in this volume as a necessary corrective that gives voice not primarily to theorists from the west who often replicate—inadvertantly or not—the discourse of "They do, We theorize" but to those do-ers who possess eloquent, theorized voices of their own.

Wired for Sound can thus be seen as a set of largely—though not exclusively—ethnographic attempts to examine local techoustemological practices in places as diverse as Indonesia, Brazil, South Africa, Australia, Nepal, and North America, often in relation to commodities that share no such distinct "placeness." Readers can certainly decide for themselves whether the material presented here suggests a set of essentially common practices with only minor—perhaps insignificant—variations (as mass-culture theorists since the Frankfurt school have warned of) or a set of tellingly local ways of using and responding to the technological mediation of sound and music (as [techno]cultural relativists have championed with equal fervor; see, for example, the essays in Lysloff and Gay 2003). Arguments between these two positions have characterized—perhaps even plagued—media and cultural studies through most of the latter half of the twentieth century and into the present and are, I suspect, unresolvable; one person's agency seems unfailingly to be another's determinism. Rather than continue to argue the point, the essays in this volume suggest several issues that, while not unrelated to such concerns, reconfigure in important ways the questions that should be asked in examining the cultural practices surrounding technologically mediated sounds.

First, sound recording technologies and practices converge to create a frequently complex relationship between the documentation of musical or sonic events and performances, and their creation in the act of recording. The distinction between documentation and creation has, of course, been important for decades: the earliest days of electronic recording, when mixing could alter the balance of instruments in an ensemble, or the advent of multitracking, which first allowed for overdubbing, both led to criticism that technology could "dupe" listeners into thinking that they were hearing an ensemble performance that, in fact, had never taken place. Such evaluative discourses are, of course, interesting data in their own right for what they reveal about local responses to technological mediation; I would go so far as to suggest that such ideological stances, and the responses and actions that feed them and flow from them with respect to technological mediation, may be the single most important extramusical basis for defining contemporary popular music genres.

But I wish to point to something more nuanced here, namely that for most recorded musics (purely electronic music may be the sole exception) the relationship between documentation and creation is always present in some configuration and is an empirical fact that necessitates close scholarly attention to its configuration on a case-by-case basis. In Louise Meintjes's chapter on South African sound engineers, for example, one learns that instruments conceptualized as traditional (for example, a calabash) are recorded via miking strategies that lead to sonic immediacy, a you-are-there-listening-to-the-musician transparency, unmediation ironically achieved via a seventeen-microphone-induced heightened mediation,[2]: all of which is to say that great value is placed on documenting their sound. Karl Neuenfeldt's discussion of Nigel Pegrum's creation of mixes that balance the "reality" of the didjeridu with "unreal" synthesized tracks again suggests that the "traditional" instrument is treated as a sonic object more to be documented than created in the recording process—not surprising given the ideological importance of authenticity in the world music market for which he is recording (see Taylor 1997: 19–31 for a discussion of the trope of authenticity in world music production and marketing). In my discussion of liveness in the recorded Austin sound, the drum kit is the instrument most held to a documentary standard. Unlike the calabash or the didjeridu, drums can make no claim in the rock or blues ensemble for the status of "authentic instrument," however. In this case, a documentary recording sensibility applied to drums signifies not an authentic time, place, or sound of indigeneity but the authenticity of an act—its live performance. In each of these cases, choices are made regarding which aspects of the recording are treated as documentary, and which can be engineered outside of a documentary framework. These choices can also be seen as conventions, when they come to define how a style of music should sound: see Jeremy Wallach's discussion of the value placed on whether or not *dangdut* remixes remain *kasar.* Attention to how and by whom such decisions are made is central to acknowledging the agency (see Taylor 2001: 25–38) that is part of contemporary techoustemological practices.

Second, sound recording technology and practice foreground issues of the permanence and the permutation of recorded music, a distinction salient for scholars as well as sound engineers, musicians, and consumers. Anthropologists and ethnomusicologists, as suggested above, have used recording devices to gather data for over a century. While the impetus for collecting that sonic data may be for purposes of future analysis, and while analysis at times may be aided by altering those recordings to make materials more audible (through, for example, equalization or other sonic processing), in general we are not accustomed to thinking of our field tapes (DATs, MiniDiscs, etc.) as raw materials for further textual reworking, nor do we assume that they should be thrown in the trash once our scholarly analysis of them is complete. As recorded text and as storage medium, they are treated as essentially completed and permanent objects—the elaborate set of institutional archives established for just such purposes would seem to confirm that field tapes are largely viewed as finished, permanent "texts."

The early history of sound recording suggests that a similar idea pervaded the approach to recording most music; that to record a performance was to "fix" it for eternity, thereby ensuring that performers could outlast their lifetimes (see Thompson 1995 and Morton 2000 for a discussion of how the Edison Corporation explicitly incorporated the concept of permanence and sonic immortality into its marketing of the added value of the phonograph). In such a framework, recordings were, if anything, the antithesis of raw materials intended for permutation; to rework them would be to violate the very intent behind committing a performance to tin foil, wax, vinyl, or acetate. And until the late 1960s, when the cassette recorder made its significant incursion into the Western consumer market, the mere idea that one would do a reworking of a "text" such as an LP—even as simple a reworking as creating a personal version of a recording that included only the parts that one truly liked—was virtually inconceivable.

Reworkings of all kinds are increasingly, of course, a staple practice of popular music production and consumption, as well as a driving force behind audio technology design and development. (One might legitimately ask whether the shift from analog to digital recording has hyperbolized a process that was already underway before its advent; that the storage not of analogs of sound but of simple bits of data simply facilitated the conceptualization of the storage medium as a source of raw material [1s and 0s] to be worked with as one might work with any other sort of data; the history of digital audio sampling use certainly suggests this to be the case.) Paul Greene and Jeremy Wallach characterize these reworkings as "sonic montage" and "techno-hybrids," respectively, and demonstrate the social implications of the sonic reconfigurations they yield. However one terms it, what is clear from a close examination of popular music practices as witnessed on dance floors and in studios around the world (to invoke Keil 1994

[1987]) is that remixing — reworking, permutation — has become one of the prime forms that agency takes in relation to technology and music.

Third, the term "sound engineering" takes on a special significance when it is moved beyond a narrow reference to the technological manipulation of sonic output. "Sound engineering" has been used throughout this volume to mean something both micro and macro: at the microlevel, production practices and the labor of sound engineers in recording studios have been examined for their aesthetic and political impact on recorded music. But equal attention has been paid to a broader sense of the term, one foregrounding engineering as the use of sound "to execute . . . social strategies" (Greene 1999). These uses may be undertaken by individuals "to construct and subtly transform meanings, symbols, and traditions in ritual performance settings," as Greene argues, but the chapters here suggest how this broader definition of sound engineering can highlight larger cultural and social impacts as well. Ingemar Grandin points to the strategic use of "modern song" and the radio in the development of a Nepali superculture; Louise Meintjes to how studio work processes, available technologies, and sonic design across South African popular music styles are indivisible from both racial discourses and global commodity flows; Timothy Taylor to radio's strategic introduction to Americans and its crucial link to the country's developing national sense of modernity in the twentieth century; and I to how sound engineering in the narrow sense becomes implicated in the production of a local music identity that in turn becomes a cornerstone for governmentally sanctioned and supported local economic development policy and practice. Whatever the specifics of the cases involved, expanding the definition of "engineering" beyond the narrow confines of technological work on music invites the investigation of how individuals, corporations, industries, and governments continually mine the nexus of music, sound, and technology for strategic social, political, economic, and aesthetic ends. Engineering can no longer simply be cast as the ethereal, nitpicking, obsessive, complex activity of the sonic technogeek; it is an everyday strategic activity demanded by living and acting in a world of mediated sound and music.

Fourth, additional ethnographic attention must be devoted to issues of gender and technology. The intimate link between technology and masculinity has been noted by numerous scholars (see Oldenziel 1999 and Wacjman 1991 for general discussions; considerations pertinent to music technologies can be found in, among others, Gay 1998, Meintjes 2003, Porcello 2003 [1998], and Sandstrom 2000). The territorializing of music technology as a masculine domain is particularly ironic because both as recordists and consumers, women have been deeply involved in the use of audio technology. Erika Brady's history of ethnographic field recording, for example, makes abundantly clear the extent to which women were centrally active in recording music and oral performances of folklore throughout the United States at the turn of the twentieth century (1999); women were also strongly targeted as consumers in early efforts to sell domestic sound recording and reproduction equipment (Morton 2000). But by the middle of the century, both professional and domestic audio technologies and practices had been reinscribed as fundamentally male domains (see, for example, Keightly 1996 on domestic practices surrounding home stereo systems; Kealy 1979 on the means by which sound engineering became a male-centered trade; and Douglas 1999 on the masculinization of radio culture).

Technologies, of course, are in and of themselves gender neutral. What genders a technology or the practices that accompany it are social actions; one literally must, as the title of Ruth Oldenziel's study of modern machines in America so aptly puts it, *make* technology gendered (1999). Beverley Diamond's piece in this volume hints at how the concept of music "production" is contested along gender lines, with women defining it broadly to include issues of collaboration and the overall flow of albums, while men argue for a narrower, technologically focused definition of the process. I have briefly argued elsewhere (2003 [1998]) that in technology-intensive phases of recording sessions, women are often expected to take directions, not to give them. These two examples suggest that the masculinization of audio technology is, at least in part, a discursive process; that is, it unfolds as part of the verbal or textual interactions that accompany music production (and consumption). Operating largely as historians engaged in archival research, feminist scholars of science and technology have recently documented some specific means by which men have claimed authority over technology; their analyses of written texts demonstrate in great detail processes ranging from men writing out of their autobiographies the contributions made by women partners to technology research and design (Oldenziel 1999: 100–105), to the process of "inventing experts"—unfailingly white men—designed to keep any and all Others marginalized from participating authoritatively in official discourses about electrical technologies in the late 1800s (Marvin 1988: 17–32). In parallel fashion, the ethnographic study of the social actions that gender audio technologies can prove a valuable resource for deconstructing not only the naturalization of maleness in the world of sound engineering but also the ways that discursive practices in technologically intensive workplaces more generally reinforce gendered relationships to technology.

Finally, another theme at play throughout this book and worthy of further exploration is the extent to which technology is assumed to pose a "problem" for music makers, music consumers, and scholars of music and musical practices. The intellectual roots of this "problematic" view of technology return us to the media theorists mentioned above. In foregrounding the link between popular music and "massness," and in casting massness in essentially negative terms, for instance, early Frankfurt school theorists (notably Adorno 1994; Horkheimer and Adorno 1991) effectively problematized the relationship between the technologies used in the creation and dissemination of popular music and the purported negative effects of the music itself. Similarly, readings given to Benjamin's "The Work of Art in the Age of Mechanical Reproduction" (1968) — a piece that is clearly important when thinking about recorded music, but that at the same time too often receives a cursory genuflection in much scholarship on the issue — often reinforce the sense that technology is problematic for music; the mass reproduction embodies a *lack* — of aura, of contextual rootedness — that derives directly from the reproductive capabilities of its constitutive technologies. This early problematization of technology has cast a long shadow into the scholarship that grapples with music/technology relationships; a particularly concise and trenchant response to how that shadow affects ethnomusicological recording practice and scholarship can be found in Steven Feld's discussion (1994) of criticisms leveled at his 1991 *Voices of the Rainforest* recording. Like Feld, not all scholars see the music/technology relationship as unremittingly problematic, of course; my observation here, rather, is that those who don't usually find themselves arguing from a persistently defensive position.

In watching Maggie Greenwald's film *Songcatcher* (2000), about an early twentieth-century (ethno)musicologist who, upon being denied tenure, heads to the Appalachian mountains to visit her sister and "discovers" mountain music that bears a striking resemblance to earlier folk music of the British Isles, I was struck by two scenes that bear directly upon many of the themes raised in the preceding chapters of this book, particularly those of the problems and potentials of music technology. In the first, having just heard the singing of a young Appalachian woman, Lily Penlaric (the scholarly character is based loosely on Olive Dame Campbell, who toured the Southern Appalachians in 1908 and published a book of English folk songs she collected on that tour in 1917) persuades her former (male) colleague to send a mechanical phonograph to the settlement school where she is staying so that she may record all of the songs the woman knows. "I need supplies," she tells him over the phone. "The collecting must be done scientifically." Upon the phonograph's arrival, she begins to record the young singer, Delatis, who explains that she had been taught a wealth of ballads by her deceased grandmother. Delatis inserts her head into the horn of the phonograph and begins to sing. We watch Delatis sing the first stanza in this fashion, and then the filmic image and sound shift so that the audience hears the second stanza being played back in recorded form and watches Lily, Delatis, and the two women who run the settlement school react to the recorded sound. What passes across their faces are expressions of satisfaction, curious amazement mixed with a hint of fear, and joy, respectively.

The scene immediately transitions to a subsequent song transcription session, which foregrounds the labor involved—for Delatis especially, but also for Lily—in writing music and lyric text to paper in real time. In stark contrast to the seamless move between performance and finished reproduction that the audience experiences while watching the cylinder recording sequence, we now witness Lily repeatedly interrupt her young singer, asking that Delatis sing two- or three-measure sections of the stanza multiple times so that Lily may write them down. "Why can't we just do this on cylinder?" Delatis complains, an apparent immediate convert to sound recording technology. Because they don't work for longer songs and will wear out, Lily informs her brusquely before asking for yet another repetition. Finally the song is all transcribed, and the young singer flops exhaustedly onto a bed, wearily and somewhat belligerently proclaiming herself "all sung out."

In a later scene, Lily wishes to make a recording of the singing of a woman who lives several rugged miles away from the school. She loads the bulky Edison machine onto a horse-drawn sled and, with the assistance of Delatis and her boyfriend, sets off across the steep, forested terrain. The audience watches the physical difficulty of the journey—dragging what appears to be several hundred pounds of equipment through dense forest, up precipitous hills, and across rocky streams. In earlier scenes, Lily has been challenged as to why she is interested in making recordings in such difficult conditions; her answer continues to invoke the quest to document and preserve the mountain music, as well as to subject the recordings to "scientific analysis." On this trip, due apparently to a continuing lovers' quarrel between her two assistants as well as to the near-impossibility of transporting the machine through such rugged terrain, the young man in a fit of anger finally hurls the sled backwards down an embankment, destroying the machine. The group continues its journey, however, and for the rest of the movie, Lily transcribes songs by hand, with a clear sense of regret at the loss of the phonograph.

In an obvious (perhaps even heavy-handed) way, the phonograph is cast as a problem in the narrative: a problem for the ethnomusicologist who must deal with its physical constraints in the field, as well as an object that she must demystify or neutralize for her "informants"; a problem for the mountain people who fear that these songs will, both in a literal and a more deeply political way, be taken from them once recorded; a problem in local social relations, as differing groups form around their responses to the presence of the ethnomusicologist and the question of whether she should be supported in her efforts to record local music; and a problem in gender relations that can seemingly be resolved only by a destructive act that unseats a woman from her professional relationship to audio technology—a reassertion of male dominance over knowledge as linked to machines. At the same time (though certainly in a less obvious way), technology is celebrated: for Lily it provides access to a form of documentation important to the goals of scholarship (and potentially to being treated as an equal in a male-dominated academy); for the people being recorded it provides a window into hearing the self and others in ways (and through time) that have previously been unavailable, and that many seem to find valuable. While the relationship between music and technology is certainly not the main focus of the movie, it becomes an interesting parallel narrative, one that ends ambiguously, never resolving whether the musical, sonic, and cultural engineering that Lily does ultimately has positive or negative repercussions for the music, the community, and herself.

That very ambiguity strikes at the heart of many of the chapters of this book, as well as at whatever shadowy assumptions about the music/technology relationship we continue to work with. Louise Meintjes describes, for instance, how technological limitations as well as the choices made about how to record different black South African musics are clearly problematic for some social actors (the engineers, mostly) but are also the very means by which the potential to get "overseas" is enabled; in Jeremy Wallach's look at *dangdut* remixes we see how digital technologies potentially threaten the presence of desirable analog timbres while nonetheless facilitating the development of more complex and interesting rhythms; my discussion of how Austin engineers craft a roomy drum sound suggests that even when a particular technology is available to produce a certain sound, other resources may be chosen instead. Other articles more clearly point to how technology provides not a problem but a remarkable resource: most notably, Harris Berger and Cornelia Fales suggest that the increased heaviness of heavy metal (as judged by fans as a desirable sonic feature of the music) is clearly about technological potentials that have changed since the early days of heavy metal, but also the chapters on Nepal by Ingemar Grandin and Paul Greene, on samba by Frederick Moehn, and on radio by Timothy Taylor largely demonstrate that not all participants in sonic cultures see technology in the problematic role that many scholars persist in casting it. When one looks carefully, it becomes evident that, even in the face of an increasingly globalized industry of music production, distribution, and consumption, local techoustemological practices are built around multiple ways of engineering and valuing the potentials, limitations, and implications of sound recording.

Notes

1. Many examples can be cited to contest this sweeping generalization, but I will mention only three. First, many rock music consumers neither watch music videos nor regularly attend concerts, particularly baby-boomers; Auslander seems to assume a younger audience, raised with MTV and VH1 (when the former still emphasized videos), as his template. My own anecdotal work with undergraduate students when teaching from Auslander's book, however, suggests that in fact very few college-age students watch videos with any regularity or view them as particularly salient in terms of the authenticity of their preferred performers/bands. Second, in tracking the upswing of engagement with MP3—whether in terms of storing music on personal computers or iPods, or in terms of file sharing—it is clear that consumers continue to gravitate toward collecting and consuming music-as-sound, not music-as-image. Third, not all musics that fit under the rubric of rock ideology as defined by Auslander (1999: 62–85) are readily available to fans in video form; I think here of local music that is outside of the economic networks that can support the production and distribution of videos but that nonetheless maintains significant fan bases.

2. See Porcello 1996: 263–287 for an extended discussion of the "masked mediation" utilized to heighten the sense of immediacy in musical performances. Although confined to a discussion of lo-fi rock and the "unplugged" phenomenon of the 1990s, that discussion highlights technological practices utilized in recording studios in many parts of the world.

References

BOOKS AND ARTICLES

Adorno, Theodor. 1994. *Philosophy of Modern Music,* transl. Anne G. Mitchell and Wesley Blomster. New York: Continuum.

Auslander, Philip. 1999. *Liveness: Performance in a Mediatized Society.* New York: Routledge.

Benjamin, Walter. 1968. "The Work of Art in the Age of Mechanical Reproduction." In *Illuminations,* transl. Hannah Arent. New York: Schocken Books, 217–251.

Bijker, Wiebe E., Thomas P. Hughes, and Trevor Pinch, eds. 1987. *The Social Construction of Technological Systems: New Directions in the Sociology and History of Technology.* Cambridge, Mass.: MIT Press.

Bolter, Jay David, and Richard Grusin. 1999. *Remediation: Understanding New Media.* Cambridge, Mass.: MIT Press.

Brady, Erika. 1999. *A Spiral Way: How the Phonograph Changed Ethnography.* Jackson, Miss.: University of Mississippi Press.

Diehl, Keila. 2002. *Echoes from Dharamsala: Music in the Life of a Tibetan Refugee Community.* Berkeley: University of California Press.

Douglas, Susan. 1999. *Listening In: Radio and the American Imagination.* New York: Times Books.

Feld, Steven. 1994. "From Schizophonia to Schizmogenesis: On the Discourses and Commodification Practices of 'World Music' and 'World Beat.'" In *Music Grooves,* ed. Charles Keil and Steven Feld. Chicago: University of Chicago Press, 257–289.

——. 1996. "Waterfalls of Song: An Acoustemology of Place Resounding in Bosavi, Papua New Guinea." In *Senses of Place,* ed. Steven Feld and Keith H. Basso. Santa Fe: School of American Research Press, 91–135.

Gay, Leslie. 1998. "Acting Up, Talking Tech: New York Rock Musicians and Their Metaphors of Technology." *Ethnomusicology* 42(1): 81–98.
Greene, Paul. 1999. "Sound Engineering in a Tamil Village: Playing Audio Cassettes as Devotional Performance." *Ethnomusicology* 43(3): 459–489.
Horkheimer, Max, and Theodor Adorno. 1991. *Dialectic of Enlightenment,* transl. John Cumming. New York: Continuum.
Kealy, Edward. 1979. "From Craft to Art: The Case of Sound Mixers and Popular Music." *Sociology of Work and Occupations* 6(1): 3–29.
Keightly, Kier. 1996. "'Turn It Down!' She Shrieked: Gender, Domestic Space, and High Fidelity, 1948–59." *Popular Music* 15(2): 149–177.
Keil, Charles. 1994 [1987]. "Participatory Discrepancies and the Power of Music." In *Music Grooves,* ed. Charles Keil and Steven Feld. Chicago: University of Chicago Press, 96–108.
Lysloff, René T.A., and Leslie C. Gay Jr., eds. 2003. *Music and Technoculture.* Middletown: Wesleyan University Press/University Press of New England.
Marvin, Carolyn. 1988. *When Old Technologies Were New: Thinking About Electric Communication in the Late Nineteenth Century.* New York: Oxford University Press.
Meintjes, Louise. 2003. *Sound of Africa! Making Music Zulu in a South African Studio.* Durham, N.C.: Duke University Press.
Morton, David. 2000. *Off the Record: The Technology and Culture of Sound Recording in America.* New Brunswick, N.J.: Rutgers University Press.
Oldenziel, Ruth. 1999. *Making Technology Masculine: Men, Women, and Modern Machines in America, 1870–1945.* Amsterdam: Amsterdam University Press.
Penley, Constance, and Andrew Ross, eds. 1992. *Technoculture.* Minneapolis: University of Minnesota Press.
Porcello, Thomas. 1996. "Sonic Artistry: Music, Discourse, and Technology in the Sound Recording Studio." Ph.D. dissertation: University of Texas at Austin.
———. 2003 [1998]. "Tails Out: Social Phenomenology and the Ethnographic Representation of Music-Making." In *Music and Technoculture,* ed. René T.A. Lysloff and Leslie C. Gay Jr., Middletown, Conn.: Wesleyan University Press/University Press of New England, 264–289.
Sandstrom, Boden. 2000. "Women Mix Engineers and the Power of Sound." In *Music and Gender,* ed. Pirkko Moisala and Beverley Diamond. Urbana: University of Illinois Press, 289–305.
Taylor, Timothy. 1997. *Global Pop: World Music, World Markets.* New York: Routledge.
———. 2001. *Strange Sounds: Music, Technology and Culture.* New York: Routledge.
Thompson, Emily. 1995. "Machines, Music, and the Quest for Fidelity: Marketing the Edison Phonograph in America, 1877–1925. *Musical Quarterly* 79(1): 131–171.
Wajcman, Judy. 1991. *Feminism Confronts Technology.* University Park: Pennsylvania State University Press.
Wong, Deborah. 2003. "Plugged In at Home: Vietnamese American Technoculture in Orange County." In *Music and Technoculture,* ed. René T.A. Lysloff and Leslie C. Gay Jr. Middletown, Conn.: Wesleyan University Press/University Press of New England, 125–152.

RECORDINGS
Voices of the Rainforest. 1991. Rykodisc RCD 10173.

VIDEOS
Songcatcher. 2000. Lion's Gate Films/Trimark Home Video VM 7543D.

Contributors

HARRIS M. BERGER is Associate Professor of Music in the Department of Performance Studies, Texas A & M University, and author of *Metal, Rock, and Jazz: Perception and Phenomenology of Musical Experience* (Wesleyan/New England).

BEVERLEY DIAMOND holds the Canada Research Chair in Traditional Music at Memorial University, Newfoundland. Since the early 1970s she has worked extensively in Inuit and First Nations communities in the Northwest Territories, Labrador, Québec, and Ontario. Her work centers on the relationship of music to issues of cultural identity, women's expressive cultures, musical instruments as cultural metaphor, and indigenous popular music.

CORNELIA FALES is an ethnomusicologist and music perception researcher, and Assistant Professor of Music at the University of California at Santa Barbara. Her research engages timbre in traditional African and high-tech American musics.

INGEMAR GRANDIN is a lecturer at the Institute for Thematic Studies at the University of Linköping, Sweden. He is author of *Music and Media in Local Life: Music Practice in a Newar Neighbourhood in Nepal* (Linköping).

PAUL D. GREENE is an ethnomusicologist and Associate Professor at Pennsylvania State University. His research examines practices of sound engineering and engineered musical cultures in both South India and Nepal, and also Buddhist musical traditions.

LOUISE MEINTJES is Associate Professor of Music at Duke University and author *Sound of Africa! Making Music Zulu in a South African Studio* (Duke 2003).

FREDERICK J. MOEHN is an ethnomusicologist specializing on musical culture in Brazil and is currently Assistant Professor of Music at the State University of New York at Stony Brook.

KARL NEUENFELDT is Senior Lecturer at Central Queensland University, Australia, and also co-editor of the journal *Perfect Beat*. His research engages Australian Aboriginal musics and technologies of sound production and commerce.

THOMAS PORCELLO is Assistant Professor of Anthropology and Co-Director of Media Studies at Vassar College and has worked as a sound recording engineer and studio musician in Texas and Arizona. His publications examine the social phenomenology of recorded music and he is currently researching studio-based discursive strategies for the description of musical timbre.

TIMOTHY D. TAYLOR is Associate Professor of Ethnomusicology and Musicology at UCLA. His publications include *Global Pop: World Music, World Markets* (Routledge 1997), *Strange Sounds: Music, Technology, Culture* (Routledge 2001), and numerous articles on various popular and classical musics.

JEREMY WALLACH is an Assistant Professor at Bowling Green State University and researches technology and music in the sound studios and underground music scenes of Jakarta, Indonesia.

Index

MUSIC / CULTURE

A series from Wesleyan University Press

Edited by George Lipsitz, Susan McClary, and Robert Walser

My Music
by Susan D. Crafts, Daniel Cavicchi, Charles Keil, and the Music in Daily Life Project

Running with the Devil: Power, Gender, and Madness in Heavy Metal Music
by Robert Walser

Subcultural Sounds: Micromusics of the West
by Mark Slobin

Upside Your Head! Rhythm and Blues on Central Avenue
by Johnny Otis

Dissonant Identities: The Rock 'n' Roll Scene in Austin, Texas
by Barry Shank

Black Noise: Rap Music and Black Culture in Contemporary America
by Tricia Rose

Club Cultures: Music, Media and Sub-cultural Capital
by Sarah Thornton

Music, Society, Education
by Christopher Small

Popular Music in Theory
by Keith Negus

Any Sound You Can Imagine: Making Music/Consuming Technology
by Paul Théberge

Listening to Salsa: Gender, Latin Popular Music, and Puerto Rican Cultures
by Frances Aparicio

A Thousand Honey Creeks Later: My Life in Music from Basie to Motown and Beyond
by Preston Love

Voices in Bali: Energies and Perceptions in Vocal Music and Dance Theater
by Edward Herbst

Musicking: The Meanings of Performing and Listening
by Christopher Small

Singing Archaeology: Philip Glass's Akhnaten
by John Richardson

Music of the Common Tongue: Survival and Celebration in African American Music
by Christopher Small

Metal, Rock, and Jazz: Perception and the Phenomenology of Musical Experience
by Harris M. Berger

Music and Cinema
Edited by James Buhler, Caryl Flinn, and David Neumeyer

"You Better Work!" Underground Dance Music in New York City
by Kai Fikentscher

Singing Our Way to Victory: French Cultural Politics and Music During the Great War
by Regina M. Sweeney

The Book of Music and Nature: An Anthology of Sounds, Words, Thoughts
Edited by David Rothenberg and Marta Ulvaeus

Recollecting from the Past: Musical Practice and Spirit Possession on the East Coast of Madagascar
by Ron Emoff

Banda: Mexican Musical Life across Borders
by Helena Simonett

Global Noise: Rap and Hip-Hop outside the U.S.A.
edited by Tony Mitchell

The 'Hood Comes First: Race, Space, and Place in Rap and Hip-Hop
by Murray Forman

Manufacturing the Muse: Estey Organs and Consumer Culture in Victorian America
by Dennis Waring

The City of Musical Memory: Salsa, Record Grooves, and Popular Culture in Cali, Colombia
by Lise A. Waxer

Symphonic Metamorphoses: Subjectivity and Alienation in Mahler's Re-Cycled Songs
by Raymond Knapp

Music and Technoculture
Edited by René T. A. Lysloff and Leslie C. Gay, Jr.

Angora Matta: Fatal Acts of North-South Translation
by Marta Elena Savigliano

False Prophet: Fieldnotes from the Punk Underground
by Steven Taylor

Phat Beats, Dope Rhymes: Hip Hop Down Under Comin' Upper
by Ian Maxwell

Locating East Asia in Western Art Music
Edited by Yayoi Uno Everett and Frederick Lau

Making Beats: The Art of Sample-Based Hip-Hop
by Joseph G. Schloss

Identity and Everyday Life: Essays in the Study of Folklore, Music and Popular Culture
by Harris M. Berger and Giovanna P. Del Negro

The Other Side of Nowhere: Jazz, Improvisation, and Communities in Dialogue
Edited by Daniel Fischlin and Ajay Heble

Setting the Record Straight: A Material History of Classical Recording
by Colin Symes

Wired for Sound: Engineering and Technologies in Sonic Cultures
Edited by Paul D. Greene and Thomas Porcello